THE CASE AGAINST
GEORGE W. BUSH

100% of the author's royalties from the sales of this book will go to the 9/11 Memorial & Museum in New York City.

THE CASE AGAINST
GEORGE W. BUSH

STEVEN C. MARKOFF

Foreword by Richard A. Clarke

RARE BIRD BOOKS
LOS ANGELES, CALIF.

THIS IS A GENUINE RARE BIRD BOOK

Rare Bird Books
453 South Spring Street, Suite 302
Los Angeles, CA 90013
rarebirdlit.com

Set in Minion
Printed in the United States

10 9 8 7 6 5 4 3 2 1

Publisher's Cataloging-in-Publication Data

Names: Markoff, Steven C., author.
Title: The Case Against George W. Bush / Steven C. Markoff.
Description: Includes bibliographical references and index. | First Hardcover Edition. | New York, NY; Los Angeles, CA: Rare Bird Books, 2020.
Identifiers: ISBN: 9781644281352 (Hardcover) | 9781644281772 (ebook)
Subjects: LCSH Bush, George W. (George Walker), 1946-. | Bush, George W. (George Walker), 1946—Political and social views. | Bush, George W. (George Walker), 1946—Influence. | United States—Politics and government—2001–2009. | United States—Foreign relations—2001–2009. | United States—Foreign relations—Moral and ethical aspects. | BISAC POLITICAL SCIENCE / American Government / Executive Branch | POLITICAL SCIENCE / Corruption & Misconduct

Classification: LCC E902 .M375 2020 | DDC 973.931092—dc23

"...the world is more threatened by those who tolerate evil or support it than the evil-doers themselves."

Albert Einstein, 1953

This book is dedicated to all those who were killed or adversely affected by 9/11, and those tortured directly or indirectly by our government after September 11, 2001, and by our 2003 invasion of Iraq.

CONTENTS

FOREWORD

FOR SOME AMERICANS, GEORGE W. Bush looks good by comparison to the incumbent, Donald Trump. In his post-presidency, Bush has devoted himself to worthy causes and acted in a bipartisan manner. The 43rd president should, however, be judged not by comparison to America's worst president, nor by what Bush may have done after leaving office. He should be evaluated for his actions in office, his nonfeasance, misfeasance, and malfeasance.

This volume from Steven Markoff provides the evidence for such an evaluation. You can judge for yourself. For me, there is little doubt. I, unfortunately, witnessed Bush and his administration make many of their most cataclysmic decisions. I was in the room when some of them occurred.

When in December 2000 the Supreme Court of the United States decided on a five to four vote that George W. Bush would become the 43rd president, I was a special assistant to the president for national security and national coordinator for security and counterterrorism for President William J. Clinton. I anticipated leaving the White House on January 20, 2001, when the Clinton presidency ended; however, I was asked by the incoming administration to stay on for an unspecified period because, as it was explained to me, there was no one on Bush's incoming team who knew much about terrorism or wanted my job.

Departing Clinton administration officials stressed to the newly arriving Bush team, and to Bush himself, the importance and urgency of dealing with the Al-Qaeda terrorist threat. Indeed, the Clinton administration had developed an extensive series of further steps to combat Al-Qaeda that it would have taken if it had continued in office, or indeed, had Vice President Gore assumed office in 2001. Within days of Bush's inauguration, I asked for an urgent meeting at Cabinet level to review both the threat and the plan to ratchet up the measures against Al-Qaeda.

No such meeting occurred until a week before 9/11. That meeting was inconclusive.

From January 2001 through the second week in September, Bush personally received frequent intelligence warnings that Al-Qaeda posed an imminent threat. He convened no meetings to address the issue. His inner circle of national security officials did nothing, despite frequent urgings by the CIA director and the national coordinator (including such vivid imagery as our asking in writing that they consider a near future in which there would be hundreds of dead bodies of the street in America). Instead, they focused on Iraq and the regime of Saddam Hussein. Bush's nonfeasance cost American lives.

Following the deaths of over three thousand innocent civilians on 9/11, the Bush administration attempted to tie the Al-Qaeda attack to Iraq, which had nothing to do with it. Despite CIA and FBI analyses that reiterated Iraq's noninvolvement, the Bush administration almost immediately following the 9/11 attack began to make plans to invade Iraq. Senior Bush officials spoke privately of the need to demonstrate our strength in the wake of the 9/11 attack, show our might by destroying the largest army in the Middle East, and thereby also prove our willingness to take US military casualties to achieve our ends.

Prior to 9/11, foreign terrorists who had attacked Americans had been successfully sought out around the world and arrested by US law enforcement authorities, assisted by the Intelligence Community. Many terrorists had been returned to US territory, given their Miranda rights, provided with counsel, tried in our civilian criminal courts, convicted, sentenced, and incarcerated in maximum security prison cells. (One, tried by the Commonwealth of Virginia, was executed). Despite this record, the Bush administration abandoned criminal process and established its own extra-judicial system for dealing with terrorists post 9/11. That new system used techniques that any objective observer would judge as torture.

Perhaps the most well-known torture technique was the procedure known as "waterboarding." The United States government had tried World War II Japanese military personnel for using that exact technique. They were found guilty and some were executed by hanging.

The United States Senate's committee on Intelligence conducted the most extensive oversight and investigative examination in its history on the issue of torture during the Bush administration. That voluminous study concluded that torture was employed and that it had not, despite administration claims to the contrary, uniquely revealed information that had prevented terrorist attacks. To the contrary, it showed that tortured prisoners unable to satisfy their interrogators with information that the terrorists did not know instead guessed at what kind of story would stop the torture and then fabricated information of the kind they thought their persecutors wanted to hear.

Bush was not only aware of the torture, he approved it. His role in giving authorization for such acts can rightly be considered criminal malfeasance, as should his orders to invade Iraq.

Among the many justifications the Bush administration considered for their invasion and occupation of Iraq, they chose finally to make the alleged existence of weapons of mass destruction their chief complaint. Other nations had weapons of mass destruction (e.g., North Korea, Pakistan), but Iraq's supposed ownership of such technology was different and allegedly justified invasion.

The United Nations, which had located and destroyed large amounts of Iraqi WMD, was still attempting to negotiate further inspections when Bush decided to initiate the invasion. Bush was unable to explain why in the absence of any demonstrable imminent threat, he would not wait for the UN inspection. Of course, had there been further UN inspections, they would have found what previous inspections had revealed: there were no more chemical, biological, nuclear weapons or long-range missiles to be found.

The needless and unjustified invasion and occupation of Iraq cost over 4,400 American lives and left over 32,000 Americans wounded, in addition to an even larger number of Americans scarred with PTSD. There are only estimates of Iraqi casualties. Those range from slightly over 100,000 dead to six times that number. The financial cost to American taxpayers, including the long-term care of wounded warriors, exceeds $2 trillion. The list of American problems that could have been addressed with funds of that magnitude is extensive—problems that remain unaddressed due in part to their financial cost.

Other costs of the Iraq War are incalculable but immense. America's power and prestige, its influence for good in the world, were damaged perhaps beyond recovery. The chain of events that the US invasion unleashed led to a new terrorist organization, IISS, resulting in hundreds of thousands of casualties and the destruction of major cities in several countries. That toll continues to mount.

While this volume is restricted to Bush's conduct on terrorism and Iraq, consideration of Bush's presidency must also include his nonfeasance and then misfeasance in the disaster of Katrina and the destruction of an American city, New Orleans.

While I may be considered by some to be prejudiced in my judgement, there are facts that any objective observer must accept.

— First, Bush ignored warnings about the serious threat from Al-Qaeda prior to 9/11.

— Second, Bush ordered the invasion of Iraq in violation of international law, when Iraq had been uninvolved in 9/11 and offered no imminent threat to the United States.

— Third, Bush authorized the use of torture and denied prisoners due process, both acts in violation of international law.

Note that in each case I say that Bush did these things, not the Bush administration. There is a revisionist school that seeks to place the blame on Bush's vice president, Richard B. Cheney. While there can be little doubt that Cheney encouraged Bush to take many of these actions, it is not true that the president was merely a tool of a mendacious and scheming subordinate. The evidence is now clear that Bush agreed with his vice president and knew full well what he was doing. He was an enthusiastic participant, a believer in the war on terror and the war on Iraq. It is true, however, that he did not master or manage the details of either war until the last few years of his eight-year presidency.

Only well into his second term did Bush begin to exhibit views at variance with his vice president and Cheney's close colleague, Secretary of Defense Donald Rumsfeld. Not until the Iraq War had been underway for over two years and the insurgency continued and worsened did Bush become actively involved in attempting as commander-in-chief to manage its conduct.

Throughout his administration, however, even after getting more involved in the management of the war in Iraq, Bush paid less personal attention to the success, or lack thereof, of US military and intelligence efforts related to those who had actually attacked us on 9/11, to the fighting in Afghanistan and the search for the leader of Al-Qaeda, Osama bin Laden. (The Al-Qaeda leader remained at large throughout Bush's presidency.) Indeed, Bush justified the closure of a CIA office dedicated to tracking bin Laden and publicly minimized the significance of the Al-Qaeda leader and, implicitly, the need to arrest or kill the man who had ordered 9/11.

There are no judges sitting in review of Bush's actions, but you can view the evidence. Read the facts in this volume and go to other sources. View PBS's *American Experience* "George W. Bush," a four-hour documentary on the Bush presidency. Read the Senate report on torture. Choose from any of the scores of books cited by Steven Markoff, many written by or quoting firsthand witnesses. Do not judge Bush in comparison to the crimes of the incumbent president, which are also legion and of the utmost seriousness. Judge Bush by what he demonstrably and undeniably failed to do, by what he clearly ordered to happen, and by the extraordinary consequences of his nonfeasance, misfeasance, and malfeasance in office. You be the judge.

Richard A. Clarke
June 2020

PREFACE

THIS BOOK PRESENTS MY case—told through almost six hundred sourced quotes from published books, writings, transcripts, and government documents and reports—that George W. Bush (a.k.a. "Bush") committed three crimes while president: criminal negligence[1] over what became 9/11, the torturing of prisoners post 9/11, and using fraud and deception to take our country into the unnecessary and devastating 2003 war against Iraq.

Although many books have been published about Bush, some lauding him, others not, those books were usually written from the eyes, experience, and background of each book's author or authors. The information in their books, however useful, was often limited to what they knew and learned from their research and how they saw or interpreted that research. This book is a story told through the actual words of almost one hundred knowledgeable authors—from Hans Blix to Bob Woodward—with my thoughts and comments included for interpretation and context.

There have been excuses made for George W. Bush's presidency over the years—for example, that *it was a difficult time to be president, we were under attack, he made some mistakes,* and *he did what he thought was right at the time.* While true, those meaningless statements cover up, belittle, or whitewash ugly and serious facts about his administration that this book brings to light. Others have downplayed, tried to forget, or buried Bush's actions by saying things such as *anything about George W. Bush is old news* and *we have moved on from his presidency.*

As you read many surprising if not shocking quotes in this book from well-known and well-placed people, you will find a straightforward and well-documented case outlining George W. Bush's guilt and complicity in committing the aforementioned crimes.

---

1   The legal concept that one needs to act responsibly depending on one's circumstances and situation.

As you work through this book, I hope that you will find it has achieved my goals:

— Documenting and explaining the three crimes of President Bush and how those crimes caused the unnecessary deaths of hundreds of thousands of people, as well as bringing untold destruction to our people, our country, and others.

— Learning how Bush's interest in and thirst for oil (for his friends and for our country) may well have been the substantive or primary reason why he attacked Iraq in 2003.

— Chronicling how Bush, as president and our commander-in-chief, used secrecy, fraud, and deceit to scare our country into the Iraq War, which helps us better understand and study his actions in hopes that the lessons learned will help keep our nation from falling prey to such presidential trickery in the future.

At the least, this book should tie together some of the facts and theories, conflicting or otherwise, that you have heard or thought about George W. Bush's presidency.

QUOTE CREDIBILITY & UNUSUAL FORMATS

CONSIDER THE CREDIBILITY OF this book and its sourced comments based on two assumptions:

— What people publish tends to be accurate, in part, because when writers put their name on a book, paper, or report those works are usually fact-checked or edited by others and even if not, few want to be embarrassed by written words later being found inaccurate or worse.

— Although hearsay isn't usually accepted as court testimony or evidence, and although some of the quotes in the book are hearsay, given the politically diverse backgrounds of the sources and the quotes from an assortment of people saying similar things, their cumulative quotes should be collectively meaningful.

UNUSUAL FORMATS

Two unusual formats important in this book:

— Gray Boxes: The quotes in gray boxes appear when positions taken or comments made by George W. Bush or those senior in his administration seem (or are) counter to known facts at the time. For example, Bush and his people continually said Saddam Hussein had weapons of mass destruction (WMD) when they had no confirmatory intelligence those words were true; Bush's administration focused on the dangers posed by Hussein and oil instead of the many reported threats from bin Laden and Al-Qaeda; Hussein was somehow connected to 9/11 and bin Laden or Al-Qaeda, when neither he nor his organization was found to be so.

— Quotes have dates or are dated in order to give you a framework of timing, while showing that the times aren't always precise.

The quotes in this book are therefore dated:

— On the specific year, month, and day when known.

— The twenty-fifth of the month is used when the quote was reported "at" or "around" the "end" of the month or "late" in the month. [Notated as "The twenty-fifth of the month used for date sorting purposes only."]

— The fifteenth of the month is used to date a quote when there was no evidence or clue as to when the quote occurred in a given month. [Notated as "The fifteenth of the month used for date sorting purposes only."]

— The fifth of the month is used when a quote was said to have happened "early" or "around" the beginning of the month, or when a quote was similarly described. [Notated as "The fifth of the month used for date sorting purposes only."]

For the other policies used in putting this book together, see Methodology.

OVERVIEW

A. BACKGROUND

AL-QAEDA, A TERRORIST GROUP founded by and associated with Osama bin Laden in 1985, was well-known as a serious threat to our country during the presidential administrations of George H. W. Bush (Bush's[2] father) and William J. "Bill" Clinton.

The threat to our country from bin Laden and Al-Qaeda was clear, given that bin Laden made many threats against the United States. Importantly, Al-Qaeda was believed to be responsible for successful terrorist acts. Those attacks included the March 1994 bombing of the New York World Trade Center (WTC 7), located next to the Twin Towers; the August 1998 bombing of our East African embassies in Tanzania and Kenya; and the October 2000 bombing of our warship the USS *Cole*. It was reported that more than 245 lives were lost and more than 5,000 were injured in those combined four pre-9/11 attacks.

When George W. Bush became president in January of 2001, I didn't think about terrorist threats to our country. If I had, I would have assumed that because we had the best intelligence agencies and the most powerful military in the world, our new president would have been on top of any serious terrorist or other threats against us.

Eight months later, like most Americans, I was shocked by the events of 9/11, when two hijacked planes crashed into Manhattan's Twin Towers. A third hijacked plane crashed into the Pentagon, and a fourth crashed in a field in Somerset County, Pennsylvania.

Almost three thousand people died in those attacks, making it, in terms of lives lost to terrorism, the worst day in our country's history. Watching some

2   The names President George W. Bush and Bush are used interchangeably. Bush's father will always be referred to as George H. W. Bush or H. W. Bush.

of those attacks on television that morning, I thought they must have been well planned and shielded from anyone knowing about them in advance, sneak attacks that no competent government could have known about, foreseen, or prepared for.

A short time after 9/11, when President George W. Bush, still in his first year in office, declared a war on terrorism, and launched missile attacks in Afghanistan against bin Laden and Al-Qaeda as retribution for 9/11, our country was overwhelmingly behind him.

Concurrently, my interest in Middle East politics was piqued as I watched and read bits of news about 9/11, Middle Eastern oil, the reported dangers of Saddam Hussein and his weapons of mass destruction, and our country's march toward attacking Iraq again—in 2003.

Still, I wasn't involved in the run-up to that war, physically or emotionally. That changed strikingly in 2007 when I read Richard A. Clarke's book *Against All Enemies: Inside America's War on Terror.* The book was a calm recitation of surprising and disturbing facts and information.

For example, Clarke revealed that George W. Bush and some of his senior staff had been warned about the dangers of Osama bin Laden and Al-Qaeda even before Bush became president in January of 2001. Clarke also wrote that Bush received subsequent warnings that bin Laden and Al-Qaeda were planning on attacking the US prior to 9/11. After 9/11, Bush disregarded or downplayed those previously received threats while focusing on removing Hussein from power. Clarke also wrote that Bush took us into the 2003 Iraq War without having credible intel that Hussein was an immediate threat to our country.

Importantly, Clarke had the necessary government background, involvement, and position to know about what he wrote.[3] When I finished Clarke's book, I was shocked. Could Bush have really disregarded threats of bin Laden and Al-Qaeda prior to 9/11? If so, was there a compelling reason that Bush spent his political capital and energy going after Hussein? Could it be that George W. Bush's Iraq War was about oil?

---

3   In 1992, President George H. W. Bush appointed Richard A. Clarke to chair the Counterterrorism Security Group and to a seat on the United States National Security Council. President Bill Clinton retained Clarke and in 1998 promoted him to the National Coordinator for Security, Infrastructure Protection, and Counterterrorism. Under President George W. Bush, Clarke initially continued in the same position and later became the special advisor to the president on cyber security. He left his government position prior to the US invasion of Iraq in 2003.

It occurred to me that while Clarke seemed knowledgeable about terrorists, 9/11, and the run up to our 2003 invasion of Iraq, he was just one person, and his knowledge was limited to what he had personally seen and learned.

I thought that if I combined details from Clarke's book with related information from other diverse sources with inside or special knowledge of those times and places, that combined information could produce new and clearer insights about 9/11 and the Iraq War. I then set out to find what additional facts and information were available on those and related topics.

With the able assistance of Steve Gaskin, my project manager for the effort, and eight part-time researchers, over the next three and a half years we scoured 130 published books, numerous speeches, newspaper articles, and government reports on Hussein, his WMD, Iraqi oil, bin Laden, and Al-Qaeda. That research, sorting and cataloging produced more than 7,350 sourced quotes.

Those quotes cover events from the 1980s onward and include facts and statements related to terrorism, Osama bin Laden, Al-Qaeda, US/Middle East policies, Middle Eastern oil, Hussein, and decisions and actions by President George W. Bush and others from his inauguration through 9/11, the Bush Administration and torture, and finally the run-up to our attacking Iraq in 2003. The quotes also cover the aftermath of the 2003 invasion, Bush's statements on the war and torture.

In order to paint a reasonably complete picture of the relevant events, Gaskin and I selected quotes from books and other sources that included authors from all sides of the political spectrum—excluding no book or source due to the politics of its author.

The authors quoted include former British Prime Minister Tony Blair; Hans Blix, head of the United Nations Monitoring, Verification and Inspection Commission from March 2000 to June 2003; President George W. Bush; former Vice President Richard "Dick" Cheney; former US Senator Russ Feingold; former Secretary of State Condoleezza Rice; former Secretary of Defense Donald Rumsfeld; and writers and journalists such as Steve Coll, Frank Rich, Craig Unger, and Bob Woodward.

We then put the selected quotes into a free online searchable database that I designed and commissioned, www.911Plus.org.[4]

---

4 Since finishing the database in 2013, I have occasionally added to it when particularly relevant information surfaced. Such information includes four articles of impeachment

Being more of an archivist than author, I waited for a writer with investigative and writing skills to find and use 911Plus.org quotes as the foundation for a book about how George W. Bush had conducted himself as our president and commander-in-chief.

Several years passed, but no such writer surfaced. Then, during a bus ride toward the coast of Chile with my wife and other traveling companions in October 2015, I decided that if I wanted a book written about how George W. Bush began his administration and my other findings, I would have to do it myself.

B. PRESIDENT GEORGE W. BUSH AND HIS ACTIONS

ON JANUARY 20, 2001, George W. Bush was sworn in as the forty-third president of the United States. The oath was administered by William Rehnquist, Chief Justice of the US Supreme Court (USSC), a ritual conducted by other chief justices at the inaugurations of many previous incoming presidents. The words of that oath:

> **"I do solemnly swear that I will faithfully execute the office of the President of the United States, and will to the best of my ability, preserve, protect and defend the Constitution of the United States."**

You will read my contention, supported by many quotes, that certain George W. Bush actions broke that oath and betrayed his office and our country.

I acknowledge that being the president of the United States is a close to impossible job. Adding to the difficulties of the job are the human mistakes we all make; however, this book is not about Bush's mistakes as president or his good intentions gone wrong. My contention is that three of George W. Bush's important mistakes were not *mistakes*, but criminal acts of omission and commission.

(of the thirty-five) in the June 2008 House resolution of impeachment of George W. Bush titled "RESOLUTION Impeaching George W. Bush, President of the United States, of high crimes and misdemeanors," introduced by Rep. Dennis J. Kucinich (D-OH-10), Congress. gov, June 10, 2008.

Despite swearing an oath to faithfully execute the responsibilities of the presidency—and, arguably, the primary responsibility of our president is to keep our country safe—these pages will show that George W. Bush as president committed the three crimes mentioned in the preface.

You will now find three chapters, each chapter outlining one of those crimes.

CRIME #1: CRIMINAL NEGLIGENCE / 9/11

President George W. Bush was well-briefed about the dangers to our country from bin Laden and Al-Qaeda even before he became president. After his inauguration he did little about those dangers until 9/11. Some knowledgeable people say 9/11 didn't need to have happened.

THE QUOTES IN THIS chapter show that beginning in the early 1980s, the presidential administrations of Ronald W. Reagan and George H. W. Bush were tracking and dealing with Iraq, Middle Eastern oil, and Hussein. From 1988 on, H. W. Bush and Clinton were additionally dealing with the growing danger from the terrorist group Al-Qaeda and its mentor and strategist Osama bin Laden.

In addition to prior presidential knowledge about bin Laden and Al-Qaeda going back ten years, some weeks before George W. Bush took office in January 2001, he and his top people received pre-inauguration intelligence briefings from President Clinton and his senior staff about the special danger posed by Osama bin Laden and Al-Qaeda. At that time, the Clinton administration thought they were the most lethal terrorist threats to our country.

Those pre-inauguration briefings made it clear that bin Laden and Al-Qaeda intended to terrorize the United States and our people again, after previously attacking our embassies in Tanzania and Kenya in 1998, the World Trade Center in 1993, and the USS *Cole* in 2000.

However, those pre-inauguration intelligence briefings about the danger of bin Laden and Al-Qaeda seemingly had little impact on our soon-to-be president.

From the first few days of Bush's inauguration, and with no credible intelligence that Hussein was an urgent, immediate, or serious threat to our country, President Bush began telling the American people about the danger posed by Hussein and his supposed weapons of mass destruction. In the months ahead, Bush would keep his focus on Saddam, despite the continuing flood of intelligence he received that showed we would be attacked again by Al-Qaeda. Almost from the day of Bush's inauguration, his administration also focused on Iraqi oil.

Mirroring President Bush's apparent lack of interest in bin Laden and Al-Qaeda prior to 9/11 were other Bush administration senior officials. They included Vice President Cheney, Secretary of Defense Rumsfeld, National Security adviser Rice, Attorney General John Ashcroft, and Foreign Policy Advisor Richard Perle.

Bush's post-inauguration focus on Hussein and Iraqi oil increased the chances that we would be attacked by Al-Qaeda, which we were on September 11, 2001. The 2,973[5] lives lost that day (excluding the nineteen hijackers who committed suicide in the attacks) constituted the greatest number of casualties from a terrorist attack on US soil in the history of our nation. The number of lives lost even surpassed the 2,403[6] killed in the December 7, 1941, Japanese attack on Pearl Harbor. In addition to the thousands killed and wounded on 9/11, many were sickened by inhaling poisoned air while trying to help those buried or injured in the rubble of the collapsed Twin Towers.

The carnage from 9/11 destroyed people, families, and businesses and set the stage for the loss of many of our civil liberties due to the policies, regulations, and laws enacted by knee-jerk (some say premeditated) responses to the panic that followed.

The quotes in this chapter will highlight some knowledgeable people who claim that were it not for Bush's lack of interest toward the ever-flowing intel about the coming terrorist attacks, 9/11 could have been disrupted or prevented.

If there had been no 9/11 to terrify our country with the fear of more attacks, Bush would not have had the political capital to push us into attacking Iraq in 2003. Without 9/11 or the Iraq War, there would not have been any reason or excuse to torture anyone.

As an indication of what was in George W. Bush's mind after his inauguration, in the 379 speeches[7] he made from January 20, 2001, through

---

5   "The 9/11 Commission Report," National Commission on Terrorist Attacks Upon the United States, 9-11commission.gov, report dated July 22, 2004

6   "A Pearl Harbor Fact Sheet," Nationalww2museum.org, accessed May 10, 2017

7   George W. Bush made a total of 379 presidential speeches from his inauguration through 9/10/2001. The speeches, compiled from George W. Bush—White House Archives online [taken offline by 2018], are considered any remarks he made when he spoke in front

9/10/2001, he never mentioned bin Laden or Al-Qaeda. However, he mentioned Saddam Hussein; Iraq; WMD; nuclear; offensive; defensive weapons; weapons of terror or mass destruction; or Saddam and imminent or immediate threats 143 times. He mentioned oil forty-one times.

In the 379 speeches George W. Bush made from January 20, 2001, to September 10, 2001	
Words or phrases mentioned in Bush's 379 speeches	Numbers of times the words or phrases were mentioned in the 379 speeches[8]
Al-Qaeda or bin Laden	0
Saddam Hussein / Iraq / WMD / Nuclear / Offensive / Defensive weapons / Weapons of Terror or mass Destruction / Saddam and imminent or immediate threats	143
Oil	41

The numbers above seem at least close to courtroom proof that George W. Bush was far more interested in Hussein and Iraq's oil than the risks to our country from Al-Qaeda and bin Laden so often communicated to him.

In sum, this chapter will show that President George W. Bush received repeated, well-documented warnings about the dangers posed by bin Laden and Al-Qaeda before and after he became president, yet he remained fixated on Hussein and Iraqi oil.

In doing so, Bush violated his presidential duty to use reasonable care (or effort) to protect us from those well-known threats.

I, therefore, contend that Bush's fixation on Saddam and Iraqi oil, instead of on the terrorist threats, met the standard for criminal negligence. Criminal negligence can be defined as:

---

of an undefined number of people, either alone or with other individuals, and includes, but are not limited to State of the Union speeches, radio addresses, press conferences, commencement ceremonies, meetings, remarks, tours, toasts, photo opportunities, visits, and events.

8   These numbers came from my assistant going through the 379 speeches listed on the George W. Bush—White House Archives website and doing word checks of those speeches.

"The failure to use reasonable care to avoid consequences that threaten or harm the safety of the public and that are the foreseeable outcome of acting in a particular manner."[9]

This chapter, broken into six sections, shows more specifically why I believe Bush was guilty of criminal negligence.

A. 1980–November 6, 2000

The time period from 1980 through November 6, 2000 (the day before George W. Bush was elected president of the United States), shows some of the complexities of US politics in the Middle East, our prior government's sustained interest in Middle Eastern oil, and our government's awareness of a growing danger to our country posed by Osama bin Laden and Al-Qaeda. During that time period, for example:

— Bin Laden founded Al-Qaeda

— Al-Qaeda bombed our two embassies in Kenya and Tanzania

— The Clinton administration put a $5M bounty on bin Laden, making him US public enemy No. 1

— The New York World Trade Center was bombed for the first time

— Al-Qaeda bombed the United States warship the USS *Cole*

---

9   "Criminal Negligence," Legal-Dictionary.TheFreeDictionary.com, accessed February 27, 2020.

While I could find no federal statute for criminal negligence, there are state statutes that include the charge of criminal negligence that do not have statutes of limitation. That means President George Bush could be charged under these state statutes at any time during his life. For example, Bush could be charged under the Texas Penal Code, Title 5 Chapter 19 on homicide. Bush spent the month of August 2001 at his "Texas White House" in Crawford, Texas, and on August 6, 2001, he was warned by the now-infamous Presidential Daily Briefing that "Bin Laden Determined to Strike in the U.S." By ignoring this warning (and other warnings leading up to 9/11) I believe that he engaged in criminally negligent homicide pursuant to Section 19.05 of the Texas Penal Code which states "(a) A person commits an offense if he causes the death of an individual by criminal negligence." Although the statute does not define criminal negligence per se, it is considered common law, i.e. part of case law. Texans are expected to comport themselves in a manner that does not endanger the safety or lives of others. Failing to do so can get them convicted in a Texas court of law. According to a website that records the names of the victims from 9/11 (http://www.911research.wtc7.net/cache/sept11/victims/victims_list.htm), eleven are listed as coming from Texas. A state charge of criminal negligence could be brought against Bush on behalf of any of the 9/11 Texas victims.

The quotes in this section also show that by November 6, 2000, there were national security experts who knew that our country faced danger from bin Laden and Al-Qaeda.

B. November 7, 2000 (the day Bush was elected[10]) through 9/11

This section shows that George W. Bush and his top people received multiple briefings and warnings about the danger to our country from bin Laden and Al-Qaeda. As mentioned, Bush received some of those warnings even before he was inaugurated. Quotes in this section show, for example, that in December of 2000 and January of 2001:

— President Clinton proposed to President-elect George W. Bush that the danger of bin Laden and Al-Qaeda be a national security priority of his administration

— Outgoing CIA [Central Intelligence Agency] leaders George Tenet and James Pavitt briefed President-elect Bush about the dangers to our country poised by bin Laden and Al-Qaeda

— Rice and Cheney were told by President Clinton's CIA leaders Tenet and Pavitt that bin Laden was one of the greatest threats to our nation

After his inauguration, even in the face of escalating threats from bin Laden and Al-Qaeda, Bush remained focused on removing Hussein from office, scaring our country by repeatedly saying that Hussein had weapons of mass destruction, and focusing on Iraqi oil instead of on our well-known enemies—bin Laden and Al-Qaeda.

C. 9/11 could have been disrupted or prevented

D. Injuries and deaths from 9/11

E. Costs related to 9/11

F. Recap

There are also important questions neither this chapter nor book attempts to answer. Those questions include: Why was George W. Bush so focused on

---

10   The official election date of GW Bush was November 7, 2000, although some use a different date because of various vote counting issues in Florida. Some argue that George W. Bush was not confirmed elected president until the US Supreme Court's seven to two decision in *Bush v. Palm Beach County Canvassing Board* on December 12, 2000. Gore conceded to Bush the next day, December 13, 2000. Britannica.com, accessed August 6, 2017.

taking out Hussein, a man not thought by our intelligence community at that time to be a serious or immediate threat to our country? Why was Bush so seemingly uninterested in the well-chronicled danger to our country from bin Laden and Al-Qaeda? And, what were his motives and interest in Iraqi oil?

A. 1980 THROUGH NOVEMBER 6, 2000 (THE DAY BEFORE G. W. BUSH WAS ELECTED PRESIDENT OF THE UNITED STATES)

THE FOLLOWING QUOTES, FROM 1980 through November 6, 2000, show America dealing with a toxic mix of shifting Middle East alliances: our efforts initially focused on having close relations with Hussein and then we went to war against him; our complicated relationship with the Saudis and Iran; our thirst for, and the perceived importance of, oil to our country; and the growing terrorist threats from bin Laden and Al-Qaeda.

1/23/1980: Carter: Persian Gulf contains more than two-thirds of world's exportable oil; of vital US interest

A month after the Soviet invasion of Afghanistan, President Jimmy Carter proclaimed what would be known as the Carter Doctrine in his State of the Union Address on January 23, 1980: "The region which is now threatened by Soviet troops in Afghanistan is of great strategic importance: It contains more than two-thirds of the world's exportable oil....We must call on the best that is in us to preserve the security of this crucial region. Let our position be absolutely clear: An attempt by any outside force to gain control of the Persian Gulf region will be regarded as an assault on the vital interests of the United States of America, and such an assault will be repelled by any means necessary, including military force."

—Jimmy Carter, "Jimmy Carter State of the Union Address 1980," Jimmy Carter Library, January 23, 1980

1/20/1981: Republican Ronald W. Reagan inaugurated as president for first term with George H. W. Bush as vice president

---

5/15/1981: Reagan administration sides with Iraq in Iraq-Iran War, supports restoring oil, US business interests

"The United States was officially neutral throughout the eight years of the Iran-Iraq war. Unofficially, however, the Reagan administration was hoping to make Iraq 'the new Iran'—or rather, what the pre-1979 revolution Iran was to the United States and its corporations....Thus, in May 1981, the State Department's William Eagleton met with Iraqi Deputy Prime

Minister Tariq Aziz. Eagleton described the meeting in a telegram to the State Department: 'I said the U.S. government supports the participation of American firms in projects designed to restore Iraq's oil facilities as rapidly as possible after the war.' He added that the meeting 'should be helpful to our position and that of U.S. business interests in Iraq.'" [*The fifteenth of the month used for date sorting purposes only.*]

—Antonia Juhasz, *The Bush Agenda*, Page 158

11/26/1983: Reagan defends critical Persian Gulf oil for US

Regarding the defense of American oil interests in the Persian Gulf, President Reagan said, in National Security Decision Directive [NSDD] 114 on November 26, 1983: "[W]e should assign the highest priority to access arrangements which would facilitate the rapid deployment of those forces necessary to defend the critical oil facilities..."

—Ronald Reagan, "U.S. Policy Toward the Iran—Iraq War," Federation of American Scientists online, NSDD 114, November 26, 1983

1/20/1985: Republican Ronald W. Reagan inaugurated as president for a second term again with George H. W. Bush as vice president [11]

3/15/1985: Reagan, George H. W. Bush administration secretly arming Iraq

"The Reagan administration and, to an even greater extent, the Bush Sr. administration, spent nearly a decade secretly arming Iraq through direct and indirect sales. The direct sales were of 'dual-use' materials, which are goods ostensibly made for civilian purposes but have military applications as well....The Reagan and Bush Sr. administrations allowed the sales over the objections of the Pentagon, which believed these products would inevitably be used for military purposes. One government official explained that in March 1985, high-technology export licenses, which previously had not been approved by the U.S. government to Iraq, 'started to go through as if someone had suddenly turned a switch.'

The indirect method involved sales of conventional and chemical weapons to third parties, generally friendly governments, who then sold the weapons to Iraq. U.S. arms dealers made out handsomely, as did dozens of U.S. multinational corporations" [*The fifteenth of the month used for date sorting purposes only.*]

—Antonia Juhasz, *The Bush Agenda*, Pages 167–168

---

11   Because January 20, 1985, fell on a Sunday, the public Inauguration ceremony was scheduled for Monday, January 21, 1985. Reagan was sworn in privately on January 20, 1985.

7/30/1986: VP George H. W. Bush transferring military intelligence to Hussein

On July 30, 1986, Vice President H. W. "Bush went to Jordan to perform the most delicate part of his [Middle East] mission, initiating the transfer of military intelligence to Saddam. According to two Reagan administration officials, Bush told King Hussein that Iraq needed to be more aggressive in the war with Iran and asked that Saddam Hussein be urged to use his air force against targets inside Iran."

—Craig Unger, *House of Bush, House of Saud*, Page 75

1/15/1987: Reagan administration approves SCUD missile sales to Iraq, increasing danger to Israel/Saudi Arabia

During January 1987, "The United States Commerce Department approved exports to Iraq's SCUD [Subsonic Cruise Unarmed Decoy] missile program. Gary Milhollin, the director of the Wisconsin Project on Nuclear Arms Control appeared before the Subcommittee on Technology and National Security of the Joint Economic Committee on the 2nd of July, 1991. He stated that: 'These exports allowed Iraq to extend SCUD range far enough to hit allied soldiers in Saudi Arabia and Israeli civilians in Tel Aviv and Haifa.'" [*The fifteenth of the month used for date sorting purposes only.*]

—Philip Taylor, *The War in Iraq—A Failure of Honesty*, Page 12

3/2/1987: VP George H. W. Bush approves sensitive US tech sales to Iraq over objections from Defense Department

On March 2, 1987, "Vice President George H.W. Bush meets with Iraqi ambassador Nizar Hamdoon and tells him that two requests by Iraq for sensitive American technology had been approved over objections from the Defense Department.'"

—Philip Taylor, *The War in Iraq—A Failure of Honesty*, Page 12

4/17/1987: Soviets bomb bin Laden's compound, marking the birth of bin Laden's public reputation as a warrior

"On April 17, 1987, Soviet helicopters and bomber jets hit Osama bin Laden's new fortified compound at Jaji [Afghanistan], an assemblage of small crevices and caves dug into rocky hills above the border village....the battle of Jaji marked the birth of Osama bin Laden's public reputation as a warrior among Arab jihadists....After Jaji he began a media campaign designed to publicize the brave fight waged by Arab volunteers who stood their ground against a superpower."

—Steve Coll, *Ghost Wars*, Pages 162–163

2/15/1988: Reagan administration gives Iraq military intel and direct military assistance in conflict with Iran

"Apart from receiving the assistance of U.S. military intelligence, the Iraqis received direct military assistance from the United States, which sent teams of military advisers to assist the Iraqi top brass direct operations at the front [during a new offensive against the Iranians in February 1988]." [*The fifteenth of the month used for date sorting purposes only.*]

—Con Coughlin, *Saddam*, Page 222

8/11/1988: Soviet occupation leads bin Laden's meeting and discussion of new military group, Al-Qaeda

Regarding the formation of Al-Qaeda, "By the end of the Soviet occupation [of Afghanistan], an estimated 35,000 Muslim radicals from forty-three Islamic countries had joined the fight [against the Soviets]....On August 11, 1988, bin Laden held a meeting in which he discussed the establishment of a new military group—al-Qaeda."

—Bob Graham with Jeff Nussbaum, *Intelligence Matters*, Page 28

8/15/1988: Bin Laden founds Al-Qaeda August of 1988

In August 1988, Osama "Bin Laden founds al Qaeda." [*The fifteenth of the month used for date sorting purposes only.*]

—Roy Gutman, *How We Missed the Story*, Page 263

1/20/1989: Republican George H. W. Bush inaugurated as president with James D. Quayle as vice president

---

10/2/1989: George H. W. Bush orders expanded US political and economic ties with Iraq

On October 2, 1989, "President [H. W.] Bush issued National Security Directive [NSD] 26, which ordered the different branches of the federal government to expand America's political and economic ties to Baghdad."

—Lawrence F. Kaplan and William Kristol, *The War Over Iraq*, Page 41

11/24/1989: Bin Laden allegedly assassinates opponent and establishes Al-Qaeda for jihad against the West when Soviets leave Afghanistan

"As the Soviets leave Afghanistan, a dispute breaks out among the 'Afghan Arabs' over the best use of the fortune that continues to pour in. [Palestinian cleric Abdullah] Azzam wants to use the money to set up an Islamic regime in Kabul. Osama bin Laden wants to use it for a worldwide jihad against the West. Mysteriously, Azzam and his two sons are murdered in a car bombing [on November 24, 1989]. Though bin Laden professes grief, intelligence analysts believe he was responsible. Within months, with the support of his Egyptian allies Dr. Ayman al-Zawahiri, Mohammed Atef, and Sheikh Omar Abdel Rahman, bin Laden takes over Azzam's Services Office network, using it as a grid for his new terror network, al Qaeda."

—Peter Lance, *Triple Cross*, Page (Timeline) 3

1/15/1990: George H. W. Bush waives restrictions on Iraq's use of Export-Import bank, overlooking Iraq stealing nuclear technology

"In January 1990, President [H. W.] Bush waived congressional restrictions on Iraq's use of the Export-Import Bank and in doing so overlooked new evidence that Iraq was testing ballistic missiles and stealing nuclear technology. All told, the Reagan and Bush administrations ended up providing Saddam Hussein with more than $5 billion in loan guarantees. In the end, American support had enabled the repressive dictator to become a major military force in the Persian Gulf. Saddam had chemical weapons and a nuclear arms program. There were now a million men in the Iraqi army." [*The fifteenth of the month used for date sorting purposes only.*]

—Craig Unger, *House of Bush, House of Saud*, Pages 81–82

1/15/1990: George W. Bush's (son of George H. W. Bush) luck with oil

After the purchase of George W. Bush's oil company Spectrum 7 by Harken Energy, Bush was offered a spot on the Harken board. "In January 1990, by which time the elder George Bush had become president, Harken came into another stroke of unexpected good luck. The beleaguered oil company had had no offshore drilling experience whatsoever and had never even drilled outside the borders of the United States. Nevertheless, tiny Harken stunned industry analysts by beating out giant Amoco to win exclusive offshore drilling rights in Bahrain—thanks to yet another BCCI [Bank of Credit and Commerce International] stockholder, the prime minister of Bahrain, Sheikh Khalifa bin Salman al-Khalifa....No one in the oil industry doubted that the Bahrain deal happened solely because Bush's father was president. Moreover, George W. Bush was one of its greatest beneficiaries and profited handsomely from it." [*The fifteenth of the month used for date sorting purposes only.*]

—Craig Unger, *House of Bush, House of Saud*, Page 122

4/12/1990: Senators relay a message from George H. W. Bush that US wants better relations with Hussein, address human rights and WMD

"[O]n April 12, 1990, Senator Bob Dole [R-KS] and a party of five other senators from agricultural states met with Saddam and provided a message from President George H. W. Bush addressing human rights and WMD and assuring the Iraqi president that Washington wanted better relations."

—Charles Duelfer, *Hide and Seek*, Page 59

7/15/1990: Iraqi tanks move toward Kuwait

"In mid-July [1990], Iraqi tanks began moving toward Kuwait, and by July 19 our satellite photos showed three heavy armored divisions within striking distance of the Kuwait border." [*The fifteenth of the month used for date sorting purposes only.*]

—Dick Cheney, *In My Time*, Page 182

7/18/1990: US determined to ensure free flow of oil through Strait of Hormuz, supporting our friends in the Gulf

As Iraq built up troops on the Kuwaiti border, "[t]he State Department declared on July 18 [1990] that the United States remained 'determined to ensure the free flow of oil through the Strait of Hormuz and to defend the principle of freedom of navigation. We also remain strongly committed to supporting the individual and collective self-defense of our friends in the Gulf with whom we have deep and longstanding ties.'"

—Richard N. Haass, *War of Necessity, War of Choice*, Page 56

7/25/1990: Glaspie to Hussein: "We have no opinion on the Arab-Arab conflicts like your border disagreement with Kuwait"

"In response to Iraqi troop movements along the border with Kuwait, the State Department dispatched Ambassador [April] Glaspie to mollify Saddam. At a July 25, 1990 meeting, the Iraqi leader predicted to Glaspie that America would not oppose his aims because 'yours is a society that cannot accept 10,000 dead in one battle.' To which Glaspie replied, 'we have no opinion on the Arab-Arab conflicts like your border disagreement with Kuwait....[Secretary of State] James Baker has directed our official spokesman to emphasize this instruction.'"

—Lawrence F. Kaplan and William Kristol, *The War Over Iraq*, Page 42

[**Note:** This simple US error or miscommunication suggesting that our country wouldn't interfere if Hussein invaded Kuwait might have accidentally blessed Iraq's invasion of Kuwait a week later.]

8/1/1990: Hussein invades Kuwait, bin Laden volunteers his services to Saudi Arabia—offer not accepted

"After Hussein's forces did invade the small, oil-rich state [of Kuwait] on August 1, 1990, and threaten the security of Saudi Arabia, bin Laden immediately volunteered his services and those of his holy warriors. The Saudi army and his own men would be enough to defend the Kingdom...The Saudis did not take this offer seriously....they turned instead for help to the U.S. government and then-President [H. W.] Bush, who had made his fortune in the oil trade and so understood exactly what was at stake in Iraq's invasion of Kuwait"

—Peter Bergen, *Holy War, Inc.*, Pages 80–81

8/5/1990: George H. W. Bush issues ultimatum to Hussein to leave Kuwait

"On August 5 [1990], President [H. W.] Bush stepped off Marine One on the White House lawn and, referring to the Iraqi invasion, uttered the most famous words of his presidency: 'This will not stand, this aggression against Kuwait.' The spontaneous remark meant one thing: war."

—Craig Unger, *House of Bush, House of Saud*, Page 133

8/6/1990: Secretary of Defense Cheney says US will defend Saudi Arabia

On August 6, 1990, "Secretary of Defense Dick Cheney flew to Riyadh [Saudi Arabia] at the head of an American delegation and read out to King Fahd bin Adbul Aziz and the senior Saudi princes a message from President George [H. W.] Bush. 'We are prepared to deploy these forces to defend the Kingdom of Saudi Arabia,' the message said. 'If you ask us to come we will come. We seek no permanent bases. And when you ask us to leave, we will go home.'"

—Jonathan Randal, *Osama*, Pages 105–106

8/8/1990: Hussein invades Kuwait; George H. W. Bush administration orders 500,000 US forces for Operation Desert Shield to prevent Saudi invasion

After Hussein invaded Kuwait, "On August 8, 1990, President George H. W. Bush ordered American troops to the region, ostensibly to prevent an invasion of Saudi Arabia. Operation Desert Shield was now under way. Eventually, that movement resulted in the buildup of approximately 500,000 U.S. forces over the next five months."

—Ricardo S. Sanchez with Donald T. Phillips, *Wiser in Battle*, Page 64

8/15/1990: George H. W. Bush: World would suffer if "world's great oil reserves fell into the hands" of Hussein

On August 15, 1990, days after Iraq invaded Kuwait on August 2, 1990, President H. W. Bush declared: "Our jobs, our way of life, our own freedom, and the freedom of friendly countries around the world would all suffer if control of the world's great oil reserves fell into the hands of that one man, Saddam Hussein."

—"Remarks to Department of Defense Employees," The American Presidency Project, Presidency.UCSB.edu, August 15, 1990

9/11/1990: Secretary of Defense Cheney about possible Iraqi stranglehold on oil and US economy

Speaking before the Senate Armed Services Committee on September 11, 1990, then-Secretary of Defense Cheney said: "Once he [Iraqi President Hussein] acquired Kuwait and deployed an army as large as the one he possesses, he was clearly in a position to be able to dictate the future of worldwide energy policy, and that gave him a strangle hold on our economy and on that of most of the other nations of the world as well."

—United States Senate, Committee on Armed Services-S.Hrg. 101–1071, "Crisis in the Persian Gulf Region: U.S. Policy Options and Implications," US Government Printing Office, books.Google.com, 1990, Page 11

11/5/1990: First document bearing the name Al-Qaeda found in terrorist's US home in aftermath of JDL assassination where plans include WTC attack

"Early in the evening of November 5, 1990, in New York City...Rabbi Meir Kahane, the fiery founder of the militant Jewish Defense League, was appearing at a meeting at the New York Marriott Hotel on West Forty-ninth Street in Manhattan....As Kahane took questions from the audience, a man of Arab descent with an odd smile on his face suddenly approached and shot Kahane dead with a silver-plated .357 handgun. The man who pulled the trigger, [Islamist] El Sayed Nosair, was...originally from Egypt.... At Nosair's apartment, police discovered bomb-making materials and instruction manuals on special warfare. They also found a list of potential

assassination targets, and maps and photos of many of New York's land-
marks—including the World Trade Center." It took more than two years
to translate documents found in Nosair's file cabinets which included "a
document that appears to be one of the very first bearing the name of bin
Laden's new organization: Al Qaeda."

—Craig Unger, *House of Bush, House of Saud*, Pages 146–148

11/29/1990: UN authorizes all means necessary to drive Iraq from Kuwait

On November 29, 1990, "the United Nations authorized the use of 'all necessary means' to drive Iraqi forces from Kuwait if they failed to withdraw
by January 15 [1991] and to 'restore international peace and security in the
area.' Security Council Resolution 678 passed by a vote of 12–2, with China
abstaining and Cuba and Yemen voting no."

—Karen DeYoung, *Soldier*, Page 201

1/15/1991: Bin Laden enraged with Saudis for allowing US, Jews, Christians, and rock music on their soil during Gulf War

"Mr. bin Laden was indignant with corruption in the government and became enraged when [Saudi] King Fahd let American forces, with their rock
music and Christian and Jewish troops, wage the Persian Gulf war from
Saudi soil in early [January] 1991." [*The fifteenth of the month used for date
sorting purposes only.*]

—Robert D. McFadden, "A NATION CHALLENGED: IN PROFILE; Bin Laden's
Journey From Rich, Pious Boy To the Mask of Evil," *The New York Times*, September 30, 2001

1/15/1991: George H. W. Bush NSD 54: Access to Persian Gulf oil is vital to US national security

On January 15, 1991, "The day before he launched the U.S. attack against
Iraq, President [H. W.] Bush signed National Security Directive 54. The first
line states, 'Access to Persian Gulf oil and the security of key friendly states
in the area are vital to U.S. national security.'"

—Antonia Juhasz, *The Tyranny of Oil*, Page 328

1/17/1991: The US and coalition forces invade Iraq to force them out of Kuwait

---

2/15/1991: George H. W. Bush signs order to topple Hussein

"After the 1991 Gulf War, President George H. W. Bush signed a presidential finding authorizing the CIA to topple Saddam [on February 15, 1991]....
the president publicly called on Iraqis to 'take matters into their own hands' to remove Saddam. When the Kurds in the north and Shiite Muslims in the south rebelled against Saddam, [H. W.] Bush declined U.S. military support. The result was another slaughter."

—Bob Woodward, *Plan of Attack*, Page 70

3/3/1991: Gulf War ends with Iraq agreeing to UN terms, and pledging to dismantle and not pursue WMD

"The Persian Gulf War officially ended on March 3, 1991...when Iraq formally agreed to accept all the terms laid out by the United Nations—including a pledge to dismantle and not pursue weapons of mass destruction. Kuwait had been liberated and the United Nations, the United States, and the coalition had realized all goals."

—Ricardo S. Sanchez with Donald T. Phillips, *Wiser in Battle*, Page 82

4/3/1991: Gulf War ended with no state allowed to import Iraqi oil unless Iraq cooperated with weapons inspections

"The [First Gulf] war ended with a cease-fire, which was confirmed by [United Nations] Security Council Resolution 687, adopted on April 3, 1991. The resolution established an inspection regime under which Iraq was to declare all its holdings of weapons of mass destruction as well as facilities and programs for their manufacture. The declarations were to be verified by the newly created UN [United Nations] Special Commission (UNSCOM) [United Nations Special Commission, the inspection group that searched for weapons of mass destruction in Iraq] in the spheres of biological and chemical weapons and long-range missiles, while the IAEA [International Atomic Energy Agency] would be responsible for the nuclear sphere. Iraq was given a strong incentive to cooperate: No state would be allowed to import oil from Iraq until the Security Council, upon the reports of the inspectors, had concluded that all prohibited items and programs were eradicated."

—Hans Blix, *Disarming Iraq*, Page 20

12/21/1991: JDL killer gets money from bin Laden for his defense, the first time FBI learns of the leader in association with WTC future bombers

Egyptian Islamist El Sayyid Nosair was sentenced for the murder of Rabbi Meier Kahane on December 21, 1991. "Nosair's cousin Ibrahim El-Gabrowny gets $20,000 from bin Laden for Nosair's defense. The FBI later admits that this is the first time bin Laden's name comes up in association with the New York cell members around the [future World Trade Center (WTC) bombing conspirator] blind Sheikh [Omar Abdel Rahman]."

—Peter Lance, *Triple Cross*, Page (Timeline) 5

3/30/1992: George H. W. Bush states reasons for not taking out Hussein in 1990/1991 Gulf War

On March 30, 1992, "President George H. W. Bush answered the question as to why we did not go on to Baghdad to take out Saddam Hussein: 'We certainly had the military capability to go on to Baghdad. But once we had prevailed and had toppled Saddam Hussein's government, we presumably would have had to stay there and put another government in place. And what would that have been: a Sunni government, a Shia government, a Kurdish government, or another Baathist regime? How long would U.S. forces have been required to stay in to prop the government up? And how effective could it have been if the government we put in had been perceived as a puppet of the U.S. military? To involve American forces in a civil war inside Iraq would have been a quagmire, because we would have gone in there with no clear-cut military objective. It's just as important to know when not to use force as it is to know when to use it.'"

—Ricardo S. Sanchez with Donald T. Phillips, *Wiser in Battle*, Pages 82–83

[**Note:** A prescient response.]

10/15/1992: CIA hires DC PR firm to turn world opinion against Hussein

"The CIA, in turn, passed along a sizable amount of money to The Rendon Group [an international strategic communications consultancy based in Washington, DC] to turn world opinion against Hussein. One of the company's first actions was to create the Iraqi National Congress [INC]... as a Hussein opposition group; and in October 1992...[Potential Iraqi President] Ahmed Chalabi was placed in charge of the group." [*The fifteenth of the month used for date sorting purposes only.*]

—James Bamford, *A Pretext for War*, Page 296

12/29/1992: Yemen hotel bombing first bin Laden attack

On December 29, 1992, "[a] bomb explodes in a hotel in Aden, Yemen, where US troops had been staying while en route to a humanitarian mission in Somalia. The bomb killed two Austrian tourists; the U.S. soldiers had already left. Two Yemeni Muslim militants, trained in Afghanistan and injured in the blast, are later arrested. US intelligence agencies allege that this was the first terrorist attack involving bin Laden and his associates."

—"Hunting Bin Laden; Who is Bin Laden & What Does He Want? A Chronology of His Political Life," *PBS Frontline*, accessed April 24, 2018

1/15/1993: Clinton: US will not oust Hussein, relations may improve even with him in power

"Bill Clinton, the president-elect, spoke to Tom Friedman of the *New York Times* in January [15,] 1993 and suggested that the United States would not work for Saddam's ouster and that relations could improve even if he remained in power. 'Based on the evidence that we have, the people of Iraq would be better off if they had a different leader. But my job is not to pick their rulers for them. I always tell everybody I'm a Baptist. I believe in deathbed conversions. If he wants a different relationship with the United States and with the United Nations, all he has to do is change his behavior.'"

—Richard N. Haass, *War of Necessity, War of Choice*, Page 155

1/20/1993: Democrat William J. Clinton inaugurated as president for first term with Albert A. Gore, Jr. as vice president

---

2/26/1993: First WTC bombing; refugee center in New York is outpost for bin Laden, Al-Qaeda operations

"On February 26 [1993], [terrorist Ramzi] Yousef…and Ismail Najim, an associate who had flown up from Texas to take part in the operation, drove a rented white Ford Econoline van to the World Trade Center and parked it in the B-2 level of the underground garage. At 12:17 p.m., the device exploded. It killed six people and injured more than a thousand others, but failed to accomplish its intended mission of knocking down both of the Twin Towers.…Also involved was the Blind Sheikh, Omar Abdel Rahman. The Al-Kifah Refugee Center in Brooklyn…was now the New York outpost of Osama bin Laden and Al Qaeda's operation."

—Craig Unger, *House of Bush, House of Saud*, Pages 149–150

3/15/1993: Bin Laden says US is trying to eradicate Islam

In an interview conducted by CNN in March 1993, Osama bin Laden said: "'America escalated its campaign against the Muslim world in its entirety, aiming to get rid of Islam itself.'" [*The fifteenth of the month used for date sorting purposes only.*]

—Daniel Benjamin and Steven Simon, *The Age of Sacred Terror*, Page 106

4/2/1993: CIA: Bin Laden works independently or with others to promote "militant Islamic causes"

"A CIA paper circulated on April 2, 1993, described bin Laden as an 'independent actor [who] sometimes works with other individuals or governments' to promote 'militant Islamic causes.'"

—Steve Coll, *Ghost Wars*, Pages 255–256

6/15/1993: Bin Laden plots killings of Middle East leaders

"From the comfort of his home in Khartoum [Sudan] bin Laden began considering plans for assassination attacks on Middle Eastern leaders he opposed. In June 1993 he was involved in an attempt to murder Crown Prince Abdullah of Jordan, now the leader of the country since the death of King Hussein in 1999." [*The fifteenth of the month used for date sorting purposes only.*]

—Simon Reeve, *The New Jackals*, Page 183

8/15/1993: CIA analyst authors paper with the first warning about Osama bin Laden

"In August 1993, while working at the Bureau of Intelligence and Research, the small intelligence shop inside the State Department, [CIA analyst Gina] Bennett had authored a paper that was the first warning of the threat posed by a man named 'Osama Bin Ladin,' who was 'enabling hundreds of jihadists and training even more' in Afghanistan, Pakistan, Sudan, and Yemen." [*The fifteenth of the month used for date sorting purposes only.*]

—Peter Bergen, *The Longest War*, Page 36

10/3/1993: Bin Laden brags to CNN of killing more than a dozen US soldiers in Somalia while in Sudan

"Bin Laden told CNN in [March] 1997 that one of his proudest achievements while he was based in Sudan was the role of his Afghan Arabs in the [October 3–4] 1993 killings of more than a dozen American soldiers stationed in Somalia."

—Peter Bergen, *Holy War, Inc.*, Page 84

1/15/1994: Bin Laden finances terrorist training camps in North Sudan

"According to US intelligence analysts, by January 1994, bin Laden was financing at least three terrorist training camps in North Sudan, where rebels from a half-dozen nations received training." [*The fifteenth of the month used for date sorting purposes only.*]

—"Hunting Bin Laden; Who is Bin Laden & What Does He Want? A Chronology of His Political Life," *PBS Frontline*, accessed April 24, 2018

3/15/1994: Wolfowitz: US and industrialized world have enormous stake in Persian Gulf oil

Former Undersecretary of Defense for Policy Paul Wolfowitz said, in March 1994: "'The United States and the entire industrialized world have an enormous stake in the security of the Persian Gulf, not primarily in order to save a few dollars per gallon of gasoline but rather because a hostile regime in control of those resources could wreak untold damage on the world's economy, and could apply that wealth to purposes that would endanger peace globally.'" [*The fifteenth of the month used for date sorting purposes only.*]

—Antonia Juhasz, *The Bush Agenda*, Page 35

6/24/1994: Pentagon reports that terrorists might simultaneously attack different targets perhaps even in different countries

One of the most important conclusions of the Pentagon's June 24, 1994, secret report titled "Terror-2000: The Future Face of Terrorism," "was that rather than bombing a single target, terrorists would soon try to conduct simultaneous bombings and attacks, perhaps even in different countries, to maximize the devastation and publicity for their cause."

—Simon Reeve, *The New Jackals*, Page 260

[**Note:** An accurate prediction.]

9/15/1994: Three discovered terror plans include killing Pope, hijacking planes, and flying them into American buildings

In September 1994, "Working out of the Philippines, [World Trade Center bomber Ramzi] Yousef conceives three plots. (1) He will kill Pope John Paul II on a visit to Manila in January 1995. (2) He will create an undetectable liquid-based bomb to be smuggled on board eleven U.S. jumbo jets entering the United States from Asia [later known as the 'Bojinka' plot]…. (3) With Abdul Hakim Murad, the pilot trained at four U.S. flight schools, Yousef will coordinate the training of Islamic pilots at U.S. schools who will then commandeer airliners and fly them into buildings in America. This third plot becomes the blueprint for the 9/11 attacks." [*The fifteenth of the month used for date sorting purposes only.*]

—Peter Lance, *Triple Cross*, Page (Timeline) 13

[**Note:** This is the first warning I found that terrorists, trained at US flight schools, would commandeer airlines, and fly them into US buildings.]

11/12/1994: Bin Laden wants Clinton killed, but knowing it is too risky to kill a sitting US president, 1993 WTC bomber sets his aim on the Pope

"Bin Laden, his emissaries explained, wanted Yousef to assassinate President Clinton when he visited the Philippines on 12 November 1994, at the start of a five-day tour of Asia. Yousef appears to have been keen on the operation, relishing the prestige of his target, but he was also concerned that assassinating the most powerful man in the world would be no easy task—far harder than taking bombs into Iran or the World Trade Center.... Deterred from his mission to kill President Clinton by the US leader's security precautions, Ramzi Yousef decided he would instead assassinate Pope John Paul II [during his mid-January visit to Manila]."

—Simon Reeve, *The New Jackals*, Pages 76, 78

12/24/1994: Bin Laden-funded GIA members' plan to fly a plane of explosives into Eiffel Tower ended when French forces stormed hijacked plane

On December 24, 1994, "members of the bin Laden-funded Armed Islamic Group (GIA), boarded Flight 8969 [in Algiers, Algeria]...storming the cockpit and wiring the airliner with explosives. After a hostage standoff, they flew to Marseilles [France] and demanded that the Airbus be fully fueled. When the GIA terrorists killed two hostages, the plane was stormed by France's elite GIGN [National Gendarmerie Intervention Group] 'super gendarmes' and the crisis ended. Passengers later told police that the hijackers intended to fly the Airbus into the Eiffel Tower."

—Peter Lance, *Triple Cross*, Page 188

1/5/1995: Laptop reveals Bojinka plot to use planes as bombs; Philippines PSG wonders why America didn't listen

"At the 1996 Bojinka trial of Yousef, Murad, and Wali Khan [Amin Shah] in the Southern District [of New York], the Feds restricted their disclosures [of Yousef's laptop's contents] to the nonsuicide Bojinka plot and to the initial plan to pilot a Cessna-like plane into CIA headquarters. But a blueprint [for virtually the entire 9/11 plot]...was also contained on that laptop and the Philippines National Police got the details in *early January 1995*. 'We told the Americans about the plans to turn planes into flying bombs as far back as 1995,' said Avelino 'Sonny' Razon, the former colonel from the Presidential Security Group (PSG) who ran the Bojinka investigation. 'Why didn't they pay attention?'" [*The fifth of the month used for date sorting purposes only.*]

—Peter Lance, *Triple Cross*, Pages 184–185

[**Note:** A warning we received that planes could become weapons flown into US buildings.]

1/15/1995: Clarke: Yousef plans to blow up planes over Pacific

In January 1995, Clarke said: "'[Yousef] was planning to blow up U.S. airliners in the Pacific with bombs smuggled on board, bombs we won't notice, using liquid explosives. They're assembled on board in the bathroom and then left there. The terrorist then gets off at the first stop and the plane continues on and blows up. The Filipinos found some of the bombs, but not all.'" [*The fifteenth of the month used for date sorting purposes only.*]

—Richard Clarke, *Against All Enemies*, Page 93

1/20/1995: Terrorists discussed flying small plane into CIA

Based on the transcript of Philippines National Police Colonel Rodolfo Mendoza's January 20, 1995, interrogation session with terrorist Ramzi Yousef's cohort Abdul Hakim Murad, the 9/11 Commission determined on April 13, 2004: "'Two of the [Bojinka] perpetrators had also discussed the possibility of flying a small plane into the headquarters of the CIA.'"

—Peter Lance, *Triple Cross*, Page 384

[**Note:** More notice of the possibility of a plane being flown into a US building.]

2/15/1995: Islamic terrorists training in US flight schools; targets include the CIA, Pentagon, WTC

In February 1995, after Philippines National Police Colonel Rodolfo Mendoza threatened to turn World Trade Center bomber Ramzi Yousef's cohort Abdul Hakim Murad over to Israeli Mossad, Murad filled him in on Yousef's third plot.

"He tells Mendoza that ten Islamic terrorists are currently training in U.S. flight schools. The ultimate targets will be the CIA, the Pentagon, the World Trade Center, the Sears Tower in Chicago, the Transamerica Tower in San Francisco, and a U.S. nuclear facility." [*The fifteenth of the month used for date sorting purposes only.*]

—Peter Lance, *Triple Cross*, Page (Timeline) 15

[**Note:** More information about terrorists training in US flight schools and intending to fly planes into US buildings.]

4/13/1995: FBI: WTC, other attacks prove Islamic extremists can operate anywhere; confession reveals plot to hijack plane, fly it into the CIA

"The FBI's [April 13, 1995] report [on global terrorism, quoted in *The Washington Post* on June 6, 2002] noted the vulnerability of the American homeland to attacks.

It specifically cited [Yousef's cohort] Murad's confessed plot to hijack a plane and fly it into CIA headquarters as an example....

The cable concluded: 'Yousef's group fits the mold for this new generation of Sunni Islamic terrorists....The WTC bombing, the Manila plot, and the recent [Islamic Group] attack against [Egyptian president Hosni] Mubarak demonstrate that Islamic extremists can operate anywhere in the world. We believe the threat is not over.'"

—Steve Coll, *Ghost Wars*, Pages 278–279

[**Note:** Still another terrorist plot to hijack a plane and fly it into a US building.]

5/11/1995: FBI: Terrorist Hakim wants to bomb WTC again

"As FBI agents Frank Pellegrino and Thomas Donlon noted in an FBI 302 [interview summary] transcribed on May 11, 1995, '[Yousef's cohort] MURAD advised that RAMZI wanted to return to the United States in the future to bomb the World Trade Center a second time.'"

—Peter Lance, *Cover Up*, Page 46

7/15/1995: NIE: Loosely organized terrorist groups with help from individuals like bin Laden are the greatest emerging threat to national security

"A [July] 1995 National Intelligence Estimate [NIE] concluded that loosely organized, transnational terrorist groups, obtaining weapons, financing, and other forms of support from various governments, factions, and individual benefactors like bin Laden, posed the greatest emerging threat to national security." [*The fifteenth of the month used for date sorting purposes only.*]

—John Farmer, *The Ground Truth*, Page 20

[**Note:** The greatest emerging threat to our national security was reported as early as 1995.]

10/15/1995: FBI had not even opened a file on bin Laden until 1995; CIA already had forty thick file folders on him

"The FBI had not even opened a file on bin Laden until October 1995" at the same time, "the CIA had forty thick file folders on bin Laden. Although much of it was raw, and often not reliable, intelligence, it was an indicator to the FBI agents of how far behind the Bureau was in focusing on bin Laden and also illustrated once again how little information the CIA had shared [the following is from a footnote in the book]." [*The fifteenth of the month used for date sorting purposes only.*]

—Gerald Posner, *Why America Slept*, Pages 114–115

[**Note:** By October 1995, the CIA has substantiated information about bin Laden.]

10/21/1995: Clinton issues secret order for intel agencies to join together and increase, integrate efforts to track bin Laden's money, but they fail

"The effort to track the bin Laden group's money began in earnest when President Bill Clinton signed a classified presidential order on Oct. 21, 1995. The secret order, Presidential Decision Directive [PDD] 42, ordered the Departments of Justice, State and Treasury, the National Security Council [NSC], the C.I.A. and other intelligence agencies to increase and integrate their efforts against international money laundering by terrorists and criminals. The government agencies joined together to try to penetrate the bin Laden network of businesses, charities, banks and front companies. They failed."

—Tim Weiner and David Cay Johnston, "Roadblocks Cited in Efforts to Trace bin Laden's Money," *The New York Times*, September 20, 2001

11/12/1995: Clinton administration confused, unable to respond to a wave of bin Laden terrorist attacks that start on a US military base in Saudi Arabia

The attack on a US Military base in Riyadh, Saudi Arabia on November 12, 1995, "was the beginning of a string of terrorist attacks by bin Laden and related terrorist groups that left the Clinton administration confused and unable to respond."

—Bill Gertz, *Breakdown*, Pages 7–9

11/13/1995: Bin Laden followers kill seven with car bomb that injures US Saudi guard advisors

"On November 13 [1995], a car bomb in Riyadh, widely attributed to followers of Osama bin Laden, kills seven people, including five Americans, and wounds several American advisers with Vinnell, the Carlyle-owned firm that trains the Saudi Arabian National Guard."

—Craig Unger, *House of Bush, House of Saud*, Page 303

1/15/1996: CIA forms elite bin Laden task force from more than eleven federal agencies, largest for a single terrorist

"In January 1996, a decision was taken by senior staff of the CIA's 200-strong Counterterrorist Center...to form a special bin Laden taskforce. Ever since, the Osama bin Laden desk, manned by elite staff of more than eleven federal agencies, has mounted the largest, most expensive and most extensive investigation ever into a single individual charged with international terrorism." [*The fifteenth of the month used for date sorting purposes only.*]

—Simon Reeve, *The New Jackals*, Pages 184–185

[**Note:** The CIA focuses on the danger of bin Laden back in 1996.]

4/30/1996: State Department report mentions bin Laden for first time, calls him "a major financier of terrorism"

"In its 1995 Patterns of Global Terrorism report [released on April 30, 1996], the State Department, for the first time, mentioned bin Laden, calling him 'a major financier of terrorism.'"

—Richard Miniter, *Losing Bin Laden*, Page 106

6/25/1996: Bin Laden suspected in truck bombing at US military housing in Saudi Arabia, dozens killed

"On June 25, 1996, a truck bomb with five thousand pounds of explosives rocked the Khobar Towers military housing complex in Dharhan, Saudi Arabia, killing dozens of people, including nineteen American soldiers, and wounding more than five hundred others....Again, bin Laden was suspected."

—Craig Unger, *House of Bush, House of Saud*, Page 173

7/10/1996: Bin Laden calls Americans "main enemy" to Muslims worldwide; world reaching "beginning of war between Muslims and the United States"

"The Americans were the 'main enemy' of Muslims worldwide, an angry bin Laden told a British journalist [Robert Fisk, for an article published in *The Independent* on July 10, 1996] who visited him in an eastern Afghan mountain camp weeks after his arrival in Jalalabad. Saudi Arabian authorities were only 'secondary enemies,' he declared. As bin Laden saw it, the world had now reached 'the beginning of war between Muslims and the United States.'"

—Steve Coll, Ghost Wars, Page 326

8/23/1996: Bin Laden declares war on the US

Osama bin Laden declared war on the United States in a treatise written from Afghanistan. "[B]in Laden said, on August 23, 1996, in his 'Declaration of War Against the Americans Occupying the Land of the Two Holy Places.' The latest indignity—'one of the worst catastrophes to befall the Muslims since the death of the Prophet'—was the presence of American and coalition troops in Saudi Arabia."

—Lawrence Wright, The Looming Tower, Page 265

[**Note:** When inaugurated, George W. Bush should have known that bin Laden had already declared war on America.]

1/6/1997: Counterterrorist Center Commentary: "[E]fforts by Bin Laden suggests...taking steps to develop the capability to use" WMD

According to a recently declassified top secret Counterterrorist Center Commentary on January 6, 1997: "[Redacted] agents of Usama Bin Ladin purchased a container of uranium [redacted] but [redacted] bogus nuclear material [redacted] efforts by Bin Ladin suggests he is taking steps to develop the capability to use weapons of mass destruction (WMD)—possibly involving chemical agents and biological toxins as well as nuclear material—for terrorist operations, or may plan to give these substances to supporters."

—CIA, "Terrorism: Usama Bin Ladin Trying to Develop WMD Capability," (Counterterrorist Center Commentary), The Central Intelligence Agency's 9/11 File: The National Security Archive, January 6, 1997

1/20/1997: Democrat William J. Clinton inaugurated as president for a second term with Albert A. Gore, Jr. as vice president

---

2/15/1997: Bin Laden: Better to kill an American soldier than waste time on other matters

"In a February 1997 Arabic-language television interview, bin Laden declared, 'If someone can kill an American soldier, it is better than wasting time on other matters.'" [*The fifteenth of the month used for date sorting purposes only.*]

—Richard Miniter, Losing Bin Laden, Page 161

3/20/1997: Bin Laden declares jihad against "unjust, criminal, and tyrannical" US

"[I]n March [20, 1997], bin Laden had told reporter Peter Arnett on CNN that he had 'declared jihad against the U.S. government because the U.S. government is unjust, criminal, and tyrannical.'"

—Peter Lance, *Triple Cross*, Page 275

5/15/1997: Tenet testifies to senate committee that US has been at war with bin Laden for a number of years

"Referring to bin Laden and other terror masters, the Director of Central Intelligence, George Tenet, had testified before a closed-door session of the Senate Appropriations Committee in May 1997. 'I think we are already at war,' he said. 'We have been on a war footing for a number of years now.'" [*The fifteenth of the month used for date sorting purposes only.*]

—Richard Miniter, *Losing Bin Laden*, Page 16

[**Note:** Tenet, who would become George W. Bush's first CIA director, knew the danger of bin Laden as early as 1997.]

1/26/1998: NeoCons write to Clinton about ousting Hussein; Clinton makes token effort; George W. Bush sympathetic to NeoCon's plea

"Following [neoconservative Douglas] Feith's call for a war against the occupied Palestinians, [former Assistant Secretary of Defense Richard] Perle, Wolfowitz, [former Secretary of Defense] Rumsfeld, and a small group of neocons signed a letter to President Clinton [on January 26, 1998] pleading with him to make the ouster of Saddam Hussein the 'aim of American foreign policy' and to use military force....Clinton, however, made only a token effort...But Perle and Wolfowitz soon found a sympathetic ear with [Texas Republican Governor] George W. Bush, and at the start of his candidacy he named them as top advisors to his foreign policy team, then being coordinated by [future National Security Advisor] Condoleezza Rice."

—James Bamford, *A Pretext for War*, Pages 281–282

2/17/1998: Clinton speaks about Iraqi WMD; Hussein clearest example of terrorist threat

"In February [17] 1998, in a speech about the dangers of Iraq's weapons of mass destruction, Bill Clinton warned of 'an unholy axis of terrorists, drug traffickers, and organized international criminals' and said 'there is no more clear example of this threat than Saddam Hussein.'"

—Stephen F. Hayes, *Cheney*, Page 319

[**Note:** Although President Clinton speaks on the danger of Hussein in early 1998, his warnings to Bush in December of 2000 were about bin Laden and Al-Qaeda.]

2/22/1998: Bin Laden fatwa: A "duty" for Muslims to kill any American, anywhere to liberate two mosques

From Osama bin Laden's February 22, 1998, statement of jihad against Jews and Crusaders: "'[I]n compliance with Allah's order, we issue the following fatwa to all Muslims: The ruling to kill the Americans and their allies—civilians and military—is an individual duty for every Muslim who can do it in any country in which it is possible to do it, in order to liberate the al-Aqsa Mosque [in Jerusalem] and the holy mosque [Mecca] from their grip.'"

—Peter Bergen, *The Osama bin Laden I Know*, Pages 195–196

5/28/1998: Bin Laden says a "black day" for US coming, states will secede, collect their dead soldiers

"[I]n late May [28, 1998], he [Osama bin Laden] appeared on prime-time network news across the country, telling ABC's John Miller, 'We predict a black day for America and the end of the United States as United States, and [they] will be separate states, and will retreat from our land and collect the bodies of its sons back to America. Allah willing.'"

—James Bamford, *A Pretext for War*, Page 187

8/7/1998: Bombing at US Embassies in Kenya and Tanzania

"On August 7 [1998], the American embassies in Kenya and Tanzania were blown up by al-Qaeda followers, killing 224 people, including 12 Americans."

—Philip Shenon, *The Commission*, Page 254

8/12/1998: Clinton told by advisors that bin Laden is seeking WMD to use against US installations

On August 12, 1998, "The Small Group of presidential advisors meet with Clinton, reportedly with evidence that bin Laden is looking to obtain weapons of mass destruction and chemical weapons to use against US installations"

—"Hunting Bin Laden; Who is Bin Laden & What Does He Want? A Chronology of His Political Life," *PBS Frontline*, accessed April 24, 2018

8/15/1998: After embassy attacks, Clinton secretly allows CIA, Afghan tribes to work together to capture, possibly kill, bin Laden

"In response to al Qaeda's August 1998 bombing of American embassies in Dar es Salaam, Tanzania, and Nairobi, Kenya, President Clinton issued several secret authorizations for the CIA to work with Afghan tribal elements to capture and if necessary kill Osama Bin Laden." [*The fifteenth of the month used for date sorting purposes only.*]

—Jack Goldsmith, *The Terror Presidency*, Page 94

[**Note:** Clinton authorized the capture or killing of bin Laden.]

8/20/1998: US Treasury adds bin Laden to list of terrorists to shut down finances subsidizing his activities

On August 20, 1998, "US adds bin Laden's name to list of terrorists whose funds are targeted for seizure by US Treasury in order to shut down the financial pipelines that allegedly subsidize bin Laden's terrorist activities."

—"Hunting Bin Laden; Who is Bin Laden & What Does He Want? A Chronology of His Political Life," *PBS Frontline*, accessed April 24, 2018

8/20/1998: Clinton sends missiles into Afghanistan and puts sanctions on Al-Qaeda

"On the same day that we sent cruise missiles into Afghanistan [August 20, 1998], President Clinton signed Executive Order[12] 13099, imposing sanctions against Usama bin Laden and al Qaeda."

—Richard Clarke, *Against All Enemies*, Page 190

9/15/1998: Reports in fall of 1998 mention bin Laden terror plans in US involving food, water, and planes

"A classified September 1998 threat report warned that in bin Laden's next strike his operatives might fly an explosive-laden airplane into an American airport and blow it up. Another report that fall, unavailable to the public, highlighted a plot involving aircraft in New York and Washington....Some of these threats against aviation targets were included in classified databases about bin Laden and his followers maintained by the FBI and the CIA.... Several classified reports that fall warned that bin Laden was considering a new attack using poisons in food, water, or the air shafts of American embassies. Aviation was an issue but not a priority." [*The fifteenth of the month used for date sorting purposes only.*]

—Steve Coll, *Ghost Wars*, Page 420

[**Note:** More intel that bin Laden's operatives might be planning on flying a plane into American targets.]

---

12   "[A]n order that comes from the US president or a government agency and must be obeyed like a law," Merriam-Webster.com, accessed September 20, 2016

10/31/1998: Clinton signs law to remove Hussein from power

"The Iraq Liberation Act declared that the goal of U.S. policy should be 'to remove the regime headed by Saddam Hussein from power.' The U.S. House of Representatives approved that legislation by a vote of 360 to 38. It passed the Senate without a single dissenting vote. Clinton signed the legislation into law [on October 31, 1998]. Regime change in Iraq was now the official policy of the United States."

—Donald Rumsfeld, *Known and Unknown*, Page 417

12/1/1998: Intel community warns of bin Laden terror plans for inside US, that he is recruiting operatives

"On December 1 [1998], an intelligence community assessment of [Usama] bin Laden [UBL] warned, 'UBL is actively planning against U.S. targets... Multiple reports indicate UBL is keenly interested in striking the U.S. on its own soil...Al Qaeda is recruiting operatives for attacks in the U.S. but has not yet identified potential targets.'"

—James Bamford, *A Pretext for War*, Page 211

12/16/1998: Clinton explains strikes against Iraq

"In a prime-time address from the Oval Office in December [16] 1998, President Clinton explained [why he launched Operation Desert Fox, a series of strikes against Iraq]: 'The hard fact is that so long as Saddam remains in power, he threatens the well-being of his people, the peace of his region, the security of the world. The best way to end that threat once and for all is with a new Iraqi government—a government ready to live in peace with its neighbors, a government that respects the rights of its people....Heavy as they are, the costs of action must be weighed against the price of inaction. If Saddam defies the world and we fail to respond, we will face a far greater threat in the future. Saddam will strike again at his neighbors. He will make war on his own people. And mark my words, he will develop weapons of mass destruction. He will deploy them, and he will use them.'"

—George W. Bush, *Decision Points*, Page 227

[Note: The above quote from George W. Bush's book doesn't mention that twenty-four months later, Clinton informed him that the biggest terrorist danger to our country was bin Laden, not Hussein.]

12/21/1998: State Department aide says bin Laden to retaliate on DC and NY for the US hitting his headquarters

"Intelligence sources tell TIME [on December 21, 1998] they have evidence that bin Laden may be planning his boldest move yet—a strike on Washington or possibly New York City in an eye-for-an-eye retaliation. 'We've hit his headquarters, now he hits ours,' says a State Department aide."

—Douglas Waller, "Inside The Hunt For Osama," *Time* magazine, December 21, 1998

12/24/1998: Administration lawyers say the president's assassination order didn't violate assassination ban on bin Laden if he is an imminent threat

"By Christmas Eve 1998, President Clinton had authorized the CIA to allow America's tribal allies [in Afghanistan] to kill bin Laden if they could not capture him, overriding the objections of some that this order violated the assassination ban. Administration lawyers concluded that the assassination ban would not be broken if the United States acted in self-defense under international law against an imminent threat of attack."

—John Yoo, *War By Other Means*, Page 59

[**Note:** Clinton tried again to kill bin Laden; the rationale being the imminent threat of an attack.]

1/11/1999: Bin Laden: Religious duty to get nukes, chemical weapons

In an interview conducted by journalist Rahimullah Yusufzai that was printed in *Time* magazine on January 11, 1999, Osama bin Laden said: "'Acquiring nuclear and chemical weapons is a religious duty.'"

—Peter Bergen, *The Osama bin Laden I Know*, Page 337

1/15/1999: Bin Laden: War on US "has just begun"

Regarding the August 1998 bombings of two American embassies in Kenya and in Tanzania, bin Laden said in a January 1999 interview: "'The war [on the United States] has just begun.'" [*The fifteenth of the month used for date sorting purposes only.*]

—James Bamford, *A Pretext for War*, Page 167

2/2/1999: Tenet: No doubt bin Laden is planning new attacks, kidnappings, assassinations, WMD use

"There was 'not the slightest doubt' that bin Laden was planning new attacks, [CIA director George] Tenet said [in a statement to the Senate Armed Services Committee on February 2, 1999, titled 'Current and Projected National Security Threats']. The CIA director issued this warning in public and in private. He saw evidence that bin Laden had contacts inside the United States. Tenet anticipated 'bombing attempts with conventional explosives,' he told Congress and the White House. Bin Laden's operatives were also 'capable of kidnappings and assassinations.' He worried that al Qaeda might acquire and use weapons of mass destruction. Tenet believed a chemical or biological [CB] attack by bin Laden or his allies was now a 'serious prospect.'"

—Steve Coll, *Ghost Wars*, Page 453

[**Note:** Two years before George W. Bush became president, Bush's CIA director-to-be had no doubt bin Laden was a threat to our country.]

3/27/1999: UN: Inspectors effective in ensuring that Iraq did not rebuild weapons program

In a report dated March 27, 1999, a United Nations panel "concluded that 'the bulk of Iraq's proscribed weapons programmes has been eliminated' and suggested that the presence of inspectors was the most effective way to provide assurance that Iraq did not retain, acquire or rebuild prohibited weapons. The panel warned against believing that any system could bring 100-percent certainty and suggested a concentration on the remaining priority tasks. The system could range from routine monitoring to very intrusive inspection. The panel cautioned that any information should be assessed 'strictly on the basis of its credibility and relevance to the mandate' and that the relationship to intelligence providers should be one-way only, even if it was recognized that some dialogue was necessary. The report demanded effectiveness, but warned against unnecessary confrontation. The legal framework for UNSCOM could remain, just in 'renovated' form."

—Hans Blix, *Disarming Iraq*, Pages 38–39

8/6/1999: CBS reports that US intel sources think that bin Laden now has resources to strike US soil

"[O]n 6 August 1999, CBS reported, 'U.S. intelligence sources say they have made a fundamental shift in their assessment of terrorist leader Osama bin Laden. Once confident that bin Laden only had enough resources to strike targets overseas, like the East Africa embassies that are still under repair, they now believe he has the money and people to strike in the continental United States as well.'"

—Michael Scheuer, *Through Our Enemies' Eyes*, Page 203

[**Note:** A notable shift in our intelligence assessment increasing the danger bin Laden could strike the United States.]

9/15/1999: LOC prepares report stating bin Laden could hijack airliner and fly them into government buildings

In September 1999, a report prepared by the Library of Congress for the National Intelligence Council (NIC) said: "Osama bin Laden's terrorists could hijack an airliner and fly it into government buildings like the Pentagon. 'Suicide bomber(s) belonging to al-Qaida's Martyrdom Battalion could crash-land an aircraft packed with high explosives (C-4 and semtex) into the Pentagon, the headquarters of the Central Intelligence Agency (CIA), or the White House,'" [*The fifteenth of the month used for date sorting purposes only.*]

—John Solomon, Associated Press, "Attack Foreseen in 1999," *The Berkeley Daily Planet*, May 18, 2002

[**Note:** Another intelligence warning that bin Laden could use planes to attack US buildings such as the Pentagon.]

10/26/1999: Clarke's Counterrerrorism Security Group "urged" to be creative about preventing bin Laden attacks on US territory

"On October 26 [1999], Clarke's CSG [Counterrerrorism Security Group] took the unusual step of holding a meeting dedicated to trying 'to evaluate the threat of a terrorist attack in the United States by the Usama bin Ladin network.' The CSG members were 'urged to be as creative as possible in their thinking' about preventing a Bin Ladin attack on U.S. territory."

—9/11 Commission, The 9/11 Commission Report, July 22, 2004, Page 127

[**Note:** Clarke working to prevent a bin Laden attack on US territory.]

12/15/1999: UN council authorizes monitoring of Iraq's weapons program

"In December 1999, the UN Security Council authorized the setting up of United Nations Monitoring, Verification and Inspection Commission (UNMOVIC) to monitor Iraq's weapons programmes and to identify any remaining disarmament tasks. Hans Blix, a veteran Swedish diplomat and former director general of the IAEA, was put in charge of UNMOVIC." [*The fifteenth of the month used for date sorting purposes only.*]

—Ali A. Allawi, *The Occupation of Iraq*, Page 71

12/15/1999: US offers $5M for information leading to arrest of bin Laden, names him "public enemy number one"

"Counterterrorism czar Richard Clarke strongly championed a plan to raise the reward for information leading to the arrest of bin Laden from $2.5 million to $5 million. At the time, it was the highest monetary amount allowed by federal law for a wanted man. President Clinton agreed to Clarke's plan.

By December 1999, bin Laden was officially public enemy number one."
[The fifteenth of the month used for date sorting purposes only.]

—Richard Miniter, *Losing Bin Laden*, Page 192

[**Note:** Clarke pushed for an increased reward for the arrest of bin Laden; Clinton agreed.]

1/31/2000: Clarke's Counterrrorism Security Group devoted to possible Al-Qaeda airline hijacking

"After the 1999–2000 millennium [terror] alerts, when the nation had relaxed, Clarke held a meeting of his Counterterrorism Security Group [on January 31, 2000] devoted largely to the possibility of a possible airline hijacking by al Qaeda."

—9/11 Commission, The 9/11 Commission Report, July 22, 2004, page 345

9/15/2000: Think tank backed by Cheney, Rumsfeld, Wolfowitz, and Jeb Bush makes clear George W. Bush administration plans to take control of Gulf region

"It is absolutely clear from the letter and other documents like 'Rebuilding America's Defences', [sic] which was written in September 2000 and drawn up by the same think-tank backed by Dick Cheney, Donald Rumsfeld, Paul Wolfowitz and Jeb Bush [the Project for the New American Century], that the [George W.] Bush administration was planning to take military control of the Gulf region. The document states that 'while the unresolved conflict with Iraq provides the immediate justification, the need for a substantial American force presence in the Gulf transcends the issue of the regime of Saddam Hussein'," *[The fifteenth of the month used for date sorting purposes only.]*

—Clare Short, *An Honourable Deception?*, Pages 92–93

[**Note:** Less than two months before George W. Bush was first elected president, he was planning to take military control of the Gulf region.]

10/12/2000: Al-Qaeda bombs USS *Cole*, seventeen sailors killed

"On the morning of October 12 [2000], two al Qaeda suicide bombers load a device made of C-4 explosive into a small skiff and take off across the harbor in Aden, Yemen. The U.S.S. *Cole*, an advanced guided missile destroyer, is at the refueling dock. As the skiff approaches the ship...the bomb detonates, blowing a four-story hole in the side of the ship. The two bombers and seventeen U.S. sailors are killed."

—Peter Lance, *Triple Cross*, Timeline, Page 29

10/15/2000: CIA: Al-Qaeda's goal is to destroy US; they will get stronger if their safe haven not attacked

"'We've got to change the rules,' the CIA's [unidentified] bin Laden unit chief argued in the aftermath [of the USS *Cole* bombing on October 12, 2000]. It was time for the agency to try to break the policy stalemate about the Taliban. Al Qaeda was growing, and its sanctuary in Afghanistan allowed ever more ambitious operations. Within the CIA and at interagency White House sessions the Counterterrorist Center officers spoke starkly. 'Al Qaeda is training and planning in Afghanistan, and their goal is to destroy the United States,' they declared, as one official recalled it. 'Unless we attack their safe haven, they are going to get continually stronger and stronger.'"

—Steve Coll, *Ghost Wars*, Page 538

10/25/2000: DOD trains for plane hitting the Pentagon

"In late October 2000, in an ironic precursor of things to come, the Department of Defense [DOD] conducted a mass casualty (MASCAL) exercise simulating the impact of a plane hitting the Pentagon." [*The twenty-fifth of the month used for date sorting purposes only.*]

—Peter Lance, *1000 Years For Revenge*, Page 400

[**Note:** Prescient DOD training.]

11/6/2000: George W. Bush: Military should be prepared to prevent war

On November 6, 2000, the day before the [presidential] election, Republican nominee George W. "Bush told an enthusiastic crowd in Chattanooga, Tennessee: 'Let me tell you what else I'm worried about: *I'm worried about an opponent who uses nation-building and the military in the same sentence* [emphasis added]. See, our view of the military is for our military to be properly prepared to fight and win war and, therefore, prevent war from happening in the first place.'"

—Stefan Halper and Jonathan Clarke, *America Alone*, Page 135

As you have read, fifteen years prior to George W. Bush's election as president, the governments of Reagan, H. W. Bush, and Clinton had experience dealing with Iraq, bin Laden, Al-Qaeda, Middle Eastern oil, and Hussein.

A few of President Clinton's concerns were touched on in the quotes of January 15, 1993, January 26, 1998, February 17, 1998, and August 12, 1998. Further proving that concern, Clinton signed the United States 1998 Iraq

Liberation Act (whose goal was Iraq regime change). In late December 1998, Clinton ordered missile strikes against Iraq.

Shifting his main focus from Hussein to bin Laden and Al-Qaeda, in late 1999 Clinton offered a $5 million reward for information leading to the arrest of bin Laden. Then, a month before Bush's inauguration, Clinton and his people told Bush and his senior staff that the number one terrorist risk our country faced, and the biggest terrorist threat Bush and his new administration, would be dealing with would be bin Laden and Al-Qaeda. It's notable that nearing the end of his presidency, Clinton, given all the intel he had received, knew that bin Laden might use planes as weapons to crash into our buildings and was focused on bin Laden and Al-Qaeda, not Hussein.

B. NOVEMBER 7, 2000 (THE DAY BUSH WAS ELECTED), THROUGH 9/11

THIS SECTION WILL SHOW that between Bush's November 7, 2000, election and 9/11, Bush and his incoming administration began receiving and continued to receive top-level briefings about the special dangers presented by bin Laden and Al-Qaeda.

In the beginning, those briefings were given by President Clinton himself, Clinton's counterterrorism czar Clarke (who would stay on in the Bush administration), outgoing Clinton National Security Agency Advisers Sandy Berger and Don Kerrick, and Clinton's CIA Director Tenet (who would also stay on with Bush).

Given the high-level briefing about the danger to our country from bin Laden and Al-Qaeda that President-elect Bush and his national security staff received even before the beginning of his presidency, what did Bush do to protect us from those serious terrorist threats he was warned about?

As you will read, little if anything.

> **11/7/2000: Republican George W. Bush elected president with Richard [Dick] Bruce Cheney as vice president**

Note: The quotes in the gray boxes show that Bush and others in his administration focused on Hussein, his supposed weapons of mass destruction, and Iraqi oil instead of the well-known danger from bin Laden and Al-Qaeda.

12/16/2000: President Clinton briefs President-elect George W. Bush on biggest security problems he will face, including Al-Qaeda

"When [President-elect George W.] Bush visited the White House on December 16, 2000, for the first time, Clinton had briefed him on 'the biggest security problems' he would face. Of the six major threats Clinton listed, three involved al Qaeda and Pakistan. These were al Qaeda itself, nuclear tensions between India and Pakistan and nonproliferation, and 'the ties of the Pakistanis to the Taliban and al Qaeda.'"

—Ahmed Rashid, *Descent Into Chaos*, Page 56

[**Note:** Neither Iraq nor Hussein was on that list.]

12/19/2000: President Clinton proposes Al-Qaeda as a priority to G. W. Bush

Clinton met with President-elect Bush at the White House on December 19, 2000. "Clinton told Bush that he had read his campaign statements carefully and his impression was that his two priorities were national missile defense and Iraq. Bush said this was correct. Clinton proposed a different set of priorities, which included Al Qaeda, Middle East diplomacy, North Korea, the nuclear competition in South Asia, and, only then, Iraq. Bush did not respond."

—Michael R. Gordon and Bernard E. Trainor, *Cobra II*, Page 15

12/20/2000: Powell briefed by Clarke and his team that Al-Qaeda is attempting a direct attack against the US

"[Colin] Powell's first official briefing on terrorism had taken place on December 20, 2000, even before he was sworn in as secretary of state. He had asked Clarke and his team—all still working under President Clinton at the time—to give him a full rundown on bin Laden. Intelligence had indicated that al-Qaeda was planning direct attacks against the United States and likely had sleeper cells already in place inside the country."

—Karen DeYoung, *Soldier*, Page 344

[**Note:** Powell was briefed about the danger from bin Laden even before Bush became president.]

12/20/2000: Clarke, Clinton's counterterrorism czar, presents plan to "roll back" Al-Qaeda postponed by NSA advisor, later presented to Rice, ignored

"On December 20 [2000], counterterrorism czar Richard Clarke presents National Security Adviser Sandy Berger with a plan to 'roll back' Al Qaeda. The plan is postponed pending the arrival of the new [Bush] administration, presented to the new national security adviser, Condoleezza Rice, and then ignored."

—Craig Unger, *House of Bush, House of Saud*, Page 304

12/29/2000: CIA offers "Blue Sky" plan to go after bin Laden

On December 29, 2000, "The [Clinton] CIA had put together what it called a 'Blue Sky' plan for additional authorities to go after Osama bin Laden and his cohorts more aggressively, and Clarke wanted the new president [Bush] to sign off on aid to the Northern Alliance, an anti-Taliban rebel group in Afghanistan, and to neighboring Uzbekistan. [Incoming National Security

Advisor] Rice authorized him to develop a strategy, but no such meeting would be held for months."

—Peter Baker, Days of Fire, Page 90

1/1/2001: Bush advisors calling for a preemptive war in the Middle East even before Bush's inauguration

"With the Pentagon now under Secretary of Defense Donald Rumsfeld and his deputy, Paul Wolfowitz—both of whom had also long believed that Saddam Hussein should have been toppled during the first [1991] Gulf War—the war planners were given free rein. What was needed, however, was a pretext—perhaps a major crisis. 'Crises can be opportunities,' wrote [advisor to Cheney, David] Wurmser in his [January 1, 2001] paper calling for an American-Israeli preemptive war throughout the Middle East."

—James Bamford, A Pretext for War, Pages 268–269

1/3/2001: Incoming G. W. Bush administration given aggressive plan to attack Al-Qaeda by Clarke; administration later denies being given a *formal* plan against Al-Qaeda

"Clarke presented the incoming Bush team with an aggressive plan to attack Al Qaeda [at a meeting on January 3, 2001]....Bush administration officials have denied being given a formal plan to take action against Al Qaeda....Most significantly of all, Clarke called for covert operations 'to eliminate the sanctuary' in Afghanistan where the Taliban was protecting bin Laden and his terrorist training camps."

—Craig Unger, House of Bush, House of Saud, Pages 220–221

1/5/2001: Outgoing NSA adviser Berger briefs successor Rice that terrorism and Al-Qaeda will be biggest subjects of incoming Bush administration

During the transitional period between the Clinton and Bush administrations in the first week of January 2001, outgoing National Security Advisor Berger met with his successor, Rice, at a briefing on terrorism. Afterwards, he told her: "'I believe that the Bush Administration will spend more time on terrorism generally, and on al-Qaeda specifically, than any other subject.'" [*The fifth of the month used for date sorting purposes only.*]

—"They Had A Plan," CNN.com, August 5, 2002

[**Note:** Could the warning to Rice have been more specific and clear?]

1/10/2001: Outgoing CIA advisors name bin Laden one of the greatest threats to our country; killing bin Laden would have impact but not stop the threat

"Early in [January 10] 2001, DCI [Director of Central Intelligence] Tenet and Deputy Director for Operations James Pavitt gave an intelligence briefing to President-elect Bush, Vice President-elect Cheney, and [incoming National Security Advisor] Rice; it included the topic of al Qaeda. Pavitt recalled conveying that Bin Ladin was one of the gravest threats to the country. Bush asked whether killing Bin Ladin would end the problem. Pavitt said he and the DCI had answered that killing Bin Ladin would have an impact, but would not stop the threat."

—9/11 Commission, The 9/11 Commission Report, July 22, 2004, Page 348

1/10/2001: *Washington Post* editorial: G. W. Bush administration needs strategy for bin Laden since it will not "inherit one"

"An editorial in the *Washington Post* [on January 10, 2001] ten days before Clinton left office noted: 'Yemeni officials say they have developed substantial evidence that the [October 12, 2000, USS *Cole*] bombing was ordered by the Saudi-born terrorist Osama bin Laden, and financed and coordinated by Muhammad Omar al-Harazi, a bin Laden associate.' The editorial concluded that the Bush administration 'will also need a coherent strategy for countering Mr. bin Laden; clearly, it will not inherit one.'"

—Stephen F. Hayes, *Cheney*, Page 322

[**Note:** My research found no George W. Bush plan or strategy to counter or try to protect us from the bin Laden or Al-Qaeda threats.]

1/15/2001: CIA secrets briefing to G. W. Bush mentions bin Laden as "tremendous threat," coming after US again

A week before Bush's inauguration in January 2001, Rice, Cheney, and George W. Bush attended a secrets briefing delivered by Tenet and Pavitt. "They told him that bin Laden and his network were a 'tremendous threat' which was 'immediate.' There was no doubt that bin Laden was coming after the United States again, they said, but it was not clear when, where or how. Bin Laden and the network were a difficult, elusive target." [*The fifteenth of the month used for date sorting purposes only.*]

—Bob Woodward, *Bush at War*, Pages 34–35

1/20/2001: Outgoing Deputy National Security Advisor Kerrick warns incoming George W. Bush administration "about the threat posed by Al-Qaeda"

According to a January 20, 2002, article in *The Washington Post*, in January 2001, Kerrick warned the incoming Bush Administration about the threat posed by Al-Qaeda. "As a courtesy, he sent a memo to the NSC front office on 'things you need to pay attention to.' About the al-Qaeda terrorist threat he wrote bluntly, 'We are going to be struck again.' He never heard back. 'I don't think it was above the waterline,' he says. 'They were gambling nothing would happen.'"

—Daniel Benjamin and Steven Simon, *The Age of Sacred Terror*, Page 336

1/20/2001: Republican George W. Bush inaugurated as president with Richard [Dick] Bruce Cheney as vice president

---

George W. Bush decided to keep Clinton's CIA Director Tenet and counterterrorism czar Clarke on in his new administration. Despite Tenet's and Clarke's wealth of knowledge and concern about the danger to our country from bin Laden and Al-Qaeda, Bush, within a few days of taking office and in the months ahead, focused on taking out Hussein (and his supposed weapons of mass destruction) and on Iraqi oil.

While I never discovered why our new president focused on Hussein and Iraqi oil instead of the recently communicated danger from bin Laden and Al-Qaeda, by not focusing on those well-known terrorist dangers, Bush increased the chance we would be attacked. Some have said 9/11 was just a freak accident, like being struck by lightning on a cloudless day, an event that no one could have foreseen or a tragedy that couldn't have been avoided. The following quotes show otherwise.

1/25/2001: Rice says "only one paragraph" in Clarke's memo attachment addressed Al-Qaeda

Rice wrote: "Dick Clarke sent…a [three-page] memorandum to me on January 25 [2001], laying out the case for stepped-up efforts against al Qaeda. Ironically, **only one paragraph, in an attachment to the memorandum, addressed al Qaeda and the homeland threat.**" [bolding added]

—Condoleezza Rice, *No Higher Honor*, Pages 64–65

[**Note:** Despite Rice writing in her book that only one paragraph in the Clarke attachment mentioned Al-Qaeda and the homeland threat, Al-

Qaeda was actually mentioned in over thirty-five of the attachment's paragraphs, and over 120 times in the memo and attachment.

It's hard to envision a more important memo an incoming president could receive, and even more so given Clarke's history with and deep knowledge about terrorism, bin Laden and Al-Qaeda, and their danger to our country.

The following is a copy of Clarke's redacted three-page memorandum to Rice with its thirteen-page attachment containing the many references to bin Laden and Al-Qaeda.]

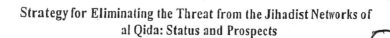

Strategy for Eliminating the Threat from the Jihadist Networks of al Qida: Status and Prospects

(D)

1. Summary

The al Qida terrorist organization lead by Usama bin Ladin has stitched together a network of terrorist cells and groups to wage jihad. Al Qida seeks to drive the United States out of the Arabian Peninsula and elsewhere in the Muslim world. It also seeks to overthrow moderate governments and establish theocracies similar to the Taliban regime in Afghanistan. The al Qida network is well financed, has trained tens of thousands of Jihadists, and has a cell structure in over forty nations. It also is actively seeking to develop and acquire weapons of mass destruction.

The United States' goal is to reduce the al Qida network to a point where it no longer poses a serious threat to our security or that of other governments. That goal can be achieved over a three to five year period, if adequate resources and policy attention are devoted to it.

Toward that end, the United States has developed a comprehensive and coordinated strategy that employs a variety of tools including: diplomacy, covert action, public information and media, law enforcement, intelligence collection, foreign assistance, financial regulation enforcement, and military means to affect al Qida to its core.

2. The Threat

Al Qida ("the base" or "the foundation") is both an independent terrorist organization and a sponsor and coordinator of a network of other semi-independent terrorist groups. The Al Qida network provides its members as well as its affiliates with a broad range of support:

--sophisticated media propaganda, through use of internet sites, videos, magazines, brochures, and speakers throughout the world

--substantial funding from its own investments and from a fund raising network throughout the world

--global recruitment and covert transportation of trainees through safe houses with false documentation

--advanced training in espionage, sabotage, weapons, and explosives at a series of al Qida camps in Afghanistan

--a multi-national pool of trained terrorists and Jihad fighters available to support Jihad in countries other than their own

--a global cell structure available to assist transport of terrorists, acquisition of materials, attack operations, and provide safe havens

The organizations substantially sponsored by the al Qida network include:

--al Ittihad in Kenya and Somalia

--Egyptian Islamic Jihad

--the Islamic Movement of Uzbekistan

--the Abu Sayyaf Group in the Philippines

--the Libyan Islamic Fighting Group

--the Abayan Islamic Army of Yemen

--the Chechnyan Mujaheedin

--the Palestinian Asbat al Ansar

--the Armed Islamic Group (GIA)

Al-Qida has recently increased its contacts with the Palestinian rejectionist gorups, including Hizbollah, Hamas and Palestine Islamic Jihad. There are substantial cells of Moroccans, Tunisians, Saudis, Pakistanis, and Algerians operating on a global basis supported by al Qida. In addition to the Arab and Central Asian nations, al Qida supports cells in the United States, Canada, Ireland, England, Israel, Italy, Turkey, Germany, Spain, Belgium, and Thailand. The cells include "sleeper agents" who marry into the local community, find local employment and engage in criminal activity to raise funds (cell phone number cloning, credit card fraud, etc.) to sustain themselves and help support the international network..

al Qida developed beginning in the late 1980s as an outgrowth of the international jihad against the Soviet Union in Afghanistan. The avowed purpose of the organization is to evict the United States from the region and to replace "unholy" governments with Islamic fundamentalist regimes.

Initially, the group's chief targets were Saudi Arabia and Egypt. The group's leader and some of its central infrastructure were located in Sudan, although the training camps were in Afghanistan. Following successful diplomatic pressure on Sudan, al Qida moved its headquarters to Afghanistan in 1996. As their network grew, al Qida began to focus more attention on supporting operations in Bosnia and Central Asia (Chechnya, Dagestan, Uzbekistan, Tajikistan), while their targeting of the US, Saudi Arabia, and Egypt continued unabated.

    o <u>Direct Attacks on US</u>: In retrospect, we have discovered ties between what we now understand to be the al Qida network and a series of high profile attacks on the US in the early 1990s. al Qida played a role in the attempted attack on US Air Force personnel in Yemen in 1992. There are indications that al Qida played a role in the World Trade Center bombing and the attack on US forces in Mogadishu, both in 1993. Sheik Rahman and the cell arrested in New York and New Jersey for planning to destroy the NY-NJ tunnels were also linked to al Qida. In fact, the Sheik's son is now a major al Qida network commander. It also appears likely that the Manila cell that was preparing bombs for six US flag 747s in 1993 was funded and trained by al Qida.

In 1998, Usama bin Ladin publicly declared war on the United States. In August, 1998 al Qida launched attacks on US embassies in Kenya and Tanzania. Attacks were also planned on US embassies in Albania and Uganda that year, but were disrupted. During 1998-99, al Qida cells were disrupted in several countries. Intelligence indicated that the al Qida network planned these attacks around the first of January, 2000, including: an al Qida network cell in Jordan where three attacks were to occur at sites where US citizens would be present; an al Qida network cell in Yemen was to attack a US Navy ship; and in December, a Canadian-based al Qida cell aligned with former GIA members was engaged in smuggling of bombs into the United States. All three sets of attacks were disrupted or failed, but the attack on a US Navy ship in Yemen was attempted again, successfully, in October, 2000.

4

o <u>Presence in the US</u>: al Qida is present in the United States. al Qida has been linked to terrorist operations in the U.S. while also conducting recruiting and fundraising activities. U.S. citizens have also been linked to al Qida.

Two al Qida members key to the planned multi-site attacks on Americans in Jordan (December 1999) were naturalized American citizens who had lived in Los Angeles and Boston. The plot to smuggle bombs from Canada to the US in 1999 revealed connections to al Qida supporters in several states. The 1993 World Trade Center and NY-NJ Tunnels conspiracies revealed an extensive terrorist presence, which we now understand was an early manifestation of al Qida in the US. A suspect in the East Africa bombings (former US Army Sergeant Ali Muhammad) has informed ██US██ that an extensive network of al Qida "sleeper" agents currently exists in the US.

o <u>Subversion of Other Governments</u>: Jihadists trained at al Qida network camps in Afghanistan are among those engaged in terrorism against several governments, notably Egypt, Algeria, Jordan, Uzbekistan, and the Philippines. The al Qida network-sponsored religious and Jihadist propaganda is spread throughout the Gulf (Kuwait, Saudi Arabia, UAE) and Arab communities in Europe. The propaganda links the US and Israel to moderate Islamic regimes, making it more difficult for some governments to cooperate openly with the US. While al Qida alone cannot overthrow a government, it can substantially assist in the creation of a climate driven by propaganda where trained indigenous oppositionists supported by al Qida will engage in violence at their behest. Up to 50,000 Jihadists from over three dozen nations have been trained in al Qida camps in Afghanistan and then returned to their home countries.

o <u>Weapons of Mass Destruction</u>: Numerous sources have reported that al Qida is attempting to develop or acquire chemical or radiological weapons. The al Qida acquisition network in Europe and the former Soviet Union have repeatedly attempted to obtain WMD components. Al Qida's Derunta camp near Jalalabad in Afghanistan has been identified as a development and testing facility for poisons and chemical weapons and poisons. References to ██████ nerve gases) have been founded on captured computers Operational detail, removed at the request of the CIA

3. The US Goal: Roll Back

The United States goal is to roll back the al Qida network to a point where it will no longer pose a serious threat to the US or its interests, as was done to previously robust terrorist groups such as the Abu Nidal Organization and the Japanese Red Army. In order to significantly reduce the threat al Qida poses to US interests, every element of its infrastructure must be considerably weakened or eliminated, most notably:

--the significant camp and facility infrastructure for training and safehaven sanctuary in Afghanistan

--access to large amounts of money and the ability to disperse it internationally to support cells and affiliated terrorist groups.

--multiple active cells capable of launching military style, large-scale terrorist operations

--a large pool of personnel willing to risk being identified as al Qida members and willing to reside at al Qida facilities.

The United States actively seeks to reduce al Qida to such a rump group in the next three to five years through a steady and coordinated program employing all relevant means.

4. Implementing the Strategy: The Record to Date

To implement this strategy, the US has used diplomacy, intelligence collection, covert action, law enforcement, foreign assistance, force protection and diplomatic security in a coordinated campaign against al Qida:

o Intelligence Collection: Beginning in 1996, the al Qida network was singled out for special treatment within the US counter-terrorism community. A "Virtual Station" was created by CIA, an organization modeled on a CIA overseas station dedicated to collection and operations against al Qida. NSA and CIA made collection against the al Qida network a major requirement, with higher priority given only to support of on-going US military operations.

o Sanctuary Sudan Eliminated: The US placed significant diplomatic pressure on Sudan, resulting in a decision by the Sudanese government to request bin Ladin to abandon Khartoum and move his headquarters to the camps in Afghanistan. US diplomacy with Saudi Arabia resulted in the Kingdom depriving bin Ladin of his Saudi citizenship and taking steps to deny him access to financial assets held in his name.

o <u>Diplomacy with Pakistan and the Taliban</u>: Repeated diplomatic efforts with Pakistan gained some limited law enforcement and intelligence cooperation against al Qida. The Pakistani government requested that the Taliban cease to provide sanctuary to al Qida, but the Pakistanis did not condition their support of the Taliban on compliance. Similarly, frequent direct diplomatic contact with the Taliban by the US has failed to gain any cooperation on ending the al Qida presence in Afghanistan. Beginning in late 1998, the US has repeatedly told the Taliban leadership that their complicity in harboring al Qida makes them equally culpable for al Qida operations against us. While some in the Taliban leadership appear willing to cooperate with the US, the ruler (Mullah Omar) has prohibited any action against al Qida.

o <u>Saudi Support Gained</u>: By 1997, CIA was identifying al Qida cells in several nations and working with local security services to disrupt them. Also that year, the Saudis disrupted a plot by the al Qida cell in the Kingdom. Operational detail, removed at the request of the CIA. Subsequently, the Saudis began taking the al Qida threat seriously and pressured the Taliban to check bin Ladin's activities. Saudi Arabia then joined in demanding bin Ladin's arrest by the Taliban and, when Saudi efforts failed, they severed diplomatic ties and terminated direct assistance to the Taliban.

o <u>UN Security Council Sanctions</u>: By 1999, the Saudis and others joined us in sponsoring limited UN sanctions on Afghanistan because of its harboring of bin Ladin. The US seized over $250,000,000 in Taliban funds. At the end of 2000, the United States and Russia co-sponsored a further round of UN sanctions that included a one sided arms embargo (only on the Taliban, not on the Northern Alliance) and expanded UN demands to include closure of the terrorist infrastructure in Afghanistan. The resolution passed 13-0-2, China and Malaysia abstaining.

o <u>Renditions and Disruptions</u>: With two, nearly simultaneous, suicide truck-bomb attacks, al Qida destroyed the US embassies in Kenya and Tanzania in 1998. The US stepped up the al Qida cell disruption effort. In addition to disrupting cells, the US found and brought to the US for trial al Qida operatives in Jordan, Egypt, Pakistan, Malaysia, South Africa, Kenya, Tanzania, Germany, and the

United Kingdom. Other al Qida operative^s not indicted in the US were brought to
██ countries ██████ where they were wanted by authorities.

o Building Partner Capability: Through the CIA's Counter-terrorism Center
(CTC) and State's Anti-Terrorism Assistance Program (ATA) the US has
enhanced the capabilities of several nations to collect intelligence on al Qida and to
disrupt their operations. █Operational detail, removed at the request of the CIA█
██
Counter-terrorism training and equipment have been provided to several nations'
security forces. As a result of these partnerships, simultaneous disruptions of over
twenty al Qida cells were conducted in December, 1999 to prevent possible
Millennium celebration period attacks. The FBI has also greatly strengthened
counter-terrorism cooperation with foreign counterparts, including stationing of
FBI personnel overseas and training partner organizations at home and abroad.

o Inside Afghanistan: CIA developed sources inside Afghanistan who were
able to report on the activities and locations of al Qida commanders. One group
was developed as a covert action team designed to forcibly apprehend al Qida
commanders and hand them off to US arrest teams. An Intelligence Finding
authorized the use of lethal force as part of operations against the al Qida
commanders. Several efforts to apprehend or attack the al Qida leadership using
Afghan personnel were unsuccessful. █A foreign█ government unit was trained and
equipped for a similar mission, but has not yet been employed in an operation.

The Afghan Northern Alliance is engaged in civil war with the Taliban. al Qida
has been a major source of the Taliban's success, providing the best fighting unit
(the 55th Brigade) and literally buying the support of provincial leaders. The
Pakistani Army has also provided the Taliban with advisors, intelligence, training,
equipment, and placed personnel in Taliban units. The US has provided very
limited intelligence and non-lethal equipment to the Northern Alliance, in
exchange for intelligence on al Qida. The Northern Alliance has not yet been able
to mount an apprehension operation against al Qida commanders.

o Military Operations: In August, 1998 the US struck al Qida facilities in
Afghanistan and an al Qida associated chemical plant in Sudan. Subsequent to
those attacks, follow-on attacks were considered and military assets deployed on
three occasions when the al Qida commanders were located in Afghanistan by
Humint sources. The Humint sources were not sufficiently reliable and a lack of
second source corroboration prevented US military action. Thus in September,

8

2000 the CIA began covert flights into Afghanistan using the Predator UAV operating out of Uzbekistan. On three occasions, the UAV provided ▮ video coverage of what appeared to be gatherings involving the senior al Qida leadership. The UAV operations were suspended ▮▮▮▮▮ but plans are now being developed to allow operations to recommence in late March. The Spring flights may be able to incorporate a new capability: Hellfire anti-tank missiles mounted aboard the Predators. This new capability would permit a "see it/shoot it" option ▮ Operational detail, removed at the request of the CIA ▮

o <u>Better Self-Defense</u>: Defense, State, and CIA have all taken steps to enhance our capability to defend US installations abroad against al Qida attacks. Physical security measures have been greatly enhanced at likely target facilities. Additional security personnel have been deployed, including covert counter-surveillance units. Intelligence reports indicate that al Qida considered attacks on several facilities, but decided that the enhanced defensive measures would prevent those attacks from succeeding. Ambassadors have been encouraged to take steps, including temporary closing of embassies and consulates, based upon intelligence without waiting for Washington approval. Embassy Dushanbe and Embassy Khartoum have been closed for security reasons. Embassy Doha was relocated on an emergency basis. New, more secure embassies are under construction or planned at several locations as part of a multi-year plan, but further funding is needed.

o <u>Financing</u>: Al Qida and several of its affiliates are legally designated Foreign Terrorist Organizations under US law, making it a felony to transfer money to them through US institutions or to raise money for them (or their front organizations) in the US. Moreover, the US can take banking sanctions against foreign banking institutions which facilitate terrorist finances. ▮▮▮ CIA has ▮ been able to collect numerous reports about alleged al Qida investments, companies, and transactions. Treasury has had pledges of cooperation from several nations, including Saudi Arabia, the UAE, and Kuwait. Based on the absence of actionable intelligence, however, Treasury has not been able to make specific requests to these countries. State has taken action against several Islamic NGOs which appear to be fronts for al Qida.

5. <u>Bringing the Strategy to Completion – The Next Three to Five Years</u>

The programs initiated in the last three years lay the basis for achieving the strategic goal of rendering the al Qida network as a non serious threat to the US, but success can only be achieved if the pace and resource levels of the programs continue to grow as planned.

Continued anti-al Qida operations at the current level will prevent some attacks, but will not seriously attrit their ability to plan and conduct attacks. Absent additional resource, cells that are disrupted will continue to be replaced, the organizational presence in the US will not be uncovered fully, and the overall capability of the al Qida networks may be held in check or may continue to grow, but will not be dismantled.

In order to implement the overall, global strategy while undermining the ability of al-Qa'ida to utilize Afghanistan, CIA has prepared a program that focuses on eliminating it as a safehaven, disrupting the mujahidin support infrastructure that connects Afghanistan to the global network, and changing the operational environment inside Afghanistan.
Possible steps include:

Safehavens

- Massive support to anti-Taliban groups such as the Northern Alliance led by Ahamd Shah Masood. This effort would be intended primarily to keep Islamic extremist fighters tied down in Afghanistan.

- Identify and destroy camps or portions of camps run by known terrorists while classes are in session. To take advantage fully of this initiative, we would need to have special teams ready for covert entry into destroyed camps to acquire intelligence for locating terrorist cells outside Afghanistan. This effort would require either a commitment from JSOC or a liaison force capable of conducting activity on-the-ground inside Afghanistan.

- In order to integrate the above elements and to fully exploit proposed new capabilities, we would need to continue and expand the Predator UAV program. If testing prove successful, we could also introduce armed UAVs into Afghanistan in the Spring.

Mujahidin Support Infrastructure

- Continue and expand efforts to arrest and disrupt recruiter, travel, and false document facilitators, and those who run the waystaions and guesthouses abroad.

████████████████████████████████

Operational detail, removed at the request of the CIA

Operational Environment Afghanistan

- Explore possible efforts to remove the more extreme wing of the Taliban from power. This could involved a combination of propaganda and covert action to further divide the Taliban by amplifying and exploiting divisions within the leadership.

CIA's program would require funding ███████████████ over five years. In addition, other U.S. assets must be incorporated into the effort.

-- State Department programs for Anti-terrorism Assistance and a new information media effort;.

-- Treasury's new interagency Terrorist Asset Tracking Center;

--a significant US role in multilateral counter narcotics operations aimed at the Afghan heroin trade, requiring increased State and DEA resources; and

-- FBI's programs to translate and analyze material obtained from domestic surveillance authorized under the Foreign Intelligence Surveillance Act (FISA) and to operate multi-agency Joint Terrorism Task Forces (JTTFs) in major metropolitan areas. And recent funding to support Customs, IRS, and INS participation in the JTTFs must be sustained and expanded.

o Near Term Policy Decisions: In addition to program above, there are also several key policy decisions on steps that hold significant prospects for reducing the al Qida threat. These policy decisions relate to attacking al Qida's center of gravity: sanctuary in Afghanistan under Taliban sponsorship.

-- Covert US assistance to the Northern Alliance to oppose the Taliban militarily. Such assistance could include funding, intelligence support, and ███ ███████ equipment. ██████ proposed a twelve month program ███ ████████ that would allow Masood to stay in the fight with the Taliban and al-Qida as a credible, conventional threat;

-- Covert US assistance to Uzbekistan ██████

Operational detail, removed at the request of the CIA

--Continued Predator UAV operations, resuming in March.

--Overt US military action to destroy al Qida command/control and infrastructure and Taliban military and command assets.

Considerations with Pakistan

These decisions involve consideration of US policy toward Pakistan. Like almost all of Pakistan's foreign and security policy, their approach to the Taliban and to terrorism flows from ███ concerns ██████ with seizing Kashmir and redressing its defeat by India in three wars. Support for the Taliban has run through three Pakistani governments – Bhutto, Sharif, and now Musharraf – and is predicated on the concept of "strategic depth," i.e. ensuring a friendly government in Kabul that will not pose a threat in the event of another war with India. The Pakistani military has consistently believed the Taliban was the best means of achieving that goal. Russian and Indian support for the Taliban's only remaining military opponent reinforces Pakistan's tendency to view Afghanistan through an Indo-Pakistani lens.

Pakistan's acquiescence in the Taliban's hosting of terrorist camps and bin Laden is a product of the nexus between Afghanistan and Pakistan's proxy war in Kashmir.

Operational detail, removed at the request of the CIA

Support for bin Laden comes also from a small but dedicated cadre of Islamist leaders whose electoral influence in Pakistan is minimal but whose street power has intimidated successive governments into fostering Islamic causes. Bin Laden has benefited as he ostentatiously supports Islamic causes as far afield as Bosnia and Chechnya.

As we seek Pakistani cooperation, we need to keep in mind that Pakistan has been most willing to cooperate with us on terrorism when its role is invisible or at least plausibly deniable to the powerful Islamist right wing. Pakistan's rendition to the US of Ramzi Yousef and Mir Aimal Kansi and to Jordan last year of Khalil Deek were sharply criticized by the Islamic parties. Overt Pakistani support for U.S. action against bin Laden, who is a hero especially in the Pushtun-ethnic border areas near Afghanistan, would be so unpopular as to threaten Musharraf's government.

We do have levers with the Pakistanis, despite the deleterious effect of overlapping sanctions (Pressler, Glenn, military coup, MTCR) that we imposed beginning in 1990:

- The blunt instrument of UNSC sanctions – Pakistan wants to be seen as a responsible member of the international community and will attempt to comply, in whole or in part
- Increasing domestic opposition to ███ clandestine campaigns. The Afghan camps train Sunni extremists whose bloody warfare against Pakistan's Shi'a community ultimately threatens the nation's future. Similarly, the fundamentalism fed by the madrassas of Pakistan and by Taliban hard-liners is anathema to the moderate military and civilian leaders of Pakistan
- Economic leverage. As Musharraf implements the economic rescue policies he hopes will pull Pakistan out of its steep decline, he needs our moral and practical support in the IMF for a medium-term economic support package.

We are already pursuing policies that have the effect – but only over a very long term – of encouraging Pakistan's distaste for its Taliban adventure:

- Lending our support to a fair but non-violent settlement of Kashmir;

- Demonstrating that there are alternatives to the Taliban (e.g., traditional leaders chosen through the Loya Jirga process) that serve Pakistan's national interests; and
- Helping to build up a secular educational system that ends rural Pakistan's exclusive reliance on the fundamentalist madrassas.

Chief Executive Musharraf has been clear in his discussions with American officials that:

--he opposes terrorism and al Qida and believes that the spread of such fundamentalism threatens Pakistani internal stability;

--Pakistan requires a Pashtun majority government in Afghanistan and the repatriation of refugees, which can best be achieved through support to Taliban;

--but there are influential radical elements in Pakistan that would oppose significant Pakistani measures against al Qida or the Taliban;

--Pakistan has been unable to persuade the Taliban to yield up bin Ladin and close the sanctuary and is unwilling to do more to persuade them.

In the wake of the attack on the USS Cole, Pakistan has called upon the US not to violate Pakistani airspace (again) to launch punitive strikes in Afghanistan.

If you were incoming National Security Advisor Rice and you received the above Clarke memo and attachment, wouldn't you immediately discuss the memo with your president and work to protect our country from attack by bin Laden and Al-Qaeda?

Speculating how or why Rice so mischaracterized the above memo in her book, perhaps she never bothered reading the memo—or maybe she told Bush about it, but he showed little interest in its contents so neither did she.

However, as this first chapter shows, regardless of what Rice did or did not do or say about the Clarke memo, George W. Bush chose to go after Hussein and Iraqi oil.

1/30/2001: Cheney Energy Task Force maps out "U.S. oil industry's interests in Iraq's oil fields"

Deputy Secretary of the Interior Stephen "Griles was a lead actor in the Cheney Energy Task Force [that first convened on January 30, 2001], serving as the Interior Department's chief representative. As such, he played a lead role in mapping out the U.S. oil industry's interests in Iraq's oil fields and developing some of the most destructive national energy bills in the nation's history, giving more than $14 billion worth of subsidies, tax breaks, and other benefits to the oil industry."

—Antonia Juhasz, *The Tyranny of Oil*, Page 260

1/30/2001: George W. Bush states deposal of Hussein in his first high-level national security team meeting

On January 30, 2001, President George W. Bush addressed the sole items on the agenda for his first high-level national security team meeting: "[T]hree key objectives: Get rid of Saddam Hussein, end American involvement in the Israeli-Palestinian peace process, and rearrange the dominoes in the Middle East....the centerpiece of their recommendations was the removal of Saddam Hussein as the first step in remaking the Middle East into a region friendly, instead of hostile, to Israel....As part of their 'grand strategy,' they recommended that once Iraq was conquered and Saddam Hussein overthrown, he should be replaced by a puppet leader friendly to Israel."

—James Bamford, *A Pretext for War*, Pages 260–262

[Note: Where was any concern about Al-Qaeda or bin Laden in this first high-level national security team meeting?]

2/1/2001: George W. Bush administration plans for post-Hussein Iraq and Iraqi oil wealth

"On February 1, 2001, two days after the [first] NSC meeting, Bush officials circulated a memo titled 'Plan for post-Saddam Iraq' and began discussing what to do with Iraq's oil wealth."

—Craig Unger, *The Fall of the House of Bush*, Page 202

[Note: Could Bush's intentions toward Iraq and Iraqi oil eleven days after his inauguration have been shown with greater clarity?]

2/3/2001: Iraq and oil discussed in top-secret document

"[A]ccording to *The New Yorker* [on February 16, 2004], a top-secret document [dated February 3, 2001] directed National Security Council staffers to cooperate fully with the Energy Task Force as it considered 'melding' two areas of policy that appeared to be unrelated: 'the review of operational policies toward rogue states,' such as Iraq, and 'actions regarding the capture of new and existing oil and gas fields.'"

—Craig Unger, *The Fall of the House of Bush*, Page 203

[Note: Iraq and oil]

2/5/2001: Rice chairs committee to consider how to ramp up intel on suspected Iraqi WMD

"On the 17th day of the Bush presidency, Monday, February 5 [2001], Rice chaired a principals committee meeting that included Cheney, Powell and Rumsfeld. Deputy CIA Director John E. McLaughlin substituted for Tenet. The purpose was to review Iraq policy, the status of diplomatic, military and covert options. Among the first taskings...consider how intelligence collection could be increased on Iraq's suspected weapons of mass destruction."

—Bob Woodward, *Plan of Attack*, Page 13

2/7/2001: Tenet's first public testimony to Senate cites immediate threat from bin Laden

Former CIA Director Tenet wrote: "In my first public testimony during the new [Bush] administration, in February [7] 2001, I told the Senate that 'The threat from terrorism is real, it is immediate, and it is evolving....[A]s we have increased security around government and military facilities, terrorists are seeking out *softer* targets that provide opportunities for mass casualties....Usama Bin Ladin and his global network of lieutenants and associates remain the most immediate and serious threat....He is capable of planning multiple attacks with little or no warning.'"

—George Tenet with Bill Harlow, *At the Center of the Storm*, Page 144

[**Note:** Despite Tenet saying publicly that bin Laden and his associates remain the most immediate and serious terrorist threats to our country, Bush and his administration continued their focus on Hussein and Iraqi oil.]

2/22/2001: George W. Bush tells reporter US will warn Hussein there will be no tolerance for his developing WMD

In a press conference at the White House on February 22, 2001, when questions from John Roberts, *CBS News*, regarding the Secretary of State's trip to the Middle East and the future modifications of the sanctions on Iraq came up, President George W. Bush had this to say:

"We're reviewing all policy in all regions of the world, and one of the areas we've been spending a lot of time on is the Persian Gulf and the Middle East. The Secretary of State is going to go listen to our allies as to how best to effect a policy, the primary goal of which will be to say to Saddam Hussein, we won't tolerate you developing weapons of mass destruction, and we expect you to leave your neighbors alone....But the primary goal is to make it clear to Saddam that we expect him to be a peaceful neighbor in the region, and we expect him not to develop weapons of mass destruction."

—"The President's News Conference: February 22, 2001," Weekly Compilation of Presidential Documents, February 26, 2001, Vol. 37, No. 8, Page 326

3/5/2001: George W. Bush campaign Foreign Policy Advisor Perle to Senate subcommittee: Support Iraqi opposition

In early March 2001, Foreign Policy Advisor to the Bush campaign Richard Perle told a Senate Foreign Relations subcommittee panel: "'Improved sanctions or smarter sanctions, none of them are going to end the threat from Saddam Hussein.' Instead, Mr. Perle said, the Iraqi National Congress, one of the opposition groups, should be supported so that it could re-establish its presence in parts of Iraq not under Mr. Hussein's control. Then, if Mr. Hussein made a 'military response,' the United States should have 'assets in the air to protect that opposition.'" [*The fifth of the month used for date sorting purposes only.*]

—Jane Perlez, "Capitol Hawks Seek Tougher Line on Iraq," *The New York Times*, March 7, 2001

3/7/2001: George W. Bush's national security team meets for first time for broad review on roll-back of Al-Qaeda

"On March 7, 2001, President Bush's national security team, cautioned by C.I.A. officials and departing aides to President Bill Clinton that terrorism would be a serious problem, met for the first time to begin a broad review of the government's approach to Al Qaeda and Afghanistan. Stephen Hadley, Ms. Rice's deputy, told the Congressional committee, 'The goal was to move beyond the policy of containment, criminal prosecution and limited retaliation for specific attacks, toward attempting to roll back Al Qaeda.'"

—David Johnston and Eric Schmitt, "Uneven Response Seen to Terror Risk in Summer '01," *The New York Times*, April 4, 2004

[**Note:** George W. Bush team finally meets about Al-Qaeda.]

4/3/2001: WSJ reports that George W. Bush admin decided to "play down bin Laden's role" in *Cole* attack

"In an article on April 3, 2001, the *Wall Street Journal* reported that the [Bush] administration had deliberately decided to play down bin Laden's role [in the October 2000 attack on the USS *Cole*] by not mentioning him in public: 'U.S. counterterrorism officials believe they inflated Mr. bin Laden's power and prestige in recent years by portraying him as the ultimate terrorist mastermind and the top threat to America's security.' Indeed, the State Department's annual *Patterns of Global Terrorism* report, which had devoted an entire page to bin Laden's life history and ambitions in 2000, omitted that page in the 2001 edition [the above is from a footnote in the book]."

—Roy Gutman, *How We Missed the Story*, Page 250

[**Note:** Publicly downplaying bin Laden's role in past terrorism may or may not have been a good call, but what did the Bush administration do to protect our country from bin Laden in the months leading up to 9/11?]

4/15/2001: Strategic Energy Policy Challenges For The 21st Century report: Iraq seen as threat to flow of oil

"President Bush's Cabinet agreed in April 2001 that 'Iraq remains a destabilizing influence to the flow of oil to international markets from the Middle East' and because this is an unacceptable risk to the US 'military intervention' is necessary.

Vice-president Dick Cheney, who chairs the White House Energy Policy Development Group, commissioned a report on 'energy security' from the Baker Institute for Public Policy, a think-tank set up by James Baker, the former US secretary of state under George Bush Sr.

The report, Strategic Energy Policy Challenges For The 21st Century, concludes: 'The United States remains a prisoner of its energy dilemma. Iraq remains a de-stabilizing influence to...the flow of oil to international markets from the Middle East. Saddam Hussein has also demonstrated a willingness to threaten to use the oil weapon and to use his own export program to manipulate oil markets.'" [*The fifteenth of the month used for date sorting purposes only.*]

—Neil Mackay, "Official: US Oil at the Heart of Iraq Crisis," *The Sunday Herald*, Archive.commondreams.org, October 6, 2002

[**Note:** It seems like early planning to create a reason to grab Iraqi oil.]

4/18/2001: FAA sends memo to US airlines that Middle Eastern terrorists might hijack and blow up an American jet

"On April 18 [2001], U.S. airlines got a memo from the FAA [Federal Aviation Administration] warning that they should demonstrate a 'high degree of alertness' because Middle Eastern terrorists might try to hijack or blow up an American plane....the threats were so frequent and, often, so vague, they had little impact on security."

—Craig Unger, *House of Bush, House of Saud*, Page 230

4/30/2001: State Department report: Iraq has terrorist group ties but no Western attack since the 1993 attempt on George H. W. Bush

"According to the 2000 edition of the State Department's annual 'Patterns of Global Terrorism' report, issued in April [30] 2001, Iraq has ties to various terrorist groups and does terrible things to dissidents, but, 'The regime has not attempted an anti-Western terrorist attack since its failed plot to assassinate former President [H. W.] Bush in 1993 in Kuwait.'"

—Michael Kinsley, "Ours Not To Reason Why," Slate.com, September 26, 2002

5/1/2001: George W. Bush: "Cold War deterrence is no longer enough"

When speaking to the students and faculty of National Defense University on May 1, 2001, President George W. Bush brought up previous issues with Iraq: "When Saddam Hussein invaded Kuwait in 1990, the world joined forces to turn him back. But the international community would have faced a very different situation had Hussein been able to blackmail with nuclear weapons. Like Saddam Hussein, some of today's tyrants are gripped by an implacable hatred of the United States of America. They hate our friends, they hate our values, they hate democracy and freedom and individual liberty. Many care little for the lives of their own people. In such a world, Cold War deterrence is no longer enough."

—Office of the Press Secretary, "Remarks by the President to Students and Faculty at National Defense University," George W. Bush—White House Archives, May 1, 2001

5/5/2001: Chevron takes Rice's name off oil supertanker

"In 1993, Chevron named a [oil] supertanker after her, the 129,000-ton SS *Condoleezza Rice*. But in the face of criticism about the Bush administration's ties to big oil—including a suit against Chevron charging human rights abuses in Nigeria—the company quietly renamed the tanker the *Altair Voyager* in the spring of 2001 [according to a *San Francisco Chronicle* article on May 5, 2001]."

—Elisabeth Bumiller, *Condoleezza Rice*, Page 109

5/15/2001: Cheney links Iraq, North Korea and Iran as threats

"Already in May 2001, in an interview with the *New Yorker*, Cheney had linked North Korea, Iran, and Iraq as threats to American security." [*The fifteenth of the month used for date sorting purposes only.*]

—Julian E. Zelizer, ed., *The Presidency of George W. Bush*, Page 94

5/16/2001: Cheney energy task force eyes Gulf oil

"The [Cheney Energy] task force released its final report, 'National Energy Policy,' in May [16] 2001. It lays out quite succinctly the priorities of the Bush administration and Big Oil [the major oil companies], paying particular attention to Middle East oil. The report found that 'by any estimation, Middle East oil producers will remain central to the world['s] oil security' and that 'the [Persian] Gulf will be a primary focus of U.S. international energy policy.' The report argues that Middle Eastern countries should be urged 'to open up areas of their energy sectors to foreign investment.'"

—Antonia Juhasz, *The Tyranny of Oil*, Page 341

5/18/2001: George W. Bush on foreign oil: "It's in our nation's interest that we diversify" oil we import from Iraq

President George W. Bush, while encouraging energy conservation and reform at Safe Harbor Water Power Corporation on May 18, 2001: "And I said to the folks there, I said, I would much rather have our economy powered by crops grown in Iowa than barrels of oil coming out of Iraq. (Applause.) It's in our nation's interest that we diversify. It's in our nation's interest that we become less dependent upon nations, some of which really don't care for what we believe in. And I believe we can do so....People have got to understand that it's possible that we could find, and likely find, 600,000 barrels of oil a day out of ANWR [Arctic National Wildlife Refuge]. That's what we import from Saudi—I mean, from Iraq. It makes sense, folks, for us to have an environmentally sensitive exploration plan in America, in order to diversify supply, not only for national security reasons, but for international reasons, as well."

—Office of the Press Secretary, "Remarks by the President at Safe Harbor Water Power Corporation," George W. Bush—White House Archives, May 18, 2001

5/25/2001: George W. Bush speech: One-third of naval forces ready for "mischief Saddam might contemplate" overseas

Remarks by President George W. Bush at the Naval Academy Commencement on May 25, 2001: "Today, nearly one-third of our naval forces are forward-deployed overseas. The USS Constellation carrier battle group and its 10,000 sailors are plying the waters of the Persian Gulf, enforcing the no-fly zone over southern Iraq. Another 3,800 sailors and Marines stand guard nearby with the Boxer amphibious ready group, deterring [any] mischief Saddam might contemplate."

—Office of the Press Secretary, Remarks by the President at US Naval Academy Commencement," George W. Bush—White House Archives, May 25, 2001

6/13/2001: Egypt's Mubarak learns of bin Laden plane threat against George W. Bush and other G8 heads; tells US

"In an interview on French television on Monday [September 24, 2001], President Hosni Mubarak of Egypt…[said:] 'on June 13 of this year [2001], we learned of a communiqué from bin Laden saying he wanted to assassinate George W. Bush and other G8 [The Group of Eight Industrialized Nations] heads of state during their summit in Italy.'…Separately, he told Le Figaro, a major French daily newspaper, that Egyptian intelligence services had told the United States about the threat and that the warning included a reference to 'an airplane stuffed with explosives.'"

—David E. Sanger, "A NATION CHALLENGED: THE CONSPIRACY; 2 Leaders Tell Of Plot to Kill Bush in Genoa," *The New York Times*, September 26, 2001

[Note: Another warning about an airplane as a possible bomb.]

6/15/2001: Bin Laden on tape: "America is much weaker than it appears"

In a tape released in June 2001, "Mr. bin Laden seemed to gloat as he spoke in Arabic of future attacks on American targets that he said would dwarf those he has directed in the past. 'With small capabilities, and with our faith, we can defeat the greatest military power of modern times,' he said at one point. 'America is much weaker than it appears.'" [*The fifteenth of the month used for date sorting purposes only.*]

—John F. Burns, "A DAY OF TERROR: THE MILITANT; America the Vulnerable Meets a Ruthless Enemy," *The New York Times*, September 12, 2001

6/15/2001: Eighteen of 298 Senior Executive Intelligence Briefs to George W. Bush administration refer to Al-Qaeda, bin Laden

"In June [2001], only 18 out of 298 classified Senior Executive Intelligence Briefs sent to Bush administration officials referred to bin Laden or al Qaeda." [*The fifteenth of the month used for date sorting purposes only.*]

—Steve Coll, *Ghost Wars*, Page 568

6/15/2001: Attorney General Ashcroft seemed more interested in background checks for gun buyers than terrorism

"He [Acting FBI Director Thomas Pickard] gave Ashcroft the first of his weekly briefings in June [2001]. Before the meeting, Pickard sent an agenda to Ashcroft's office of the issues to be discussed. Terrorism was the number one item on the list....Ashcroft listened, but he seemed far more intrigued by other items on the agenda, especially the latest on the FBI's efforts to end delays on background checks for gun buyers." [*The fifteenth of the month used for date sorting purposes only.*]

—Philip Shenon, *The Commission*, Pages 246–247

[**Note:** Given that Ashcroft reported to President Bush, it seems probable that Ashcroft mirrored his boss' secondary concern for the terrorism threat.]

6/21/2001: Journalist told by Al-Qaeda chief of important surprises that will target American and Israeli interests

On June 21, 2001, journalist Bakr Atyani was invited to interview Osama bin Laden in Afghanistan. While bin Laden did not wish to be quoted, al Qaeda military chief "Muhammad Atef gave Atyani the news in the form of a stark warning. 'The coming weeks will hold important surprises that will target American and Israeli interests in the world,' he said. Atyani knew that meant a coming attack. 'I am 100 percent sure of this, and it was absolutely clear they had brought me there to hear this message,' he later said."

—James Bamford, *The Shadow Factory*, Page 54

6/22/2001: NSA intercepts conversations of imminent major attack on US military forces in Middle East

"On June 22 [2001], U.S. military forces in the Persian Gulf and the Middle East were once again placed on alert after NSA intercepted a conversation between two al Qaeda operatives in the region, which indicated that 'a major attack was imminent.' All U.S. Navy ships docked in Bahrain, homeport of the U.S. Fifth Fleet, were ordered to put to sea immediately."

—Matthew M. Aid, *The Secret Sentry*, Page 214

[Note: Someone did something about the Al-Qaeda threat to our country.]

6/22/2001: CIA: Bin Laden attack on America imminent

"On Friday [June 22, 2001], the CIA sent out a cable to all its stations. 'Threat UBL [Usama Bin Laden] Attack Against US Interests Next 24–48 Hours,' it said. The same day the FBI issued its own warning to its field offices in its daily 'UBL/Radical Fundamentalist Threat Update.'"

—James Bamford, *The Shadow Factory*, Page 56

6/22/2001: FAA: Potential threat of terrorist airline hijacking

"*June 22, 2001*: FAA issues an information circular to private air carriers. 'Although we have no specific information that this threat is directed at civil aviation, the potential for terrorist operations, such as an airline hijacking to free terrorists incarcerated in the U.S., remains a concern.'"

—Gerald Posner, *Why America Slept*, Pages 190–191

[Note: FAA warnings to private air carriers are useful, but what else did the Bush government do to protect us from such attacks?]

6/23/2001: Middle East report: With a smile bin Laden confirms plan to attack America, Israeli interests

Middle East Broadcasting Centre reporter Baker Atyani was invited to meet with bin Laden near Kandahar, Afghanistan. As he reported on June 23, 2001, "bin Laden specified in his invitation that he would discuss his latest pledge of loyalty to [Taliban leader] Mullah [Mohammad] Omar. When Atyani arrived, the script changed. 'In the next few weeks we will carry out a big surprise, and we will strike or attack American and Israeli interests,' [Al-Qaeda military commander] Abu Hafs told Atyani. When Atyani asked bin Laden to confirm the plan, he smiled but did not speak."

—Roy Gutman, *How We Missed the Story*, Pages 250–251

6/23/2001: SEIB: Bin Laden attack may be imminent

A SEIB (Senior Executive Intelligence Brief) headline on June 23, 2001, read: "Bin Ladin Attacks May Be Imminent."

—Philip Shenon, *The Commission*, Page 152

[Note: If you were president and you received the above referenced SEIB, wouldn't those words and the previous warnings about bin Laden cause you to focus on protecting our country from him?]

6/24/2001: Foreign broadcast report: Bin Laden preparing to strike US and Israeli interests

A Foreign Broadcast Information Service (FBIS) report on June 24, 2001, focused on a MBC (Middle East Broadcasting Center) TV interview with Usamah Bin-Ladin: "The followers of Usamah Bin-Ladin are conducting continuous military maneuvers and training in the desert of Afghanistan in preparation for a military strike against US interests in the world....In the desert of Qandahar [Afghanistan], we were able to meet Usamah Bin-Ladin. The meeting was attended by [al-Zawahiri]...The meeting was also attended by Usamah Bin-Ladin's right-hand man, Abu-Hafs, who preferred not to appear on camera....Bin-Ladin was happy at the statements of his followers that the next weeks will witness important surprises and that US and Israeli interests in the world will be targeted."

—CIA, "DCI Report: The Rise of UBL and Al—Qa'ida And the Intelligence Community Response," (Draft, Central Intelligence Agency Analytic Report), The Central Intelligence Agency's 9/11 File:, The National Security Archive, March 19, 2004

6/25/2001: Clarke warns Rice about six intel reports on pending calamitous Al-Qaeda attack

"On June 25 [2001], Clarke warned Rice and Hadley that six separate intelligence reports showed al Qaeda personnel warning of a pending attack.... The intelligence reporting consistently described the upcoming attacks as occurring on a calamitous level, indicating that they would cause the world to be in turmoil and that they would consist of possible multiple—but not necessarily simultaneous—attacks."

—9/11 Commission, The 9/11 Commission Report, July 22, 2004, Page 257

[Note: What, if anything, did Rice do about Clarke's warnings?]

6/28/2001: Clarke writes to Rice about likely attacks in July

On June 28, 2001, Clarke wrote to Rice that the pattern of activity suggesting an attack by Al-Qaeda over the previous six weeks "'had reached a crescendo.'" He was convinced that "'a major terrorist attack or series of attacks is likely in July,'...One al Qaeda intelligence report warned that something 'very, very, very, very' big was about to happen, and most of Bin Ladin's network was reportedly anticipating the attack."

—9/11 Commission, The 9/11 Commission Report, July 22, 2004, Page 257

[Note: What did Rice *do* with or because of that information?]

6/28/2001: CIA alert memo: Al-Qaeda attack imminent,

On June 28, 2001, "the CIA issued what was called an Alert Memorandum, which stated that the latest intelligence indicated the probability of imminent al Qaeda attacks that would 'have dramatic consequences on governments or cause major casualties.'"

—Matthew M. Aid, *The Secret Sentry*, Page 214

[Note: What did George W. Bush *do* to protect our country in the face of that scary warning?]

6/29/2001: SEIB: "Terrorism: Bin Ladin Threats Are Real" and not part of "disinformation campaign"

According to a top secret report from Tenet on March 19, 2004: "On June 29, 2001, our [CIA] analysts published a piece in the SEIB entitled 'Terrorism: Bin Ladin Threats Are Real' which concluded that recent indications of near-term attacks were not part of a disinformation campaign, but were consistent with other reporting and public statements by Bin Ladin."

—CIA, "DCI Report: The Rise of UBL and Al—Qa'ida And the Intelligence Community Response," (Draft, Central Intelligence Agency Analytic Report), The Central Intelligence Agency's 9/11 File:, The National Security Archive, March 19, 2004

[Note: Given all the reported threats in June 2001 from bin Laden and Al-Qaeda, what did George W. Bush *do* to try and protect the US from those threats?]

7/1/2001: To CNN, Feinstein mentions major probability of bin Laden attack by intel staff

"On July 1 [2001], Senators [Dianne] Feinstein (D-CA) and Richard Shelby (R-AL) appeared on CNN's *Late Edition with Wolf Blitzer*, warning of a potential attack by Osama bin Laden. 'Intelligence staff have told me,' said Feinstein, 'that there is a major probability of a terrorist incident within the next three months.'"

—Peter Lance, *1000 Years For Revenge*, Page 405

[Note: Was George W. Bush or his senior people listening?]

7/2/2001: Tenet: Liaisons overseas urged to "redouble" efforts against Al-Qaeda, arrests made

Tenet provided a written statement for the 9/11 Commission on March 24, 2004. He wrote: "During the week of July 2, 2001, reacting to a rash of intelligence threat reports, I contacted by phone a dozen of my foreign liaison counterparts to urge them to redouble their efforts against al-Qa'ida. The chief of the Counterterrorist Center, the chief of Near East Division, and others made additional urgent calls. These calls resulted in several arrests and detentions in Bahrain, Yemen, and Turkey."

—CIA, "Statement for the Record of the Director of Central Intelligence Before the National Commission on Terrorist Attacks Upon the United States," (Office of Public Affairs, CIA), The Central Intelligence Agency's 9/11 File:, The National Security Archive, March 24, 2004

[Note: Tenet took some action by himself.]

7/2/2001: SEIB: Heightened US security delayed attacks, but did not deter plans by bin Laden

According to a Senior Executive Intelligence Brief titled "Terrorism: Planning for Bin Ladin Attacks Continues, Despite Delay [Excised]" on July 2, 2001: "Attacks planned by Usama Bin Ladin's al-Qa'ida organization may have been delayed by heightened US security [redacted] the attacks will occur soon. [Redacted] necessary to pursue jihad against Americans and that operations would soon be carried out against US and Jewish interests, [redacted]."

—CIA, "Terrorism: Planning for Bin Ladin Attacks Continues, Despite Delay [Excised]," (Senior Executive Intelligence Brief), The Central Intelligence Agency's 9/11 File:, The National Security Archive, July 2, 2001

7/3/2001: Tenet: Intel revealed bin Laden's imminent attack

Former CIA Director Tenet wrote: "[O]n July 3 [2001], we learned as a result of intelligence that Bin Ladin had promised colleagues that an attack was near."

—George Tenet with Bill Harlow, At the Center of the Storm, Page 149

7/4/2001: July fourth reported attack may have been disrupted

"American counterterrorism analysts eventually concluded that an attack might come around the Fourth of July [2001] holiday, most likely aimed at American interests overseas....When no July attack occurred, some American officials began to believe that whatever had been in the works had somehow been disrupted or aborted."

—James Risen, "A NATION CHALLENGED: INTELLIGENCE; In Hindsight, C.I.A. Sees Flaws That Hindered Efforts on Terror," *The New York Times*, October 7, 2001

7/5/2001: George W. Bush asks Rice what is being done about the *chatter* of an imminent terrorist attack

"By July 5, 2001, National Security Advisor Condoleezza Rice reported that, while 'nonspecific,' the intelligence [regarding an impending terrorist attack] was 'sufficiently robust' that President George W. Bush asked her 'to go back and to see what was being done about all of the chatter.' But White House terrorism adviser Richard Clarke had a more urgent view. In a meeting that same day with a series of agencies including the FBI, FAA, and INS [Immigration and Naturalization Service], he warned that 'something really spectacular is going to happen here, and it's going to happen soon.'"

—Peter Lance, *Triple Cross*, Page 368

[Note: The word *chatter* suggests unimportant communications, which I submit as further evidence that President George W. Bush, despite the flood of intelligence he was receiving, didn't think or *do* much about those warnings.]

7/5/2001: No specifics in the thirty-three NSA-intercepted messages on bin Laden future US attacks

"Beginning in May and continuing through early July 2001, NSA intercepted thirty-three separate messages indicating that bin Laden intended to mount one or more terrorist attacks against U.S. targets in the near future. But the intercepts provided no specifics about the impending operation other than that 'Zero Hour was near.'" [*The fifth of the month used for date sorting purposes only.*]

—Matthew M. Aid, *The Secret Sentry*, Page 214

7/6/2001: George W. Bush says he would talk to Putin about Iraq

When asked during a press conference at Cape Arundel Golf Club in Kennebunkport, Maine, on July 6, 2001, if he would be discussing the situation in Iraq with the Russian President [Vladimir] Putin, President George W. Bush stated: "We left some—you know, I told him [Putin] I'd stay in touch with him. I want to talk to him about Iraq. So to answer your question, yes, I'm going to talk to him about Iraq. I'm going to talk to him about the Balkans, Macedonia. I know it's on his mind; it's on my mind, as well."

And I look forward to listening to what he has to say. It'll just be a series of conversations we have over the summer."

—Office of the Press Secretary, "President Bush and Former President Bush Speak to the Press—Remarks by the President and Former President Bush in Photo Opportunity, Cape Arundel Golf Club, Kennebunkport, Maine," George W. Bush— White House Archives, July 6, 2001

[**Note:** With the air filled with concern about bin Laden and Al-Qaeda attacking our country, Bush continues to pursue Iraq.]

7/6/2001: Clarke email to Rice: FBI, CIA, Pentagon asked to develop plan in event of simultaneous attacks

Clarke sent an email to Rice on July 6, 2001, which covered details from their meeting on the previous day. "One senior administration official said Mr. Clarke wrote that several agencies, including the F.B.I., the C.I.A. and the Pentagon, had been directed to develop what the official said were 'detailed response plans in the event of three to five simultaneous attacks.'"

—David Johnston and Eric Schmitt, "Uneven Response Seen to Terror Risk in Summer '01." *The New York Times*, April 4, 2004

[**Note:** I found no evidence or reference that those plans were ever prepared.]

7/6/2001: Cofer Black: "We know something terrible is going to happen [to US interests]," chatter filled with code words

Meeting with members of an unidentified Middle Eastern military on July 6, 2001, Director of the Counterterrorist Center Cofer Black said: "'We know something terrible is going to happen...We don't know when and we don't know where. We do know it's going to be against U.S. interests and it's going to be big, perhaps bigger than anything we've seen before.... The mood in the al-Qaeda training camps is one of jubilation,' he went on. 'We've never seen them as excited and as happy as they are now.' Cofer said that the chatter we were picking up was filled with code words and phrases that our analysts regarded as frightening. 'There's going to be a great wedding.' 'There's going to be a great soccer game.' 'The salesman is coming with great quantities of honey.' 'These are all code for a terrorist attack,' Cofer maintained. 'We're sure it's going to happen, we just don't know where.'"

—John Kiriakou with Michael Ruby, *The Reluctant Spy*, Page 100

7/9/2001: Phoenix FBI: "The Phoenix memo," eight Middle Eastern men studying at Arizona flight schools

On July 9, 2001, "Phoenix FBI Agent Ken Williams sent a memo to FBI headquarters. He reportedly identified eight Middle Eastern men studying at Arizona flight schools, and urged that the Bureau do background checks. Williams suggested that the pilots-in-training were associated with a London Islamic group with close ties to Osama bin Laden. The communiqué, which would go down in history as 'the Phoenix memo,' was also sent to investigators in the FBI's New York office, the FBI's office of origin for all bin Laden-related terrorism cases. At least three people in the office saw the memo, but no action was taken."

—Peter Lance, *1000 Years For Revenge*, Page 406

7/10/2001: Tenet: CIA consolidated report on impending US terror threats "made my hair stand on end"

In the summer of 2001, "the warnings [of an impending terrorist attack] continued to build at such a rate that the CIA's counterterrorism team, led by Cofer Black, felt compelled to consolidate the threats into a single, strategic assessment for Tenet. On July 10 [2001], Black presented his findings to the CIA director, who had been losing sleep over the terrorist warnings and now was shocked by what he heard. Al Qaeda was going to attack American interests, possibly within the United States itself. 'The briefing he gave me literally made my hair stand on end,' Tenet recalled."

—Elisabeth Bumiller, *Condoleezza Rice*, Page 156

7/10/2001: Tenet and Black believe that Rice may not have taken terror warnings seriously

"On July 10 [2001], Tenet and the head of the CIA's Counterterrorism Center, J. Cofer Black, met with National Security Advisor Rice to underline how seriously they took the chatter being picked up by NSA. Both Tenet and Black came away from the meeting believing that Rice did not take their warnings seriously."

—Matthew M. Aid, *The Secret Sentry*, Page 215

[Note: Tenet and Black's views on that meeting are consistent with my view that Rice, probably because of Bush's lack of concern, didn't take their bin Laden and Al-Qaeda warnings seriously.]

7/12/2001: FBI Director Pickard: Raised concern of Al-Qaeda threat but Ashcroft no longer wanted such briefs

Pickard raised the concern of the threat of an Al-Qaeda attack in a July 5, 2001, meeting with Ashcroft. "Yet, Pickard testified to the 9/11 commission that when he tried to brief Ashcroft just a week later, on July 12 [2001], about the terror threat inside the United States, he got the brush-off. 'Mr. Ashcroft told you that he did not want to hear about this anymore,' Democratic commission member Richard Ben-Veniste asked on April 13 [2004]. 'Is that correct?' 'That is correct,' Pickard replied."

—Lisa Myers, "Did Ashcroft Brush off Terror Warnings?," NBCNews.com, June 22, 2004

[**Note:** Our FBI director not wanting to hear any more about terrorist attack warnings again probably mirrored the lack of concern about such warnings from his boss, George W. Bush.]

7/13/2001: SEIB: US could only delay attacks

According to a Senior Executive Intelligence Brief titled, "Terrorism: Bin Ladin Plans Delayed but Not Abandoned [Excised]" on July 13, 2001: "[Redacted] results could still be expected [redacted] US security measures would delay operations [redacted] but that plans to attack are still in train."

—CIA, "Terrorism: Bin Ladin Plans Delayed but Not Abandoned [Excised]," (Senior Executive Intelligence Brief), The Central Intelligence Agency's 9/11 File:, The National Security Archive, July 13, 2001

7/15/2001: Secret Taliban emissary warns of "huge attack on American soil," but because of massive failure of intelligence the warnings were ignored because of "warning fatigue"

In July 2001, "the United States and the United Nations ignored warnings from a secret Taliban emissary that Osama bin Laden was planning a huge attack on American soil. The warnings were delivered by an aide of Wakil Ahmed Muttawakil, the Taliban Foreign Minister at the time, who was known to be deeply unhappy with the foreign militants in Afghanistan, including Arabs. [Mr.] Muttawakil, now in American custody, believed the Taliban's protection of [Mr.] bin Laden and the other al-Qa'ida militants would lead to nothing less than the destruction of Afghanistan by the US military. He told his aide: 'The guests are going to destroy the guesthouse.' The minister then ordered him to alert the US and the UN about what was going to happen. But in a massive failure of intelligence, the message was disregarded because of what sources describe as 'warning fatigue'." [*The fifteenth of the month used for date sorting purposes only.*]

—Kate Clark, "Revealed: The Taliban Minister, the US Envoy and the Warning of September 11 that was Ignored," *The Independent*, September 7, 2002

7/15/2001: CIA learns "everyone" in Afghanistan is talking about impending attack on America

In July 2001, "the CIA had learned that in Afghanistan 'everyone is talking about an impending attack [on America].'" [*The fifteenth of the month used for date sorting purposes only.*]

—Frank Rich, *The Greatest Story Ever Sold*, Page 66

7/18/2001: Russians, Tenet warn of bin Laden attack threat regarding G8 summit and FAA

"In late July [2001], as the G-8 Summit [The Group of Eight Industrialized Nations] approached in Genoa, Italy, there was another spike in the [terrorism] threat level. The head of Russia's Federal Bodyguard Service reported that Osama bin Laden had directly targeted President [George W.] Bush for assassination at the Summit. CIA Director Tenet expressed concern about the Genoa meeting, and warned again of a 'major attack' by al Qaeda. Two days before the summit [July 18, 2001], the FBI issued another warning to U.S. law enforcement agencies, and the FAA urged airlines to 'use the highest level of caution.'"

—Peter Lance, *1000 Years For Revenge*, Page 408

7/18/2001: FBI: Counterterrorism budget increase denied

"In its annual budget request, the FBI had asked for a sizable budget increase for only one of its divisions—counterterrorism. But on July 18 [2001], Ashcroft sent a letter to Pickard saying the request had been turned down and that several FBI divisions faced budget cuts, including counterterrorism."

—Philip Shenon, *The Commission*, Page 248

[**Note:** Another indication of a lack of concern about terrorism by Ashcroft, who reported to George W. Bush.]

7/19/2001: FBI acting director didn't ask if there were US plots

"On July 19 [2001], on a periodic conference call with the FBI's field offices, Acting Director Thomas Pickard mentioned that, in light of the increased threat reporting, the Bureau needed to have 'evidence response teams ready' in case of an attack. 'He did not ask field offices to try to determine whether any plots were being considered within the United States.'"

—John Farmer, The Ground Truth, Page 57

7/20/2001: Egyptian intel warns of plane attack at G-8 summit

On July 20, 2001, "as the G-8 [The Group of Eight Industrialized Nations] leaders met in Genoa [Italy]…Egyptian intelligence warned the CIA of a potential suicide attack, in which hijackers might try to crash a plane into one of the host buildings at the summit. Believing the threat credible, the Agency reportedly asked the Italian military to ring the summit site with surface-to-air missiles."

—Peter Lance, 1000 Years For Revenge, Page 409

7/24/2001: Tenet: Jordan's king offered to help deal with Al-Qaeda, but would have to be part of larger strategy

Former CIA Director Tenet wrote: "In a briefing I received on July 24 [2001], I learned that Jordan's King Abdullah had sent word that, in his view, Bin Ladin and his command structure in Afghanistan must be dealt with in a decisive and military fashion. To that end, he offered to send two battalions of Jordanian Special Forces to go door to door in Afghanistan, if necessary, to deal with al-Qa'ida. The offer was a wonderful gesture but would have to have been part of a larger overall strategy in order to succeed."

—George Tenet with Bill Harlow, At the Center of the Storm, Page 156

7/25/2001: SEIB: Suspicious terrorist activity continues

According to a Senior Executive Intelligence Brief titled, "Terrorism: One Bin Ladin Operation Delayed, Others Ongoing [Excised]" on July 25, 2001: "[Redacted] indicates that an Usama Bin Ladin-sponsored terrorist operation has been postponed. [Redacted] still planned but had been delayed a few months. [Redacted] results still would be forthcoming [redacted]. Preparations for other attacks remain in train. Suspicious activity continued late last week [redacted]. Longer-term planning for terrorist operations against US and Israeli interests also continues, [redacted]"

—CIA, "Terrorism: One Bin Ladin Operation Delayed, Others Ongoing [Excised]," (Senior Executive Intelligence Brief), The Central Intelligence Agency's 9/11 File:, The National Security Archive, July 25, 2001

7/25/2001: CIA operative: "They're coming here"

According to former CIA Director Tenet, in late July 2001, "as we speculated about the kind of attacks we could face, Rich B. [a covert CIA operative] suddenly said, with complete conviction, 'They're coming here.' I'll never forget the silence that followed." [*The twenty-fifth of the month used for date sorting purposes only.*]

—George Tenet with Bill Harlow, *At the Center of the Storm*, Page 158

7/25/2001: Tenet: All channels of warnings "blinking red"

Tenet told the 9/11 Commission that by late July 2001, "the threat level could not 'get any worse'—'the system was blinking red.'...The collection efforts of the CIA and other organizations were not only bombarded with signs and reports of threatening activity, but the warning system itself—all those channels of communication intended to rouse the president [Bush] and the White House staff to alarm and activity—was 'blinking red.'" [*The twenty-fifth of the month used for date sorting purposes only.*]

—Thomas Powers, *The Military Error*, Page 32

[**Note:** Given "the system was blinking red," what steps did George W. Bush try to *take* to protect us?]

7/26/2001: George W. Bush on Iraq: Must ensure we "have a sanction policy that will work" after U-2 plane incident, will keep pressure on Iraq

After an incident with a U-2 plane, a member of the press questioned what the US may do about it during a photo opportunity in the Oval Office with Virginia Gubernatorial Candidate Mark Earley on July 26, 2001, and President George W. Bush responded: "Well, we're going to keep the pressure on Iraq. The no-fly zone strategy is still in place. We are in—plus, I'm analyzing the data from the incident you talked about. I look forward to finding out all the facts. But there's no question that Saddam Hussein is still a menace and a problem. And the United States and our allies must put the pressure on him. That's why I brought up to Mr. Putin in Genoa, the need for us to work in concert at the United Nations, to make sure that we have a sanction policy that will work."

—Office of the Press Secretary, "Remarks by the President and Virginia Gubernatorial Candidate Mark Earley in Photo Opportunity," George W. Bush—White House Archives, July 26, 2001

7/27/2001: Clarke to NSA: Coming Al-Qaeda attack postponed a few months, but will still happen

"On July 27 [2001], Clarke informed Rice and Hadley that the spike in intelligence about a near-term al Qaeda attack had stopped." He warned "that another report suggested an attack had just been postponed for a few months 'but will still happen.'"

—9/11 Commission, The 9/11 Commission Report, July 22, 2004, Page 260

7/27/2001: Rumsfeld: Iraqi sanctions not effective, open a dialogue; suggests ousting Hussein

"In a four-page memo marked 'Secret' that he [Rumsfeld] sent to Cheney, Rice, and Powell on the afternoon of July 27 [2001], the defense chief proposed meeting to discuss three options [for dealing with Iraq]: give up the no-fly zones and sanctions since they were no longer effective; approach 'our moderate Arab friends' to explore 'a more robust policy' aimed at toppling Saddam Hussein; or open a dialogue with Hussein to see if he was ready 'to make some accommodation.' Rumsfeld painted a picture of gathering danger. 'Within a few years the U.S. will undoubtedly have to confront a Saddam armed with nuclear weapons,' he wrote. While he did not suggest direct military action, Rumsfeld concluded that 'if Saddam's regime were ousted, we would have a much-improved position in the region and elsewhere.'"

—Peter Baker, *Days of Fire*, Page 109

[**Note:** Was Rumsfeld being honest when he suggested Hussein has no current nuclear weapons?]

7/30/2001: Taliban and Pakistan on Al-Qaeda

"When neither the Taliban nor Pakistan complied with [United Nations Resolution] 1333, follow-up Resolution 1363 was passed on July 30, 2001, with the support of the new Bush administration in Washington. It created a monitoring team to oversee the implementation of 1333, thus becoming the last of five UN resolutions after the African [embassy] bombings that called on the Taliban and Pakistan to take action against al Qaeda."

—Bruce Riedel, *The Search for Al Qaeda*, Page 75

7/31/2001: Taliban foreign minister aide: Bin Laden "planning a massive attack on U.S. soil"

"[A]t the end of July [2001], an aide to the Taliban foreign minister told an unnamed U.S. official in Peshawar, Pakistan, that bin Laden was planning a massive attack on U.S. soil."

—Peter Lance, *1000 Years For Revenge*, Page 409

[**Note:** Would such intel get your attention if you were the president of the United States?]

8/3/2001: Advisory: Al-Qaeda waiting to attack

"On August 3 [2001], the intelligence community issued an advisory concluding that the threat of impending al Qaeda attacks would likely continue indefinitely. Citing threats in the Arabian Peninsula, Jordan, Israel, and Europe, the advisory suggested that al Qaeda was lying in wait and searching for gaps in security before moving forward with the planned attacks."

—9/11 Commission, The 9/11 Commission Report, July 22, 2004, Page 260

8/6/2001: Rice: George W. Bush had to ask about Al-Qaeda threats

Regarding the August 6, 2001, President's Daily Brief [PDB], which warned of the potential for bin Laden to attack the US, Rice wrote: "The report had been developed only after the President [Bush] himself had asked whether there was any information on a possible al Qaeda attack on the U.S. homeland. The very fact that he'd had to ask suggested that the intelligence community thought it an unlikely event."

—Condoleezza Rice, *No Higher Honor*, Page xv

[**Note:** Given the preceding flood of warnings from the intelligence community that we would be attacked, why would Rice write in her book "the intelligence community thought it an unlikely attack"?]

8/6/2001: Bin Laden supporters in US planning attack

According to the President's Daily Brief on August 6, 2001, "in May 2001... the American embassy in Abu Dhabi [United Arab Emirates] had received a call claiming 'that a group of bin Laden supporters was in the US planning attacks with explosives.'"

—Elisabeth Bumiller, *Condoleezza Rice*, Page 161

8/6/2001: Bush receives requested brief on US threat level; threat of bin Laden attack in US current, serious

"During the spring and summer of 2001, President Bush had on several occasions asked his briefers whether any of the threats pointed to the United States. Reflecting on these questions, the CIA decided to write a briefing article summarizing its understanding of this danger.

Two CIA analysts involved in preparing this briefing article believed it represented an opportunity to communicate their view that the threat of a Bin Ladin attack in the United States remained both current and serious.

The result was an article in the August 6 [2001] Presidential Daily Brief titled 'Bin Ladin Determined to Strike in US.' It was the 36th PDB item briefed so far that year that related to Bin Ladin or al Qaeda, and the first devoted to the possibility of an attack in the United States."

—9/11 Commission, The 9/11 Commission Report, July 22, 2004, Page 260

[**Note:** It was the thirty-sixth PDB item brief in 2001 that related to bin Laden or Al-Qaeda.]

8/6/2001: PDB: Bin Laden determined to strike in the US; no further meetings on terror in next thirty days

The August 6, 2001, President's Daily Brief was titled 'Bin Laden Determined to Strike in the U.S.' Though it was a classified document, *NBC* reported that chemical and biological weapons were discussed. "Over the next thirty days, President Bush had no further meetings about terrorism."

—Craig Unger, *House of Bush, House of Saud*, Page 238

[**Note:** After Bush received the frightening briefings of August 6, 2001, he had no more meetings on terrorism for thirty days.]

8/6/2001: George W. Bush receives PDB "Strike in US," leaves work early, goes fishing

"Contemporaneous reports on the day that [President] Bush received the intelligence report [the President's Daily Brief, titled 'Bin Laden Determined to Strike in U.S.'], August 6 [2001], indicated that he had broken off from work early and gone fishing."

—Frank Rich, *The Greatest Story Ever Sold*, Page 47

8/6/2001: After 192 PDBs, George W. Bush in Texas when first mention of homeland attack issued in PDF memo

Regarding the August 6, 2001, President's Daily Brief, which warned of the potential for bin Laden to attack the US, Rice wrote: "That memo was the only PDB item that addressed the homeland threat in the 192 PDBs that the President [Bush] had seen since assuming office. On August 6 the President was in Crawford [Texas] and George Tenet was, as he put it to me in 2003, 'on a beach in New Jersey.' A homeland threat was simply not the focus of the myriad intelligence briefings the President received."

—Condoleezza Rice, *No Higher Honor*, Page 69

[**Note:** What about all the other intel that we would be attacked?]

8/7/2001: SEIB keeps PDF "Strike" title, but no further references and no meetings on potential threat

"Although the following day's [August 7, 2001] SEIB repeated the title of this [the August 6] PDB [titled 'Bin Ladin Determined to Strike in U.S.'], it did not contain the reference to hijackings, the alert in New York, the alleged casing of buildings in New York, the threat phoned in to the embassy, or the fact that the FBI had approximately 70 ongoing bin Ladin-related investigations. No CSG [Counterterrorism Security Group] or other NSC meeting was held to discuss the possible threat of a strike in the United States as a result of this report."

—9/11 Commission, The 9/11 Commission Report, July 22, 2004, Pages 260–262

8/7/2001: George W. Bush mentions that Hussein is still a "menace"

In a discussion with the press at the Ridgewood Country Club in Waco, Texas, on August 7, 2001, about the situation with Iraq, President George W. Bush said: "As I said, Saddam Hussein is a menace, he's still a menace and we need to keep him in check, and will."

Followed by a question from the press: "Are they ratcheting it up, though? We've had a lot of incidents lately."

President George W. Bush: "No—are they, the Iraqis? He's been a menace forever, and we will do—he needs to open his country up for inspection, so we can see whether or not he's developing weapons of mass destruction."

—Office of the Press Secretary, "Remarks by the President to the Pool—Ridgewood Country Club Waco, Texas," George W. Bush—White House Archives, August 7, 2001

8/10/2001: US, British jets bomb sites in Iraq

"On August 10 [2001], U.S. and British jets bombed three air defense sites in Iraq, the largest strikes since February."

—Bob Woodward, *Plan of Attack*, Page 23

8/13/2001: Potential plane hijacker starts flight school in Minneapolis; FBI alerted two days later

"On August 13 [2001], he [potential hijacker Zacarias Moussaoui] started his new [flight] training [near Minneapolis, Minnesota]....Two days later, the school called the local FBI office, telling agents they had what they thought was a potential hijacker on their hands....By the next afternoon, the FBI was at the school. By nightfall, Moussaoui was in jail on immigration charges. By the following day, the Minnesota agents had alerted counterterrorism officials in Washington...One agent even wrote in the margin of his interview notes that Moussaoui was the type of guy who might hijack an airplane and fly it into the World Trade Center."

—Terry McDermott, *Perfect Soldiers*, Page 226

8/15/2001: FBI and CIA Advisory: US itself very vulnerable to hundreds of bin Laden–linked terrorists

"FBI and CIA officials were advised in August [2001] that as many as 200 terrorists were slipping into this country and planning 'a major assault on the United States,' a high-ranking law enforcement official said Wednesday [September 19, 2001]. The advisory was passed on by the Mossad, Israel's intelligence agency. It cautioned that it had picked up indications of a 'large-scale target' in the United States and that Americans would be 'very vulnerable,' the official said.

It is not known whether U.S. authorities thought the warning to be credible, or whether it contained enough details to allow counter-terrorism teams to come up with a response. But the official said the advisory linked the information 'back to Afghanistan and [exiled Saudi militant] Osama bin Laden.'" [*The fifteenth of the month used for date sorting purposes only.*]

—Richard A. Serrano and John-Thor Dahlburg, "Officials Told of 'Major Assault' Plans," *Los Angeles Times*, September 20, 2001

[**Note:** If the FBI and CIA were notified, how could Bush not have received that information? If he did, I found no information that he did anything about it.]

8/15/2001: CIA: Bin Laden shifting to US attack plans

"[I]n August [2001], the Central Intelligence Agency issued a secret report warning senior policy makers that Al Qaeda, Mr. bin Laden's network, hoped to launch a strike against the domestic United States. The report combined both new and older intelligence gathered by the C.I.A. and other American intelligence agencies to depict Mr. bin Laden's long-term desire to shift from attacks on American interests overseas to targets in the United States." [*The fifteenth of the month used for date sorting purposes only.*]

—James Risen and Don Van Natta Jr., "Authorities Have Learned the Identities Of 18 Hijackers, Attorney General Says," *The New York Times*, September 14, 2001

8/15/2001: CIA tells Pentagon US will be "struck soon"

"'We are going to be struck soon,' Cofer Black told the Pentagon's classified annual conference on counterterrorism [on August 15, 2001] nine days later [than the August 6, 2001, President's Daily Brief]. 'Many Americans are going to die, and it could be in the U.S.'" [*The fifteenth of the month used for date sorting purposes only.*]

—Steve Coll, *Ghost Wars*, Page 569

8/15/2001: George W. Bush warned at least twice in August about Al-Qaeda threat

In former CIA Director Tenet's memoir *At the Center of the Storm*, he wrote: "'a few weeks after the Aug. 6 [2001] PDB was delivered, I followed it to Crawford [Texas] to make sure the president [Bush] stayed current on events.'...If [9/11 Commission member Tim] Roemer's suspicions were right, that meant that the CIA had warned Bush not once but at least twice in August 2001 that al-Qaeda was planning to attack in the United States." [*The fifteenth of the month used for date sorting purposes only.*]

—Philip Shenon, *The Commission*, Page 363

8/15/2001: Minnesota FBI agent warns of potential suicide hijacker crashing plane into NY WTC

On August 15, 2001, "a flight school in Minnesota contacted the local FBI field office to express concern about a student, Zacarias Moussaoui. He had asked suspicious questions about the flight patterns around New York City and whether the doors of a cockpit could be opened during flight. The local bureau quickly determined that Moussaoui was an Islamic radical who had been to Pakistan and probably to Afghanistan....The FBI agents investigating the case sought permission from headquarters to examine Moussaoui's laptop, which was denied because the agents couldn't show a probable cause for their search. When the Minneapolis supervisor pressed the matter with headquarters, he was told he was trying to get people 'spun up.' The supervisor defiantly responded that he was 'trying to keep someone from taking a plane and crashing into the World Trade Center'"

—Lawrence Wright, *The Looming Tower*, Page 396

[**Note:** If our government was on high alert, might the supervisor have changed the 9/11 history?]

8/19/2001: FBI agent notifies supervisor of Islamic extremist

"[A]n FBI field agent e-mailed his supervisors on August 19, 2001, that flight-school attendee Zacarias Moussaoui was 'an Islamic extremist preparing for some future act in furtherance of radical fundamentalist goals.'"

—Al Gore, *The Assault on Reason*, Page 179

8/23/2001: CIA review titled 'Islamic Extremist Learns to Fly [747]' details Moussaoui's capture

The CIA released a DCI Update Terrorist Threat Review on August 23, 2001. It mentioned details on the recent arrest of potential hijacker Zacarias

Moussaoui. Under the headline "Islamic Extremist Learns to Fly," its bullet points read:

"—Islamic fundamentalist travels to US to learn to fly a 747 in Minnesota
—Pays for training in cash
—Interested to learn that 747 doors don't open in flight
—Wanted training on London-JFK [New York] flights
—FBI arrested him based on the fact that he overstayed his 90 day visa"

—CIA, "DCI Update Terrorist Threat Review," (CIA), The Central Intelligence Agency's 9/11 File:, The National Security Archive, August 23, 2001

8/23/2001: Tenet sees flight school student arrest as an FBI issue and doesn't inform White House of possible connection to greater threat to US

"On August 23 [2001], DCI Tenet was briefed about the Moussaoui case in a briefing titled 'Islamic Extremist Learns to Fly.'...He was told that the FBI had arrested Moussaoui because of a visa overstay and that the CIA was working the case with the FBI. Tenet told us that no connection to al Qaeda was apparent to him at the time. Seeing it as an FBI case, he did not discuss the matter with anyone at the White House or the FBI. No connection was made between Moussaoui's presence in the United States and the threat reporting during the summer of 2001."

—9/11 Commission, The 9/11 Commission Report, July 22, 2004, Page 275

[**Note:** Was Tenet infected with Bush's apparent lack of concern with terrorism?]

8/25/2001: Bin Laden brags to paper about US attack plans

"[I]n late August [2001], [Mr.] bin [Laden boasted] in an interview with the London-based newspaper al-Quds al-Arabi that he was planning an unprecedentedly large strike against the United States." [*The twenty-fifth of the month used for date sorting purposes only.*]

—Andrew Gumbel, "Bush did not heed several warnings of attacks," *The Independent*, September 17, 2001

[**Note:** It seems that bin Laden boasting in an interview with a newspaper that he was planning an unprecedented large strike against the US should have caught the attention of our president or someone in his administration.]

8/28/2001: CIA lead on terror pair passed to FBI agents untrained in counterterrorism, labeled "routine"

"In July [2001], when a CIA officer finally told an FBI analyst about the pair [future 9/11 hijackers Khalid al-Midhar and Nawaf Alhazmi], he asked her to check on them 'in her spare time.' She concluded that if the two men were in the U.S., they were probably in New York, so she forwarded the information there on August 28 [2001], where an agent without any prior experience in counterterrorism was assigned the case. Since the lead was marked 'routine,' the agent had up to thirty days to open the case, by which time 9/11 intervened."

—Gerald Posner, *Why America Slept*, Page xiv

[**Note:** Although June, July, and August 2001 brought many new warnings that we would be attacked by bin Laden and Al-Qaeda, I found no evidence that Bush did anything substantive about those warnings.]

9/4/2001: Clarke presents strategy at one of only two "Principals Committee" meetings on terrorism in seven and a half months

"On September 4 [2001], Clarke was finally given the chance to present his strategy [for attacking Al-Qaeda] at a meeting of the administration's so-called Principals Committee, a group of high-level cabinet-ranking policy makers....it was only their second meeting about terrorism [in seven and a half months]—out of ninety to a hundred meetings since [President] Bush had taken office."

—Craig Unger, *House of Bush, House of Saud*, Page 239

[**Note:** Given that our government had received so many warnings that we would be attacked by terrorists, the fact that this was only the second high-level meeting about terrorism in seven and a half months is bizarre, at best.]

9/4/2001: Clarke memo of frustration asking Rice if George W. Bush administration is serious about dealing with the Al-Qaeda threat

On September 4, 2001, Clarke wrote Rice a memo "in which Clarke seemed to predict what was just about to happen. It was a memo that seemed to spill out all of Clarke's frustration about how slowly the Bush White House had responded to the cascade of terrorist threats that summer. The note was terrifying in its prescience. 'Are we serious about dealing with the Al Qaeda threat?' he asked Rice. 'Decision makers should imagine themselves on a future day when CSG [Counterterrorism Security Group] has not succeeded in stopping Al Qaeda attacks and hundreds of Americans lay dead in several countries, including the U.S. What would those decision makers wish that they had done earlier? That future day could happen at any time.'"

—Philip Shenon, The Commission, Page 148

[**Note:** Clarke had the background, the intel, the position; Bush had the intel that we would be attacked by Al-Qaeda. Why wasn't Bush or his people listening?]

9/7/2001: State Department issues worldwide terror warning

"Most recently, on Friday, Sept. 7, [2001] the State Department issued a worldwide alert warning 'American citizens may be the target of a terrorist threat from extremist groups with links to [Osama bin Laden's] al Qaeda organization.'"

—David Ruppe, "Analysts Suspect Bin Laden Group ," ABCNews.go.com, September 11, 2001

[**Note:** At least a warning—four days before 9/11.]

9/9/2001: FBI agent: "Bin Laden is appeasing the Taliban. Now the big one is coming," after hearing of Northern Alliance leader assassination

On September 9, 2001, head of the Northern Alliance "Ahmed Shah Massoud agreed to see two Arab television journalists...He was the best hope Afghanistan had of a moderate Islamist alternative to the Taliban. [Al Qaeda second-in-command Aywan al-] Zawahiri's forged letter had gotten the two phony journalists into Massoud's office. The cameraman's battery pack was filled with explosives. The bomb tore the assassins apart, killed a translator, and drove two pieces of metal into Massoud's heart. When [FBI Agent] Ali Soufan heard the news in Yemen, he told another agent, 'Bin Laden is appeasing the Taliban. Now the big one is coming.'"

—Lawrence Wright, The Looming Tower, Pages 400–401

9/9/2001: Two days before 9/11, Rumsfeld said he would recommend counterterrorism budget veto

"When the Senate Armed Services Committee proposed to strip $600 million from the missile defense budget, and spend it instead on counterterrorism priorities identified by military commanders, Rumsfeld said he would recommend a veto. The veto threat came on September 9 [2001]."

—Barton Gellman, Angler, Page 113

[**Note:** Was Rumsfeld channeling Bush when he was recommending against increasing the budget for identified counterterrorism priorities?]

9/10/2001: FBI Director Ashcroft denies request for more money for counterterrorism the day before 9/11

On September 12, 2001, Pickard received a letter from Ashcroft. "It was a denial of his request for more money for the counterterrorism division. The letter was dated September 10, 2001."

—Philip Shenon, *The Commission*, Page 24

[**Note:** Would Ashcroft have denied a request for more counterterrorism money if he thought his boss George W. Bush was concerned or focused on the terrorism risk?]

The preceding quotes again bring up the question of what President Bush did, tried to do, or didn't do to protect us from the expected terrorist attacks while he was focusing on Hussein and Iraqi oil.

C. 9/11 COULD HAVE BEEN DISRUPTED OR PREVENTED

THE FOLLOWING QUOTES WILL show that if Bush had focused on trying to protect our country from the many documented concerns and threats from bin Laden and Al-Qaeda, 9/11 might have been disrupted or prevented.

6/15/2001: Fox News: "Missed leads" on terrorism from Germany, UK given to administration before 9/11

"[There are] many examples of 'missed leads' that the Bush administration was given prior to Sept. 11....German intelligence alerted the Central Intelligence Agency, Britain's MI-6 intelligence service, Israel's Mossad in June 2001 that Middle Eastern terrorists were training for hijackings and targeting American and Israeli interests." [*The fifteenth of the month used for date sorting purposes only.*]

—Carl Cameron, Fox News, "Clues Alerted White House to Potential Attacks," reprinted in "BEST ARTICLES EVER Want To Know COMPLETE ARCHIVE News Articles 3, 950," Archive.org, May 17, 2002

7/10/2001: Tenet: Pre-9/11 meet with Rice a lost opportunity

"Tenet looked back on his July 10, 2001, meeting with Rice, two months before 9/11, as a tremendous lost opportunity to prevent or disrupt the 9/11 attacks."

—Bob Woodward, *State of Denial*, Page 79

7/10/2001: FBI agent: 9/11 may have been "prevented" if five-page memo on flight schools was heeded

The FBI office in "'PHOENIX BELIEVES THAT THE FBI should accumulate a listing of civil aviation universities/colleges around the country,' FBI special agent Kenneth Williams wrote to FBI headquarters...on July 10, 2001....His five-page memorandum would be a key warning that went unheeded by the FBI. If it had been acted upon, there is a chance the deadly September 11 plot might have been prevented."

—Bill Gertz, *Breakdown*, Page 83

12/17/2003: Kean in CBS News interview: Leaders prior to 9/11 failed, 9/11 preventable

"In an interview with CBS News on December 17 [2003], he [9/11 Commission Chairman Thomas Kean] suggested that the 9/11 attacks might have been preventable. 'As you read the report,' Kean said, 'you're going to have a pretty clear idea what wasn't done and what should have been done. This was not something that had to happen.' Even more surprising, from the mild-mannered Kean, was the suggestion that those at fault should be held accountable. 'There are people that, if I was doing the job, would certainly not be in the position they were in at that time because they failed,' he said."

—Peter Lance, *Cover Up*, Pages 143–144

[**Note:** It's some indictment—to have the chairman of the 9/11 Commission (a Republican) saying if some people had done their job, 9/11 might have been preventable.]

1/21/2004: Former CIA deputy director tells 9/11 Commission that the Bush White House was unwilling to believe in terror threats before 9/11

The 9/11 Commission's staff conducted a private interview on January 21, 2004, with former Deputy CIA Director John McLaughlin. He said, there was "'great tension' at the CIA...over what seemed to be the refusal of the White House to deal with warnings of an imminent terrorist attack in 2001. The White House had just seemed unwilling to believe there was a problem—or at least no problem that required immediate attention, and certainly no problem on American soil."

—Philip Shenon, *The Commission*, Pages 394–395

[**Note:** What former Deputy CIA Director McLaughlin told the 9/11 Commission is consistent with my contention that President George W. Bush, up to 9/11, was not taking the bin Laden and Al-Qaeda threats seriously.]

3/21/2004: Clarke tells *60 Minutes* that Bush, Rice ignored his urgent warnings, did nothing about Al-Qaeda before 9/11, then tried to link it to Iraq to justify war

Clarke appeared on *60 Minutes* on March 21, 2004. He said that President "Bush and Rice had ignored his urgent warnings throughout the spring and summer of 2001 about an imminent attack....He was merciless about Rice. Like others in the administration, she was obsessed with cold war issues, not with the terrorist threats in front of her. President Bush, Clarke said, had 'done nothing' about al-Qaeda before 9/11 and then, after the attacks, tried desperately to link 9/11 to Saddam Hussein to justify an invasion of Iraq."

—Philip Shenon, *The Commission*, Page 277

[**Note:** Clarke, with an inside seat in Bush's administration, saying that Bush had done nothing about Al-Qaeda until 9/11.]

4/4/2004: Kean and Lee of the 9/11 Commission: 9/11 could and should have been prevented

"On April 4, 2004, Tom Kean and Lee Hamilton went on *Meet the Press* and reluctantly acknowledged—in response to [host Tim] Russert's questions—what many on the commission's staff believed had been obvious since the early days of the investigation: The 9/11 attacks could have been prevented. They should have been prevented."

—Philip Shenon, *The Commission*, Page 262

[**Note:** Could there have been a stronger indictment of Bush than to say the 9/11 attacks could and should have been prevented?]

7/22/2004: 9/11 Commission final report found that the Bush administration never mobilized in response to the domestic terrorist threat

In its section on "Government Response to the Threats" in the 9/11 Commission's final Report, which was issued on July 22, 2004, although the Bush administration was warned of a terrorist threat, "The September 11 attacks fell into the void between the foreign and domestic threats....No one was looking for a foreign threat to domestic targets," and that "In sum, the domestic agencies never mobilized in response to the threat. They did not have direction, and did not have a plan to institute. The borders were not hardened. Transportation systems were not fortified. Electronic surveillance was not targeted against a domestic threat. State and local law enforcement were not marshaled to augment the FBI's efforts. The public was not warned."

—9/11 Commission, The 9/11 Commission Report, July 22, 2004, Pages 263, 265

[**Note:** Given all the actions the Commission found were not taken to try and protect our country from the well-chronicled coming terrorist attacks, what did Bush do to try and protect us, if anything?]

11/15/2004: Review of FBI shows only one intel research specialist assigned to bin Laden, that researcher was gone after July 2001, no one else assigned

"In 1996, the FBI had hired 36 IRSs [Intelligence Research Specialists] in an effort to bolster its international terrorism analytical program. According to witnesses, within a year approximately half of the IRSs had left the program.

By mid-1999, there were only approximately 15 international terrorism IRSs, and by mid-2000 there were only 10 IRSs devoted to counterterrorism analysis.

Former IRS managers confirmed to us that only one IRS was assigned to UBL [Usama Bin Laden] matters in 2001, but she transferred to another unit in July 2001.

Thus, in the summer of 2001 when the Phoenix EC [Electronic Communication] was received, no IRS was assigned to work on Bin Laden matters." [*The fifteenth of the month used for date sorting purposes only.*]

—"A Review of the FBI's Handling of Intelligence Information Prior to the September 11 Attacks," Office of the Inspector General in the U.S. Department of Justice, OIG.Justice.gov, November 2004, Page 87

[Note: After July 2001, the FBI having no research specialist assigned to bin Laden shows bin Laden was anything but a high priority to the FBI.]

6/10/2008: George W. Bush "Repeatedly Ignored and Failed to Respond to High Level Intelligence Warnings of Planned Terrorist Attacks in the U.S., Prior to 9/11"

"[Bush] Repeatedly Ignored and Failed To Respond to High Level Intelligence Warnings of Planned Terrorist Attacks in the U.S., Prior to 9/11... The White House's top counter-terrorism adviser, Richard A. Clarke, has testified that from the beginning of George W. Bush's presidency until September 11, 2001, Clarke attempted unsuccessfully to persuade President Bush to take steps to protect the nation against terrorism. Clarke sent a memorandum to then-National Security Advisor Condoleezza Rice on January 24, 2001, 'urgently' but unsuccessfully requesting 'a Cabinet-level meeting to deal with the impending al Qaeda attack.'

In April 2001, Clarke was finally granted a meeting, but only with second-in-command department representatives, including Deputy Secretary of Defense Paul Wolfowitz, who made light of Clarke's concerns.

Clarke confirms that in June, July, and August 2001, the Central Intelligence Agency (CIA) warned the president in daily briefings of unprecedented indications that a major al Qaeda attack was going to happen against the United States somewhere in the world in the weeks and months ahead. Yet, Clarke was still unable to convene a cabinet-level meeting to address the issue.

Condoleezza Rice has testified that George Tenet met with the president 40 times to warn him that a major al Qaeda attack was going to take place, and that in response the president did not convene any meetings of top officials. At such meetings, the FBI could have shared information on possible terrorists enrolled at flight schools. Among the many preventive steps that could have been taken, the Federal Aviation Administration, airlines, and airports might have been put on full alert.

According to Condoleezza Rice, the first and only cabinet-level meeting prior to 9/11 to discuss the threat of terrorist attacks took place on September 4, 2001, one week before the attacks in New York and Washington.

On August 6, 2001, President Bush was presented a President's Daily Brief (PDB) article titled 'Bin Laden Determined to Strike in U.S.' The lead sentence of that PDB article indicated that Bin Laden and his followers wanted to 'follow the example of World Trade Center bomber Ramzi Yousef and *bring the fighting to America*'. The article warned:

'Al-Qa'ida members—including some who are U.S. citizens—have resided in or traveled to the U.S. for years, and the group apparently maintains a support structure that could aid attacks.'

The article cited a 'more sensational threat reporting that Bin Laden wanted to hijack a U.S. aircraft', but indicated that the CIA had not been able to corroborate such reporting. The PDB item included information from the FBI indicting 'patterns of suspicious activity in this country consistent with preparations for hijackings or other types of attacks, including recent surveillance of Federal buildings in New York'. The article also noted that the CIA and FBI were investigating 'a call to our embassy in the UAE in May saying that a group of Bin Laden supporters was in the U.S. planning attacks with explosives'.

The president spent the rest of August 6, and almost all the rest of August 2001 on vacation. There is no evidence that he called any meetings of his advisers to discuss this alarming report. When the title and substance of this PDB article were later reported in the press, then-National Security Adviser Condoleezza Rice began a sustained campaign to play down its significance, until the actual text was eventually released by the White House.

New York Times writer Douglas Jehl, put it this way: 'In a single 17-sentence document, the intelligence briefing delivered to President Bush in August 2001 spells out the who, hints at the what and points towards the where of the terrorist attacks on New York and Washington that followed 36 days later.'

Eleanor Hill, Executive Director of the joint congressional committee investigating the performance of the U.S. intelligence community before September 11, 2001, reported in mid-September 2002 that intelligence reports a year earlier 'reiterated a consistent and constant theme: Osama bin Laden's intent to launch terrorist attacks inside the United States'.

That joint inquiry revealed that just two months before September 11, an intelligence briefing for 'senior government officials' predicted a terrorist attack with these words: 'The attack will be spectacular and designed to inflict mass casualties against U.S. facilities or interests. Attack preparations have been made. Attack will occur with little or no warning.'

Given the White House's insistence on secrecy with regard to what intelligence was given to President Bush, the joint-inquiry report does not divulge whether he took part in that briefing. Even if he did not, it strains credulity to suppose that those 'senior government officials' would have kept its alarming substance from the president.

Again, there is no evidence that the president held any meetings or took any action to deal with the threats of such attacks."

—Article XXXIII of H.Res.1258 "RESOLUTION Impeaching George W. Bush, President of the United States, of high crimes and misdemeanors," introduced by Rep. Dennis J. Kucinich (D-OH-10), June 10, 2008, and referred to the Committee on the Judiciary, Congress.gov, June 11, 2008

[**Note:** The above article of impeachment in the House resolution to impeach Bush confirms what my independent research found— that George W. Bush did little or nothing to protect our country in response to the flood of intel he received in the first eight months of his presidency stating in various ways that we would be attacked by Al-Qaeda.]

As the previous quotes show—and are broadly confirmed by article XXXIII of the June 2008 resolution to impeach George W. Bush—Bush and others in his administration received many warnings that bin Laden and Al-Qaeda were coming to attack our country. Some of those warnings also mentioned the possibility that hijacked planes might be flown into buildings, including the Twin Towers and the Pentagon.

One would have thought that our president and commander-in-chief should have reacted strongly to the flood of intel warning that our country would be attacked by terrorists.

D. INJURIES AND DEATHS FROM 9/11

THE ESTIMATED NUMBER OF injuries and deaths from 9/11 differs widely from organization to organization, and I could find no official credible numbers. The following quotes show the range of those estimates, calculated in different ways.

9/1/2011: More than 18,000 people suffering from 9/11 linked illnesses as a result of toxic dust

"More than 18,000 people are suffering from illnesses linked to the dust from the attacks on New York's World Trade Center on 11 September 2001. The figure comes from the US government's monitoring and treatment programme for 9/11 emergency workers, volunteers and local residents. The most common afflictions are respiratory problems including asthma and sinusitis, but muscular and intestinal conditions are reported as well. The senior US official managing the health legacy of the attacks warns that early deaths are possible among the survivors."

—David Shukman, "Toxic dust legacy of 9/11 plagues thousands of people," BBC. com, September 1, 2011

9/11/2001: 2,977 9/11 deaths

"At the World Trade Center (WTC) site in Lower Manhattan, 2,753 people were killed when hijacked American Airlines Flight 11 and United Airlines Flight 175 were intentionally crashed into the north and south towers, or as a result of the crashes.…

At the Pentagon in Washington, 184 people were killed when hijacked American Airlines Flight 77 crashed into the building.

Near Shanksville, Pennsylvania, 40 passengers and crew members aboard United Airlines Flight 93 died when the plane crashed into a field."

—CNN Library, "September 11 Terror Attacks Fast Facts," CNN.com, June 13, 2019

6/29/2011: Decade after War on Terror, 225,000 people killed; cost to America between $3.2 and $4 trillion including medical care and vet disability

"Nearly 10 years after the declaration of the War on Terror [declared by Bush on September 20, 2001], the wars in Afghanistan, Iraq, and Pakistan have killed at least 225,000 people, including men and women in uniform, contractors, and civilians. The wars will cost Americans between $3.2 and $4 trillion, including medical care and disability for current and future war veterans, according to a new report by the Eisenhower Research Project based at Brown University's Watson Institute for International Studies....

Among the group's main findings:

—The U.S. wars in Afghanistan, Iraq, and Pakistan will cost between $3.2 and $4 trillion, including medical care and disability for current and future war veterans. This figure does not include substantial probable future interest on war-related debt.

—More than 31,000 people in uniform and military contractors have died, including the Iraqi and Afghan security forces and other military forces allied with the United States.

—By a very conservative estimate, 137,000 civilians have been killed in Iraq and Afghanistan by all parties to these conflicts.

—The wars have created more than 7.8 million refugees among Iraqis, Afghans, and Pakistanis.

—Pentagon bills account for half of the budgetary costs incurred and are a fraction of the full economic cost of the wars.

—Because the war has been financed almost entirely by borrowing, $185 billion in interest has already been paid on war spending, and another $1 trillion could accrue in interest alone through 2020.

—Federal obligations to care for past and future veterans of these wars will likely total between $600-$950 billion. This number is not included in most analyses of the costs of war and will not peak until mid-century."

—Deborah Baum, "Estimated cost of post-9/11 wars: 225,000 lives, up to $4 trillion," Brown.edu, June 29, 2011

9/6/2015: Nearly 21,000 have filed eligibility claims with the September 11 Victims Compensation Fund

"The 9/11 death and injury toll is still rising as this week's 14th anniversary of the terrorist attacks approaches.

Nearly 21,000 people have filed eligibility claims with the September 11th Victims Compensation Fund as of Sept. 6, up more than 4,000 from this time last year, according to updated data that fund officials released Wednesday."

—Kevin McCoy, "9/11 death and injury total still rising," USA Today, September 9, 2015

9/11/2016: WTC Health Program established in 2011 has 75,000 registered, 87% were rescue workers at WTC; 1,140 have died but no causes are tracked

In a 2016 anniversary article on the aftermath of the September 11, 2001, World Trade Center (WTC) collapse: "In 2011, the federal World Trade

Center Health Program (WTCHP) was established. It has 75,000 registered members, 87% of whom worked on rescue, recovery and clean-up. The rest are New York residents or workers. A total of 1,140 registered members have died since the program was created in 2011, WTCHP spokeswoman Christy Spring said....Causes of death are not recorded by the WTCHP. There is no central record for how many people died between 2001 and 2011 from illnesses linked to 9/11 fumes and debris, Spring said, nor any way of knowing exactly how many other people have died without any record of their illnesses having been caused by exposure near Ground Zero."

—Joanna Walters, "9/11 health crisis: death toll from illness nears number killed on day of attacks," *The Guardian*, September 11, 2016

E. COSTS RELATED TO 9/11

THIS SECTION SHOWS THE costs of the 9/11 attacks calculated differently.

Some calculations of 9/11 costs have included the property damaged, increased medical care for those disabled when the Twin Towers fell, a downturn in the tourism and airline businesses, increased costs and resources for airport security, lost wages, and increased military budgets for the 2003 Iraq War.

Other calculations have included the cost of the War on Terror in other Middle Eastern countries such as Afghanistan and Syria, and the interest accrued for those expenditures.

9/1/2011: Aljazeera.com interactive chart shows 9/11 cost America more than $5 trillion

Aljazeera.com created an interactive chart titled "September 11: Counting the costs to America" online: "$5 trillion, and counting: Osama bin Laden spoke often of a strategy of 'economic warfare' against the United States, a low-level war aimed at bankrupting the world's economic superpower.

A decade after the 9/11 attacks, it's hard to argue that bin Laden's strategy was ineffective.

The attacks themselves, according to the September 11 commission, cost Al Qaeda between $400,000 and $500,000 to execute.

They have cost America, by our estimate, more than $5 trillion—a 'return on investment' of 10,000,000 to one."

—Gregg Carlstrom, "Interactive: How much did 9/11 cost the US?" Aljazeera.com, September 1, 2011

9/8/2011: Al-Qaeda spent half a million dollars to attack on 9/11, which has cost the US $3.3 trillion

"Al Qaeda spent roughly half a million dollars to destroy the World Trade Center and cripple the Pentagon. What has been the cost to the United States? In a survey of estimates by *The New York Times*, the answer is $3.3 trillion."

—Shan Carter and Amanda Cox, "One 9/11 Tally: $3.3 Trillion," *The New York Times*, September 8, 2011

9/8/2011: Some 9/11 costs, like lives lost, are incalculable; $4 trillion in total war costs estimated through 2050

"The terrorists who crashed into the World Trade Center and the Pentagon on Sept. 11, 2001 spent an estimated $400,000 to $500,000 to kill nearly 3,000 people. The total costs of the attack for U.S. companies and taxpayers are much more difficult to ascertain. The cost of losing so many human lives is incalculable. And the economic toll is difficult to tally, given the ongoing and indirect expense of war.

Here are a few of the 9/11 line items:

[1] $7 billion: Amount paid out through the 9/11 Victims Compensation Fund to the survivors of the 2,880 people killed and 2,680 injured in the attacks.

[2] $8.7 billion: Estimated lifetime potential earnings lost of the victims who perished in the World Trade Center towers.

[3] $500 million: Amount the city of New York paid in overtime compensation to clean up Ground Zero.

[4] $19.6 billion: The drop in U.S. airline revenue between 2001 and 2002.

[5] $5 billion: Direct government aid to U.S. airlines to cover losses incurred during three days of grounded flights immediately after 9/11 and sustained through the end of the year. The government also extended $10 billion in future loan guarantees.

[6] $21.8 billion: Cost to replace the buildings and infrastructure in New York destroyed in the attacks.

[7] $500 million: Cost to repair the Pentagon after the attack.

[8] $40 billion: Insured losses related to the 9/11 attacks, including property, business interruption, aviation, workers compensation, life and liability insurance.

[9] $192 million: Cost to run the NYPD's counter-terrorism and intelligence activities for one year.

[10] $5 million: Amount the NYPD has earmarked from a Homeland Security grant to buy a high-speed, bullet-proof boat designed to respond to a suicide or live shooter attack in the city's port area.

[11] $408 billion: Cost to operate the Department of Homeland Security since it was created in 2002.

[12] $80.1 billion: Civilian and military intelligence gathering costs in 2010—more than double what was spent in 2001.

[13] $43 billion: Minimum cost of 10 years worth of U.S. airport security. Passengers cover roughly 40 percent each year through the passenger security tax of $2.50 per flight.

[14] $1.1 billion: Estimated price to modify and add stealth features to a fleet of 73 MH-60 Black Hawk helicopters, two of which are thought to have been used in the raid that killed Osama Bin Laden, according to Richard Aboulafia, an aviation analyst at the Teal Group Corporation.

[15] $1.3 trillion: Cost of the wars in Iraq, Afghanistan, and Pakistan to date in 2011 dollars, according to Pentagon appropriations.

[16] $4 trillion: Total war costs through 2050, if you include veterans' care, war-related foreign aid, and interest paid on Pentagon appropriations."

—Lindsay Blakely, "The cost of 9/11—in dollars," CBSNews.com, September 8, 2011

2/28/2017: IAGS report: Big ticket 9/11 costs also from loss of four civilian aircraft, cleanup costs, job losses; price tag approaches $2 trillion

"Counting the value of lives lost as well as property damage and lost production of goods and services, losses already exceed $100 billion. Including the loss in stock market wealth—the market's own estimate arising from expectations of lower corporate profits and higher discount rates for economic volatility—the price tag approaches $2 trillion.

Among the big-ticket items:

—The loss of four civilian aircraft valued at $385 million.

—The destruction of major buildings in the World Trade Center with a replacement cost of from $3 billion to $4.5 billion.

—Damage to a portion of the Pentagon: up to $1 billion.

—Cleanup costs: $1.3 billion.

—Property and infrastructure damage: $10 billion to $13 billion.

—Federal emergency funds (heightened airport security, sky marshals, government takeover of airport security, retrofitting aircraft with anti-terrorist devices, cost of operations in Afghanistan): $40 billion.

—Direct job losses amounted to 83,000, with $17 billion in lost wages.

—The amount of damaged or unrecoverable property hit $21.8 billion.

—Losses to the city of New York (lost jobs, lost taxes, damage to infrastructure, cleaning): $95 billion.

—Losses to the insurance industry: $40 billion.

—Loss of air traffic revenue: $10 billion.

—Fall of global markets: incalculable."

—"How much did the September 11 terrorist attack cost America?" The Institute for the Analysis of Global Security, IAGS.org, accessed February 28, 2017

11/4/2018: Study: US post 9/11 war-related spending "allocated through FY2019 is $4.9 trillion"; author estimates "through FY2023, the US will spend and take on obligations to spend more than $6.7 trillion"

"Including the other areas of war-related spending, the estimate for total US war-related spending [FY2001, post 9/11, to FY2019] allocated through FY2019 is $4.9 trillion. But because the US is contractually and morally obligated to pay for the care of the post-9/11 veterans through their lifetimes,

it is prudent to include the costs of care for existing post-9/11 veter
through the next several decades. This means that the US has spent or is
ligated to spend $5.9 trillion in current dollars through FY2019....Furt
the US military has no plans to end the post-9/11 wars in this fiscal year or
the next. Rather, as the inclusion of future years spending estimates in the
Pentagon's budget indicates, the DOD anticipates military operations in
Afghanistan, Pakistan, Iraq and Syria necessitating funding through at least
FY2023. Thus, including anticipated OCO and other war-related spending,
and the fact that the post-9/11 veterans will require care for the next several
decades, I estimate that through FY2023, the US will spend and take on
obligations to spend more than $6.7 trillion."

—Neta C. Crawford, "United States Budgetary Costs of the Post-9/11 Wars Through
FY2019: $5.9 Trillion Spent and Obligated," Watson Institute for International and
Public Affairs, Brown University, Watson.Brown.edu, November 14, 2018

8/6/2001 ; Bush "OK you've
delivered your message,
now you can go"
Scott Ritter — Iraq—Confidential

William Rivers Pitt-
Was Don Imag—

Susan Lindauer, — Lies —
Extreme Prejudice —

F.   RECAP

Years before George W. Bush was elected president, bin Laden founded Al-Qaeda and declared war on the United States. As part of that war, Al Qaeda bombed the World Trade Center in 1993, our embassies in Kenya and Tanzania in 1998, and our navy ship the USS *Cole* in 2000. Those attacks alone cost hundreds of American lives, over 1,000 Americans wounded, and many others killed and injured. In addition, at the end of 1999, less than a year before Bush was elected president, Clinton's administration offered a $5 million reward for the arrest of Osama bin Laden, calling him our "public enemy number one."

Then, between the election of George W. Bush on November 7, 2000, and his inauguration on January 20, 2001, Bush and his incoming team of senior advisors and others were given personal intelligence briefings about the special terrorist danger to our country posed by bin Laden and Al-Qaeda. Those briefings were conducted by President Clinton and included counterterrorism czar Clarke; Berger, the outgoing National Security Advisor; Tenet, Director of Central Intelligence; Pavitt, Deputy Director for (CIA) Operations; and General Kerrick, outgoing Deputy National Security Advisor.

Bush, as our president, retained in his new administration some senior Clinton people knowledgeable in terrorism, including Tenet and Clarke, both of whom were well aware of the dangers bin Laden and Al-Qaeda represented to our country.

The incoming President Bush and his top people were clearly briefed about the specific terrorist danger to our country. However, instead of immediately working to try to protect our country from bin Laden and Al-Qaeda, for the next eight months, Bush studied Iraq's oil while publicly demonizing Hussein and scaring our nation into falsely believing that Hussein had weapons of mass destruction. Bush also implied that Hussein intended to use those weapons against us while not concerning himself with bin Laden and Al-Qaeda.

Bush's administration even deleted the information about bin Laden in the State Department's annual report, *Patterns of Global Terrorism*. The prior year's edition had a full page dedicated to bin Laden.

Perhaps Bush thought that by not discussing or answering questions about bin Laden and Al-Qaeda, he could better sell his message of the danger of Hussein and his WMD to our Congress and country. Perhaps by focusing on his message about the dangers of Hussein, Bush increased the chances of securing Iraqi oil.

Bush's efforts to downplay or dismiss the threats from bin Laden and Al-Qaeda are perhaps best evidenced by the fact that he never uttered the words "Al-Qaeda" or "bin Laden" in the 379 speeches he gave from his inauguration to 9/11.

The following three quotes are reminders of why I believe that Bush was guilty of criminal negligence as president:

— 12/17/2003: 9/11 was not something that had to happen. "In an interview with CBS News on December 17 [2003], he [9/11 Commission Chairman Thomas Kean] suggested that the 9/11 attacks might have been preventable. 'As you read the [9/11] report,' Kean said, 'you're going to have a pretty clear idea what wasn't done and what should have been done. This [9/11] was not something that had to happen.' Even more surprising, from the mild-mannered Kean, was the suggestion that those at fault should be held accountable. 'There are people that, if I was doing the job, would certainly not be in the position they were in at that time because they failed,' he said."

— 3/21/2004: Bush and Rice ignored urgent warnings prior to 9/11. Clarke appeared on *60 Minutes* on March 21, 2004. He said that President "Bush and Rice had ignored his urgent warnings throughout the spring and summer of 2001 about an imminent attack....He was merciless about Rice. Like others in the administration, she was obsessed with cold war issues, not with the terrorist threats in front of her. President Bush, Clarke said, had 'done nothing' about al-Qaeda before 9/11 and then, after the [9/11] attacks, tried desperately to link 9/11 to Saddam Hussein to justify an invasion of Iraq."

— 7/22/2004: In its section on "Government Response to the Threats" in the 9/11 Commission's final Report, which was issued on July 22, 2004, although the Bush administration was warned of a terrorist threat, "The September 11 attacks fell into the void between the foreign and domestic threats...No one was looking for a foreign threat to domestic targets," and that, "In sum, the domestic agencies never mobilized in response to the threat. They did not have direction, and did not have a plan to institute. The borders were not hardened. Transportation systems were not fortified. Electronic surveillance was not targeted against a domestic threat. State and local law enforcement was not marshaled to augment the FBI's efforts. The public was not warned."

The following undated quote is from President George W. Bush about his lack of response to the August 6, 2001, President's Daily Brief [and other intel he had received before 9/11], as conveyed by Peter Baker, on page 113 of his book, *Days of Fire*. It sums up my findings and contention that Bush never took the terrorism threats he had received prior to 9/11 seriously:

> **"Looking back, Bush admitted that he did not react with the alarm he should have. He did not summon the directors of the FBI and the CIA. He did not order heightened alerts. Nor was any action requested of him in the [August 6, 2001] memo. 'I didn't feel that sense of urgency,' Bush said."**

The evidence in this chapter has made it clear that had Bush taken the many bin Laden and Al-Qaeda warnings seriously, and had he moved reasonably to try and protect us from their possible outcome, 9/11 might have been prevented, disrupted, or its effect diminished.

Because he did not use reasonable care in trying to prevent damage to our people and our country from the many notices that we would be attacked, I posit that George W. Bush was criminally negligent by turning a blind eye to those warnings and in so doing left our country naked to terrorist risks he knew about and at least should have tried to stop.

CRIME #2: TORTURE / TORTURING PRISON-ERS / SENDING PRISONERS TO BE TORTURED BY OTHERS / RELATED ISSUES

George W. Bush approved and encouraged the torture of detainees (a.k.a. prisoners and unlawful enemy combatants) and sent detainees to other countries to be tortured—all while Bush and senior members of his administration proclaimed publicly that their government didn't torture.

THE ISSUE OF TORTURE was arguably addressed by our new nation soon after the US Constitution was ratified in 1789.

The Eighth Amendment (one of the first ten Amendments to the Constitution that made up the Bill of Rights) became law on December 15, 1791. It read:

> **"Excessive bail shall not be required, nor excessive fines imposed, nor cruel and unusual punishments inflicted."**

Those six words, *nor cruel and unusual punishments inflicted*, are broad and vague (like many phrases in the Constitution and its Amendments). Consequently, the US Supreme Court has had to give guidance on interpreting that phrase in a number of cases.[13]

Meanwhile, over time, our country has stopped meting out some past punishments under the law such as branding an adulterer or dunking/drowning someone accused of being a witch. The interpretation of what the words *cruel and unusual punishment* in specific circumstances will surely continue to be argued about and tested in our courts, but to many, certain acts are clearly torture.

---

13   "Cruel and Unusual Punishment," Cornell Law School, Law.Cornell.edu, https://www.law.cornell.edu/wex/cruel_and_unusual_punishment.

A. ATTEMPTING TO DEAL WITH THE ABUSE AND TORTURE OF SOLDIERS AND PRISONERS DURING WAR AND IN THE TREATMENT OF MAN OVERALL

GENEVA CONVENTIONS 1864 TO 1949

THE ORIGINAL GENEVA CONVENTION became a group of four international agreements, signed and ratified by many countries, including the United States.[14] The conventions dealt with the humane treatment of prisoners during wars of various kinds.

The first Geneva Convention was organized in 1863 by the Red Cross and its founder, Henri Dunant. Dunant was moved to protect injured soldiers because he had witnessed widespread carnage and suffering after Italy's second war for Independence at the Battle of Solferino in 1859, described as one of the bloodiest battles of the century.

Here are five of the 143[15] articles of the Third Geneva Convention regarding the obligatory treatment of prisoners of war:

— "Art 13. Prisoners of war must at all times be humanely treated."

— "Art 17. Every prisoner of war, when questioned on the subject, is bound to give only his surname, first names and rank, date of birth, and army, regimental, personal or serial number, or failing this, equivalent information....No physical or mental torture, nor any other form of coercion, may be inflicted on prisoners of war to secure from them information of any kind whatever. Prisoners of war who refuse to answer may not be threatened, insulted, or exposed to unpleasant or disadvantageous treatment of any kind."

---

14 When the United States signed the 1949 Geneva Conventions, it indicated that the US wouldn't honor parts of the Convention. For example, the convention prohibiting use of the death penalty. "Convention (III) relative to the Treatment of Prisoners of War. Geneva, 12 August 1949...Reservation made upon signature and maintained upon ratification." ICRC. org, accessed May 22, 2019

15 "Convention (III) relative to the Treatment of Prisoners of War." Geneva, 12 August 1949," ICRC.org, accessed May 22, 2019

— "Art 25. Prisoners of war shall be quartered under conditions as favourable as those for the forces of the Detaining Power who are billeted in the same area. The said conditions shall make allowance for the habits and customs of the prisoners and shall in no case be prejudicial to their health."

— "Art 27. Clothing, underwear and footwear shall be supplied to prisoners of war in sufficient quantities by the Detaining Power, which shall make allowance for the climate of the region where the prisoners are detained. Uniforms of enemy armed forces captured by the Detaining Power should, if suitable for the climate, be made available to clothe prisoners of war."

— "Art 38. While respecting the individual preferences of every prisoner, the Detaining Power shall encourage the practice of intellectual, educational, and recreational pursuits, sports and games amongst prisoners, and shall take the measures necessary to ensure the exercise thereof by providing them with adequate premises and necessary equipment.

Prisoners shall have opportunities for taking physical exercise, including sports and games, and for being out of doors. Sufficient open spaces shall be provided for this purpose in all camps."

Each of the four 1949 Conventions also contained a section known as "Common Article 3: Conflicts Not of an International Character." That Article for the first time addressed conflicts that cannot easily be classified, for example where the statehood of one of the parties involved is uncertain. Those conflicts "include traditional civil wars, internal armed conflicts that spill over into other States or internal conflicts in which third States or a multinational force intervenes alongside the government."[16]

Common Article 3 contained prohibited acts against prisoners, including:

(a) violence to life and person, in particular murder of all kinds, mutilation, cruel treatment, and torture

(b) taking of hostages

---

16   "The Geneva Conventions of 1949 and their Additional Protocols," ICRC.org, October 29, 2010

(c) outrages upon personal dignity, in particular humiliating and degrading treatment

(d) the passing of sentences and the carrying out of executions without previous judgment pronounced by a regularly constituted court, affording all the judicial guarantees, which are recognized as indispensable by civilized peoples.[17]

The Geneva Conventions could roughly be described as *you treat your prisoners properly, and don't torture them, and we will treat our prisoners equally.* Unfortunately, after 9/11, under Bush the United States violated and tried to work around their Geneva and other treaty obligations.

For example, during the US invasion of Afghanistan in November 2001, militia forces captured Salim Ahmed Hamdan, a Yemeni national who was alleged to have worked as a personal aide to Osama bin Laden. Hamdan was transported to Guantánamo Bay, where he was interrogated using "coercive" tactics. He was tried by a military commission, a new judicial system created by President Bush in order to allow the admission of evidence obtained by torture; in a regular US court system, such evidence would be rejected as unreliable, since torture victims will often say anything to end the torture.[18] The military commission deemed Hamdan an "enemy combatant" and tried and convicted him of conspiracy.[19]

Hamdan's attorneys challenged the constitutionality of their client's trial by a military commission because the commission didn't offer Hamdan adequate due process protections. His attorneys argued that he should be tried in United States courts based on Common Article 3(d) of the 1949 Geneva Conventions. That legal question ended at the Supreme Court, with Justice Stevens, on June 29, 2006, writing for the majority in *Hamdan v. Rumsfeld* that, in part, Common Article 3 was applicable and required that Hamdan be tried by a "regularly constituted court, affording all the judicial guarantees which are recognized as indispensable by civilized peoples."[20]

---

17   1949 Conventions (I, II, III, IV) Article 3, "Conflicts Not Of An International Character," ICRC.org, accessed May 22, 2019

18   Charlotte Dennett, *The People v. Bush* (Chelsea Green) 2010. Page 130

19   National Constitution Center staff, "*Hamdan v. Rumsfeld*: Applying the Constitution to Guantánamo prisoners," Constitutioncenter.org, June 29, 2017

20   "*Hamdan v. Rumsfeld*, "Opinion of the Court," June 29, 2006," Supreme.Justia.com, accessed February 17, 2020

In response to the court's decision, the Military Commissions Act of 2006 was signed into law by President George W. Bush, which expanded the power of the executive "to authorize trial by military commission for violations of the law of war, and for other purposes."[21] It stated that any detainee classified as an "unlawful enemy combatant" could be tried by a military commission.[22] In 2007, under the new act, Hamdan was reclassified as an "unlawful enemy combatant," given revised charges, and authorized to be tried by a military commission. In 2008, the military commission found Hamdan guilty of "material support for terrorism" and sentenced him to five and a half years, with time served. He was finally released on January 8, 2009,[23] and permitted to live with his family in Yemen.[24]

On October 16, 2012, the US Court of Appeals DC Circuit vacated Hamdan's entire conviction.[25] The court ruled in part that, because the Constitution prohibits Congress from passing "laws that retroactively punish conduct that was not previously prohibited,"[26] the government was not authorized to prosecute Hamdan for "providing material support for terrorism," which was not a war crime[27] at the time of Hamdan's actions, only being codified as a war crime in US law by the Military Commission Act in 2006.[28]

---

21   "S. 3930 an act to authorize trial by military commission for violations of the law of war, and for other purposes." LoC.gov; Public Law No: 109-366, October 17, 2006, Congress.gov, accessed May 20, 2019

22   Sgt. Sara Wood, "Judge Dismisses Charges Against Second Guantánamo Detainee," Archive.Defense.gov, accessed May 20, 2019

23   "Lesson Plan: Debate Which Civil Liberties Should Be Provided to Those in Prison at Guantánamo," PBS.org, accessed May 20, 2019

24   Reuters, "Yemen Releases Former bin Laden Driver From Jail," NYTimes.com, January 11, 2009

25   *Hamdan v United States*, CADC.uscourts.gov, accessed May 22, 2019

26   *Hamdan v United States* referencing U.S. Const. art. I, § 9, cl. 3 ("No Bill of Attainder or ex post facto Law shall be passed."), Caselaw.Findlaw.com

27   The court here notes that a war crime is defined as a violation of the laws of war, and that the US codified laws of war (10 U.S.C. § 821) refer to the international laws of war; the court cites Justice Stevens' majority opinion in *Hamdan v. Rumsfeld* to define a violation of international laws of war as "'when universal agreement and practice both in this country and internationally' recognize it as such" *Hamdan v. United States*, 19–20

28   *Hamdan v. United States*, (III, B) 22: "There is no international-law proscription of material support for terrorism…there are no relevant international treaties that make material support for terrorism a recognized international-law war crime. Neither the Hague Convention nor the Geneva Conventions—the sources that are 'the major treaties on the

BELGIUM'S 1993 UNIVERSAL JURISDICTION LAW

ON JUNE 16, 1993, Belgium passed a law[29] giving their courts universal jurisdiction over international crimes that were in violation of the 1949 Geneva Conventions and its additional protocols. The law was later amended in 1999 to include genocide and crimes against humanity.

The law was hailed by international human rights groups because it allowed victims of atrocities committed abroad to file complaints in Belgium, thus challenging the long-standing impunity of tyrants and war criminals.[30]

This law was then used as the basis to file legal complaints against, among others, former President H. W. Bush and some of his senior advisers, including Chairman of the Joint Chiefs of Staff Powell, for alleged illegal actions in the 1991 Gulf War. In response, on March 18, 2003, Powell (who was by then serving as secretary of staff under President George W. Bush) "cautioned our Belgian colleagues that they need to be very careful about this kind of...legislation" because it would make it "hard" for US officials to travel to NATO (North Atlantic Treaty Organization) headquarters in Brussels[31]—a veiled threat against Brussels continuing as headquarters of NATO. In response, Belgium amended the law again, this time restricting its jurisdiction. The amendment, in part, gave Belgian courts discretion to dismiss criminal complaints when they were not directly tied to Belgium, and stated that Belgian courts "should refrain" from prosecuting matters that would be "better brought before either an international tribunal or before another national tribunal."[32]

---

laws of war' [quoting Justice Stevens' opinion in *Hamdan v. Rumsfeld*]—acknowledge material support for terrorism as a war crime." Caselaw.Findlaw.com

29   "Observations by Belgium on the scope and application of the principle of universal jurisdiction," UN.org, accessed February 17, 2020

30   "Belgium Universal Jurisdiction Law Repealed," Human Rights Watch, HRW.org, https://www.hrw.org/news/2003/08/01/belgium-universal-jurisdiction-law-repealed

31   US Department of State Press Release on Interview by International Wire Services, State.gov, March 18, 2003

32   "US Reaction to Belgian Universal Jurisdiction Law." *The American Journal of International Law*, vol. 97, no. 4, 2003, pp. 984–987, JSTOR.org, October 2003

On May 14, 2003, a group of Iraqi and Jordanian nationals filed a criminal complaint against United States General Tommy Franks for alleged war crimes during the invasion of Iraq in 2003. In the following months, complaints were filed against President George W. Bush, Rumsfeld, and again against Secretary of State Powell. In response, United States officials expressed strong disapproval with those filings, with Rumsfeld now directly threatening Belgium's status as host to NATO. According to Rumsfeld:

> **"Belgium needs to realize that there are consequences to its actions. This law calls into serious question whether NATO can continue to hold meetings in Belgium and whether senior U.S. officials, military and civilian, will be able to continue to visit international organizations in Belgium....we will have to oppose any further spending for construction for a new NATO headquarters here in Brussels until we know with certainty that Belgium intends to be a hospitable place for NATO to conduct its business."[33]**

Belgium changed its law again on August 5, 2003, to once again severely restrict its jurisdiction over international crime, with the exception of a few open cases, to instances where "the accused is Belgian or has his primary residence in Belgium; if the victim is Belgian or has lived in Belgium for at least three years at the time the crimes were committed; or if Belgium is required by treaty to exercise jurisdiction over the case."[34] That August 5, 2003, amendment further prohibits filing complaints against "sitting heads of state and foreign ministers, as well as against other individuals enjoying immunity in Belgium based on treaties."[35]

On September 24, 2003, Belgium dismissed all pending cases against United States officials.[36]

---

33 "US Reaction to Belgian Universal Jurisdiction Law." *The American Journal of International Law*, vol. 97, no. 4, 2003, p. 986, JSTOR.org, October 2003

34 "Belgium: Universal Jurisdiction Law Repealed," Human Rights Watch, HRW.org, August 1, 2003

35 "US Reaction to Belgian Universal Jurisdiction Law." *The American Journal of International Law*, vol. 97, no. 4, 2003, p. 987, JSTOR.org, October 2003

36 Glenn Frankle, "Belgian War Crimes Law Undone by Its Global Reach," *Washington-Post.com*, September 30, 2003

Belgian officials had stated publicly that without pressure from the United States, their government "would be unlikely to change the law."[37]

THE WAR CRIMES ACT OF 1996

THE WAR CRIMES ACT of 1996, signed into law by President Clinton on August 21, 1996,[38] is the first federal law passed in the United States that imposes criminal penalties for war crimes under the Geneva Conventions by nonmilitary members.[39]

The purpose of the law was to define war crimes such that they could be prosecutable in United States court, and was intended for use against potential acts committed against US troops in countries such as Bosnia, El Salvador, and Somalia, though the Defense Department advocated expanding the law to encompass a broader range of war crimes. According to its sponsor, Republican Rep. Walter B. Jones Jr. of North Carolina, the incentive for the law was his and others' frustration with the inability of the United States to prosecute north Vietnamese perpetrators of torture against United States POWs during the Vietnam War.

The law defines "war crime" as a "grave breach" of any international convention to which the United States is party, with specific reference to violations of Common Article 3 of the 1949 Geneva Conventions. Included in the definition of "war crime" was any act constituting "torture" as defined by United States law. The Act applied in situations where the victim or perpetrator was an American national or member of the US military.[40]

Congress passed the Act with overwhelming bipartisan support, never anticipating that a decade later, as noted by Salon.com, the law might also be used against a US administration "accused of systematic war crimes." As

---

37   Craig S. Smith, "Belgium Plans to Amend Law on War Crimes," *NYTimes.com*, June 23, 2003

38   Weekly Compilation of Presidential Documents, Vol. 32, No. 34, GovInfo.gov, Page 1482

39   R. Jeffrey Smith, "Detainee Abuse Charges Feared...," *WashingtonPost.com*, July 28, 2006; Michael Scherer, "Will Bush and Gonzalez Get Away With It?" Salon.com, August 2, 2006

40   "War Crimes Act of 1996," July 24, 1996, GovInfo.gov, accessed May 23, 2019

would happen, White House Counsel Alberto Gonzales fretted that President Bush's policies "could trigger prosecution under the act."[41]

Not surprisingly, the law was amended by the Military Commissions Act (MCA) of 2006, which, in part, explicitly denied the protections of the Geneva Conventions, including Common Article 3, to those deemed "unlawful enemy combatants."[42] In 2008, in *Boumediene v. Bush*, the Supreme Court decided that the MCA unconstitutionally denied terror suspects their rights to *habeas corpus*.[43] Following that decision, a further amendment was made with the Military Commissions Act of 2009,[44] signed into law by President Barack Obama on October 28, 2009, which limited the ability of the US government to use hearsay or coerced evidence, and afforded detainees suspected of terrorism greater access to defense and due process rights.[45]

THE 1998 ROME STATUTE—INTERNATIONAL CRIMINAL COURT

THE 1998 ROME STATUTE is the treaty that founded the International Criminal Court (ICC) and established the four main international crimes that the court would prosecute: genocide, crimes against humanity, war crimes, and the crime of aggression. It authorized the court to prosecute those crimes under the following conditions: if they were committed by a national of a state party or in the territory of a state party; if the states are "unable" or "unwilling" to prosecute the crimes in their domestic courts; or if the court is authorized to do so by the United Nations Security Council. The treaty further stated that those four core crimes do not have a statute of limitations. (It should be noted

---

41 Michael Scherer, "Will Bush and Gonzales get away with it?" Salon.com, August 2, 2006. https://www.salon.com/2006/08/02/cronin/

42 "Military Commissions Act of 2006," October 17, 2006, LoC.gov, accessed May 23, 2019

43 "*Boumediene v Bush*," Oyez.org and law.cornell.edu

44 "Title XVIII: Military Commissions—Military Commissions Act of 2009" of the "National Defense Authorization Act for Fiscal Year 2010," H.R.2647, Public Law 111–84, Congress.gov, October 28, 2009

45 Jaclyn Belczyk, "House passes amendments to Military Commissions Act," law.Jurist.org, October 9, 2009

that the crime of aggression was only added as the fourth core crime in 2017 after lengthy debate and deliberation.)

The treaty was signed at an international convention in Rome on July 17, 1998 (despite votes against it from the United States, Iraq, Israel, Libya, China, Qatar, and Yemen), and went into effect on July 1, 2002. Although President Clinton eventually signed the treaty, on December 31, 2000, he did not submit it to the senate for ratification, citing "significant flaws" within it and a wish to "protect US officials from unfounded charges."[46]

On May 6, 2002, weeks before the statute would go into effect, Under Secretary of State for Arms Control and International Security John Bolton, on behalf of the Bush administration, "unsigned"[47] the treaty, stating that "the United States does not intend to become a party to the treaty," and that "the United States has no legal obligations arising from its signature on December 31, 2000."[48] Further, In June of 2002, the United States threatened to veto the renewal of all United Nations peacekeeping missions unless they passed United Nations Security Council Resolution 1422, which would grant immunity from the ICC to United States troops on peacekeeping missions. United States ambassador to the United Nations John Negroponte stated on July 12, 2002, that the United States Government "will never permit Americans to be jailed"[49] by the ICC. The resolution passed unanimously that same day but required yearly renewal. On June 18, 2004, two months after the release of photos of United States troops abusing prisoners in Abu Ghraib prison, the United Nations Security Council denied the United States its request for renewal.[50]

On August 2, 2002, the Bush administration signed into law the American Service-Members' Protection Act (ASPA), which completely cut off funding for the ICC[51] and put in place a provision requiring that the United States

46   "Clinton's statement on war crimes court," BBC.co.uk, December 31, 2000

47   Whether or not a president can unilaterally rescind signature of a treaty is still a matter of legal debate.

48   Richard Boucher, Spokesman, "International Criminal Court: Letter to UN Secretary General Kofi Annan," 2001-2009.state.gov, May 6, 2002

49   John D. Negroponte, U.S. Permanent Representative to the United Nations, "Vote About the International Criminal Court," 2001-2009.state.gov, July 12, 2002

50   "What does the International Criminal Court do?" BBC.com, June 25, 2015

51   Kiel Ireland and Julian Bava, "The American Service-Members' Protection Act: Pathways to, and Constraints on, U.S. Cooperation with the International Criminal Court," Stanford Law School: Law and Policy Lab, law.Stanford.edu, June 2016, Page 13

enter into agreements with all ICC state signatories giving American citizens immunity from ICC prosecution while in those states.[52]

The Obama administration softened the United States' relations with the ICC. On January 13, 2009, during her confirmation hearing as Secretary of State for the Obama administration, Hillary Clinton said "we will end hostility toward the ICC, and look for opportunities to encourage effective ICC action... by bringing war criminals to justice."[53] The United States continued to engage with the ICC "in ways that promote U.S. interests"[54] including supporting referral of war crimes to the ICC. For example, on February 26, 2011, the UN Security Council voted in favor of "referring the situation in Libya to the International Criminal Court (ICC)," after which warrants of arrest were granted by ICC judges on June 27, 2011, against Muammar Gaddafi and others in Libya for their alleged crimes against humanity.[55]

On September 3, 2018, John Bolton, back in the White House as President Trump's National Security Adviser, stated that the United States "will fight back" against the ICC if the court attempts to prosecute Americans for alleged war crimes committed in Afghanistan. He threatened to place sanctions on any funds the ICC has in the US financial system, ban judges from entering the United States, and prosecute them in American courts.[56]

The four treaties just mentioned (1949 Geneva Conventions, Belgium 1993 law, the 1996 War Crimes Act, and the 1998 Rome Statute—or the ICC) represent some of the world trying to bring humanistic sanity to the chaos, tragedies, and horrors of war. As shown, George W. Bush most assuredly knew some of his administration's actions on and off the battlefield were crimes or he wouldn't have worked so creatively to sidestep, stifle, or gut the intent, if not the words, of those treaties.

---

52   "American Service-Members' Protection Act," *The American Journal of International Law*, Vol. 96, No. 4, October 2002, JSTOR.org, Page 976

53   Steven Groves and Brett Schaefer, "The U.S. Should Not Join the International Criminal Court," Heritage.org, August 18, 2009

54   Ibid.

55   "Libya: Q&A on the Arrest and Surrender of the Three International Criminal Court Suspects," HRW.org, August 26, 2011; and Harold Hongju Koh, Legal Advisor U.S. Department of State, New York City "International Criminal Justice 5.0," 2009-2017.state.gov, November 8, 2012

56   Steve Holland, "Trump administration takes aim at International Criminal Court, PLO," Reuters.com, September 9, 2018

US FEDERAL LAWS AGAINST TORTURE

Our federal law on torture is found in three sections of "18 US Code § 2340A. Torture."[57]

The law is organized into three sections: §2340. Definitions; §2340A. Torture; and §2340B. Exclusive remedies.

Section "§2340. Definitions," last amended in 1994 and 2004, reads:

"(1) 'torture' means an act committed by a person acting under the color of law specifically intended to inflict severe physical or mental pain or suffering (other than pain or suffering incidental to lawful sanctions) upon another person within his custody or physical control;

(2) 'severe mental pain or suffering' means the prolonged mental harm caused by or resulting from—

(A) the intentional infliction or threatened infliction of severe physical pain or suffering;

(B) the administration or application, or threatened administration or application, of mind-altering substances or other procedures calculated to disrupt profoundly the senses or the personality;

(C) the threat of imminent death; or

(D) the threat that another person will imminently be subjected to death, severe physical pain or suffering, or the administration or application of mind-altering substances or other procedures calculated to disrupt profoundly the senses or personality; and

---

57   "18 U.S. Code § 2340. Definitions," Law.Cornell.edu, accessed May 18, 2019

(3) 'United States' means the several States of the United States, the District of Columbia, and the commonwealths, territories, and possessions of the United States."[58]

Section "§2340A. Torture" was amended in 1994 and 2001 and reads:

"(a) Offense.—Whoever outside the United States commits or attempts to commit torture shall be fined under this title or imprisoned not more than 20 years, or both, and if death results to any person from conduct prohibited by this subsection, shall be punished by death or imprisoned for any term of years or for life.

(b) Jurisdiction.—There is jurisdiction over the activity prohibited in subsection (a) if—

(1) the alleged offender is a national of the United States; or

(2) the alleged offender is present in the United States, irrespective of the nationality of the victim or alleged offender.

(c) Conspiracy.—A person who conspires to commit an offense under this section shall be subject to the same penalties (other than the penalty of death) as the penalties prescribed for the offense, the commission of which was the object of the conspiracy."[59]

Section "§2340B. Exclusive remedies" reads:

"Nothing in this chapter shall be construed as precluding the application of State or local laws on the same subject, nor shall anything in this chapter be construed as creating any substantive or procedural right enforceable by law by any party in any civil proceeding."[60]

The preceding overview mainly looked at some laws and treaties intended to stop torture and other abuses of those captured or in government custody. Also, the section gave some examples of what has been done to thwart or weaken those treaties. Now let's look at waterboarding from a few different perspectives.

---

58   "18 U.S. Code § 2340. Definitions," Law.Cornell.edu, accessed June 7, 2020

59   "18 U.S. Code § 2340A. Torture," Law.Cornell.edu, accessed June 7, 2020

60   "18 U.S. Code § 2340B. Exclusive remedies," Law.Cornell.edu, accessed June 7, 2020

B. WATERBOARDING HAS BEEN ILLEGAL IN THE UNITED STATES

WHILE MANY STRUGGLE WITH the meaning of "cruel and unusual punishments," United States law has been clear that waterboarding (a.k.a. the water treatment or water cure) has been considered torture for many years.

In the 1922 Mississippi murder case, *White v. State* (182, 91 So. 903, 904; Miss. 1922), defendant Gerrard White, a young African-American male, appealed his murder conviction in the state of Mississippi and was sentenced to death. He based his appeal upon the argument that his original confession was coerced through the use of the "water cure." White won his appeal. Judge Holden explained in the appeals court ruling how the "water cure" was administered:

> "[T]he hands of appellant were tied behind him, he was laid upon the floor upon his back, and, while some of the men stood upon his feet, Gilbert, a very heavy man, stood with one foot entirely upon appellant's breast, and the other foot entirely upon his neck. While in that position what is described as the 'water cure' was administered to him in an effort to extort a confession as to where the money was hidden which was supposed to have been taken from the dead man. The 'water cure' appears to have consisted of pouring water from a dipper into the nose of appellant, so as to strangle him, thus causing pain and horror, for the purpose of forcing a confession. "[61]

That court held that:

> "Confessions induced by fear, though not aroused by spoken threats, are nevertheless involuntary, because the fear which takes away the freedom may arise solely from the conditions and circumstances surrounding the confessor."[62]

---

61   Daily Dish "Waterboarding In Mississippi," TheAtlantic.com, November 14, 2007

62   "American Law Reports Annotated, Volume 24," books.Google.com, Page 700, copyright 1928

In another Mississippi case, the 1926 murder conviction in *Fisher v. State* (110 So. 361, 362; Miss. 1926) was reversed in the Mississippi Supreme Court and sent back for a new trial because the appellant's confession had been coerced by the "water cure":

In the Mississippi Supreme Court ruling, the sheriff is referenced as testifying that:

> **"he was sent for one night to come and receive a confession of the appellant in the jail; that he went there for that purpose; that when he reached the jail he found a number of parties in the jail; that they had the appellant down upon the floor, tied, and were administering the water cure, a species of torture well known to the bench and bar of the country....Several persons were introduced by the appellant who testified as to the presence of the parties in the jail and the administering of the water cure to Fisher and others jointly charged with the offense with him."[63]**

Mississippi Supreme Court Judge William Nathaniel Ethridge Jr. wrote that the lower court "erred in receiving the confessions" of the appellant, noting that:

> **"the Constitution of the state provides in section 26, among other things, that 'the accused shall not be compelled to give evidence against himself.' This guaranty is violated whenever a confession is illegally extorted from a person accused of crime."[64]**

The court went on to cite from the 1922 Mississippi case described above, *White v. State*, which ruled against involuntary confessions.

In 1947, the United States prosecuted the use of waterboarding by the Japanese against a United States civilian, wrote *The Washington Post's* Walter Pincus:

> **"in 1947, the United States charged a Japanese officer, Yukio Asano, with war crimes for carrying out another form of waterboarding on a U.S. civilian. The subject was strapped on a stretcher that was tilted so that his feet were in the air and**

---

63   "Fisher v. State, 110 So. 361 (Miss. 1926) Mississippi Supreme Court," CourtListener. com, accessed May 18, 2019

64   Ibid.

head near the floor, and small amounts of water were poured over his face, leaving him gasping for air until he agreed to talk.

> 'Asano was sentenced to 15 years of hard labor,' Sen. Edward M. Kennedy (D-Mass.) told his colleagues [in 2006] during the debate on military commissions legislation. 'We punished people with 15 years of hard labor when waterboarding was used against Americans in World War II,' he said."[65]

In 1948, relying on the third Geneva Convention in 1929, the 1946–1948 International Military Tribunal for the Far East convicted twenty-five Japanese leaders of war crimes and crimes against humanity, specifically including torture by waterboarding, referred to as the "water treatment," as published on WashingtonPost.com:[66]

> "After World War II, we convicted several Japanese soldiers for waterboarding American and Allied prisoners of war. At the trial of his captors, then-Lt. Chase J. Nielsen, one of the 1942 Army Air Forces officers who flew in the Doolittle Raid and was captured by the Japanese, testified: 'I was given several types of torture....I was given what they call the water cure.' He was asked what he felt when the Japanese soldiers poured the water. 'Well, I felt more or less like I was drowning,' he replied, 'just gasping between life and death.'"

Lt. Nielsen's experience, the article continued, "was not unique. Nor was the prosecution of his captors":

> "After Japan surrendered, the United States organized and participated in the International Military Tribunal for the Far East, generally called the Tokyo War Crimes Trials. Leading members of Japan's military and government elite were charged, among their many other crimes, with torturing Allied military personnel and civilians. The

---

65   Walter Pincus, "Waterboarding Historically Controversial," Politics, WashingtonPost.com, October 5, 2006

66   Evan Wallach, "Waterboarding Used to Be a Crime," Outlook & Opinions, WashingtonPost.com, November 4, 2007

principal proof upon which their torture convictions were based was conduct that we would now call waterboarding."

During the Vietnam war in 1968, a US soldier from the 1st Cavalry Division in Vietnam was documented as having waterboarded a Vietnamese soldier under interrogation.

Walter Pincus of *The Washington Post* wrote about waterboarding in an article titled "Fine Print: U.S. can't seem to shake the 'water cure' as a method of interrogation" published May 1, 2014:

> *"The Washington Post* **on Jan. 21, 1968, ran a front-page photo of a U.S. soldier supervising the waterboarding of a captured North Vietnamese soldier. The caption says the technique induced 'a flooding sense of suffocation and drowning, meant to make him talk.' Because of the photo, the U.S. Army initiated an investigation and the soldier was court-martialed and convicted of torturing a prisoner."**

In 1983, another instance of waterboarding in the United States came to light in a report by National Public Radio. That year, James Parker (Texas Sheriff for San Jacinto County) and three of his deputies were charged by the Department of Justice for their use of "water torture" on prisoners,[67] and convicted and sentenced to four years in prison.[68]

11/15/2005: CIA kept hundreds of hours of interrogation tapes, that included waterboarding, from 9/11 Commission; tapes the CIA destroyed in 2005

"From the start of [Al-Qaeda logistics chief Abu] Zubayda's capture, the CIA videotaped hundreds of hours of his interrogation, including his waterboarding....Although the Agency insisted that the Program was legally and politically defensible, it withheld these tapes from both the 9/11 Commission and a federal court judge in the Moussaoui case. And in [November] 2005, on orders from the head of the Clandestine Services, the Agency destroyed them."

—Jane Mayer, *The Dark Side,* Pages 174–175

---

67   "*UNITED STATES of America, Plaintiff-Appellee, v. Carl LEE, Defendant-Appellant*," (744 F.2d 1124), OpenJurist.org, October 12, 1984; and The University Of Chicago Law School Faculty Blog, "Back to Posner and Vermeule on Torture," uChicagoLaw.typepad. com, May 7, 2009

68   Eric Weiner, "Waterboarding: A Tortured History," NPR.org, November 3, 2007

C. THE BUSH ADMINISTRATION TORTURING AND HAVING DETAINEES TORTURED: JUSTIFICATION, DENIAL, AND THE HEADLINE FROM THE FIRST FINDING IN THE SENATE INTEL-LIGENCE COMMITTEE REPORT OF APRIL 2014

THIS CHAPTER WILL SHOW that whether out of fear, sadism, revenge, or thinking he was above the law, President George W. Bush approved the torturing of prisoners captured by or turned over to us (sometimes for a bounty) after 9/11.

Bush and those in his administration often called what they did (which included waterboarding) *enhanced interrogation* and *rendition,* not torture. The detainee treatment was aimed largely in part at what his administration deemed "unlawful enemy combatants"—loosely defined as fighters not wearing the uniform of a sovereign country.

The administration said such combatants were not legitimate soldiers, so they had no legal rights or protections of any kind under any law or treaty.

Bush told us that *enhanced interrogation* was necessary because it provided our military with important intelligence from detainees that could not be gained any other way; the intel gained from such *enhanced interrogation* or *rendition* was vital to keeping our country safe from further terrorist attacks.

As you will read, some knowledgeable about interrogations have said that enhanced interrogation and torture are ineffective and not necessary, as there are better methods to gather intel.

More specifically, you will read in this chapter that:

— Bush and his administration sent prisoners around the world for enhanced interrogation, called "rendition"[69] or "extraordinary rendition,"[70] code words in the intelligence community for

---

69   According to Lexico.com, the definitions of "rendition" include: "1. a performance or interpretation, especially of a dramatic role or piece of music....2. (also **extraordinary rendition**)...the practice of sending a foreign criminal or terrorist suspect covertly to be interrogated in a country with less rigorous regulations for the humane treatment of prisoners," accessed June 2, 2020

70   "**Extraordinary rendition,** extrajudicial practice, carried out by U.S. government agencies, of transferring a prisoner to a foreign country for the purposes of detention and interrogation. Those agencies asserted that the practice exempted detainees from the legal

We knew it was you all along

kidnapping detainees and sending them to other countries that abuse and torture them for us.

— Contrary to established United States and international law, President Bush claimed that waterboarding was not torture, a claim mirrored by Bush's vice president, Cheney. Bush subsequently admitted (actually appeared to brag) that he personally approved waterboarding.

— While Bush and a few others in his administration were torturing people, or having them tortured, he, Rice, and Cheney proclaimed publicly that the Bush administration did not torture.

Torture has never been accepted under our legal system. However, after 9/11, some people, either in anger over those attacks or in fear of more attacks, justified torture, in part, to gain information they said would protect us from future attacks.

Others have said that torture is never acceptable, while others have said it was okay to torture unlawful enemy combatants, but not fighters wearing the uniforms of sovereign countries.

Whatever your views on George W. Bush and torture, you may find the pages ahead eye-opening if not shocking.

Note: The quotes in gray boxes are misleading, without credible basis or false.

9/15/2001: George W. Bush administration sanctions torture for first time in US history

"[A]lmost immediately after September 11, 2001…for the first time in its history, the United States sanctioned government officials to physically and psychologically torment U.S.-held captives, making torture the official law of the land in all but name." [*The fifteenth of the month used for date sorting purposes only.*]

—Jane Mayer, *The Dark Side*, Pages 7–8

1/11/2002: Rumsfeld says detainees in Guantánamo would not be handled as "prisoners of wars" but as "unlawful combatants"

During a Pentagon Briefing on January 11, 2002, Rumsfeld responded to a journalist's question about whether the ICRC [International Committee of

safeguards afforded to prisoners under U.S. and international law." Kenneth J. Ryan, "Extraordinary rendition," Britannica.com, October 20, 2011

143

the Red Cross] and other non-governmental organizations would be given access to the detainees in Guantánamo: "They will be handled not as prisoners of wars, because they're not, but as unlawful combatants. The—as I understand it, technically unlawful combatants do not have any rights under the Geneva Convention. We have indicated that we do plan to, for the most part, treat them in a manner that is reasonably consistent with the Geneva Conventions, to the extent they are appropriate, and that is exactly what we have been doing."

—Federal News Service Transcript at 9:50 on video, "Defense Department Briefing," Pentagon Briefing, C-SPAN.org, January 11, 2002

3/31/2002: FBI sees CIA's detainee treatment as disgraceful, disastrously counterproductive, and criminal

Although President George W. Bush noted that the Department of Justice had declared the CIA's treatment of Al-Qaeda operations chief Abu Zubayda as legal, "FBI agents, who were the first to question Zubayda [on March 31, 2002] at the black site, before the CIA interrogation team arrived…thought that what they glimpsed of the CIA's treatment of him was disgraceful, disastrously counterproductive, and criminal."

—Jane Mayer, The Dark Side, Page 155

8/1/2002: Bybee memo to Rizzo: Walling, facial slaps, insects placed in a confined box, and waterboarding are not torture

In Assistant Attorney General Jay Bybee's August 1, 2002, memo to Acting General Counsel to the CIA John Rizzo, "The OLC [Department of Justice, Office of Legal Counsel] concluded that the use of the following ten interrogation techniques by the CIA would not constitute torture: 1) attention grasp, 2) walling, 3) facial hold, 4) facial slap, 5) cramped confinement, 6) wall standing, 7) stress positions, 8) sleep deprivation, 9) insects placed in a confinement box, and 10) waterboarding."

—M. Cherif Bassiouni, The Institutionalization of Torture by the Bush Administration, Page 22

8/1/2002: Justice Department's memo allowed torture against enemy combatants: International laws forbidding torture don't apply to the commander in chief

The Justice Department's August 1, 2002, memo allowed for the use of torture against enemy combatants. "The radical legal reasoning in the document held that international laws forbidding torture did not apply to the commander in chief because Congress 'may no more regulate the Presi-

144

dent's ability to detain and interrogate enemy combatants than it may regulate his ability to direct troop movements on the battlefield."'

—Elisabeth Bumiller, *Condoleezza Rice*, Page 241

11/27/2002: FBI Legal Counsel: Some interrogation techniques "not permitted by the US Constitution"

FBI Legal Counsel Marion Bowman sends "Interrogation Techniques" in "Legal Analysis of Interrogation Techniques" categorizing techniques into four categories and outlining which were "not permitted by the U.S. Constitution" such as "Legal Analysis...Category II...5. Hooding detainee."

—Marion Bowman, "Legal Analysis of Interrogation Techniques," NSarchive.gwu.
edu, November 27, 2002

2/5/2003: Deputy Judge Advocate: Several interrogation techniques "violations of domestic criminal law and the UCMJ"

"In November 2002, military lawyers were already expressing reservations about the interrogation techniques proposed for use at Guantánamo....

Major General Jack Rives, the Deputy Judge Advocate General of the United States Air Force, was more pointed in his analysis, and observed that several of the exceptional interrogation techniques 'on their face, amount[ed] to violations of domestic criminal law and the UCMJ [Uniform Code of Military Justice].' General Rives also urged that consideration 'be given to the possible adverse effects on U.S. Armed Forces culture and self-image.' He noted that American armed forces had been 'consistently trained to take the legal and moral *high-road* in the conduct of our military operations regardless of how others may operate.'"

—"Two Narratives of Torture," *Northwestern Journal of International Human Rights*, Vol. 7, Issue 1, Article 2, ScholarlyCommons.law.Northwestern.edu, Spring 2009, Pages 62–63

3/1/2003: George W. Bush said, "Damn right" when asked if he gave permission for use of waterboarding

Former President George W. Bush recalled, after the capture of 9/11 mastermind Khalid Sheikh Mohammed [KSM] on March 1, 2003, CIA Director "George Tenet asked if he had permission to use enhanced interrogation techniques, including waterboarding, on Khalid Sheikh Mohammed. I thought about my meeting with [slain journalist] Danny Pearl's widow, who was pregnant with his son when he was murdered. I thought about the 2,973 people stolen from their families by al Qaeda on 9/11. And I

We knew it was you all along

thought about my duty to protect the country from another act of terror. 'Damn right,' I said."

—George W. Bush, *Decision Points*, Page 170

[**Note:** Bush's admission of the crime of torturing.]

3/6/2003: Defense review to provide legal basis for "exceptional interrogations"

"In 2003, the Defense Department conducted its own review of the limits that govern torture, in consultation with experts at the Justice Department and other agencies. The aim of the March 6, 2003, review, conducted by a working group that included representatives of the military services, the Joint Chiefs of Staff and the intelligence community, was to provide a legal basis for what the group's report called 'exceptional interrogations.'"

—Dana Priest and R. Jeffrey Smith, "Memo Offered Justification for Use of Torture," *The Washington Post*, June 8, 2004

3/14/2003: Yoo memo: Arguably legal interrogation techniques were gouging a prisoner's eyes out, dousing him with "scalding water, corrosive acid, or caustic substance," or "slitting an ear, nose, or lip"

Deputy Chief of the Office of Legal Counsel John "Yoo's March [14] 2003 opinion...declared that federal laws prohibiting assault, maiming, and other crimes did not apply to the military interrogators in Guantánamo.... Among the practices the memo discussed as arguably legal were gouging a prisoner's eyes out, dousing him with 'scalding water, corrosive acid, or caustic substance,' or 'slitting an ear, nose, or lip, or disabling a tongue or limb.'"

—Jane Mayer, *The Dark Side*, Pages 230–231

[**Note:** Would you want our soldiers, if they were captured in war, to be treated by the enemy as the above memo suggests our military could treat captives in Guantánamo?]

3/15/2003: CIA curbs enhanced interrogation as political support wanes; no waterboarding past March 2003

Regarding enhanced interrogation techniques: "Acutely aware that the agency would be blamed if the policies lost political support, nervous C.I.A. officials began to curb its practices much earlier than most Americans know: no one was waterboarded after March 2003, and coercive interrogation methods were shelved altogether in 2005." [*The fifteenth of the month used for date sorting purposes only.*]

—Mark Mazzetti and Scott Shane, "Interrogation Debate Sharply Divided Bush White House," *The New York Times*, May 3, 2009

3/15/2003: State Department only knew of Rumsfeld's new interrogation rules from news stories in 2003 that two Afghans were beaten to death while in US custody

"[T]he State Department knew nothing of the new interrogation rules approved by Rumsfeld and had no confirmation of mistreatment until news stories in March 2003 revealed that two Afghans had been beaten to death while in U.S. custody. Although the military had initially reported that the men had died of natural causes at a U.S. 'holding facility' in Bagram, Afghanistan, death certificates given to their families had listed the cause as homicide. The military's own autopsies described multiple internal and external 'blunt force injuries.'" [*The fifteenth of the month used for date sorting purposes only.*]

—Karen DeYoung, *Soldier*, Page 504

[**Note:** Wasn't it foreseeable that Bush's enhanced interrogation policy would cause deaths?]

4/4/2003: DOD working group, headed by Mary Walker, issues report that perpetuated plan to authorize torture and other coercive measures

"The DOD Working Group, headed by Air Force General Counsel Mary Walker, issued a report on April 4, 2003, that perpetuated the common plan to authorize torture and other coercive measures and to deny protections and violate the Geneva Conventions by reiterating two completely and manifestly false but familiar conclusions within the [Bush] administration: (1) that members of al Qaeda are supposedly not protected 'because, *inter alia*, al Qaeda is not a High Contracting Party to the Convention,' and (2) that with respect to members of the Taliban the Geneva Civilian Convention supposedly 'does not apply to unlawful combatants,'"

—Jordan J. Paust, *Beyond the Law*, Page 14

4/16/2003: DOD: "What is legal and what is put into practice is a different story"; Rumsfeld approved twenty-four of thirty-five interrogation techniques, the twenty-four not made public

"A Defense Department spokesman said last night [June 7, 2004] that the March 2003 [Pentagon] memo [on interrogation procedures at Guantánamo] represented 'a scholarly effort to define the perimeters of the law' but added: 'What is legal and what is put into practice is a different story.' Pentagon officials said the group examined at least 35 interrogation techniques, and Rumsfeld later approved using 24 of them in a classified directive on April 16, 2003, that governed all activities at Guantánamo Bay. The Pentagon has refused to make public the 24 interrogation procedures."

—Dana Priest and R. Jeffrey Smith, "Memo Offered Justification for Use of Torture," *The Washington Post*, June 8, 2004

5/9/2003: Two assistant US attorneys deny any recording of CIA interrogations in War on Terror; CIA admissions prove interrogations were recorded and those tapes were not destroyed until 2005

"[O]n May 9, 2003, two Assistant U.S. Attorneys denied that any CIA interrogations [of detainees in the War on Terror] were recorded when they were asked about it by District Court Judge Leonie Brinkema, CIA admissions prove that not only were the interrogations recorded, but that the tapes were not destroyed until 2005."

—M. Cherif Bassiouni, *The Institutionalization of Torture by the Bush Administration*, Page 199

6/26/2003: George W. Bush: "Torture anywhere is an affront to human dignity everywhere."

On June 26, 2003, the 'United Nations International Day in Support of Victims of Torture,' President George W. Bush said:

"[T]he United States declares its strong solidarity with torture victims across the world. Torture anywhere is an affront to human dignity everywhere. We are committed to building a world where human rights are respected and protected by the rule of law. Freedom from torture is an inalienable human right. The Convention Against Torture and Other Cruel, Inhuman or Degrading Treatment, ratified by the United States and more than 130 other countries since 1984, forbids governments from deliberately inflicting severe physical or mental pain or suffering on those within their custody or control. Yet torture continues to be practiced around the world by rogue regimes whose cruel methods match their determination to crush the human spirit. Beating, burning, rape, and electric shock are some of the grisly tools such regimes use to terrorize their own citizens. These despicable crimes cannot be tolerated by a world committed to justice.... The United States is committed to the world-wide elimination of torture and we are leading this fight by example. I call on all governments to join with the United States and the community of law-abiding nations in prohibiting, investigating, and prosecuting all acts of torture and in

12/23/2003: Neither Tenet nor others at CIA mention hundreds of hours of taped interrogations to 9/11 Commission

"In a meeting on December 23, 2003, [Executive Director of the 9/11 Commission Philip] Zelikow demanded that the CIA...provide any and all documents responsive to its requests...But in an omission that would later become part of a criminal investigation, neither Tenet nor anyone else from the CIA in the meeting mentioned that, in fact, the Agency had in its possession at that point hundreds of hours of videotapes of the interrogations."

—Jane Mayer, *The Dark Side*, Page 279

1/13/2004: Sergeant Darby, an Army MP, left note and CD of photographic evidence of prisoner abuse to CID

"On January 13, 2004, Sergeant (SGT) Joseph M. Darby, a twenty-three-year-old U.S. Army MP [Military Police] who worked in the office at Abu Ghraib, left a note with a CD containing photographs of prisoner abuses on the desk of a Criminal Investigation Division (CID) agent.

Darby received the material from Corporal (CPL) Charles Graner and agonized about whether or not to bring it to the attention of the authorities. In the end, as he later said to a congressional committee, his decision was made because '[the abuses] violated everything I personally believed in and all I'd been taught about the rules of war.'"

—Ricardo S. Sanchez with Donald T. Phillips, *Wiser in Battle*, Page 303

[**Note:** Thank goodness for such people who have a sense of morality and a backbone.]

2/15/2004: ICRC report: Abu Ghraib prison abuses not confined to a few rogue guards; Bush administration authorized techniques

"A [February 2004] report by the International Committee of the Red Cross, first disclosed by *The Wall Street Journal*, found that the [Iraqi prisoner] abuses were not confined to a handful of rogue guards at Abu Ghraib but appeared to be 'part of the standard operating procedures by military intelligence personnel to obtain confessions and extract information.'

Over the next month, leaks in the major newspapers revealed that the [Bush] administration had effectively authorized the interrogation techniques at Abu Ghraib in a series of secret memos and legal opinions that condoned torture or other acts of cruelty." [*The fifteenth of the month used for date sorting purposes only.*]

—Elisabeth Bumiller, *Condoleezza Rice*, Page 240

5/5/2004: Bush: I view torture as "abhorrent"

When President Bush was questioned about the torture of Iraqi prisoners in Abu Ghraib Prison by Alhurra Television on May 5, 2004, he said: "First, people in Iraq must understand that I view those practices as abhorrent. They must also understand that what took place in that prison does not represent America that I know.

The America I know is a compassionate country that believes in freedom. The America I know cares about every individual. The America I know has sent troops into Iraq to promote freedom—good, honorable citizens that are helping the Iraqis every day. It's also important for the people of Iraq to know that in a democracy, everything is not perfect, that mistakes are made.

But in a democracy, as well, those mistakes will be investigated and people will be brought to justice. We're an open society. We're a society that is willing to investigate, fully investigate in this case, what took place in that prison."

—Office of the Press Secretary, "President Bush Meets with Alhurra Television on Wednesday," George W. Bush—White House Archives, May 5, 2004

[**Note:** Bush misleads or lies to Alhurra Television viewers about his administration's torturing.]

5/7/2004: Tenet halts harshest techniques over CIA Inspector General Helgerson's report on legality

On May 7, 2004, "C.I.A. inspector general, John L. Helgerson, completed a devastating report. In thousands of pages, it challenged the legality of some interrogation methods, found that interrogators were exceeding the rules imposed by the Justice Department and questioned the effectiveness of the entire program. C.I.A. officials had sold the interrogation program to the White House. Now, the director of central intelligence, George J. Tenet, knew that the inspector general's report could be a noose for White House officials to hang the C.I.A. Mr. Tenet ordered a temporary halt to the harshest interrogation methods."

—Mark Mazzetti and Scott Shane, "Interrogation Debate Sharply Divided Bush White House," *The New York Times*, May 3, 2009

5/12/2004: Rumsfeld to Senate investigating committee: Geneva Convention doesn't apply to Guantánamo "terrorists"

"As late as May [12] 2004, Secretary Rumsfeld told a Senate Committee investigating widely publicized, widespread and criminal interrogation abuses in Iraq and reports of abuse at Guantánamo that the Geneva Conventions apply to all detainees in Iraq but, in his (and the President's [Bush's]) manifestly erroneous view, they do not apply to persons held at Guantánamo because they are all 'terrorists.'"

—Jordan J. Paust, *Beyond the Law*, Page 14

5/17/2004: Former CIA Agent Baer: "If you want someone to disappear...you send them to Egypt."

Former CIA Agent Robert Baer told the *New Statesman* on May 17, 2004: "'If you want a serious interrogation, you send a prisoner to Jordan. If you want them to be tortured, you send them to Syria. If you want someone to disappear, never to see them again, you send them to Egypt.'"

—M. Cherif Bassiouni, *The Institutionalization of Torture by the Bush Administration*, Page 141

[**Note:** A view on rendition.]

6/7/2004: Human Rights Watch: Torturers looking for ways to legally avoid "accountability" of war crimes

"Human rights groups expressed dismay at the Justice Department's legal reasoning [for the torture of captured terrorists] yesterday [June 7, 2004]. 'It is by leaps and bounds the worst thing I've seen since this whole Abu Ghraib scandal broke [in Iraq],' said Tom Malinowski of Human Rights Watch. 'It appears that what they were contemplating was the commission of war crimes and looking for ways to avoid legal accountability. The effect is to throw out years of military doctrine and standards on interrogations.'"

—Dana Priest and R. Jeffrey Smith, "Memo Offered Justification for Use of Torture," *The Washington Post*, June 8, 2004

6/8/2004: Leaked Bybee memo links Abu Ghraib abuses to Bush administration's policy of "everything short of near-death"

On June 8, 2004, "Someone leaked the August 2002 [John] Yoo/[Jay] Bybee torture memo to the *Wall Street Journal* and the *Washington Post*. The papers published devastating stories linking the scandalous abuses in Abu Ghraib to the Bush Administration's stunning legal policy authorizing everything short of near-death."

—Jane Mayer, *The Dark Side*, Page 292

6/12/2004: Senior military officer in Iraq Lt. Gen. Ricardo Sanchez authorized certain interrogation techniques in Abu Ghraib including military dogs and extreme temperatures

According to a June 12, 2004, *Washington Post* article: "Documents obtained by the *Washington Post* and the American Civil Liberties Union showed that the senior military officer in Iraq, Lt. Gen. Ricardo Sanchez, authorized the use of military dogs, extreme temperatures, reverse sleep patterns, and sensory deprivation as interrogation techniques in Abu Ghraib."

—Deepak Tripathi, *Overcoming the Bush Legacy in Iraq and Afghanistan*, Page 83

6/26/2004: Bush: "Freedom from torture is an inalienable human right"

In President George W. Bush's June 26, 2004, statement on the UN International Day in Support of Victims of Torture: "[T]he United States reaffirms its commitment to the worldwide elimination of torture. The non-negotiable demands of human dignity must be protected without reference to race, gender, creed, or nationality. Freedom from torture is an inalienable human right, and we are committed to building a world where human rights are respected and protected by the rule of law.

To help fulfill this commitment, the United States has joined 135 other nations in ratifying the Convention Against Torture and Other Cruel, Inhuman or Degrading Treatment or Punishment. America stands against and will not tolerate torture. We will investigate and prosecute all acts of torture and undertake to prevent other cruel and unusual punishment in all territory under our jurisdiction. American personnel are required to comply with all U.S. laws, including the United States Constitution, Federal statutes, including statutes prohibiting torture, and our treaty obligations with respect to the treatment of all detainees."

—Office of the Press Secretary, "President's Statement on the U.N. International Day in Support of Victims of Torture," George W. Bush—White House Archives, June 26, 2004

[Note: Bush saying that freedom from torture is an inalienable human right while having people tortured.]

6/28/2004: US Supreme Court requires that American citizens captured abroad must have access to lawyer and a fair hearing before a neutral judge

On June 28, 2004, "In *Hamdi v. Rumsfeld*, the [Supreme] Court required that American citizens captured abroad must have access to a lawyer and a fair hearing before a neutral judge."

—John Yoo, *War By Other Means*, Page 130

7/7/2004: Mora's twenty-two-page memo on efforts to push Pentagon from cruelty policy kept secret, private

On July 7, 2004, General Counsel of the US Navy, Alberto Mora "finished writing an extraordinary twenty-two-page memo chronicling his wide-ranging and persistent efforts in the winter of 2002 to push the Pentagon back from an official policy of cruelty [regarding detainee interrogation]. The memo...was marked secret and kept from public view."

—Jane Mayer, *The Dark Side*, Page 236

7/15/2004: ICRC report to the Bush administration: Guantánamo interrogation is "an intentional system of cruel, unusual and degrading treatment and a form of torture"

"Newer revelations about interrogation tactics at Guantánamo were revealed in an ICRC report to the Bush administration in July 2004.

The ICRC labeled the Guantánamo interrogation process as 'an intentional system of cruel, unusual and degrading treatment and a form of torture.'" [*The fifteenth of the month used for date sorting purposes only.*]

—Jordan J. Paust, *Beyond the Law*, Page 17

8/24/2004: DOD: Rumsfeld's interrogation techniques migrated from Guantánamo to other countries, and chain of command ignored reports of abuse

According to the Independent Panel to Review Department of Defense Detention Operations' report on August 24, 2004, "Rumsfeld's 'augmented [interrogation] techniques for Guantánamo migrated to Afghanistan and Iraq where they were neither limited nor safeguarded,' that 'the chain of command ignored reports' of abuse, and that '[m]ore than once a commander was complicit.'"

—Jordan J. Paust, *Beyond the Law*, Page 17

8/25/2004: Maj. Gen. Fay on Abu Ghraib abuse: "We discovered serious misconduct and a loss of moral values"

"The latest investigation into the Abu Ghraib scandal found 44 instances of abuse by soldiers and civilian contractors at the prison in Iraq, some of which amounted to torture, one of the two generals who led the Army effort said Wednesday [August 25, 2004]. 'There were some instances where torture was being used,'

Maj. Gen. George Fay told reporters at a Pentagon news conference about the investigation. 'We discovered serious misconduct and a loss of moral values,' said Gen. Paul Kern, who as the overseer of the effort presented an executive summary of the investigation report at the news conference....

The Army report cited 27 people who are accused of being associated with abuses at Abu Ghraib, 23 soldiers from a military intelligence unit and four civilian contractors working with them, Kern said."

—"General: Some Abu Ghraib Abuse was Torture," CNN.com, August 26, 2004

12/30/2004: White House Legal Counsel Gonzales extorted OLC Levin to justify earlier interrogations

Regarding Chief of the Office of Legal Counsel Dan Levin's December 30, 2004, memo, which reformed interrogation practices, White House Legal Counsel Alberto Gonzales "made clear to Levin that unless he included language in his new legal memo declaring that nothing the Bush Administration had done in earlier interrogations was illegal, the Justice Department would not accept his opinion.

In essence Levin, the top legal adviser to the executive branch, was being virtually extorted for a written legal pardon. Levin was worried that unless he gave Gonzales what he wanted, the Bush Administration would scrap his memo, abandoning the whole effort to reform interrogation practices."

—Jane Mayer, *The Dark Side*, Page 307

1/15/2005: Gonzales on torture rumors in rendition program during AG confirmation hearing: George W. Bush administration "can't fully control" what other nations do

In January 2005, when asked about rumors of torture in the rendition program during his confirmation hearings for Attorney General, Alberto Gonzales "chuckled and noted that the [Bush] administration 'can't fully control' what other nations do." [*The fifteenth of the month used for date sorting purposes only.*]

—Jane Mayer, *The Dark Side*, Page 110

1/27/2005: Bush: "Torture is never acceptable"

"In a 40-minute conversation in the Oval Office with correspondents from The New York Times, Mr. Bush, seated in front of a crackling fire, ranged across a number of issues that he is expected to discuss in his State of the Union address next week....On whether the administration had looser standards for interrogating terrorist suspects outside the United States, he said, 'Torture is never acceptable,' adding, 'nor do we hand over people to countries that do torture.'"

—Elisabeth Bumiller, David E. Sanger, and Richard W. Stevenson, "Bush Says Iraqi Leaders Will Want U.S. Forces to Stay to Help," *The New York Times*, January 28, 2005

[**Note:** Bush misleads or lies about his administration's torture in Oval Office conversation with correspondents from *The New York Times*.]

3/7/2005: AG Gonzales: Diplomatic assurances against torture are unreliable, can't control a country

From information in an *Associated Press* article on March 7, 2005: "In a candid, but damning moment, Attorney General Gonzales admitted that diplomatic assurances against torture are unreliable.

'We can't fully control what a country might do. We obviously expect a country to which we have rendered a detainee to comply with their representation to us...If you're asking me, *Does a country always comply?* I don't have to answer that.'"

—M. Cherif Bassiouni, *The Institutionalization of Torture by the Bush Administration*, Page 163

3/16/2005: Bush: "We [the US] don't believe in torture"

President Bush and his stance on torture during a news conference on March 16, 2005: "The post-9/11 world, the United States must make sure we protect our people and our friends from attack. That was the charge we have been given. And one way to do so is to arrest people and send them back to their country of origin with the promise that they won't be tortured. That's the promise we receive. This country does not believe in torture. We do believe in protecting ourselves. We don't believe in torture."

—"The President's News Conference, March 16, 2005," Weekly Compilation of Presidential Documents, March 21, 2005, Vol. 41, No. 11, Pages 443–447

[**Note:** More Bush lies about his administration and torturing people.]

5/30/2005: Bradbury memo to Rizzo: Approved "walling" technique, not "significantly painful"

"Another [interrogation] technique approved by OLC was 'walling.' An interrogator repeatedly slammed the detainee against a false wall made of plywood or a similar material.

Steven Bradbury, a protégé of Ken Starr who became acting head of OLC in 2005, acknowledged [in a memo to CIA Senior Deputy General Counsel John A. Rizzo on May 30, 2005] that walling 'wears down [the detainee] physically...and undoubtedly may startle him.' Bradbury maintained, however, that walling is not 'significantly painful.' The OLC discounted the impact of walling even when informed that a detainee could be 'walled...twenty to thirty times consecutively when the interrogator requires a...response.'"

—Peter Margulies, *Law's Detour*, Pages 39–40

6/24/2005: Italian judge issues warrant charging thirteen CIA agents with kidnapping

On June 24, 2005, "an Italian judge in Milan issued arrest warrants for thirteen CIA agents on charges of kidnapping, stemming from the CIA's 2003 rendition of an Islamic cleric known as 'Abu Omar.' Italy had given the Muslim cleric asylum, but the American operation had snatched him and flown him to Egypt, where he claimed he had been brutally tortured."

—Jane Mayer, *The Dark Side*, Page 314

6/29/2005: Bush administration to Convention Against Torture: "President of the United States has made clear that the United States...will not tolerate torture"

"While the acts of torture were happening, the Bush Administration, pursuant to Article 19 of the CAT [United Nations Convention Against Torture], submitted on June 29, 2005 a report to the Committee Against Torture, established by the CAT's Article 17.

In that report, the U.S. expressed its total conformity with the provisions of the [Geneva] Convention. It claimed, among other things, that: 'In fighting terrorism, the U.S. remains committed to respecting the rule of law, including the U.S. Constitution, federal statutes, and international treaty obligations, including the Torture Convention....The President of the United States has made clear that the United States stands against and will not tolerate torture under any circumstances'"

—M. Cherif Bassiouni, *The Institutionalization of Torture by the Bush Administration*, Pages 7–8

[**Note:** Bush administration misleads or lies about torture to Committee Against Torture.]

7/15/2005: Acting OLC Chief Bradbury approves simultaneous interrogation techniques including waterboarding and sleep deprivation

"When Bradbury finished his opinion [on the legality of interrogation practices] in the late spring of 2005 [which was signed by President Bush in July 2005], it expanded the CIA's legal latitude so that interrogators could use ten or fifteen different techniques at once, including waterboarding, head and belly slapping, sensory deprivation, sleep deprivation, temperature extremes, and stress positions, among others...Gone, sources said, were the careful limits that had been imposed by [former Chief of the Office of Legal Counsel David] Levin." [*The fifteenth of the month used for date sorting purposes only.*]

—Jane Mayer, *The Dark Side*, Page 309

[**Note:** George W. Bush signing off of waterboarding as late as July 2005.]

7/19/2005: Yoo: "[I]t seems to me that if something is necessary for self-defense, it's permissible to deviate from the principles of Geneva."

In an appearance on *PBS Frontline* on July 19, 2005, "When asked why President Bush would prefer that Geneva law strictures not apply, John Yoo, who had been a Deputy Assistant Attorney General in the Bush administration and primary author of the infamous Yoo-Delahunty 2002 memo, responded:

'Think about what you want to do when you have captured people from the Taliban and Al Qaeda. You want to interrogate them....[T]he most reliable source of information comes from the people in Al Qaeda you captured....[I]t seems to me that if something is necessary for self-defense, it's permissible to deviate from the principles of Geneva [including the prohibition of torture].'"

—Jordan J. Paust, *Beyond the Law*, Page 29

[**Note:** John Yoo upending the Geneva Convention treaties and in essence, the rule of law.]

7/21/2005: VP Cheney meets with Republican senators to block legislation preventing cruelty to detainees

"On July 21 [2005]...Cheney had met with three senior Republicans on the Senate Armed Services Committee to urge them to block legislation that would prevent the continued 'cruel, inhuman or degrading treatment' of detainees by the U.S. military."

—Eugene Jarecki, *The American Way of War*, Pages 78–79

7/24/2005: Cheney went up to Congress to lobby against McCain's proposed torture ban

"On July 24, 2005, McCain introduced an amendment to the Defense Department's budget prohibiting military interrogators from using more force than allowed by the traditional limits in the *Army Field Manual*, even if the commander in chief ordered it.

The proposed bill also prohibited other U.S. personnel—including the CIA—from engaging in torture and other forms of cruel, inhuman, and degrading treatment of U.S.-held prisoners anywhere in the world.

Cheney personally went up to Congress to lobby against McCain's proposed torture ban."

—Jane Mayer, *The Dark Side*, Page 319

[**Note:** Cheney continuing his support of torture.]

8/3/2005: Karpinski confirms that Miller was sent to Iraq to assure Rumsfeld's authorized Guantánamo's interrogation tactics were used in Iraq

"In an August [3] 2005 interview, Brigadier General Janis Karpinski confirmed that Major General Geoffrey Miller was sent to Iraq in 2003 to assure that Secretary Rumsfeld's authorized interrogation tactics were used in Iraq.

As Karpinski stated, 'he said that he was going to use a template from Guantánamo Bay to *Gitm-oize* the operations out at Abu Ghraib' and that a Rumsfeld memo was posted on a pole outside at Abu Ghraib: 'It was a memorandum signed by Secretary of Defense Rumsfeld, authorizing a short list, maybe 6 or 8 techniques: use of dogs; stress positions; loud music; deprivation of food; keeping the lights on, those kinds of things.

And then a handwritten message over to the side that appeared to be the same handwriting as the signature, and that signature was Secretary Rumsfeld's. And it said, *Make sure this happens* with two exclamation points.'"

—Jordan J. Paust, *Beyond the Law*, Pages 26–27

10/5/2005: Bush threatens to veto McCain bill on fair treatment of prisoners if it passed

"On October 5, 2005, [President] Bush threatened to exercise his veto pow-er—the first veto of his presidency—to kill the McCain bill [regarding fair treatment of prisoners] if it passed."

—Jane Mayer, The Dark Side, Page 320

11/29/2005: Rumsfeld: American troops should report, not stop, inhumane actions

Joint Chiefs of Staff Chairman Peter Pace was questioned at a Pentagon press briefing on November 29, 2005. "Asked about the recent discovery by American troops of torture victims in an Iraqi-run Baghdad jail, he said it was 'absolutely the responsibility of every U.S. service member, if they see inhumane treatment being applied, to intervene to stop it.' Rumsfeld did not think much of this idea. 'But I don't think you mean they have an obligation to physically stop it,' he intervened, 'it's to report it.'"

—Andrew Cockburn, Rumsfeld, Page 213

11/29/2005: Bush: The US "does not torture"

During a tour of the Texas border on November 29, 2005, when questioned about US-run terrorist detention centers abroad and what was being done there, President Bush stated: "The United States of America does not tor-ture. And that's important for people around the world to understand."

—Office of the Press Secretary, "President Tours Border, Discusses Immigration Reform in Texas," George W. Bush—White House Archives, November 29, 2005

[**Note:** Bush continually lying about his administration's torturing.]

12/1/2005: AG Gonzales, who as White House Counsel abetted denials of detainee rights, says Abu Ghraib interrogation techniques "shocking," "horrific," not allowed

"On December 1, 2005, during a speech at the Council on Foreign Rela-tions Attorney General Alberto Gonzales, who as White House Counsel had previously abetted denials of detainee rights and protections under the laws of war, stated that what happened at Abu Ghraib was 'shocking,' 'hor-rific,' and not allowed.

Despite his denial of authorizations to use certain tactics depicted in the Abu Ghraib photos, by the time of his speech it was well known that Secretary of Defense Donald Rumsfeld had expressly authorized the stripping of persons naked, use of dogs, and hooding as interrogation tactics, among other unlawful tactics, in an action memo on December 2, 2002..."

—Jordan J. Paust, Beyond the Law, Page 26

According to a State Department transcript, on December 5, 2005, Rice said, regarding accusations of the torture of detainees in secret prisons: "'The United States does not permit, tolerate or condone torture under any circumstances...The United States does not transport and has not transported detainees from one country to another for the purpose of interrogation using torture.'"

—Elisabeth Bumiller, *Condoleezza Rice*, Page 276

[Note: Rice's ignorance about the Bush administration's torturing or lying about it.]

12/6/2005: Human Rights Watch: Bush administration redefined torture to exclude techniques they used

"'The reason she [Rice] is able to say that the United States does not engage in torture is that the [Bush] administration has redefined torture to exclude any technique that they use,' said Tom Malinowski, Washington director of Human Rights Watch. 'What makes this awkward for Secretary Rice is that the state department has continued to condemn as torture techniques such as waterboarding when they are used by other countries—in other words the very techniques the CIA has used against these high level detainees.'"

—Suzanne Goldenberg, "US defence of tactic makes no sense says legal expert," *The Guardian*, December 5, 2005

12/8/2005: Rice to NATO: "At no time did the United States agree to inhumane acts or torture"

"'At no time did the United States agree to inhumane acts or torture,' Ms. Rice said in a public portion of her presentation to the NATO foreign ministers [on December 8, 2005].

'Even if terrorists are not covered by the Geneva Conventions, they have still applied the principles governing those Geneva Conventions,' she said."

—Richard Bernstein, "Rice's Visit: Official Praise, Public Doubts," *The New York Times*, December 11, 2005

[Note: Rice's ignorance about torture by the Bush administration or lying to NATO about it.]

12/15/2005: Yoo admits defense of admin's "legal approach" to worst torture reserved for Al-Qaeda suspects

Appearing on *National Public Radio* on December 15, 2005, former Deputy Chief of the Office of Legal Counsel John Yoo "admitted that 'some of the worst possible interrogation methods we've heard of in the press have been reserved for the leaders of al-Qaeda that we've captured' and, with remarkable candor and abandonment, 'I've defended the [Bush] administration's legal approach to the treatment of al-Qaida suspects and detainees,' including the use of torture."

—Jordan J. Paust, *Beyond the Law*, Pages 29–30

12/18/2005: Cheney: Interrogation technique that "shocks the conscience" is "in the eye of the beholder"

In defense of enhanced interrogation techniques, Vice President Cheney told *ABC News*, on December 18, 2005:

"'The rule is whether or not it shocks the conscience…Now, you can get into a debate about what shocks the conscience and what is cruel and inhuman. And to some extent, I suppose that's in the eye of the beholder. But I believe, and we think, it's important to remember that we are in a war against a group of individuals, a terrorist organization, that did, in fact, slaughter 3,000 innocent Americans on 9/11, that it's important for us to be able to have effective interrogation of these people when we capture them.'"

—Peter Baker, *Days of Fire*, Pages 435–436

12/30/2005: White House commissions Bradbury at OLC to write secret memo stating that CIA's interrogation techniques, including waterboarding, are not inhumane; memo nullifies McCain Act signed into law by Bush that only allows humane treatment of prisoners

After David Addington, Cheney's legal counsel, revised McCain's Detainee Treatment Act, which President Bush signed into law on December 30, 2005, "A new, secret legal memo commissioned by the White House from Steven Bradbury at the OLC provided a stealthy means of undercutting McCain's intent.

On its face, McCain's Detainee Treatment Act seemed to prohibit all abuse—allowing only humane treatment of prisoners by all officials of the U.S. government, including the CIA.

But Bradbury argued that none of the CIA's interrogation techniques were cruel, inhumane, or degrading. Not even waterboarding. His secret opinion nullified McCain's public victory."

—Jane Mayer, *The Dark Side*, Page 321

1/22/2006: Council of Europe report blasts US and European countries for "outsourcing" torture

On January 22, 2006, "The Council of Europe issues a report condemning both the U.S. and European countries for the practice of 'extraordinary rendition', referring to the practice as the ' *outsourcing* of torture.'"

—M. Cherif Bassiouni, *The Institutionalization of Torture by the Bush Administration*, Page xlv

1/26/2006: Bush: "if they're [Human Rights Watch and Amnesty International] saying we tortured people, they're wrong"

President Bush in response to a question during a press conference at the White House on January 26, 2006, on the reports by the Human Rights Watch and Amnesty International criticizing the U.S. on their handling of terrorist suspects: "I haven't seen the report, but if they're saying we tortured people, they're wrong. Period....No American will be allowed to torture another human being anywhere in the world."

—Office of the Press Secretary, "Press Conference of the President—James S. Brady Briefing Room" George W. Bush—White House Archives, January 26, 2006

[Note: Another false Bush statement about torture.]

2/16/2006: UN Human Rights Commission calls for US to shut down Guantánamo, confusion over what constitutes torture "particularly alarming"

On February 16, 2006, "the United Nations Human Rights Commission called for the United States to shut down the detention center at Guantánamo, where it said some practices 'must be assessed as amounting to torture.' The U.N. report described 'the confusion with regard to authorized and unauthorized interrogation techniques' as 'particularly alarming.'"

—Jane Mayer, *The Dark Side*, Page 237

5/18/2006: UN says US should stop use of secret prisons, which it considers tantamount to torture

On May 18, 2006, "A United Nations Committee Against Torture report calls for the U.S. to stop use of 'enhanced interrogation' techniques and the use of secret prisons, which it considers to amount to torture."

—M. Cherif Bassiouni, *The Institutionalization of Torture by the Bush Administration*, Pages xlv–xlvi

9/6/2006: Bush to Couric: "I've said to the people that we don't torture, and we don't"

On September 6, 2006, President Bush discussed the high-value detainees transferred to Guantánamo in an interview with *CBS Evening News* anchor Katie Couric.

When Bush mentioned that the CIA was no longer interrogating the detainees, "Couric asked Mr. Bush if this is a tacit acknowledgement that the way these detainees were handled was wrong.

'No. Not at all. It's a tacit acknowledgement that we're doing smart things to get information to protect the American people,' the President said. 'I've said to the people that we don't torture, and we don't.'"

—Melissa McNamara, "Bush: 'We Don't Torture,'" CBSNews.com, September 6, 2006

[**Note:** Bush's misleading if not false statement about his administration's torturing.]

9/15/2006: Bush: Geneva Convention Article 3 phrase "no outrages upon human dignity" too vague

During a press conference in the Rose Garden on September 15, 2006, President George W. Bush's answer to a question on the Supreme Court ruling that the US must adhere to Article 3 of the Geneva Convention:

"This debate is occurring because of the Supreme Court's ruling that said that we must conduct ourselves under the Common Article III of the Geneva Convention. And that Common Article III says that there will be no outrages upon human dignity. It's very vague. What does that mean, 'outrages upon human dignity'? That's a statement that is wide open to interpretation. And what I'm proposing is that there be clarity in the law so that our professionals will have no doubt that that which they are doing is legal."

—Office of the Press Secretary, "Press Conference of the President—The Rose Garden," George W. Bush—White House Archives, September 15, 2006

10/17/2006: Bush signs Military Commissions Act; ACLU says Bush can now "indefinitely hold people without charge"; act provides a retroactive, nine-year immunity for US officials

"On October 17, 2006, President Bush signed the Military Commissions Act of 2006, providing for the continued controversial practices in its detention and treatment of 'unlawful combatants.'

'The president can now,' wrote American Civil Liberties Union [ACLU] executive director Anthony D. Romero, 'with the approval of Congress—indefinitely hold people without charge, take away protections against horrific abuse, put people on trial based on hearsay evidence, authorize trials that can sentence people to death based on testimony literally beaten out of witnesses, and slam shut the courthouse door for habeas petitions.'...

[T]he Military Commissions Act provides a retroactive, nine-year immunity for U.S. officials who authorized, ordered, or committed possible acts of abuse on detainees prior to its enactment."

—Eugene Jarecki, *The American Way of War*, Pages 233–234

[**Note:** Bush signs "a retroactive, nine-year immunity for US officials" who might have abused detainees (which I read as tortured).]

10/24/2006: VP Cheney: "We don't torture," "dunk in water" a.k.a. waterboarding a "no-brainer" to save lives

Cheney discussed the subject of waterboarding in an interview with conservative radio talk show host Scott Hennen on October 24, 2006.

"'Would you agree a dunk in water is a no-brainer if it can save lives?' the host asked. 'It's a no-brainer for me,' Cheney said. 'But for a while there, I was criticized as being the Vice President for Torture. We don't torture. That's not what we're involved in.

We live up to our obligations in international treaties that we're party to and so forth. But the fact is, you can have a fairly robust interrogation program without torture.'"

—Peter Baker, *Days of Fire*, Page 495

[**Note:** Cheney: Waterboarding is not torture, nor is it a fairly robust interrogation program.]

11/14/2006: ACLU says CIA "formally acknowledged" two classified docs, one on foreign detention sites signed by George W. Bush, another specifies techniques to use for top Al-Qaeda members

"After years of denials, the CIA has formally acknowledged the existence of two classified documents governing aggressive interrogation and detention policies for terrorism suspects, according to the American Civil Liberties Union.

But CIA lawyers say the documents—memos from President Bush and the Justice Department—are still so sensitive that no portion can be released to the public....

The ACLU describes the first as a 'directive' signed by [George W.] Bush governing CIA interrogation methods or allowing the agency to set up detention facilities outside the United States....

The second document is an August 2002 legal memo from the Justice Department's Office of Legal Counsel to the CIA general counsel.

The ACLU describes it as 'specifying interrogation methods that the CIA may use against top al-Qaeda members.' (This document is separate from another widely publicized Justice memo, also issued in August 2002, that narrowed the definition of torture. The Justice Department has since rescinded the latter.)"

—Dan Eggen, "CIA Acknowledges 2 Interrogation Memos," *The Washington Post*, November 14, 2006

6/25/2007: Army Major General Antonio M. Taguba: "We violated the tenets of the Geneva Convention... civilian and military leaders responsible should be held accountable"

"'From the moment a soldier enlists, we inculcate loyalty, duty, honor, integrity, and selfless service,' [Army Major General Antonio] Taguba said. 'And yet when we get to the senior-officer level we forget those values. I know that my peers in the Army will be mad at me for speaking out, but the fact is that we violated the laws of land warfare in Abu Ghraib. We violated the tenets of the Geneva Convention. We violated our own principles and we violated the core of our military values. The stress of combat is not an excuse, and I believe, even today, that those civilian and military leaders responsible should be held accountable [for torture].'" [*The twenty-fifth of the month used for date sorting purposes only.*]

—Seymour M. Hersh, "THE GENERAL'S REPORT," *The New Yorker*, June 25, 2007

7/20/2007: Bush Executive Order states Art. 3 of the Geneva Convention doesn't apply to terrorists.

On July 20, 2007, President George W. Bush signed Executive Order 13440: "By the authority vested in me as President and Commander in Chief of the Armed Forces by the Constitution and the laws of the United States of America, including the Authorization for Use of Military Force (Public Law 107-40), the Military Commissions Act of 2006 (Public Law 109-366), and section 301 of title 3, United States Code, it is hereby ordered as follows:

Section 1. General Determinations. (a) The United States is engaged in an armed conflict with al Qaeda, the Taliban, and associated forces. Members of al Qaeda were responsible for the attacks on the United States of September 11, 2001, and for many other terrorist attacks, including against the United States, its personnel, and its allies throughout the world. These forces continue to fight the United States and its allies in Afghanistan, Iraq, and elsewhere, and they continue to plan additional acts of terror throughout the world. On February 7, 2002, I determined for the United States that members of al Qaeda, the Taliban, and associated forces are unlawful enemy combatants who are not entitled to the protections that the Third Geneva Convention provides to prisoners of war. I hereby reaffirm that determination."

—George W. Bush, "Executive Order 13440 of July 20, 2007," Federation of American Scientists online, July 20, 2007

8/13/2007: American Bar Association: Bush's Executive Order on extraordinary rendition is inconsistent with Geneva Convention Art. 3 obligations

"In August [13–14] 2007, the ABA [American Bar Association] spoke to the President's [Bush's] Executive Order [No. 13400] of July 20, 2007, which authorized the CIA's 'extraordinary rendition' program.

It argued that the Executive Order was inconsistent with U.S. obligations under Article 3 of the Geneva Conventions.

In a Recommendation adopted by its House of Delegates, the ABA again urged the U.S. to commit itself to treating all detainees in accordance with the minimum protections afforded by Common Article 3."

—M. Cherif Bassiouni, *The Institutionalization of Torture by the Bush Administration*, Page 235

12/10/2007: Kiriakou, former CIA officer at Guantánamo: Each slap, shake coordinated with operations director; never denied request to use more force

In a December 10, 2007, interview with Charles Gibson of *ABC's World News*, former CIA officer at Guantánamo Bay John Kiriakou said, regarding interrogation techniques:

"'It was not up to the individual interrogator to decide *I'm going to slap him* or *I'm going to shake him.* Each one of these, though they're minor, had to have the approval of the Deputy Director for Operations,' who during most of this period was James Pavitt.

'Before you could lay a hand on him, you had to send a cable saying, *He's uncooperative. Request permission to do X.* And permission would come, saying *You're allowed to slap him one time in the belly with an open hand...*' There was, however, no known instance of the supervisors denying a request to use more force."

—Jane Mayer, *The Dark Side*, Page 167

1/2/2008: 9/11 Commission accuses CIA of obstructing their investigation, a federal crime

"The commission's mandate was sweeping and it explicitly included the intelligence agencies. But the recent revelations that the C.I.A. destroyed videotaped interrogations of Qaeda operatives leads us to conclude that the agency failed to respond to our lawful requests for information about the 9/11 plot. Those who knew about those videotapes and did not tell us about them obstructed our investigation."

—Thomas H. Kean and Lee H. Hamilton, "Stonewalled by the C.I.A.," *The New York Times*, January 2, 2008

3/8/2008: George W. Bush vetoes Senate bill limiting CIA's interrogation techniques stating possible loss of "vital" info and American lives

"Limiting the CIA's interrogation methods to those in the Army Field Manual would be dangerous because the manual is publicly available and easily accessible on the Internet. Shortly after 9/11, we learned that key al Qaida operatives had been trained to resist the methods outlined in the manual. And this is why we created alternative procedures to question the most dangerous al Qaida operatives, particularly those who might have knowledge of attacks planned on our homeland. The best source of information about terrorist attacks is the terrorists themselves. If we were to shut down this program and restrict the CIA to methods in the Field Manual, we could lose vital information from senior al Qaida terrorists, and that could cost American lives.

The bill Congress sent me would not simply ban one particular interrogation method, as some have implied. Instead, it would eliminate all the alternative procedures we've developed to question the world's most dangerous and violent terrorists. This would end an effective program that Congress authorized just over a year ago."

—George W. Bush, "President's Radio Address," George W. Bush—White House Archives, March 8, 2008

4/9/2008: Senior Bush administration officials in dozens of top-secret White House talks and meetings discussed and approved details of the CIA's interrogation of high-value Al-Qaeda suspects, including waterboarding

"In dozens of top-secret talks and meetings in the White House, the most senior Bush administration officials discussed and approved specific details of how high-value al Qaeda suspects would be interrogated by the Central Intelligence Agency, sources tell ABC News.

The so-called Principals who participated in the meetings also approved the use of 'combined' interrogation techniques—using different techniques during interrogations, instead of using one method at a time—on terrorist suspects who proved difficult to break, sources said.

Highly placed sources said a handful of top advisers signed off on how the CIA would interrogate top al Qaeda suspects—whether they would be slapped, pushed, deprived of sleep or subjected to simulated drowning, called waterboarding.

The high-level discussions about these 'enhanced interrogation techniques' were so detailed, these sources said, some of the interrogation sessions were almost choreographed—down to the number of times CIA agents could use a specific tactic."

—Jan Crawford Greenburg and Howard L. Rosenberg, "Sources: Top Bush Advisors Approved 'Enhanced Interrogation'," ABCNews.go.com, April 9, 2008

6/10/2008: The president has publicly admitted that since 9/11 the US has been kidnapping and transporting those captured against their will to prisons operated in other countries

"The president has publicly admitted that since the 9/11 attacks in 2001, the U.S. has been kidnapping and transporting against the will of the subject (renditioning) in its so-called 'war' on terror—even people captured by U.S. personnel in friendly nations like Sweden, Germany, Macedonia and Italy—and ferrying them to places like Bagram Airbase in Afghanistan, and to prisons operated in Eastern European countries, African countries and Middle Eastern countries where security forces are known to practice torture.

These people are captured and held indefinitely, without any charges being filed, and are held without being identified to the Red Cross, or to their families. Many are clearly innocent, and several cases, including one in Canada and one in Germany, have demonstrably been shown subsequently to have been in error, because of a similarity of names or because of misinformation provided to U.S. authorities.

Such a policy is in clear violation of U.S. and International Law, and has placed the United States in the position of a pariah state. The CIA has no law enforcement authority, and cannot legally arrest or detain anyone. The program of 'extraordinary rendition' authorized by the president is the substantial equivalent of the policies of 'disappearing' people, practices widely practiced and universally condemned in the military dictatorships of Latin America during the late 20th Century.

The administration has claimed that prior administrations have practiced extraordinary rendition, but, while this is technically true, earlier renditions were used only to capture people with outstanding arrest warrants or convictions who were outside in order to deliver them to stand trial or serve their sentences in the U.S. The president has refused to divulge how many people have been subject to extraordinary rendition since September, 2001....

Hundreds of flights of CIA-chartered planes have been documented as having passed through European countries on extraordinary rendition missions like that involving Maher Arar, but the administration refuses to state how many people have been subjects of this illegal program.

The same U.S. laws prohibiting aiding and abetting torture also prohibit sending someone to a country where there is a substantial likelihood they may be tortured. Article 3 of CAT prohibits forced return where there is a 'substantial likelihood' that an individual 'may be in danger of' torture, and has been implemented by Federal statute. Article 7 of the ICCPR prohibits return to country of origin where individuals may be 'at risk' of either torture or cruel, inhuman or degrading treatment.

Under international Human Rights law, transferring a POW to any nation where he or she is likely to be tortured or inhumanely treated violates article 12 of the Third Geneva Convention, and transferring any civilian who is a protected person under the Fourth Geneva Convention is a grave breach and a criminal act.

In situations of armed conflict, both international human rights law and humanitarian law apply. A person captured in the zone of military hostilities 'must have some status under international law; he is either a prisoner of war and, as such, covered by the Third Convention, [or] a civilian covered by the Fourth Convention....There is no intermediate status; nobody in enemy hands can be outside the law.' Although the state is obligated to repatriate prisoners of war as soon as hostilities cease, the ICRC's commentary on the 1949 Conventions states that prisoners should not be repatriated where there are serious reasons for fearing that repatriating the individual would be contrary to general principles of established international law for the protection of human beings. Thus, all of the Guantánamo detainees as well as renditioned captives are protected by international human rights protections and humanitarian law.

By his actions as outlined above, the President has abused his power, broken the law, deceived the American people, and placed American military personnel, and indeed all Americans—especially those who may travel or live abroad—at risk of similar treatment. Furthermore, in the eyes of the rest of the world, the President has made the U.S., once a model of respect for human rights and respect for the rule of law, into a state where international law is neither respected nor upheld."

—Article XIX "Rendition: Kidnapping People and Taking Them Against Their Will to 'Black Sites' Located in Other Nations, Including Nations Known To Practice Torture" of H.Res.1258 "RESOLUTION Impeaching George W. Bush, President of the United States, of high crimes and misdemeanors," introduced by Rep. Dennis J. Kucinich (D-OH-10), Congress.gov, June 10, 2008

6/10/2008: The Bush administration violated US and international law by authorizing and encouraging the use of torture

"In violation of the Constitution, U.S. law, the Geneva Conventions (to which the U.S. is a signatory), and in violation of basic human rights, torture has been authorized by the President and his administration as official policy. Water-boarding, beatings, faked executions, confinement in extreme cold or extreme heat, prolonged enforcement of painful stress positions, sleep deprivation, sexual humiliation, and the defiling of religious articles have been practiced and exposed as routine at Guantánamo, at Abu Ghraib Prison and other U.S. detention sites in Iraq, and at Bagram Air Base in Afghanistan.

The president, besides bearing responsibility for authorizing the use of torture, also as Commander in Chief, bears ultimate responsibility for the failure to halt these practices and to punish those responsible once they were exposed.

The administration has sought to claim the abuse of captives is not torture, by redefining torture. An August 1, 2002, memorandum from the Administration's Office of Legal Counsel Jay S. Bybee addressed to White House Counsel Alberto R. Gonzales concluded that to constitute torture, any pain inflicted must be akin to that accompanying 'serious physical injury, such as organ failure, impairment of bodily function, or even death.' The memorandum went on to state that even should an act constitute torture under that minimal definition, it might still be permissible if applied to 'interrogations undertaken pursuant to the President's Commander-in-Chief powers.' The memorandum further asserted that 'necessity or self-defense could provide justifications that would eliminate any criminal liability.'

This effort to redefine torture by calling certain practices simply 'enhanced interrogation techniques' flies in the face of the Third Geneva Convention Relating to the Treatment of Prisoners of War, which states that 'No physical or mental torture, nor any other form of coercion, may be inflicted on prisoners of war to secure from them information of any kind whatever. Prisoners of war who refuse to answer may not be threatened, insulted, or exposed to any unpleasant or disadvantageous treatment of any kind.'

Torture is further prohibited by the Universal Declaration of Human Rights, the paramount international human rights statement adopted unanimously by the United Nations General Assembly, including the United States, in 1948. Torture and other cruel, inhuman or degrading treatment or punishment is also prohibited by international treaties ratified by the United States: the International Covenant on Civil and Political Rights (ICCPR) and the Convention Against Torture and Other Cruel Inhuman or Degrading Treatment or Punishment (CAT).

is for sanitary purposes and 'not used for the purpose of humiliating the detainee.' Maximum permissible period is 180 hours, or more than one week. Then eight hours of uninterrupted sleep are required.

13. Waterboarding. The detainee is strapped to a board and his feet elevated. A cloth is placed over the detainee's face, and water is poured over the cloth for no more than 40 seconds. This is not physically painful, but 'it usually does cause fear and panic,' creating the sensation of drowning. Waterboarding can only be used if there is credible intelligence that a terrorist attack is imminent and the detainee might possess actionable intelligence that could stop the attack.

A detainee could only be subjected to two distinct two-hour waterboarding sessions a day for no more than five days, with a maximum of 12 minutes of waterboarding in a 24-hour period. (Khalid Sheik Mohammed, the mastermind of the 9/11 attacks, was waterboarded 183 times.)"

—Bob Woodward, *Obama's Wars*, Pages 395–397

[**Note:** The administration admitting having used or to using waterboarding.]

12/11/2008: Senate report: Interrogation methods condemned internationally as torture were approved by the Bush administration high-level officials

The Senate Armed Services Committee report of December 11, 2008 said: "[H]igh-level officials in the Bush administration were intimately involved in reviewing and approving interrogation methods that have since been explicitly outlawed and that have been condemned internationally as torture."

—Greg Miller, "Cheney OK'd Harsh CIA Tactics," *Los Angeles Times*, December 16, 2008

12/15/2008: Cheney says "I do" when asked whether he thought the waterboarding technique use was appropriate

"Vice President Dick Cheney said Monday [December 15, 2008] that he was directly involved in approving severe interrogation methods used by the CIA, and that the prison at Guantánamo Bay, Cuba, should remain open indefinitely....Cheney's comments...mark the first time that he has acknowledged playing a central role in clearing the CIA's use of an array of controversial interrogation tactics, including a simulated drowning method known as waterboarding.

'I was aware of the program, certainly, and involved in helping get the process cleared,' Cheney said in an interview with ABC News. Asked whether he still believes it was appropriate to use the waterboarding method on terrorism suspects, Cheney said: 'I do.'"

—Greg Miller, "Cheney OK'd Harsh CIA Tactics," *Los Angeles Times*, December 16, 2008

| 1/20/2009: Democrat Barack Hussein Obama inaugurated |
| president with Joseph Robinette Biden Jr. as vice president |

2/5/2009: Cheney says extralegal policies including water-boarding kept US safe after 9/11

"[F]ormer vice president Cheney—in the course of defending the Bush administration's use of water-boarding and other such measures—claimed in February [5] 2009 that such an attack [with weapons of mass destruction] was 'a high probability,' adding that 'whether or not they can pull it off depends on whether or not we keep in place policies that have allowed us to defeat all further attempts, since 9/11, to launch mass-casualty attacks against the United States.'

In other words, if there were an attack on the United States that killed many tens of thousands, it would be the Obama administration's fault, since, in Cheney's telling, it was the Bush administration's extralegal policies that kept America safe after 9/11, including safe from terrorists wielding weapons of mass destruction."

—Peter Bergen, *The Longest War*, Pages 228–229

[**Note:** I read "extralegal" as "not legal."]

3/2/2009: CIA admits destroying ninety-two tapes purportedly showing CIA agents using harsh interrogation techniques such as waterboarding

"The CIA has destroyed nearly 100 interrogation tapes of terror suspects, a number far greater than was previously acknowledged by the agency.

The agency's admission came in new documents filed in a lawsuit seeking details about the treatment of detainees in U.S. custody outside the country.

The agency 'can now identify the number of videotapes that were destroyed' stated a letter from government attorneys to the judge presiding over the case. 'Ninety-two videotapes were destroyed.'

The tapes purportedly show CIA agents using harsh interrogation techniques, such as waterboarding, on terror suspects."

—Pierre Thomas and Jason Ryan, "CIA Destroyed 92 Interrogation Tapes," ABCNews.go.com, March 2, 2009

[**Note:** Bush's CIA admitting to destroying evidence.]

2/14/2010: Cheney strongly defends waterboarding, opposes Obama administration move to do away with it

In an interview on ABC's *This Week* on February 14, 2010, former Vice President "Cheney strongly defended waterboarding, the enhanced interrogation technique assailed by [President] Obama and what many consider to be torture.

'I was a big supporter of waterboarding. I was a big supporter of the enhanced interrogation techniques,' he said. Cheney added that he opposed the current administration's move to do away with it."

—Huma Kahn and Rachel Martin, "Vice Presidents Face Off: Dick Cheney and Joe Biden Go on the Offensive," ABCNews.go.com, February 15, 2010

[**Note:** If the CIA destroyed ninety-two tapes showing CIA agents using harsh interrogation techniques, one can only imagine the lawlessness they showed.]

3/24/2010: Wilkerson: Guantánamo detainees not captured by US directly are not enemy combatants

In a declaration on March 24, 2010, former chief of staff to Secretary of State Powell, Col. Lawrence B. Wilkerson claimed many Guantánamo detainees were not enemy combatants.

One of the reasons was: "'U.S. forces were not the ones who were taking the prisoners in the first place.

Instead, we relied upon Afghans, such as General [Abdul Rashid] Dostum's forces, and upon Pakistanis, to hand over prisoners whom they had apprehended, or who had been turned over to them for bounties, sometimes as much as $5,000 per head.

Such practices meant that the likelihood was high that some of the Guantánamo detainees had been turned in to U.S. forces in order to settle local scores, for tribal reasons, or just as a method of making money.'"

—M. Cherif Bassiouni, *The Institutionalization of Torture by the Bush Administration*, Pages 272–273

[**Note:** Given that our government was offering as much as a $5,000 bounty to the Afghans for turning "terrorists" over to our soldiers, imagine the abuse those payments must have caused.]

11/5/2010: Bush in his memoirs: Two interrogation techniques "went too far, even if they were legal," and CIA was directed "not to use them"

In former President George W. Bush's upcoming memoirs, he justified the use of enhanced interrogation techniques, writing:

"'CIA experts drew up a list of interrogation techniques....At my direction, Department of Justice and CIA lawyers conducted a careful legal review. The enhanced interrogation program complied with the Constitution and all applicable laws, including those that ban torture. 'There were two that I felt went too far, even if they were legal. I directed the CIA not to use them.

Another technique was waterboarding, a process of simulated drowning. No doubt the procedure was tough, but medical experts assured the CIA that it did no lasting harm.'"

—Adam Aigner-Treworgy, John Helton, Ed Hornick, Gabriella Schwarz, and Rebecca Sherman, "Bush on Waterboarding: 'Damn Right,'" CNN.com, November 5, 2010

[**Note:** Bush admitting he reviewed and approved *enhanced interrogation techniques.*]

11/15/2010: Powell: After 9/11, "waterboarding was, if not over the line, that at least very close to the line"

Former Secretary of State Powell discussed waterboarding in an appearance on *Larry King Live* on November 15, 2010:

"When its use came up after 9/11, Powell said 'all of us felt that waterboarding was, if not over the line, that at least very close to the line.' He said that he understood why [President] Bush authorized waterboarding, but said he himself wouldn't support something he said 'could be called now torture.'"

—CNN Wire Staff, "Powell: Obama failed to focus on what's 'most Important,'" CNN.com, November 16, 2010

5/2/2011: Rumsfeld: "First of all, no one was waterboarded at Guantánamo Bay. That's a myth"

"Asked if harsh interrogation techniques at Guantánamo Bay played a role in obtaining intelligence on bin Laden's whereabouts, [Former Defense Secretary] Rumsfeld declares:

'First of all, no one was waterboarded at Guantánamo Bay. That's a myth that's been perpetrated around the country by critics. 'The United States Department of Defense did not do waterboarding for interrogation purposes to anyone. It is true that some information that came from normal interrogation approaches at Guantánamo did lead to information that was beneficial in this instance. But it was not harsh treatment and it was not waterboarding.'"

—Jim Meyers and Ashley Martella, "Rumsfeld Exclusive: There Was No Waterboarding at Gitmo," Newsmax.com, May 2, 2011

[**Note:** A denial and stepping back from torturing and waterboarding.]

4/3/2014: Senate Intelligence Committee Report on torture

The "Report of the Senate Select Committee on Intelligence Committee Study of the Central Intelligence Agency's Detention and Interrogation Program together with Foreword by Chairman Feinstein and Additional and Minority Views" confirmed that the Bush Administration had tortured many detainees, and that torture was not an effective way of gathering intelligence.

The following are the first three headline summaries from the report's 20 findings:

"#1: The CIA's use of its enhanced interrogation techniques was not an effective means of acquiring intelligence or gaining cooperation from detainees."

"#2: The CIA's justification for the use of its enhanced interrogation techniques rested on inaccurate claims of their effectiveness."

"#3: The interrogations of CIA detainees were brutal and far worse than the CIA represented to policymakers and others."

—"Report Of The Senate Select Committee On Intelligence Committee Study Of The Central Intelligence Agency's Detention And Interrogation Program Together With Foreword By Chairman Feinstein And Additional And Minority Views," Intelligence.Senate.gov, ordered to be printed December 9, 2014, Pages xi–xii

[**Note:** The report confirmed that the Bush administration had tortured many detainees. (Summaries of all twenty of the Report's findings are in Appendix D.)]

D. THE EFFECTIVENESS OF TORTURE

Putting aside the legal and moral questions about torture, its stated need and effectiveness are in doubt when held up to professional scrutiny.

4/15/2008: FBI Director Mueller knows of no attacks on America disrupted by intel gained from "enhanced techniques"

"[W]hen the FBI director Robert Mueller was asked [in a *Vanity Fair* interview in April] in 2008 if he was aware of any attacks on America that had been disrupted thanks to intelligence obtained through 'enhanced techniques,' Mueller replied: 'I don't believe that has been the case.'" [*The fifteenth of the month used for date sorting purposes only.*]

—Peter Bergen, *The Longest War*, Pages 118–119

5/31/2009: Former commander of all coalition forces in Iraq: "there was not one instance of actionable intelligence that came out of these [enhanced] interrogation techniques"

"In front of a packed audience on Sunday night [May 31, 2009] at the Times Center in New York City, General Ricardo Sanchez, the former commander of all coalition forces in Iraq, called for a truth commission to investigate the abuses and torture which occurred there. The General described the failures at all levels of civilian and military command that led to the abuses in Iraq, 'and that is why I support the formation of a truth commission.' The General went on to say that, 'during my time in Iraq there was not one instance of actionable intelligence that came out of these [enhanced] interrogation techniques.'"

—Jack Hidary, "General Ricardo Sanchez Calls for War Crimes Truth Commission," *The Huffington Post*, May 31, 2009

4/3/2014: The first finding of the April 3, 2014, Senate Intelligence Committee on Torture[71]

"The CIA's use of its enhanced interrogation techniques was not an effective means of acquiring intelligence or gaining cooperation from detainees....

---

71 The Committee's twenty findings are in Appendix D.

For example, according to CIA records, seven of the 39 CIA detainees known to have been subjected to the CIA's enhanced interrogation techniques produced no intelligence while in CIA custody....CIA officers regularly called into question whether the CIA's enhanced interrogation techniques were effective, assessing that the use of the techniques failed to elicit detainee cooperation or produce accurate intelligence."

—"Report Of The Senate Select Committee On Intelligence Committee Study Of The Central Intelligence Agency's Detention And Interrogation Program Together With Foreword By Chairman Feinstein And Additional And Minority Views," Intelligence.Senate.gov, ordered to be printed December 9, 2014, Page xi

[**Note:** More than ten years after Bush's invasion of Iraq, a review of the CIA's use of enhanced interrogation found that those techniques were not even effective in gathering intelligence, and his CIA was, in effect, lawless.]

E. POTENTIAL FUTURE ADVERSE EFFECTS FROM GEORGE W. BUSH AND HIS ADMINISTRATION TORTURING PRISONERS

SOME WITH PROFESSIONAL BACKGROUNDS believe the pain and suffering of those tortured, and the long-term effects of that torture, hurt our efforts in the war against terror because when we torture, we become "one of them." Additionally, torturing others violates the rules of war we had agreed to live by. Torturing prisoners takes away or impedes our ability to object when our military personnel are captured and tortured by others. By torturing detainees, in addition to breaking laws, the Bush administration lost any high moral ground we had at home and in the international community from 9/11 and as you have just read, torture didn't even seem to work.

5/12/2004: Vatican Foreign Minister: Abu Ghraib torture "a more serious blow to the United States than September 11"

On May 12, 2004, "The Vatican's foreign minister [Archbishop Giovanni Lajolo], invoking the word 'torture,' called Abu Ghraib 'a more serious blow to the United States than September 11.'"

—Donald Rumsfeld, *Known and Unknown*, Page 546

11/4/2005: McCain on the implications of torturing prisoners: "because abuse of prisoners harms, not helps, us in the war against terror," often produces bad intel

In a Senate floor statement on the "National Defense Authorization Act for FY 06," McCain addressed President Bush on the implications of torturing prisoners: "But to do differently not only offends our values as Americans but undermines our war efforts because abuse of prisoners harms, not helps, us in the war against terror. First, subjecting prisoners to abuse leads to bad intelligence because under torture a detainee will tell his interrogator anything to make the pain stop. Second, mistreatment of our prisoners endangers U.S. troops who might be captured by the enemy, if not in this war then in the next. And third, prisoner abuses exact on us a terrible toll in the war of ideas because inevitably these abuses become public, as was revealed—or at least a prison system was revealed; I don't know what goes on in them—on the front page of one of our major newspapers."

—"National Defense Authorization Act For Fiscal Year 2006," Congressional Record, November 4, 2005, Vol. 151, No. 145, Congress.gov, Page S12381

8/15/2006: Rice: George W. Bush administration had to close secret sites, which were doing more harm than good

A National Security Council meeting in mid-August 2006 focused on the holding of detainees in secret prisons around the world.

"The [Bush] administration had to close the secret sites, Rice said forcefully.

They were doing more harm than good. America was a nation of laws, and it was important for the United States to bring the issue to closure, both on foreign policy and moral grounds." [*The fifteenth of the month used for date sorting purposes only.*]

—Elisabeth Bumiller, *Condoleezza Rice*, Page 297

[**Note:** Bush's secret sites holding detainees around the world had to be closed because we were a nation of laws.]

6/17/2008: Senator Levin: Enhanced interrogation techniques put "our troops at greater risk of being abused if they're captured"

Chairman of the Armed Services Committee, Senator Carl Levin (D-MI), discussed enhanced interrogation techniques on June 17, 2008. "'If we use those same techniques offensively against detainees, it says to the world that they have America's stamp of approval,' said Levin at the start of a committee hearing.

'That puts our troops at greater risk of being abused if they're captured. It also weakens our moral authority and harms our efforts to attract allies to our side in the fight against terrorism.'"

—*Daily Mail* Reporter, "U.S. official on terror interrogation: 'If the detainee dies, you're doing it wrong'," *Daily Mail*, June 17, 2008

5/3/2010: Brig. General Finnegan: Abu Ghraib photos, publicity surrounding Guantánamo, and waterboarding, created more terrorists

"Brigadier General Patrick Finnegan, Dean of the Academic Board at West Point, wrote in a letter to the Editor of *The New Yorker* magazine [on May 3, 2010]: 'the pictures from Abu Ghraib and the publicity surrounding Guantánamo, waterboarding, and other 'enhanced interrogation techniques' have created far more terrorists than most people understand.

For a country that professes to stand for the rule of law and individual rights, we look like the worst kind of hypocrites.'"

—M. Cherif Bassiouni, *The Institutionalization of Torture by the Bush Administration*, Pages xix–xx

5/12/2011: McCain opposes waterboarding; says any form of torture damages our character and reputation

"McCain said he opposes waterboarding, a technique that simulates drowning, and any form of torture tactics.

He said that they could be used against Americans and that their use damages the nation's character and reputation.

'I do not believe they are necessary to our success in our war against terrorists, as the advocates of these techniques claim they are,' he said.

'Ultimately, this is about morality. What is at stake here is the very idea of America—the America whose values have inspired the world and instilled in the hearts of its citizens the certainty that, no matter how hard we fight, no matter how dangerous our adversary, in the course of vanquishing our enemies we do not compromise our deepest values,' he said. 'We are America, and we hold ourselves to a higher standard. That is what is really at stake.'"

—Donna Cassata, Associated Press, "McCain Says Torture did not Lead to bin Laden," *The San Diego Union-Tribune*, May 12, 2011

Even though knowledgeable people said that torture creates more terrorists, is not necessary for intel gathering, puts our troops at future risk, and is against our America values, George W. Bush and others in his administration tortured.

F. INJURIES AND DEATHS FROM TORTURE

THE FOLLOWING QUOTES SHOW some of the probable or actual injuries or death caused by the Bush administration's use of enhanced interrogation (including waterboarding) and rendition.

8/15/2002: CIA waterboarded prisoners more times than they reported

"C.I.A. interrogators used waterboarding, the near-drowning technique...266 times on two key prisoners from Al Qaeda, far more than had been previously reported. The C.I.A. officers used waterboarding at least 83 times in August 2002 against Abu Zubaydah, according to a 2005 Justice Department legal memorandum." [*The fifteenth of the month used for date sorting purposes only.*]

—Scott Shane, "Waterboarding Used 266 Times on 2 Suspects," *The New York Times*, April 19, 2009

3/15/2003: Justice Dept.: CIA waterboarded Khalid Shaikh Mohammed 183 times

A 2005 Justice Department memo said: "the C.I.A. used waterboarding 183 times in March 2003 against Khalid Shaikh Mohammed, the self-described planner of the Sept. 11, 2001, terrorist attacks." [*The fifteenth of the month used for date sorting purposes only.*]

—Scott Shane, "Waterboarding Used 266 Times on 2 Suspects," *The New York Times*, April 19, 2009

[**Note:** How would our country react if another country tortured an American soldier captured during war?]

10/15/2003: Canadian rendition detainee Maher Arar tortured, cleared of terrorism link in Canada, but kept on terrorist watch list by US.

"[I]n October 2003, [approximately a year after his September 26, 2002, rendition and torture by the CIA, Canadian telecommunications engineer Maher] Arar was released without charges, after his wife forced the Canadian government to take up his cause....A thorough official investigation by the Canadian government cleared Arar of any links to terrorism and concluded that he had...been egregiously tortured....the Canadian government awarded him $10.5 million in compensatory damages....[and] also sternly disciplined the responsible public officials. In contrast, the United States government refused to clear Arar's name from its terrorist watch list but would not explain why." [*The fifteenth of the month used for date sorting purposes only.*]

—Jane Mayer, *The Dark Side*, Page 133

11/4/2003: CIA apparently tortures detainee Manadel al-Jamadi to death at Abu Ghraib

In Iraq, "on the night of November 4, 2003, a death occurred [to prisoner Manadel al-Jamadi] at Abu Ghraib—apparently caused by torture at the hands of a CIA interrogator."

—Ricardo S. Sanchez with Donald T. Phillips, *Wiser in Battle*, Page 277

1/15/2004: Germany's Merkel: George W. Bush administration admitted they had mistakenly abducted a German citizen to Afghanistan and *abused* him there

"German Chancellor Angela Merkel said on Oct. 5, 2005, that the Bush administration had admitted to her that it had mistakenly abducted a German citizen, Khaled Masri, from Macedonia in January 2004. Masri reportedly was flown to a secret prison in Afghanistan, where he allegedly was abused while being interrogated. He was released in May 2004 and dumped on a remote road in Albania." [*The fifteenth of the month used for date sorting purposes only.*]

—Jonathan S. Landay and Warren P. Strobel, "Cheney's Speech Ignored Some Inconvenient Truths," The McClatchy Newspapers, Tri-City Herald, May 21, 2009

4/28/2004: *60 Minutes* breaks news of Abu Ghraib scandal; Rumsfeld says, "I didn't know you were allowed to bring cameras into a prison!"

60 Minutes first broke the news of the Abu Ghraib scandal in Iraq in a report on April 28, 2004. "When Rumsfeld first learned that there were pictures extant of naked, humiliated, and terrified prisoners being abused by cheerful Americans, he said, according to an official who was present, 'I didn't know you were allowed to bring cameras into a prison!'"

—Andrew Cockburn, *Rumsfeld*, Page 194

7/9/2004: FBI's Office of Inspections: More than two-dozen agents observed numerous instances of detainee abuse approved by Rumsfeld and Wolfowitz

"On July 9, 2004, the FBI's Office of Inspections distributed an e-mail asking its agents who were stationed at Guantánamo whether they had witnessed, 'Aggressive treatment, interrogations or interview techniques... which were not consistent with FBI interview policy / guidelines.'

More than two-dozen agents responded that they observed numerous instances of detainee abuse.

One FBI agent wrote that, despite Rumsfeld's public statements to the contrary, the interrogation methods 'were approved at high levels w/ in DoD [Department of Defense].'

In addition to Rumsfeld, the FBI e-mails said Paul Wolfowitz, one Bush administration official who has largely escaped scrutiny in the torture debate, approved the methods at Guantánamo."

—Jason Leopold, "Gonzales Memo Advised Bush How to Avoid War Crimes Charges," PubRecord.org, June 13, 2009

[**Note:** Detainee *abuse* at Guantánamo.]

9/10/2004: Exact number of CIA detainees unknown; at least one hundred had been held in facilities operated by the CIA in undisclosed locations globally

According to information in a *Los Angeles Times* article on September 10, 2004: "While the exact number of prisoners detained in the CIA program is unknown, by 2004 it was estimated that at least 100 had been held in facilities operated by the agency in undisclosed locations around the world."

—M. Cherif Bassiouni, *The Institutionalization of Torture by the Bush Administration*, Page 163

2/14/2005: CIA "rendered" up to 150 people between 2001–2005

"Scott Horton, an expert on international law who helped prepare a report on renditions issued by N.Y.U. Law School and the New York City Bar Association, estimates that a hundred and fifty people have been rendered since 2001. Representative Ed Markey, a Democrat from Massachusetts and a member of the Select Committee on Homeland Security, said that a more precise number was impossible to obtain. 'I've asked people at the C.I.A. for numbers,' he said. 'They refuse to answer. All they will say is that they're in compliance with the law.'"

—Jane Mayer, "Outsourcing Torture: The secret history of America's 'extraordinary rendition' program." *The New Yorker*, February 14, 2005

3/2/2005: Church Report on detainee interrogation called a "whitewash" by human rights organizations

On March 2, 2005, "The Vice Admiral Albert T. Church Report on Detainee Interrogation and Incarceration is released. The panel examined 187 investigations of allegations of detainee abuse that had been completed as of September 30, 2004.

Of those, 117 cases were unsubstantiated or did not constitute abuse, and of the 70 remaining completed cases of substantiated abuse, six were deaths, 26 were considered serious, and 38 were called minor abuse cases.

Church declines to single out any specific persons to be held accountable, and human rights organizations call the report a 'whitewash'.

Within a week of the Church report, officials from the Army and Navy admit that 26, not 6, detainee deaths merited charges of homicide."

—M. Cherif Bassiouni, *The Institutionalization of Torture by the Bush Administration*, Pages xliv–xlv

[**Note:** According to officials from the Army and Navy, Bush's military killed or tortured to death twenty-six detainees.]

11/2/2005: More than one hundred suspected Al-Qaeda terrorists sent by CIA to "black sites," and Egypt, Jordan, Morocco, and Afghanistan for interrogation

Regarding the CIA's use of covert 'black sites' to detain and interrogate Al-Qaeda prisoners:

"More than 100 suspected terrorists have been sent by the CIA into the covert system, according to current and former U.S. intelligence officials and foreign sources.

This figure…does not include prisoners picked up in Iraq.

The detainees break down roughly into two classes, the sources said. About 30 are considered major terrorism suspects and have been held under the highest level of secrecy at black sites financed by the CIA and managed by agency personnel, including those in Eastern Europe and elsewhere, according to current and former intelligence officers and two other U.S. government officials….

A second tier—which these sources believe includes more than 70 detainees—is a group considered less important, with less direct involvement in terrorism and having limited intelligence value.

These prisoners, some of whom were originally taken to black sites, are delivered to intelligence services in Egypt, Jordan, Morocco, Afghanistan and other countries, a process sometimes known as 'rendition.' While the first-tier black sites are run by CIA officers, the jails in these countries are operated by the host nations, with CIA financial assistance and, sometimes, direction."

—Dana Priest, "CIA Holds Terror Suspects in Secret Prisons," *The Washington Post*, November 2, 2005

6/9/2006: US guards: Three simultaneous, mysterious Guantánamo detainee deaths not suicides

On June 9, 2006, detainees "Yasser Al-Zahrani, Mani Al-Utaybi, and Salah Ahmed Al-Salami are found dead in their cells at Guantánamo under mysterious circumstances, and determined to have simultaneously committed suicide.

In 2009, guards who were on duty that evening come forward with evidence that the men were murdered."

—M. Cherif Bassiouni, *The Institutionalization of Torture by the Bush Administration*,
Page xlvi

[**Note:** Three detainees probably murdered by Bush's military.]

9/6/2006: George W. Bush: Only about 770 ever sent to Guantánamo, which is called a "model prison" by one member of the Organization for Security and Cooperation in Europe

In a speech in the East Room on September 6, 2006, on the subject of Guantánamo, President Bush had this to say: "I know Americans have heard conflicting information about Guantánamo. Let me give you some facts. Of the thousands of terrorists captured across the world, only about 770 have ever been sent to Guantánamo. Of these, about 315 have been returned to other countries so far—and about 455 remain in our custody. They are provided the same quality of medical care as the American service members who guard them. The International Committee of the Red Cross has the opportunity to meet privately with all who are held there. The facility has been visited by government officials from more than 30 countries, and delegations from international organizations, as well. After the Organization for Security and Cooperation in Europe came to visit, one of its delegation members called Guantánamo 'a model prison' where people are treated better than in prisons in his own country. Our troops can take great pride in the work they do at Guantánamo Bay—and so can the American people."

—Office of the Press Secretary, "President Discusses Creation of Military Commissions to Try Suspected Terrorists," George W. Bush—White House Archives,
September 6, 2006

1/26/2007: European report tracks 1,245 CIA flights where suspects could face torture, violating CAT Art. 3

On January 26, 2007, "A European Parliament report concludes that the CIA has conducted 1,245 flights, many of them to destinations where suspects could face torture, in violation of Article 3 of the CAT [United Nations Convention Against Torture]."

—M. Cherif Bassiouni, *The Institutionalization of Torture by the Bush Administration*, Page xlvii

2/14/2007: Red Cross report: KSM said CIA brought him to the "verge of death and back again"

On February 14, 2007, the International Committee of the Red Cross released a report on the fourteen "high value detainees" who were transferred from secret CIA prisons to Guantánamo.

In the report, 9/11 mastermind Khalid Sheikh Mohammed described his treatment by the CIA: "'As the interrogation again resumed I was told by one of the *emirs* [CIA interrogators] that they had received the greenlight from Washington to give him *a hard time*. They never used the word *torture* and never referred to *physical pressure*, only to *a hard time*, I was never threatened with death, in fact I was told that they would not allow me to die, but that I would be brought to the *verge of death and back again*.'"

—"ICRC Report on the Treatment of Fourteen 'High Value Detainees' in CIA Custody," International Committee of the Red Cross, February 14, 2007, Page 35

6/7/2007: Swiss Senator concludes that "large numbers of people had been abducted [by CIA] across the world" and transferred to countries like Poland and Romania that have secret torture centers

"An investigation by the Council of Europe in June [7] 2007 confirmed reports of secret CIA prisons in Europe and other locations, which had first surfaced in 2005. The investigation, conducted by Swiss senator Dick Marty, concluded that 'large numbers of people had been abducted across the world' and transferred to countries where 'torture is common practice.'

Others were kept in 'arbitrary detention without any precise charge' and without any judicial oversight.

Still others had 'disappeared for indefinite periods, held in secret prisons, including in member-states of the Council of Europe, the existence and operation of which had been concealed.'

Marty reported that these people were subjected to degrading treatment and torture in order to extract information, however unsound, that America claimed 'had protected our common security.'

Prisoners were interrogated ceaselessly and were physically and psychologically abused before being released because they were 'plainly not the people being sought.'

The report said that these were the terrible consequences of the war on terror. It specifically named Romania and Poland as places where the CIA ran secret prisons and torture centers."

—Deepak Tripathi, *Overcoming the Bush Legacy in Iraq and Afghanistan*, Page 78

[**Note:** George W. Bush as our commander-in-chief approved and supported abduction and torturing.]

12/6/2007: CIA: Some Interrogation tapes destroyed in 2005 because officers were concerned that videos showing harsh interrogation methods could expose CIA officials to legal risks

"The Central Intelligence Agency in 2005 destroyed at least two videotapes documenting the interrogation of two Qaeda operatives in the agency's custody, a step it took in the midst of Congressional and legal scrutiny about its secret detention program, according to current and former government officials.

The videotapes showed agency operatives in 2002 subjecting terrorism suspects including Abu Zubaydah, the first detainee in C.I.A. custody to severe interrogation techniques.

The tapes were destroyed in part because officers were concerned that video showing harsh interrogation methods could expose agency officials to legal risks, several officials said.

In a statement to employees on Thursday [December 6, 2007], Gen. Michael V. Hayden, the C.I.A. director, said that the decision to destroy the tapes was made 'within the C.I.A.' and that they were destroyed to protect the safety of undercover officers and because they no longer had intelligence value."

—Mark Mazzetti, "C.I.A. Destroyed 2 Tapes Showing Interrogations," *The New York Times*, December 7, 2007

5/15/2008: Pentagon releases "20th hijacker" from Guantánamo; prolonged inhumane treatment weakened case, charges dismissed

"In May 2008, the Pentagon announced that it was dismissing charges against Mohammed al-Qahtani, the Saudi suspected of having been the '20th hijacker' apparently because the inhumane treatment to which he had been subjected during his long interrogation in Guantánamo, all of which had been authorized by Rumsfeld, had destroyed the credibility of his confession, hopelessly tainting the case." [*The fifteenth of the month used for date sorting purposes only.*]

—Jane Mayer, *The Dark Side*, Page 333

[**Note:** Bush's Rumsfeld meting out inhumane treatment either on his own or on behalf of his commander-in-chief]

6/2/2008: Secret US floating prisons holding at least 26,000 without trial, up to 80,000 have been "through the system" since 2001

"The United States is operating 'floating prisons' to house those arrested in its war on terror, according to human rights lawyers, who claim there has been an attempt to conceal the numbers and whereabouts of detainees....

Clive Stafford Smith, Reprieve's legal director, said: 'They choose ships to try to keep their misconduct as far as possible from the prying eyes of the media and lawyers. We will eventually reunite these ghost prisoners with their legal rights.

'By its own admission, the US government is currently detaining at least 26,000 people without trial in secret prisons, and information suggests up to 80,000 have been *through the system* since 2001. The US government must show a commitment to rights and basic humanity by immediately revealing who these people are, where they are, and what has been done to them.'"

—Duncan Campbell and Richard Norton-Taylor, "US accused of holding terror suspects on prison ships," *The Guardian*, June 1, 2008

[**Note:** Secret floating prisons, holding tens of thousands without trial, were another part of Bush's war.]

1/14/2009: *Washington Post*: Susan Crawford is first senior George W. Bush administration official reviewing Guantánamo practices to publicly state detainee was tortured

From a *Washington Post* article on January 14, 2009: "The top Bush administration official in charge of deciding whether to bring Guantánamo Bay detainees to trial has concluded that the U.S. military tortured a Saudi national who allegedly planned to participate in the Sept. 11, 2001, attacks, interrogating him with techniques that included sustained isolation, sleep deprivation, nudity and prolonged exposure to cold, leaving him in a 'life-threatening condition.'

'We tortured [Mohammed al-] Qahtani,' said Susan J. Crawford, in her first interview since being named convening authority of military commissions by Defense Secretary Robert M. Gates in February 2007.

'His treatment met the legal definition of torture. And that's why I did not refer the case' for prosecution.

Crawford...is the first senior Bush administration official responsible for reviewing practices at Guantánamo to publicly state that a detainee was tortured."

—Bob Woodward, "Guantánamo Detainee Was Tortured, Says Official Overseeing Military Trials," *The Washington Post*, January 14, 2009

[**Note:** Senior Bush administration official stating publicly that a detainee was tortured at Guantánamo.]

11/4/2009: Italy convicts CIA agents *in absentia* for acts of torture as a result of "extraordinary rendition"

In 2003, CIA members unlawfully rendered Egyptian imam Hassan Mustafa Osama Nasr from Italy to Egypt, where he underwent torture. On November 4, 2009, "Twenty-two CIA agents are convicted in absentia in Milan, Italy for violations of Italian and international law with regard to acts of torture as a result of the practice of 'extraordinary rendition.'"

—M. Cherif Bassiouni, *The Institutionalization of Torture by the Bush Administration*, Page xlix

[**Note:** Bush's CIA illegally torturing a detainee via extraordinary rendition.]

3/22/2010: Military prosecutor determines evidence from interrogation of suspected high-value Al-Qaeda detainee at Guantánamo was torture and can't lawfully be used by US; detainee released

"A suspected al Qaeda organizer [Mohamedou Ould Slahi] once called 'the highest value detainee' at Guantánamo Bay was ordered released by a federal judge in an order issued Monday [March 22, 2010]....

U.S. District Judge James Robertson [of the U.S. District Court for the District of Columbia] granted Mr. Slahi's petition for habeas corpus, effectively finding the government lacked legal grounds to hold him....

Plans to try him by military commission were derailed after prosecutors learned that Mr. Slahi had been subjected to a 'special interrogation plan' involving weeks of physical and mental torment, including a death threat and a threat to bring Mr. Slahi's mother to Guantánamo Bay where she could be gang-raped, officials said.

Although the treatment apparently induced Mr. Slahi's compliance, the military prosecutor, Marine Lt. Col. V. Stuart Couch, determined that it constituted torture and evidence it produced could not lawfully be used against Mr. Slahi."

—Jess Bravin, "Key Gitmo Detainee Ordered Released," *The Wall Street Journal*, March 22, 2010

[**Note:** Bush's military prosecutor determining the Guantánamo detainee was tortured.]

11/9/2010: "Damn right!" George W. Bush says on personally authorizing use of waterboarding

"Asked by *The Times* [*of London*] if he [former President George W. Bush] personally authorized the use of waterboarding—effectively drowning the suspect by pouring water on to his face—against the al-Qaeda suspect Khalid Sheikh Mohammed, Mr. Bush said: 'Damn right!'"

—Jenny Booth and Ben Macintyre, "Bush waterboarding claims queried by ex minister," *The Times of London*, thetimes.co.uk, November 9, 2010

[**Note:** Another admission by Bush authorizing waterboarding.]

3/5/2020: ICC rules its chief prosecutor can open investigation into "allegations of war crimes in Afghanistan including any that may have been committed by Americans"

"The International Criminal Court ruled on Thursday [March 5, 2020] that its chief prosecutor could open an investigation into allegations of war crimes in Afghanistan including any that may have been committed by Americans, a step that infuriated the Trump administration....Secretary of State Mike Pompeo...called the ruling a 'truly breathtaking action by an unaccountable, political institution masquerading as a legal body.'...The [ICC] prosecutor has said that the court had enough information to prove that U.S. forces had 'committed acts of torture, cruel treatment, outrages upon personal dignity, rape and sexual violence' in Afghanistan in 2003 and 2004, and later in clandestine C.I.A facilities in Poland, Romania and Lithuania."

—Elian Peltier and Fatima Faizi, "I.C.C. Allows Afghanistan War Crimes Inquiry to Proceed, Angering U.S.," *The New York Times*, March 5, 2020

G. COSTS RELATING TO TORTURE

11/2/2005: At least eight countries hosted CIA "black sites," medieval-like dungeons, for financial reward that US taxpayers unknowingly funded

According to *The Washington Post* on November 2, 2005: "at least eight countries have participated [in hosting clandestine prisons known as 'black sites']...For the host countries, there were both political and legal liabilities.

State enforced disappearances are not only illegal in the United States, but such practices also violate laws in almost all of the allied countries whose cooperation the United States sought.

There were financial rewards for the host countries, however. One year of the Afghan prison operation alone cost an estimated $100 million, which Congress hid in a classified annex of the first supplemental Afghan appropriations bill in 2002.

Among the services that U.S. taxpayers unwittingly paid for were medieval-like dungeons, including a reviled former brick factory outside of Kabul known as 'The Salt Pit.'"

—Jane Mayer, *The Dark Side*, Page 148

[**Note:** The twentieth finding from the 4/3/2014 Senate Intelligence Committee report on torture read:

"The CIA's Detention and Interrogation Program damaged the United States' standing in the world, and resulted in other significant monetary and non-monetary costs.

The CIA's Detention and Interrogation Program created tensions with U.S. partners and allies, leading to formal demarches to the United States, and damaging and complicating bilateral intelligence relationships....More broadly, the program caused immeasurable damage to the United States' public standing, as well as to the United States' longstanding global leadership on human rights in general and the prevention of torture in particular....CIA records indicate that the CIA's Detention and Interrogation Program cost well over $300 million in non-personnel costs....To encourage governments to clandestinely host CIA detention sites, or to increase support for existing sites, the CIA provided millions of dollars in cash payments to foreign government officials."]

H. RECAP

HERE IS A SAMPLING of quotes you have read that show Bush and others in his administration approved of, if not promoted, torturing prisoners after 9/11 and during his Iraq War while saying publicly that our country doesn't believe in torture:

— 3/31/2002: Although President Bush noted that the Department of Justice had declared the CIA's treatment of Al-Qaeda operations chief Abu Zubayda as legal, "FBI agents, who were the first to question Zubayda at the black site, before the CIA interrogation team arrived…thought that what they glimpsed of the CIA's treatment of him was disgraceful, disastrously counterproductive, and criminal."

— 8/1/2002: In Assistant Attorney General Jay Bybee's August 1, 2002, memo to Acting General Counsel to the CIA John Rizzo, "The OLC concluded that the use of the following ten interrogation techniques by the CIA would not constitute torture: 1) attention grasp, 2) walling, 3) facial hold, 4) facial slap, 5) cramped confinement, 6) wall standing, 7) stress positions, 8) sleep deprivation, 9) insects placed in a confinement box, and 10) waterboarding."

— 3/1/2003: Former President George W. Bush recalled, after the capture of 9/11 mastermind Khalid Sheikh Mohammed on March 1, 2003, CIA Director "George Tenet asked if he had permission to use enhanced interrogation techniques, including waterboarding, on Khalid Sheikh Mohammed. I thought about my meeting with Danny Pearl's widow, who was pregnant with his son when he was murdered. I thought about the 2,973 people stolen from their families by al Qaeda on 9/11. And I thought about my duty to protect the country from another act of terror. 'Damn right,' I said."

— 7/15/2004: "The ICRC labeled the Guantánamo interrogation process as 'an intentional system of cruel, unusual and degrading treatment and a form of torture.'"

— 3/16/2005: President Bush and his stance on torture: "The post-9/11 world, the United States must make sure we protect our people and our friends from attack. That was the charge we have been given. And one way to do so is to arrest people and send them back to their country of origin with the promise that they won't be tortured. That's the promise we receive. This country does not believe in torture. We do believe in protecting ourselves. We don't believe in torture."

The quotes in the preceding chapter (and in this recap) show that President George W. Bush approved, if not encouraged, the torturing (including waterboarding) of prisoners, while he and others in his administration were stating publicly that torture is immoral, un-American, and wrong, and that the Bush administration wasn't doing it.

Given the fear of another 9/11 there were different opinions about torture. Some said, for example, that there were legitimate reasons to torture to gain intel to protect our country, intel not otherwise accessible; that waterboarding isn't torture; that having someone else torture for you is different than doing it yourself; and that it's okay to torture illegal combatants.

Regardless, I believe the quotes in this chapter show that Bush approved of and promoted torture, that torture has been and continues to be a crime, and that because George W. Bush was responsible for approving the torturing of our detainees, he should be held accountable.

CRIME #3: WAR CRIMES / CRIMES AGAINST HUMANITY / MURDER OVER THE FALSELY SOLD 2003 IRAQ WAR

After 9/11, George W. Bush and some of his administration's people continually and falsely told the American public and Congress that our country was in immediate danger from Hussein, that Hussein had weapons of mass destruction, and falsely implied that Hussein was connected to 9/11 and bin Laden.

THIS CHAPTER WILL SHOW that from taking office in January of 2001, until our invasion of Iraq on June 19, 2003, Bush and his senior people (including Vice President Cheney, Vice Presidential Chief of Staff I. Lewis "Scooter" Libby, National Security Advisor Rice, Director of Central Intelligence Tenet, Secretary of State Powell, and Secretary of Defense Rumsfeld) repeatedly said that Hussein was a serious and immediate threat to our country, had weapons of mass destruction, and implied that Hussein was connected to bin Laden, Al-Qaeda, and 9/11 without having facts or credible intel that those statements were true.

While selling our country on the need to attack Iraq, Bush hid from the American people and our Congress the fact that most, if not all, of the *evidence* he and others in his administration were presenting was out of date, taken out of context, and known to be overstated, unreliable, or false.

For ease of understanding the quotes showing how George W. Bush falsely sold America on the necessity of the unnecessary 2003 Iraq War, and the war's consequences, the quotes in this chapter are broken into sections:

A. George W. Bush's interest in Iraqi oil, beginning a week after he became president

B. Ten false and misleading reasons Bush gave as support for ‹
to attack Iraq

C. The risks and damages to our country from the 2003 Iraq War

D. Injuries and deaths from our attacking Iraq

E. Costs related to our attacking Iraq

F. Recap

Note: The quotes in gray boxes are misleading, without credible basis, or false.

A. GEORGE W. BUSH'S INTEREST IN IRAQI OIL BEGINNING A WEEK AFTER HE BECAME PRESIDENT

THE FOLLOWING QUOTES SHOW that George W. Bush and his administration's interest in Iraqi oil began almost from the day he took office.

1/30/2001: Deputy Sec. of Interior Stephen Griles played "lead role in mapping out the U.S oil industry's interests in Iraq's oil fields"

Deputy Secretary of the Interior Stephen "Griles was a lead actor in the Cheney Energy Task Force [that first convened on January 30, 2001], serving as the Interior Department's chief representative. As such, he played a lead role in mapping out the U.S. oil industry's interests in Iraq's oil fields and developing some of the most destructive national energy bills in the nation's history, giving more than $14 billion worth of subsidies, tax breaks, and other benefits to the oil industry."

—Antonia Juhasz, *The Tyranny of Oil*, Page 260

[**Note:** The Cheney Energy Task Force was convened ten days after George W. Bush became president.]

2/1/2001: Two days after first National Security Council meeting, Bush officials began discussing what to do with Iraq's oil wealth

"On February 1, 2001, two days after the [first] NSC meeting, Bush officials circulated a memo titled 'Plan for post-Saddam Iraq' and began discussing what to do with Iraq's oil wealth."

—Craig Unger, *The Fall of the House of Bush*, Page 202

[**Note:** An indication of Bush's intent to go after Iraq's oil.]

2/3/2001: *New Yorker* reporter Mayer revealed top-secret February 3, 2001, memo directing NSC to work with Energy Task Force in "melding" two unrelated policies: rogue states, such as Iraq, and actions for capture of new and existing oil and gas fields

"In [February 16] 2004 *New Yorker* magazine reporter Jane Mayer revealed a top-secret memo written [on February 3, 2001] by a high-level National Security Council (NSC) official directing the NSC staff to cooperate fully with the Energy Task Force as it considered the 'melding' of two seemingly unrelated areas of policy: 'the review of operational policies towards rogue states,' such as Iraq, and 'actions regarding the capture of new and existing oil and gas fields.'"

—Antonia Juhasz, *The Tyranny of Oil*, Page 341

[**Note:** Two weeks after Bush became president, Iraq and its oil continued to be important to the Bush administration.]

3/15/2001: Conservative Judicial Watch found that VP Cheney's energy task force was studying map of Iraqi oil fields and charts detailing "Foreign Suitors for Iraqi Oilfield Contracts"

Conservative foundation Judicial Watch "found that Cheney's energy task force had been studying a map of Iraqi oil fields, pipelines, refineries, and terminals, along with charts detailing 'Foreign Suitors for Iraqi Oilfield Contracts.' The context for these documents, dated March 2001, was never explained." [*The fifteenth of the month used for date sorting purposes only.*]

—Barton Gellman, *Angler*, Page 106

4/15/2001: James A. Baker Institute report: "Iraq remains a destabilizing influence…to the flow of oil to international markets from the Middle East."

According to the April 2001 report, "Strategic Energy Policy: Challenges for the 21st Century," which was prepared by the James A. Baker Institute for Public Policy and the US Council on Foreign Relations at the request of Vice President Cheney: "Iraq remains a destabilizing influence…to the flow of oil to international markets from the Middle East. Saddam Hussein has also demonstrated a willingness to threaten to use the oil weapon and to use his own export program to manipulate oil markets….The United States should conduct an immediate policy review toward Iraq, including military, energy, economic, and political/diplomatic assessments." [*The fifteenth of the month used for date sorting purposes only.*]

—Odeh Aburdene, Graham Allison, et. Al., "Strategic Energy Policy: Challenges for the 21st Century," The James A. Baker III Institute for Public Policy at Rice University and the Council on Foreign Relations, April 2001, Page 46

[**Note:** Bush's administration focusing on Iraq and its oil.]

9/16/2001: Bush reaffirmed a decision for creating contingency plans to deal with Iraq, including plan to seize Iraq's oil fields

"On Sunday September 16 [2001], [President] Bush called Condoleezza Rice. He wanted the focus to be on Afghanistan but also wanted plans drawn up in case it turned out that Iraq was somehow implicated in the 9/11 attacks. The next day [September 17], the president convened a meeting of his National Security Council during which there was some discussion of what might follow an Afghan campaign. Bush reaffirmed his decision that contingency plans should be drawn up to deal with Iraq, including a plan to seize Iraq's oilfields."

—Michael R. Gordon and Bernard E. Trainor, Cobra II, Pages 19–20

[**Note:** Eight months into his presidency, and five days after 9/11, Bush wanted a plan to seize Iraqi oil.]

9/17/2001: George W. Bush "phase two" of war on terrorism to include plan for "possibly occupying Iraqi oil fields" if Iraq "acted against U.S. interests"

"At the September 17 [2001] NSC meeting, there was some further discussion of 'phase two' of the war on terrorism. President Bush ordered the Defense Department to be ready to deal with Iraq if Baghdad acted against U.S. interests, with plans to include possibly occupying Iraqi oil fields."

—9/11 Commission, The 9/11 Commission Report, July 22, 2004, Page 335

[**Note:** It is Iraqi oil, not Iraq, that is a danger to America.]

10/7/2001: Major consideration of Bush administration for attacking Afghanistan appeared to be supporting the dual oil and gas pipelines through Afghanistan

"[S]ocial scientist Chalmers Johnson has commented, 'Support for this enterprise [the dual oil and gas pipelines [through Afghanistan]] appears to have been a major consideration in the Bush administration's decision to attack Afghanistan on October 7, 2001.' Political commentator Kevin Phillips has agreed that 'plans were discussed in the spring and summer of 2001—well before the events of September [11]—for hamstringing Iraq and convincing the Taliban in Afghanistan to accept construction of an American (Unocal) pipeline from Turkmenistan through Kabul to Karachi, Pakistan.'"

—Peter Dale Scott, The Road to 9/11, Page 167

[**Note:** Could Bush's attack of Afghanistan less than a month after 9/11 have been to support an oil and gas pipeline through that country?]

10/12/2001: Bush administration official: "Wolfowitz cabal" plans included having American troops seize oil fields around Basra to finance Iraqi opposition

According to the plans to invade Iraq set forth by the "Wolfowitz cabal," "American troops would also seize the oil fields around Basra, in southeastern Iraq, and sell the oil to finance the Iraqi opposition in the south and the Kurds in the north, one senior [Bush Administration] official said. 'The takeover would not be dissimilar to the area we occupied in the gulf war,' the official said."

—Elaine Sciolino and Patrick E. Tyler, "A NATION CHALLENGED: SADDAM HUSSEIN; Some Pentagon Officials and Advisers Seek to Oust Iraq's Leader in War's Next Phase," *The New York Times*, October 12, 2001

2/7/2002: Neoconservative William Kristol Senate testimony: "A friendly, free, and oil-producing Iraq would leave Iran isolated and Syria cowed"

In testimony before the Senate Foreign Relations Committee on February 7, 2002, neoconservative political analyst William Kristol said: "'A friendly, free, and oil-producing Iraq would leave Iran isolated and Syria cowed; the Palestinians more willing to negotiate seriously with Israel; and Saudi Arabia with less leverage over policymakers here and in Europe. Removing Saddam Hussein and his henchmen from power presents a genuine opportunity—one President Bush sees clearly—to transform the political landscape of the Middle East.'"

—Jeffrey Record, *Wanting War*, Page 85

[**Note:** What about Iraq's danger to America?]

4/8/2002: George W. Bush talks about preventing Hussein from trying "to cut off energy supply to affect" the US

President George W. Bush during remarks to business leaders in the Eisenhower Executive Office Building calling for a change in energy policy: "I know energy policy is very important, and we spent a great deal of time with Jimmy [James P. Hoffa, general president, International Brotherhood of Teamsters] and Ed[ward C. Sullivan, president, Building and Construction Trades Department, AFL-CIO (The American Federation of Labor and Congress of Industrial Organizations)] talking about how to get a good energy bill out of the Congress.

It's an energy bill, by the way, that is needed more than ever, particularly given the fact that there's been some threats recently by Saddam Hussein that he's going to try to cut off energy supply to affect the United States. I mean, what more reason do we need than to have good energy policy in the United States, to diversify away from somebody like him?"

—Office of the Press Secretary, "President Calls on Senate to Act on Terrorism Insurance Legislation—Remarks by the President to Business Leaders," George W. Bush—White House Archives, April 8, 2002

9/20/2002: George W. Bush reassures no Iraqi oil flow disruption, "looking at all options to enhance oil flow"

"'Don't fall into the argument that there is no one to replace Saddam Hussein,' said [President] Bush [on September 20, 2002]. 'And our planning will make sure there is no oil disruption; we are looking at all options to enhance oil flow.'"

—Scott McClellan, *What Happened*, Page 139

[**Note:** Six months before Bush invaded Iraq, he was concerned with Iraq oil disruption.]

10/11/2002: Pentagon "already had plans" to control Iraqi oil

"On October 11, 2002 the *New York Times* reported that the Pentagon already had plans to occupy and control Iraq's oilfields."

—Dilip Hiro, "How Bush's Iraqi Oil Grab Went Awry," *The Nation*, September 26, 2007

10/30/2002: George W. Bush wanted a working group about Iraq oil

"On October 30 [2002], Oil and Gas International revealed that the Bush administration wanted a working group of twelve to twenty people to (a) recommend ways to rehabilitate the Iraqi oil industry 'in order to increase oil exports to partially pay for a possible U.S. military occupation government,' (b) consider Iraq's continued membership of OPEC [Organization of Petroleum Exporting Countries], and (c) consider whether to honor contracts Saddam Hussein had granted to non-American oil companies."

—Dilip Hiro, "How Bush's Iraqi Oil Grab Went Awry," *The Nation*, September 26, 2007

[**Note:** Bush administration planning to take and redistribute Iraqi oil.]

2/24/2003: NSC secret briefing "Planning for the Iraqi Petr'
Infrastructure" attended by George W. Bush

"The morning of Monday, February 24 [2003], the president [Bush] attended a secret NSC briefing called 'Planning for the Iraqi Petroleum Infrastructure: Issues for Decision.' The president and the others had high hopes that
the Iraqi oil industry, if freed from U.N. sanctions, could be the fast track
for a new regime to reenter the world economy. Pamela Quanrud, a State
Department economist working on the NSC staff...[said] in the event of
war...they might face a cost of $7 billion to $8 billion to rebuild the oil
infrastructure if Saddam blew up the wells as he had done in 1991....Recov-
ery would have three phases. First, the military would secure the oil infrastructure. Then, the U.S. would work with a growing Iraqi civil administration to establish a temporary oil authority and resume production. The oil
authority would have an Iraqi chief operating officer and an advisory board
of Iraqi and international experts. Finally, once a new Iraqi government
took power, Iraqi management would be completely in control."

—Bob Woodward, *Plan of Attack*, Pages 322–323

[**Note:** Less than one month before attacking Iraq, a secret meeting
with George W. Bush about Iraqi oil.]

3/21/2003: George W. Bush: Iraq War day one "40 percent of the
country...85 percent of the oil fields" gained

"At 6 a.m. Iraq time on Friday, March 21 [2003], the 1st Marine Division
crossed the Kuwait-Iraq border, followed shortly by the Army's 3rd Infantry
Division....He [President Bush] told [British Prime Minister Tony] Blair,
'I would say we have 40 percent of the country easily and 85 percent of the
oil fields, and those are two unbelievable accomplishments for day one.'"

—Bob Woodward, *Plan of Attack*, Page 403

[**Note:** No word about casualties or WMD, just about oil.]

3/22/2003: Rumsfeld: US to secure oil fields which Iraqi people
"will need to develop their country"

On March 22, 2003, Rumsfeld said at a Pentagon news briefing: "'Our goal
is to defend the American people, and to eliminate Iraq's weapons of mass
destruction, and to liberate the Iraqi people.'" Additionally, "Military forces
also will 'secure Iraq's oil fields and resources, which belong to the Iraqi
people, and which they will need to develop their country after decades of
neglect by the Iraqi regime...'"

—Thom Shanker and Eric Schmitt, "A NATION AT WAR: THE PENTAGON;
Rumsfeld Says Iraq Is Collapsing, Lists 8 Objectives of War," *The New York Times*,
March 22, 2003

3/23/2003: George W. Bush reveals he had long term policy on Iraqi southern oil fields

President George W. Bush's concerns regarding the Operation Iraqi Freedom during a March 23, 2003, press question and answer session upon returning from Camp David: "One of the big concerns early on was the Southern oil fields. As you all remember, we had discussions about that. There was a lot of speculation about whether or not coalition forces would be able to get to the Southern oil fields in time, before—so that Saddam Hussein wouldn't destroy them. As a matter of fact, I had frequently talked about the Southern oil fields—or oil fields in general—in my declaratory policy."

—Office of the Press Secretary, "President Discusses Military Operation: Remarks by the President in Press Availability Upon Return From Camp David," George W. Bush—White House Archives, March 23, 2003

[**Note:** Bush's big concerns–Southern Iraq oil fields.]

3/24/2003: Pentagon announces potential $7 billion oil contract to subsidiary of Halliburton

"On 24 March, 2003 the Pentagon announced that it had awarded a contract to Kellogg Brown and Root (KBR), the engineering subsidiary of the multinational energy services company, Halliburton, for a sum that might total $7 billion. The contracts were to rebuild Iraq's oil infrastructure and, controversially, to import fuel for the domestic Iraqi market. Dick Cheney, the US vice-president, had served as Halliburton's chairman in the 1990s"

—Ali A. Allawi, *The Occupation of Iraq*, Page 252

3/27/2003: Wolfowitz says Iraqi oil will pay for Iraq war

Deputy Secretary of Defense Paul "Wolfowitz duly assured the House Appropriations Committee on March 27 [2003] that reconstruction would largely be covered by proceeds from Iraqi oil. Congress was told that oil revenues in Iraq could yield between $50 billion to $100 billion over the following two to three years. Wolfowitz argued, 'There's a lot of money to pay for this. It doesn't have to be U.S. taxpayer money.'"

—Stefan Halper and Jonathan Clarke, *America Alone*, Page 223

3/29/2003: George W. Bush: "We have secured more than 600 oil wells...Our efforts to protect the [oil] wealth that belongs to the Iraqi people are paying off"

President George W. Bush updating the world on the War in Iraq during a Radio Address on March 29, 2003: "In recent days, we have cleared mines from the water and taken control of a key port city, to allow humanitarian aid to begin flowing into the country. We have secured more than 600 oil wells and have begun putting out the few oil well fires set by the enemy. Our efforts to protect the wealth that belongs to the Iraqi people are paying off."

—Office of the Press Secretary, "President Discusses Iraqi Freedom Progress in Radio Address," George W. Bush—White House Archives, March 29, 2003

[**Note:** Ten days after invading Iraq, no mention of American casualties or WMD, just a word about our capturing Iraqi oil.]

4/9/2003: US troops guard Oil Ministry in Iraq specifically

"On entering Baghdad on April 9 [2003], the American troops stood by as looters burned and ransacked public buildings, including government ministries—except for the Oil Ministry, which they guarded diligently. Within the next few days, at a secret meeting in London, the Pentagon's scheme of the sale of all Iraqi oil fields got a go-ahead in principle."

—Dilip Hiro, "How Bush's Iraqi Oil Grab Went Awry," *The Nation*, September 26, 2007

4/15/2003: US oil companies take turns "guiding" Iraq's oil

"Executives of ConocoPhillips, ExxonMobil, Chevron, Shell, and BP each took a turn guiding Iraq's oil industry. Philip Carroll of Shell and Gary Vogler, a former ExxonMobil executive, were the first on the ground. They arrived in April 2003, just one month after the invasion. Officially, the two were the ranking U.S. advisers to the Iraqi Oil Ministry. Unofficially, the two ran the ministry." [*The fifteenth of the month used for date sorting purposes only.*]

—Antonia Juhasz, *The Tyranny of Oil*, Page 346

5/8/2003: Halliburton: Hopes Iraq first domino to fall so company can gain entry into other oil markets

John Gibson, chief executive of Halliburton Energy Service Group, said on May 8, 2003: "'We hope Iraq will be the first domino and that Libya and Iran will follow. We don't like being kept out of markets because it gives our competitors unfair advantage.'"

—Antonia Juhasz, *The Bush Agenda*, Page 147

[**Note:** Seemingly brutal commercial honesty.]

5/15/2003: George W. Bush executive order gives only oil companies "immunity against contractual disputes"

"In May 2003, President Bush signed an executive order that provides oil industry companies—and *only* oil companies—unprecedented immunity against contractual disputes or lawsuits resulting from discrimination, labor law abuses, environmental disasters, and human rights violations. [As reported in the August 8, 2003, edition of the *San Francisco Chronicle*] 'In terms of legal liability,' says Tom Devine, legal director of the Government Accountability Project, 'the executive order cancels the concept of corporate accountability and abandons the rule of law. It is a blank check for corporate anarchy, potentially robbing Iraqis of both their rights and their resources.'" [*The fifteenth of the month used for date sorting purposes only.*]

—Amy Goodman with David Goodman, *The Exception to the Rulers*, Page 68

[**Note:** A gift from Bush to oil companies in Iraq.]

5/22/2003: US and Britain, as "occupying powers," awarded themselves total control of Iraq's oil revenue to rebuild Iraq

"The US and Britain produced a blueprint for postwar Iraq. In this document, which was adopted by the UN in Resolution 1483 on 22 May 2003, the allies not only identified themselves as 'occupying powers' but awarded themselves total control of Iraq's oil revenues on the basis that it would be needed to rebuild Iraq's infrastructure. The US was aware that there would be a lot of resistance to oil privatization, which would see Iraqi oil handed over to multinational corporations. But quite apart from the enormous financial incentive, there is a crucial political goal. If the US can implement privatization of the Iraqi oil industry this will undermine the enormous power that the OPEC cartel currently wields on the global energy market—and perhaps OPEC countries might follow suit, with an oil privatization bonanza in the Middle East."

—Abdel Bari Atwan, *The Secret History of al Qaeda*, Page 198

[**Note:** Although prior to attacking Iraq, Bush and others in his administration sold us on the dangers of Hussein and his never-found WMD. Looking back, even soon after the invasion, it's hard to believe that Bush's Iraq War wasn't about Iraqi oil.]

6/4/2003: Wolfowitz: "The most important difference between North Korea and Iraq is that economically, we just had no choice in Iraq. The country swims on a sea of oil."

According to an article in *The Guardian* on June 4, 2003, Deputy Secretary of Defense Paul Wolfowitz said, at an Asian security summit in Singapore: "'The most important difference between North Korea and Iraq is that economically, we just had no choice in Iraq. The country swims on a sea of oil.'"

—Stefan Halper and Jonathan Clarke, *America Alone*, Page 155

[**Note:** It was oil, not WMD, not Hussein, just oil.]

7/17/2003: Judicial Watch finds that Cheney's Energy Task Force had detailed maps of Iraqi oil sites

A press release on July 17, 2003, by the public interest group Judicial Watch, which investigates and prosecutes governmental corruption, said that in proceedings against the Cheney Energy Task Force, they found "a highly detailed map of Iraq—showing none of the cities, none of the places where people lived, but showing in great detail the location of every single oil deposit known to exist in the country, with dotted lines demarcating blocks for promising exploration"

—Al Gore, *The Assault on Reason*, Page 118

9/6/2003: Britain's former Environmental Minister: The overriding motivation for US War on Terror is that US and UK are running out of energy supply, and demand for oil is increasing

According to a *Guardian* article written by Britain's former Environmental Minister Michael Meacher, on September 6, 2003: "'The overriding motivation [for the US war on terror]...is that the U.S. and the UK are beginning to run out of secure hydrocarbon energy supplies. By 2010 the Muslim world will control as much as 60% of the world's oil production and, even more importantly, 95% of remaining global oil export capacity. As demand is increasing, so supply is decreasing, continually since the 1960s.'"

—Amy Goodman with David Goodman, *The Exception to the Rulers*, Page 39

8/19/2005: Report shows US got over half of Iraq's oil exports

On August 19, 2005, "Energy Intelligence Research reported that more than 50 percent of all Iraq's oil exports went to the United States that month [August 2005]."

—Antonia Juhasz, *The Tyranny of Oil*, Page 352

8/30/2005: George W. Bush to protestors: US troops must protect Iraqi oil or terrorists would control it

"President Bush answered growing antiwar protests yesterday [August 30, 2005] with a fresh reason for US troops to continue fighting in Iraq: protection of the country's vast oil fields, which he said would otherwise fall under the control of terrorist extremists."

—Jennifer Loven, Associated Press, "Bush Gives New Reason for Iraq War," *The Boston Globe*, August 31, 2005

[**Note:** What about protecting our troops?]

11/5/2006: George W. Bush cites threat of terrorists using oil as weapon as reason to stay in Iraq

President "Bush has been citing oil as a reason to stay in Iraq. If the United States pulled its troops out prematurely and surrendered the country to insurgents, he warns audiences, it would effectively hand over Iraq's considerable petroleum reserves to terrorists who would use it as a weapon against other countries."

—Peter Baker, "Bush Says U.S. Pullout Would Let Iraq Radicals Use Oil as a Weapon," *The Washington Post*, November 5, 2006

[Note: Americans fighting and dying for US control of Iraqi oil.]

1/7/2007: *The Independent*: DC helped Baghdad write legislation in favor of US, UK controlling oil

According to *The Independent*, on January 7, 2007: "[I]n early 2007, the government that the United States helped to establish in Baghdad enacted legislation that was written in Washington to give U.S. and British oil companies the dominant role in exploiting the massive oil reserves of Iraq."

—Al Gore, *The Assault on Reason*, Page 119

1/23/2007: George W. Bush SOTU: Foreign oil dependence "leaves us more vulnerable to hostile regimes"

In his January 23, 2007, State of the Union address, President George W. Bush said: "For too long our nation has been dependent on foreign oil. And this dependence leaves us more vulnerable to hostile regimes, and to terrorists—who could cause huge disruptions of oil shipments, and raise the price of oil, and do great harm to our economy."

—George W. Bush, "President Bush Delivers State of the Union Address," George W. Bush—White House Archives, January 23, 2007

[Note: Oil, in Bush's State of the Union address.]

9/16/2007: Greenspan cites Iraq War as largely about oil

"America's elder statesman of finance, Alan Greenspan, has shaken the White House by declaring that the prime motive for the war in Iraq was oil.

In his long-awaited memoir, to be published tomorrow [September 17, 2007], Greenspan, a Republican whose 18-year tenure as head of the US Federal Reserve was widely admired, will also deliver a stinging critique of President George W Bush's economic policies. However, it is his view on the motive for the 2003 Iraq invasion that is likely to provoke the most controversy.

'I am saddened that it is politically inconvenient to acknowledge what everyone knows: the Iraq war is largely about oil,' he says.

Greenspan, 81, is understood to believe that Saddam Hussein posed a threat to the security of oil supplies in the Middle East."

—Graham Paterson, "Alan Greenspan claims Iraq war was really for oil," *The Times of London*, thetimes.co.uk, September 16, 2007

[**Note:** A widely admired Republican saying the Iraq War is largely about oil.]

10/15/2007: Abizaid, retired head of US Central Command and military operations in Iraq, about Iraq War: "Of course it's about oil, we can't really deny that"

According to the October 15, 2007, edition of the *Standard Daily*, General John Abizaid, the retired head of US Central Command and military operations in Iraq, said of the Iraq War: "'Of course it's about oil, we can't really deny that.'"

—Antonia Juhasz, *The Tyranny of Oil*, Page 319

[**Note:** A high-ranking Bush administration general with on-the-ground Iraq War experience saying the war was about oil.]

Misleading or lying to us in order to take our country into an unnecessary war with Iraq is a strong charge. If true, that action should carry a strong penalty for causing so much unnecessary death and destruction.

Were those brave American soldiers who joined the Iraq War to protect our country from Hussein and his supposed WMD conned into putting their lives on the line for oil? Given the preceding quotes, I submit it is hard to conclude otherwise.

Would the Americans who volunteered to fight in Iraq have done so if they knew the war was about oil?

Would parents have supported their young adults going to war for Iraqi oil?

Would our Congress have voted to give George W. Bush the power to attack Iraq if they knew the war was about oil?

Few would say yes to the above questions.

Unfortunately, neither our soldiers who fought in the 2003 Iraq War nor the parents of those kids nor Congress had a chance to say no to a war for oil given Bush and some in his administration continually told our country and Congress that going into Iraq was necessary to protect us from Hussein and his WMD.

B. TEN FALSE AND MISLEADING REASONS BUSH GAVE AS SUPPORT FOR OUR NEED TO ATTACK IRAQ

As PRESIDENT, AND AS our commander-in-chief, George W. Bush gave various reasons of why we needed to attack Iraq.

Unfortunately, those reasons were unsubstantiated, misleading, or false when Bush gave them. Nor did they hold up to scrutiny after we invaded Iraq—when we could go anywhere, inspect anything, and talk with virtually anyone.

1. Bush: Iraq is a serious and immediate threat
2. Bush: Saddam Hussein has WMD
3. Bush: Iraq was connected with 9/11, bin Laden or Al-Qaeda
4. Bush: Saddam Hussein tried to buy uranium from Niger
5. Bush: Saddam Hussein has nuclear programs
6. Bush: Saddam Hussein has biological and chemical weapons
7. Bush: Congress knew what I knew when they voted to give me the power to attack Iraq
8. Bush: Saddam Hussein gassed his own and other people
9. Bush: Saddam Hussein attacked Kuwait
10. Summary: Bush used cherry-picked, false, and misleading information to lead our country into war with Iraq

1. Bush: Iraq is a serious and immediate threat

IMMEDIATELY AFTER BECOMING PRESIDENT, George W. Bush and others in his administration began saying that Iraq was a serious and immediate threat to our country. However, Bush's scaremongering wasn't supported by credible facts or intel.

The following quotes show that Iraq wasn't a serious or immediate threat while the gray box quotes show Bush and others spreading false facts and fears about the danger from Hussein.

9/19/2002: Rumsfeld: "no terrorist state poses a greater or more immediate threat to the security of our people than the regime of Saddam Hussein"

Rumsfeld during opening statements of a Senate hearing on September 19, 2002, titled "U.S. Policy On Iraq": "There are a number of terrorist states pursuing weapons of mass destruction—Iran, Libya, North Korea, Syria, just to name a few—but no terrorist state poses a greater or more immediate threat to the security of our people than the regime of Saddam Hussein in Iraq."

—Defense Secretary Donald Rumsfeld, "U.S. Policy On Iraq: Hearings Before The Committee On Armed Services United States Senate One Hundred Seventh Congress Second Session," US Government Printing Office, September 19, 2002

10/2/2002: George W. Bush: "On its present course, the Iraqi regime is a threat of unique urgency."

President George W. Bush in the Rose Garden on October 2, 2002, announcing that the House and the Senate had agreed on a course of action regarding Iraq: "On its present course, the Iraqi regime is a threat of unique urgency. We know the treacherous history of the regime. It has waged a war against its neighbors; it has sponsored and sheltered terrorists; it has developed weapons of mass death; it has used them against innocent men, women and children. We know the designs of the Iraqi regime. In defiance of pledges to the U.N., it has stockpiled biological and chemical weapons. It is rebuilding the facilities used to make those weapons. U.N. inspectors believe that Iraq could have produce enough biological and chemical agent to kill millions of people. The regime has the scientists and facilities to build nuclear weapons, and is seeking the materials needed to do so."

—Office of the Press Secretary, "President, House Leadership Agree on Iraq Resolution—The Rose Garden," George W. Bush—White House Archives, October 2, 2002

10/7/2002: George W. Bush: "The danger is already significant... does it make any sense for the world to wait to confront [Hussein] as he...develops even more dangerous weapons?"

President George W. Bush's remarks on October 7, 2002, from the Cincinnati Museum Center—Cincinnati Union Terminal in Ohio: "While there are many dangers in the world, the threat from Iraq stands alone—because it gathers the most serious dangers of our age in one place.

Iraq's weapons of mass destruction are controlled by a murderous tyrant who has already used chemical weapons to kill thousands of people. This same tyrant has tried to dominate the Middle East, has invaded and brutally occupied a small neighbor, has struck other nations without warning, and holds an unrelenting hostility toward the United States.... Some ask how urgent this danger is to America and the world. The danger is already significant, and it only grows worse with time. If we know Saddam Hussein has dangerous weapons today—and we do—does it make any sense for the world to wait to confront him as he grows even stronger and develops even more dangerous weapons?"

—Office of the Press Secretary, "President Bush Outlines Iraqi Threat—Remarks by the President on Iraq, Cincinnati Museum Center—Cincinnati Union Terminal, Cincinnati, Ohio," George W. Bush—White House Archives, NSarchive2.gwu.edu, October 7, 2002

[Note: Bush again said that Iraq had weapons of mass destruction, without credible intel to support that claim. No such weapons were ever found.]

11/20/2002: George W. Bush: Iraq a "unique and urgent threat," should not be allowed to produce, possess WMD

In a statement from Prague, Czech Republic, on November 20, 2002, President Bush said: "Today the world is also uniting to answer the unique and urgent threat posed by Iraq. A dictator who has used weapons of mass destruction on his own people must not be allowed to produce or possess those weapons."

—"Remarks to the Prague Atlantic Student Summit in Prague: November 20, 2002," Public Papers of the Presidents of the United States, 2002, Book II, July 1 to December 31, 2002, US Government Printing Office, books.Google.com, Page 2103

[Note: Bush's words "unique and urgent threat" were scary, but no intel to support those claims was ever found.]

1/15/2003: George W. Bush administration ratcheting up its claims of Iraq's imminent threat while intelligence reports were continuing to say the opposite

"By January 2003, when the Bush administration was ratcheting up its claims of Iraq's imminent threat, the intelligence reports were continuing to say the exact opposite—that Saddam Hussein had no intention of attacking the United States, unless he was about to be attacked first.

The intelligence assessment found that 'Saddam probably will not initiate hostilities for fear of providing Washington with justification to invade Iraq. Nevertheless, he might deal the first blow, especially if he perceives that an attack intended to end his regime is imminent.' But intelligence estimates are only predictions, and when they don't agree with a president's preconceived views, they are often ignored." [*The fifteenth of the month used for date sorting purposes only.*]

—James Bamford, *A Pretext for War*, Pages 382–383

7/9/2004: The 2002 NIE Report implies that the "exaggerations, overstatements, and misreadings of the CIA's estimate writers all fail in one direction—describing Iraq as more dangerous than it really was"

"The [Senate Intelligence Committee] report [released on July 9, 2004] reaches 117 separate conclusions about the October 2002 NIE and other matters relating to prewar intelligence about Iraq, and it is fair to say that almost every one contains a more or less stinging rebuke of the CIA. The report does not say, but unmistakably implies with persuasive detail, that the exaggerations, overstatements, and misreadings of the CIA's estimate writers all fail in one direction—describing Iraq as more dangerous than it really was."

—Thomas Powers, *The Military Error*, Page 19

[**Note:** The October 2002 NIE and its exaggerations and misrepresentations were one of the reasons Congress voted to give Bush the authority to attack Iraq.]

2. Bush: Saddam Hussein has WMD

DURING THE RUN-UP TO our attacking Iraq on March 19, 2003, George W. Bush and a few of his people repeatedly told Americans that Saddam had WMD.

The following quotes illustrate why Bush couldn't find any Iraqi WMD.

The quotes in gray boxes show Bush and his staff, regardless of the intel he was receiving to the contrary, continuing to convince our country that we needed to attack Iraq because of their WMD.

8/7/1995: Hussein's son-in-law says Iraq destroyed all weapons (biological, chemical, missile, nuclear) in 1991

"On the night of August 7, 1995, Hussein Kamel, the son-in-law of Saddam Hussein, fled Baghdad [Iraq] and sought asylum in Jordan. Two weeks later, he sat down in an Amman villa with senior U.N. inspectors who had spent years trying to ferret out details of Iraq's nuclear, chemical, and biological weapons programs. Now they had the ultimate source,

had no reason to lie. Kamel had been the second most power-
Iraq until he fled in fear of Saddam's psychopathic son Uday.
rtant, he had been directly in charge of all military industry.
stion…was the location and quantity of Saddam's remaining
or the so-called weapons of mass destruction. There were none,
he replied, none at all. In 1991, following some initial successes by the
inspectors, on Saddam's instructions he had 'ordered destruction of all
chemical weapons. All weapons—biological, chemical, missile, nuclear
were destroyed' and the programs for producing them dismantled. He
told exactly the same story to the CIA and Britain's MI6 [foreign intelligence service]."

—Andrew Cockburn, *Rumsfeld*, Pages 145–146

3/15/1999: UN concludes Iraq dismantled bulk of weapons program, but Iraq still needed monitoring

"Barred from Iraq, UNSCOM's mandate ended when a UN panel concluded, in March 1999, that the bulk of Iraq's weapons programmes had been
dismantled, but that Iraq continued to require an ongoing monitoring and
verification system for whatever WMD might have eluded UNSCOM's inspectors." [*The fifteenth of the month used for date sorting purposes only.*]

—Ali A. Allawi, *The Occupation of Iraq*, Page 71

10/31/1999: Iraq says it will cooperate unconditionally with UNSCOM, but UNSCOM Chairman Butler says Iraq was withholding full cooperation

"By the end of October, 1999, Iraq had asked for the departure of the weapons inspection team from its territory, but then in an about-turn announced
its intention to cooperate unconditionally with UNSCOM. This was not
sufficient, however, to stop the UNSCOM chairman, Richard Butler, from
declaring that Iraq was withholding its full cooperation."

—Ali A. Allawi, *The Occupation of Iraq*, Page 71

2/22/2001: George W. Bush says of Hussein that "if we catch him developing weapons of mass destruction, we'll take the appropriate action"

"Echoing Blair, [President] Bush said [on February 22, 2001], 'A change in
sanctions should not in any way, shape, or form, embolden Saddam Hussein. He has got to understand that we are going to watch him carefully
and, if we catch him developing weapons of mass destruction, we'll take
the appropriate action.'…Saddam was viewed more as a 'problem' to deal

with than a 'grave and gathering danger' in the early days. Talk centered on if he was developing WMD, not that he was developing them."

—Scott McClellan, *What Happened*, Page 94

[**Note:** Bush and his administration watching to see *if* Hussein would develop WMD.]

2/24/2001: Powell: "[S]anctions exist...for the purpose of keeping in check...Hussein's ambitions toward developing weapons of mass destruction"

On February 24, 2001, Powell remarked to Egyptian Foreign Minister Amre Houssa: "[S]anctions exist—not for the purpose of hurting the Iraqi people, but for the purpose of keeping in check Saddam Hussein's ambitions toward developing weapons of mass destruction. We should constantly be reviewing our policies, constantly be looking at those sanctions to make sure that they are directed toward that purpose. That purpose is every bit as important now as it was 10 years ago when we began it. And frankly they have worked. He has not developed any significant capability with respect to weapons of mass destruction. He is unable to project conventional power against his neighbors."

—Joe Conason, "That Smoking Powell Video," Salon.com, September 26, 2003

[**Note:** A month into the Bush presidency, Powell confirms the sanctions have worked as Hussein "has not developed any significant capability with respect to" WMD, as stated in the quote above.]

3/11/2002: Blair: "Let's be under no doubt whatever, Saddam Hussein has acquired weapons of mass destruction over a long period of time."

In a March 11, 2002, press conference at 10 Downing Street after meeting with Vice President Cheney, UK Prime Minister Tony Blair said: "'Let's be under no doubt whatever, Saddam Hussein has acquired weapons of mass destruction over a long period of time. He's the only leader in the world that's actually used chemical weapons against his own people. He is in breach of at least nine UN Security Council resolutions about weapons of mass destruction.' Blair concluded, 'That there is a threat from Saddam Hussein and the weapons of mass destruction that he has acquired is not in doubt at all.'"

—Dick Cheney, *In My Time*, Pages 373–374

[**Note:** The words *has acquired* artfully suggest the past is the present.]

6/15/2002: Rumsfeld to NATO: The "absence of evidence [of WMD] is not evidence of absence"

"Rumsfeld has articulated the justification for preemptive action [in Iraq] by stating [before NATO officials in Brussels, Belgium, in June 2002] that the 'absence of evidence is not evidence of absence of weapons of mass destruction.'" [*The fifteenth of the month used for date sorting purposes only.*]

—Foreign Affairs, *The U.S. vs. al Qaeda*, Pages 122–123

[**Note:** In effect, Rumsfeld saying he has no evidence of Iraqi WMD less than a year before we attacked Iraq for having WMD.]

8/26/2002: Cheney: There is no doubt Hussein *now has* WMD

In "a speech Vice President Cheney gave to the Veterans of Foreign Wars on August 26, 2002...he said, 'Simply stated, there is no doubt that Saddam Hussein now has weapons of mass destruction. There is no doubt he is amassing them to use against our friends, against our allies, and against us.' Later in the speech, the vice president would tell the VFW, 'Many of us are convinced that [Saddam] will acquire nuclear weapons fairly soon.'"

Then-CIA Director George Tenet said: "The [VFW] speech caught me and my top people off guard for several reasons. For starters, the vice president's staff had not sent the speech to CIA for clearance, as was usually done with remarks that should be based on intelligence. The speech also went well beyond what our analysis could support. The intelligence community's belief was that, left unchecked, Iraq would probably not acquire nuclear weapons until near the end of the decade."

—George Tenet with Bill Harlow, *At the Center of the Storm*, Page 315

[**Note:** When Cheney made his claim that Hussein *now has WMD*, he had no credible intel that Hussein had them.]

9/6/2002: Franks: "[W]e've been looking for Scud missiles and other weapons of mass destruction for ten years and haven't found any yet"

On September 6, 2002, Central Command leader General Tommy Franks and Rumsfeld "briefed the president [Bush] and the NSC on the latest war planning....But General Franks had something important to add. 'Mr. President,' he said, 'we've been looking for Scud missiles and other weapons of mass destruction for ten years and haven't found any yet, so I can't tell you that I know that there are any specific weapons anywhere. I haven't seen Scud one.'"

—Bob Woodward, *Plan of Attack*, Page 173

9/15/2002: Tenet: A member of Hussein's inner circle reported that Iraq had no active WMD program

"At a [mid-September 2002] meeting with [President] Bush, Cheney, and Rice, CIA director Tenet says that a member of Saddam Hussein's inner circle, his foreign minister Naji Sabri, had made a deal to reveal Iraq's military secrets to the CIA and reported that there was 'no active weapons of mass destruction program.'" [*The fifteenth of the month used for date sorting purposes only.*]

—Frank Rich, *The Greatest Story Ever Sold*, Pages 246–247

9/19/2002: Bush: "The biggest threat, however, is Saddam Hussein and his weapons of mass destruction."

"On September 19 [2002], the president [Bush] met with 11 House members in the Cabinet Room. 'The war on terrorism is going okay; we are hunting down al Qaeda one-by-one,' Bush began. 'The biggest threat, however, is Saddam Hussein and his weapons of mass destruction. He can blow up Israel and that would trigger an international conflict....We will take over the oil fields early—and mitigate the oil shock'"

—Bob Woodward, *Plan of Attack*, Page 186

[Note: Bush said that Hussein has WMD, but none were ever found; Bush did find the Iraqi oil.]

10/4/2002: Tenet's 'Iraq's Weapons of Mass Destruction Programs' document represented an unqualified case that Hussein possessed WMD

Following the release of the classified National Intelligence Estimate on October 1, 2002, Senator Bob Graham (D-FL) called for an unclassified version as well. "In response, on October 4 [2002], Tenet presented a twenty-five-page document called 'Iraq's Weapons of Mass Destruction Programs.' But it was exactly the opposite of what Graham had requested. According to Graham, 'It represented an unqualified case that Hussein possessed [weapons of mass destruction]...and omitted the dissenting opinions contained in the classified version. Its conclusions, such as *If Baghdad acquired sufficient weapons-grade fissile material from abroad, it could make a nuclear weapon within a year,* underscored the White House's claim that exactly such material was being provided from Africa to Iraq.'"

—Craig Unger, *The Fall of the House of Bush*, Page 265

11/8/2002: George W. Bush: Hussein must fully disclose and destroy his WMD

President Bush on the United Nations vote on Resolution 1441 on November 7, 2002: "Good morning. With the resolution just passed, the United Nations Security Council has met important responsibilities, upheld its principles and given clear and fair notice that Saddam Hussein must fully disclose and destroy his weapons of mass destruction. He must submit to any and all methods to verify his compliance."

—George W. Bush, "President Pleased with U.N. Vote," George W. Bush—White House Archives, November 8, 2002

[**Note:** Bush again stating Hussein had WMD.]

12/5/2002: Ari Fleischer confirming George W. Bush and Rumsfeld claims that Iraq *has* WMD

"White House spokesman Ari Fleischer said on December 5, 2002: 'The president of the United States [Bush] and the secretary of defense [Rumsfeld] would not assert as plainly and bluntly as they have that Iraq has weapons of mass destruction if it was not true, and if they did not have a solid basis for saying it.'"

—Bob Woodward, *State of Denial*, Page 139

1/25/2003: Libby reports Iraq concealing, moving, and buying items—they had to be WMD; Hussein ties to Al-Qaeda were extensive

"On January 25 [2003], in the White House Situation Room...Libby claimed that intercepts and human intelligence reports indicated that Iraq had been concealing, moving, and burying items....they had to be WMDs. He reported that Saddam's ties to al-Qaeda were extensive."

—Michael Isikoff and David Corn, *Hubris*, Page 175

[**Note:** Despite Libby's claims, neither was found to be true.]

1/31/2003: UK memo claims George W. Bush, Blair came up with second plan for attack for when no WMD found

"The memo, written [by UK Chief Foreign Policy Advisor David Manning] on 31 January 2003, almost two months before the invasion [of Iraq] and seen by the Observer, confirms that as the two men [President Bush and UK Prime Minister Blair] became increasingly aware UN inspectors would fail to find weapons of mass destruction (WMD) they had to contemplate alternative scenarios that might trigger a second resolution legitimising military action. Bush told Blair the US had drawn up a provocative plan 'to fly U2 reconnaissance aircraft painted in UN colours over Iraq with fighter cover'. Bush said that if Saddam fired at the planes this would put the Iraqi leader in breach of UN resolutions."

—Jamie Doward, Gaby Hinsliff and Mark Townsend, "Confidential Memo Reveals US Plan to Provoke an Invasion of Iraq," *The Guardian*, June 21, 2009

[**Note:** Two months before invading Iraq, Bush and Blair were so concerned no WMD would be found in Iraq that Bush concocted a plan to further con the American people into the Iraq War.]

2/8/2003: Hussein to UK's Benn: No WMD "whatsoever"

According to the *National Journal* on February 8, 2003: "Saddam Hussein told Tony Benn, a visiting British member of Parliament, '[t]here is only one truth....As I have said on many occasions before…Iraq has no weapons of mass destruction whatsoever.'"

—Karen DeYoung, *Soldier*, Page 450

2/14/2003: The UN team found no WMD in Iraq

"Saddam [Hussein] had presented a massive document to the UN [in December 2002], claiming that he had no WMD [weapons of mass destruction]. [Chief UN weapons inspector] Hans Blix had corroborated this, by stating to the Security Council on 14 February, 2003, that the UN team had found no WMD in Iraq."

—Ali A. Allawi, *The Occupation of Iraq*, Page 88

[**Note:** The UN team found no WMD about five weeks before Bush's invasion.]

3/5/2003: Rice: Interviews after liberation *would* reveal location of the WMD

"On March 5 [2003], Blix on the phone with Rice asked her point-blank if the United States knew where Iraq's WMDs were hidden. 'No, she said, but interviews after liberation would reveal it.'"

—Thomas Powers, *The Military Error*, Page 121

[**Note:** No such WMD were ever found.]

3/15/2003: Tel Aviv University study: No banned weapons in Iraq

"[A] study produced by Tel Aviv University's Jaffee Center for Strategic Studies [in November 2003] indicates that Israel's vaunted intelligence services could find no indication that Iraq possessed banned weapons, despite their location and access to Middle East sources. 'On the eve of the war [March 2003],' said the report, 'Israeli intelligence on Iraqi capabilities resembled its counterparts in the United States and other Western countries. It had not received any information regarding weapons of mass destruction and surface-to-surface missiles for nearly eight years.'" [*The fifteenth of the month used for date sorting purposes only.*]

—James Bamford, *A Pretext for War*, Page 309

3/16/2003: George W. Bush: The dictator of Iraq and *his* WMD are a threat to the security of free nations

On March 16, 2003, during a press conference in Portugal with President Bush, Prime Minister Blair, President Aznar, and Prime Minister Barroso, Bush said: "The dictator of Iraq [Saddam] and his weapons of mass destruction are a threat to the security of free nations."

—George W. Bush, "President Bush: Monday 'Moment of Truth' for World on Iraq," George W. Bush—White House Archives, March 16, 2003

[**Note:** George W. Bush, at a press conference three days before he invaded Iraq, again saying that Hussein had WMD, a statement never found to be true.]

3/16/2003: Cheney: We believe Hussein has, in fact, reconstituted nuclear weapons, and has a long-standing relationship with Al-Qaeda

On March 16, 2003, Vice President Cheney appeared on NBC's *Meet the Press* and "told Tim Russert that Saddam was hoarding unconventional weapons and had 'a long-standing relationship' with al-Qaeda. Cheney dismissed the IAEA's finding that Saddam had not revived its nuclear weapons program. 'We believe,' Cheney said, 'he has, in fact, reconstituted nuclear weapons.'"

—Michael Isikoff and David Corn, *Hubris*, Page 208

[**Note:** No "reconstituted nuclear weapons" or a long-standing relationship with Al-Qaeda were ever found.]

3/17/2003: George W. Bush to Senate and House leaders: Will invade even if Hussein leaves so we can get the WMD

On March 17, 2003, President "Bush greeted the Senate and House leaders in the Roosevelt Room...He described his [upcoming] speech, the 48-hour ultimatum [for Saddam and his sons to leave Iraq]....'The Iraqi generals are war criminals,' he told them and added a new and significant twist. 'If Saddam Hussein leaves, we'll go in anyway. That way we can avoid ethnic cleansing.'...Going in was important to get the WMD and to deal with the Baath Party leadership."

—Bob Woodward, *Plan of Attack*, Pages 368–369

[**Note:** George W. Bush confirming two days before attacking Iraq, that they had WMD—which were never found.]

3/17/2003: George W. Bush: *No doubt* Iraq regime possesses and conceals "most lethal weapons ever devised"

In President George W. Bush's Address to the Nation on March 17, 2003, stating that Saddam had forty-eight hours to leave Iraq, he said: "Intelligence gathered by this and other governments leaves no doubt that the Iraq regime continues to possess and conceal some of the most lethal weapons ever devised. This regime has already used weapons of mass destruction against Iraq's neighbors and against Iraq's people....The United States and other nations did nothing to deserve or invite this threat."

—Office of the Press Secretary, "President Says Saddam Hussein Must Leave Iraq Within 48 Hours," George W. Bush—White House Archives, March 17, 2003

[**Note:** Despite Bush saying there was "no doubt" Iraq continued to possess the most lethal weapons ever devised, no such weapons were ever found.]

3/18/2003: UK's Cook: "Iraq probably has no [WMD] in the commonly understood sense of the term"

As reported by *CNN* on March 18, 2003, during a speech to announce his resignation in protest of the planned invasion of Iraq, British House of Commons leader Robin Cook stated: "'Iraq probably has no weapons of mass destruction in the commonly understood sense of the term—namely a credible device capable of being delivered against a strategic city target. It probably still has biological toxins and battlefield chemical munitions, but it has had them since the 1980s when US companies sold Saddam anthrax agents and the then British Government approved chemical and munitions factories.'"

—Philip Taylor, *The War in Iraq—A Failure of Honesty*, Page 132

[**Note:** An important statement—unfortunately only given a day before we attacked Iraq.]

3/19/2003: The US and coalition forces invade Iraq[72]

---

[72] The start of the Iraq War is March 19, 2003, when President Bush announced the invasion to the US. The start date of the Iraq invasion is March 20, 2003.

3/21/2003: George W. Bush, Cheney: Intend to liberate Iraq, remove WMD

Following a meeting with congressional leaders on March 21, 2003, President Bush said: "I've asked the members of Congress to come up so that members of my administration can keep the leadership up-to-date as the war to liberate Iraq and to remove weapons of mass destruction out of Iraq proceeds. The military briefings, of course, will continue to be given out of the Pentagon. Secretary Rumsfeld will be briefing this afternoon....

As Secretary Rumsfeld said, we're making progress. We will stay on task until we've achieved our objective, which is to rid Iraq of weapons of mass destruction, and free the Iraqi people so they can live in a society that is hopeful and democratic and at peace in its neighborhood."

—Office of the Press Secretary, "President Thanks Congress—Remarks by the President in Meeting with Congressional Leaders," George W. Bush—White House Archives, March 21, 2003

3/22/2003: George W. Bush: Mission to disarm Iraq of WMD

President Bush on the beginning of Operation Iraqi Freedom: "American and coalition forces have begun a concerted campaign against the regime of Saddam Hussein. In this war, our coalition is broad, more than 40 countries from across the globe. Our cause is just, the security of the nations we serve and the peace of the world. And our mission is clear, to disarm Iraq of weapons of mass destruction, to end Saddam Hussein's support for terrorism, and to free the Iraqi people."

—George W. Bush, "President Discusses Beginning of Operation Iraqi Freedom—President's Radio Address," George W. Bush—White House Archives, March 22, 2003

[**Note:** No WMD were ever found to disarm.]

3/25/2003: George W. Bush: More than 200,000 men and women engaged in Operation Iraqi Freedom that could kill thousands

After submitting the Wartime Budget, on March 25, 2003, President Bush stated: "I've just met with our leaders here at the Pentagon, who are monitoring the course of our battle to free Iraq and rid that country of weapons of mass destruction. Our coalition is on a steady advance. We're making good progress....Our coalition is strong. It's bound together by the principle of protecting not only this nation, but all nations from a brutal regime that is armed with weapons that could kill thousands of innocent people. America has more than 200,000 men and women engaged in Operation Iraqi Freedom."

—George W. Bush, "President Submits Wartime Budget," George W. Bush—White House Archives, March 25, 2003

3/26/2003: George W. Bush: "We are also taking every actio[n] can to prevent the Iraqi regime from using its hi[dden] weapons of mass destruction"

From MacDill Air Force Base President George W. Bush responded to questions about Iraq: "We are also taking every action we can to prevent the Iraqi regime from using its hidden weapons of mass destruction. We are attacking the command structure that could order the use of those weapons. Coalition troops have taken control of hundreds of square miles of territory to prevent the launch of missiles, and chemical or biological weapons."

—George W. Bush, "President Rallies Troops at MacDill Air Force Base in Tampa," George W. Bush—White House Archives, March 26, 2003

[Note: Bush still saying that Iraq had WMD, but none were ever found.]

3/27/2003: Bush and Prime Minister Blair; Hussein had twelve years to get rid of his WMD and didn't

During a press conference with President Bush and Prime Minister Blair, where Bush outlined plans for Iraq, Blair said: "that I understand why people hesitate before committing to conflict and to war. War is a brutal and a bloody business. But we are faced with the situation where Saddam Hussein has been given 12 years to disarm voluntarily of weapons of mass destruction, that the whole of the international community accepts is a threat, and he has not done so. Instead, what we have had is 12 years in which he has remained in power with these weapons intact and brutalized his own people."

—George W. Bush, "President Bush, Prime Minister Blair Hold Press Availability," George W. Bush—White House Archives, March 27, 2003

[Note: Despite Bush's claim, evidence shows that Hussein had years before disarmed his country of WMD.] *Blocade!*

3/30/2003: Rumsfeld: I made a *misstatement* and should've said "suspect" WMD sites

Rumsfeld wrote: "Early in the war [March 30, 2003], while major combat operations were still underway, I was asked on a news program if I was concerned about the failure to find WMD in Iraq. I had always tried to speak with reserve and precision on intelligence matters, but on this occasion, I made a misstatement. Recalling the CIA's designation of various 'suspect' WMD sites in Iraq, I replied, 'We know where they are. They're in the area around Tikrit and Baghdad.' I should have used the phrase 'suspect sites.' My words have been quoted many times by critics of the war as an example of how the Bush administration misled the public."

—Donald Rumsfeld, *Known and Unknown*, Page 435

[**Note:** Can you imagine your son or daughter being killed or wounded in the Iraq War defending our country from the Iraq WMD they were told many times were there? Then the Secretary of Defense says, *Oops, I should have said we "suspect" Iraq has them.*]

5/7/2003: Press Sec. Fleischer: "One of the reasons that we went to war" was because of Iraq's possession of weapons of mass destruction

White House Press Secretary Ari Fleischer was questioned during a press briefing on Iraq on May 7, 2003:

"Q: Well, we went to war, didn't we, to find these—because we said that these weapons were a direct and imminent threat to the United States? Isn't that true?

MR. FLEISCHER: Absolutely. One of the reasons that we went to war was because of their possession of weapons of mass destruction. And nothing has changed on that front at all. We said what we said because we meant it."

—"Press Briefing by Ari Fleischer," The American Presidency Project, Presidency.
UCSB.edu, May 7, 2003

5/29/2003: George W. Bush: We have found WMD, two mobile labs

"'We have found the weapons of mass destruction,' [President] Bush proclaimed the next day [May 29, 2003] in an interview with a Polish television journalist....'You remember when Colin Powell stood up in front of the world, and he said, Iraq has got laboratories, mobile labs to build biological weapons...and we've so far discovered two. And we'll find more weapons as time goes on.'"

—Michael Isikoff and David Corn, *Hubris,* Page 227

[**Note:** Several months later it was confirmed that those two mobile WMD labs were found to produce hydrogen for weather balloons—they literally produced hot air.]

7/29/2003: CIA: No WMD, but George W. Bush seemed disengaged

On July 29, 2003, CIA chief weapons inspector in Iraq David Kay briefed President Bush and his cabinet on his findings. "Kay tried to be gentle.... But he couldn't avoid the bottom line: He had found nothing....But the president seemed disengaged.

'I'm not sure I've spoken to anyone at that level who seemed less inquisitive,' Kay recalled....'I cannot stress too much,' he subsequently remarked, 'that the president was the one in the room who was the least unhappy and the least disappointed about the lack of WMDs.'"

—Michael Isikoff and David Corn, *Hubris*, Pages 310–311

[**Note:** A tragic but profound observation.]

12/16/2003: George W. Bush didn't see difference between Iraq actually having weapons and their capacity to make them

"Asked by Diane Sawyer of ABC News in December [16] 2003 about the assertion that Saddam possessed actual weapons, as opposed to the capacity to make or get them, [President] Bush replied, 'So what's the difference?' In that interview and others, he hewed to one version or another of the line: 'Saddam Hussein was a threat, and the fact that he is gone means that America is a safer country.'"

—Todd S. Purdum and *The New York Times* Staff, *A Time of Our Choosing*, Page 290

[**Note:** The families and friends of the thousands of Americans and of the hundreds of thousands from other nations who died or were wounded because of the Iraq War surely knew the difference between *having* WMD and having the *capacity* to make or get them. It was as if Bush didn't care if Hussein had WMD or might get them—he got his war and the Iraqi oil.]

1/23/2004: Kay replaced, says Iraqi WMD stockpiles cited as justification for war "did not exist"

"On Friday, January 23 [2004], the CIA announced without explanation that David Kay had been replaced as head of the Iraq Survey Group [ISG] hunting for weapons of mass destruction.

In an interview that afternoon, Kay told reporters that the weapons stockpiles cited as justification for the war did not exist."

—Karen DeYoung, *Soldier*, Pages 487–488

10/6/2004: Kay's successor as ISG Head Duelfer presents comprehensive report to Congress: Hussein's WMD capability destroyed in 1991

"On October 6 [2004], Charles Duelfer, David Kay's successor as head of the WMD-hunting Iraq Survey Group, presented his comprehensive report to Congress....Saddam's WMD capability, it said, 'was essentially destroyed in 1991.'"

—Michael Isikoff and David Corn, *Hubris*, Page 374

[**Note:** When was Bush first told that Saddam's WMD were destroyed in 1991?]   *Worst day of his life*

12/13/2004: Powell: If I had known there were no WMD, "I never would have said there were stockpiles"

In an interview with *Paris Match* on December 13, 2004, Powell said: "'If I had known there were no stockpiles [of weapons of mass destruction (WMD) in Iraq], I never would have said there were stockpiles.'"

—Karen DeYoung, *Soldier*, Page 485

[**Note:** First Rumsfeld, now Powell, *correcting* his prior *misstatement* about Iraq having WMD, the basis for pushing our country into the Iraq War.]

4/25/2005: CIA closes investigation after no WMD found

"CIA's top weapons inspector in Iraq [Duelfer] said Monday [April 25, 2005] that the hunt for weapons of mass destruction has 'gone as far as feasible' and has found nothing, closing an investigation into the purported programs of Saddam Hussein that were used to justify the 2003 invasion."

—Associated Press, "CIA's Final Report: No WMD Found in Iraq," NBCNews.com, April 25, 2005

[**Note:** Hundreds of thousands of people died because Bush and senior members of his administration falsely told our country that Hussein had those WMD when they had no credible intel supporting their statements. Can Bush's actions not be a crime?]

2/18/2008: BBC: UK final dossier for Iraq War "sexed up" with insertion of misleading WMD claim

"The [UK] Government has today [February 18, 2008] been forced to publish the secret first draft of the infamous dodgy dossier which led the country into war with Iraq.

Ministers have fought through the courts for three years to prevent the revelation of the draft, written in September 2002 by John Williams, then-head of communications at the [British] Foreign Office.

The final dossier became notorious amid allegations by the BBC that it had been 'sexed up' with the insertion of the misleading claim that Saddam Hussein had been poised to launch weapons of mass [WMD] leading.

Ultimately, the row led to the suicide of Government scientist Dr David Kelly, said to be the BBC's source for the claim.

The subsequent Hutton inquiry ruled important caveats to intelligence reports had been removed from the dossier, but cleared Downing Street spin doctor Alastair Campbell of responsibility for his death."

—Rosa Prince, "Government forced to publish dodgy dossier," *The Telegraph*, February 18, 2008

[**Note:** The UK government using fraud and deceit to scare the British and others into the Iraq War.]

Many in our country believed Bush and others in his administration when they were told that Hussein had WMD. This last section should have made it clear that while Bush and some senior people in his administration were telling our country that Hussein had WMD, they were misleading or lying about that important fact. Bush had no credible intel to back up those statements.

Those statements were never found to be accurate.

Those misleading, *inaccurate* or false statements were undoubtedly a substantial cause, if not *the* reason, that Congress gave Bush the authority to attack Iraq.

Bush's false statements about the never-found Hussein WMD cost the lives of thousands of US soldiers along with the lives of hundreds of thousands of others.

3. Bush: Iraq was connected with 9/11, bin Laden, or Al-Qaeda

OUR COUNTRY WAS TRAUMATIZED by 9/11, and it was clear bin Laden and Al-Qaeda were involved in those attacks. Bush and his administration suggesting that Hussein was somehow connected to bin Laden, Al-Qaeda, and 9/11 scared the American people and our Congress into believing there were good reasons to attack Iraq.

However, as you're about to read, no credible connection has ever been found between Hussein and bin Laden, Al-Qaeda, or 9/11.

The quotes in this section both suggest and confirm that Hussein had nothing to do with those terrorist activities or 9/11. Those quotes are interspersed with gray box quotes that will show how the Bush administration bent, twisted, and distorted words to guide Americans into falsely believing there was a Hussein connection to 9/11 or the terrorists.

4/9/2001: 9/11 Commission thinks it has "debunked" Prague meeting supposedly connecting Iraq to 9/11

"The [9/11] commission's staff believed that it had debunked, once and for all, the widely circulated intelligence report about the so-called Prague meeting—a supposed encounter in the Czech capital between a senior Iraq spy and Mohammed Atta, the 9/11 ringleader, on April 9, 2001.

The report had been circulated by the Czech intelligence service and embraced by the Bush administration...to suggest an Iraqi link to 9/11.... The Czech report was based on a single, uncorroborated witness account."

—Philip Shenon, *The Commission*, Pages 380–381

9/15/2001: CIA analyst: Bush needs "better reason" to go after Hussein, no 9/11 connection

"Only a few days after September 11 [2001], Tenet writes, a CIA analyst attended a White House meeting where he was told that [President] Bush wanted to remove Saddam. The analyst's response, according to Tenet: 'If you want to go after that son of a bitch to settle old scores, be my guest. But don't tell us he is connected to 9/11 or to terrorism because there is no evidence to support that. You will have to have a better reason.'" [*The fifteenth of the month used for date sorting purposes only.*]

—Thomas Powers, *The Military Error*, Page 106

[**Note:** Could it be that the Iraq War was just a way in part to settle old scores regarding the Bush family and Hussein?]

9/18/2001: Clarke memo: "No compelling case" that Iraq was involved in 9/11 attacks

Clarke and his deputy Roger Cressey sent a memo "to Condoleezza Rice a week after 9/11 [September 18, 2001]; titled 'Survey of Intelligence Information of Any Iraqi Involvement in the September 11 Attacks,' it concluded that there was 'no compelling case' that Iraq was involved [in 9/11]."

—Peter Bergen, *The Longest War*, Page 52

9/21/2001: George W. Bush is told there's no evidence linking Hussein to 9/11; Hussein "viewed Al Qaeda...as a potential threat to his secular regime"

"President Bush was told in a highly classified briefing [on September 21, 2001] that the U.S. intelligence community had no evidence linking the Iraqi regime of Saddam Hussein to the [9/11] attacks and that there was scant credible evidence that Iraq had any significant collaborative ties with

Al Qaeda…the few credible reports of contacts between Iraq and Al Qaeda involved attempts by Saddam Hussein to monitor the terrorist group. Saddam viewed Al Qaeda as well as other theocratic radical Islamist organizations as a potential threat to his secular regime."

—Murray Waas, "Key Bush Intelligence Briefing Kept From Hill Panel," *National Journal*, November 22, 2005

11/28/2001: Joint Intelligence Council: Hussein "refused to permit" Al-Qaeda presence in Iraq

"On 28 November 2001, the JIC [Joint Intelligence Council] assessed that:
    —Saddam Hussein had 'refused to permit any Al Qaida presence in Iraq'.
    —Evidence of contact between Iraq and Usama Bin Laden (UBL) was 'fragmentary and uncorroborated'; including that Iraq had been in contact with Al Qaida for exploratory discussions on toxic materials in late 1988."

—Commissioned by the Prime Minister The Right Honourable Gordon Brown MP, "The Report of the Iraq Inquiry: Executive Summary," IraqInquiry.org.uk, July 6, 2016, Page 43

6/15/2002: Cheney, Libby argued and reargued for Hussein-9/11 link until eve of war

Vice President "Cheney and his personal national security adviser, I. Lewis Libby, known by his nickname as Scooter, argued and reargued the case for the link [between Saddam and 9/11] until the eve of war. Often they went to the agency [CIA] personally, bringing fresh allegations acquired from their own sources, and pressing CIA analysts to 're-look' the evidence…. In June 2002, the deputy director for intelligence, Jami Miscik, complained to Tenet that Scooter Libby and Paul Wolfowitz would not let the subject drop. Tenet reports that he told Miscik to 'just say *we stand by what we previously wrote.*'" [*The fifteenth of the month used for date sorting purposes only.*]

—Thomas Powers, *The Military Error*, Page 105

[**Note:** No credible evidence that Hussein was linked to 9/11 was ever found. On 6/5/2007, Libby was convicted of "one count of obstruction of justice, two counts of lying under oath and one count of making false statements" in the leak of CIA officer Valerie Plame Wilson's name, according to Politico.com on 6/5/2018. His sentence was commuted by President George W. Bush on 7/2/2007, and he was granted a full pardon by President Donald Trump on 4/13/2018.]

9/8/2002: Cheney: Al-Qaeda had contacts with Iraq, Prague

Appearing on NBC's *Meet the Press* on September 8, 2002, Cheney said: "'I'm not here today to make a specific allegation that Iraq was somehow responsible for 9/11. I can't say that. On the other hand, since we did that interview [discussing possible Iraqi involvement in 9/11 on December 9, 2001], new information has come to light. And we spent time looking at that relationship between Iraq, on the one hand, and the al Qaeda organization on the other. And there has been reporting that suggests that there have been a number of contacts over the years. We've seen in connection with the hijackers, of course, Mohamed Atta, who was the lead hijacker, did apparently travel to Prague [Czech Republic] on a number of occasions. And on at least one occasion, we have reporting that places him in Prague with a senior Iraqi intelligence official a few months before the attack on the World Trade Center.'"

—Stephen F. Hayes, *Cheney*, Page 443

[Note: Cheney *suggests* the *possible visit* between lead 9/11 hijacker Mohamed Atta and an Iraqi intelligence officer in Prague. However, the *Newsweek* article by Michael Isikoff—four and a half months before September 8, 2002—"quoted a 'senior U.S. law enforcement official' saying, 'We looked at this real hard because, obviously, if it were true, it would be huge. But nothing had matched up.' Isikoff allowed that new information suggesting a link could turn up, but concluded, 'for now, at least, the much-touted *Prague connection* appears to be an intriguing, but embarrassing, mistake.'"—*Stephen F. Hayes, The Connection, Pages 148–149*]

9/27/2002: Rumsfeld: "Bulletproof" evidence of an Iraq-Al-Qaeda connection

On September 27, 2002, "Secretary of Defense Donald Rumsfeld said that there was 'bulletproof' evidence of an Iraq-al-Qaeda connection."

—Peter Bergen, *The Longest War*, Page 132

[Note: Another Rumsfeld *misstatement*. That "bulletproof" evidence was never found.]

10/7/2002: George W. Bush: Hussein cheered 9/11 attack on US; Al-Qaeda had contacts in Iraq; some Al-Qaeda leaders fled to Iraq

President George W. Bush, when outlining the Iraqi threat in a speech at the Cincinnati Museum Center-Cincinnati Union Terminal in Ohio on October 7, 2002: "We know that Iraq and the al Qaeda terrorist network share a common enemy—the United States of America. We know that Iraq and al Qaeda have had high-level contacts that go back a decade. Some al Qaeda leaders who fled Afghanistan went to Iraq. These include one very senior al Qaeda leader who received medical treatment in Baghdad this year, and who has been associated with planning for chemical and biological attacks. We've learned that Iraq has trained al Qaeda members in bomb-making and poisons and deadly gases. And we know that after September the 11th, Saddam Hussein's regime gleefully celebrated the terrorist attacks on America."

—Office of the Press Secretary, "President Bush Outlines Iraqi Threat," George W. Bush—White House Archives, October 7, 2002

[Note: Bush's statement was made up of *innuendos suggesting* that Iraq was somehow connected to Al-Qaeda and 9/11. That connection was never found.]

10/7/2002: Senator Graham: Bush misled country "to build support for a war against an unrelated threat"

Referring to a speech made by President Bush on October 7, 2002, Senator Bob Graham (D-FL) said that President Bush's rhetoric was misleading the public toward war with Iraq: "These claims [of an Iraq/Al-Qaeda connection] were effective. At the time, a poll showed that 70 percent of Americans believed that Saddam Hussein was involved in or directly responsible for the attacks of September 11; rather than disabusing people of the notion, the President tried to solidify it. Instead of using his presidency to teach America about the real terrorist threats we faced, Bush was using it to mislead the country in order to build support for a war against an unrelated threat."

—Bob Graham with Jeff Nussbaum, *Intelligence Matters*, Page 193

[Note: The Bush misleading statements worked: "70 percent of Americans believed that Hussein was involved in or directly responsible for the attacks of September 11." That connection, if it existed, was never found.]

1/26/2003: Powell: State Dept. questioned Hussein/Al-Qaeda ties

"In his Davos [Switzerland] speech [at the World Economic Forum on January 26, 2003] he [Powell] had cited allegations that his own State Department analysts questioned, including the attempts [by Iraq] to import uranium and nuclear-related aluminum tubes as well as the ties between Saddam and al-Qaeda."

—Karen DeYoung, *Soldier*, Page 441

1/28/2003: George W. Bush SOTU: "Saddam Hussein aids and protects terrorists, including…al-Qaeda."

"In his January [28] 2003 State of the Union address, President Bush said, 'Saddam Hussein aids and protects terrorists, including members of al-Qaeda.'"

—Peter Bergen, *The Longest War*, Page 132

[Note: Bush's statement that Hussein aids and protects members of Al-Qaeda was never found to be true.]

1/29/2003: CIA report did not connect Iraq with 9/11

A January 29, 2003, CIA report on potential links between Iraq and Al-Qaeda "concluded there had been contacts over the years and moments when Iraq seemed to provide safe haven for terrorists. But it did not connect Iraq with September 11 and found no evidence of 'command linkages.'"

—Peter Baker, *Days of Fire*, Page 245

2/5/2003: In UN presentation, Powell cites suspected Al-Qaeda terror camp in Iraq as "sinister nexus"

"[I]n his presentation to the UN Security Council on February 5 [2003], Secretary of State Colin Powell failed to produce any compelling proof that Baghdad was even remotely connected to the 9/11 attacks. Powell pointed to a suspected al Qaeda terror camp located near Kurdish-held northern Iraq. Contending that the facility trained al Qaeda operatives to carry out attacks with explosives and poisons, Powell insisted that there was a 'sinister nexus between Iraq and the al Qaeda terror network.'"

—Peter Lance, *Triple Cross*, Pages 476–477

[Note: Powell's Iraq and Al-Qaeda "sinister nexus" was never found to be true.]

2/5/2003: Terror camp cited by Powell is in part of Iraq not controlled by Hussein

On February 5, 2003, "On ABC's *World News Tonight* just hours after the [Powell's] testimony [to the UN Security Council], investigative reporter Brian Ross raised questions about Powell's claims of Iraqi links to [Kurdish Sunni Islamist group] Ansar al Islam.…'There's no doubt Ansar al Islam is a radical Islamic terror group,' Ross said. 'Their own videos show it. Their ties to al Qaeda are also well documented. But they operate in a part of Iraq not controlled by Saddam Hussein and their leaders say they seek to overthrow Saddam Hussein and his government.' The piece cut to Mullah

Krekar, Ansar's longtime leader and religious authority, then living openly in Norway. '[The Iraqi leaders] are our enemy,' Krekar said. 'Really, they are also our enemy.' Krekar also said he had no association with [Al-Qaeda in Iraq leader Abu Musab] al Zarqawi. Ross noted that British intelligence was skeptical of the links: 'another blow to the U.S. case.'"

—Stephen F. Hayes, *The Connection*, Page 168

[**Note:** More Bush administration misleading words that took us to war.]

2/5/2003: UK defense intel sees no Hussein/Al-Qaeda link

A British Defense Intelligence Staff (DIS) document, which was leaked in early February 2003, "indicated that British intelligence believed there were no current links between Saddam Hussein and al-Qaeda and that any contact between officials in the Iraqi regime and the al-Qaeda network yielded nothing due to reciprocal mistrust and incompatible ideologies." [*The fifth of the month used for date sorting purposes only.*]

—Stefan Halper and Jonathan Clarke, *America Alone*, Page 215

2/11/2003: Tenet: "Credible and reliable sources" show link between Iraq and Al-Qaeda

On February 11, 2003, Tenet told the Senate Intelligence Committee: "'Iraq has in the past provided training in document forgery and bomb making to al Qaeda. It also provided training in poisons and gasses to two al Qaeda associates...this information is based on a solid foundation of intelligence. It comes to us from credible and reliable sources.'"

—Richard Miniter, *Losing Bin Laden*, Page 234

[**Note:** Tenet's credible and reliable sources showing a link between Iraq and Al-Qaeda were never found.]

2/16/2003: *LA Times*: The "most hotly debated" issue for invading Iraq is Hussein/Al-Qaeda connection

"A [February 16, 2003] *Los Angeles Times* story quoting supporters and critics of the potential Baghdad attack concluded: 'Of all the charges the United States has made, the most hotly debated are those linking Iraq and the Al Qaeda network. Without such a connection, the logic of invading Iraq as a response to September 11th seems weak to many Americans.'"

—Peter Lance, *1000 Years For Revenge*, Page 438

[**Note:** No credible connections between Iraq and Al-Qaeda were ever found.]

3/6/2003: George W. Bush in pre-war news conference interchanged Iraq with 9/11 attacks eight times

On March 6, 2003, "President Bush holds his last prewar news conference. The New York Observer writes that he interchanged Iraq with the attacks of 9/11 eight times, 'and eight times he was unchallenged.' The ABC News White House correspondent, Terry Moran, says the Washington press corps was left 'looking like zombies.'"

—Frank Rich, "The Ides of March 2003," *The New York Times*, March 18, 2007

[**Note:** Bush suggesting or implying connections between Iraq and 9/11 that were never found.]

3/9/2003: Rice: A detainee said Al-Qaeda sought, got help from Iraq on chemical weapons

"On the 9th of March 2003, on the *CBS* program *Face the Nation*, National Security Adviser Condoleezza Rice was asked about the alleged link between Saddam and al-Qa'ida training: 'We know from a detainee that—the head of training for al-Qa'ida, that they sought help in developing chemical and biological weapons because they weren't doing very well on their own. They sought it in Iraq. They received the help.'"

—Philip Taylor, *The War in Iraq—A Failure of Honesty*, Page 91

[**Note:** Rice told *Face the Nation* there was a connection between Al-Qaeda and Hussein relying on the words of a detainee. No such connection was ever found.]

3/15/2003: Tenet: "CIA found absolutely no linkage between Saddam and 9/11."

After informing Bush in March 2003 that Cheney was going to make an erroneous speech regarding the Iraq-Al-Qaeda link, Tenet said: "CIA found absolutely no linkage between Saddam and 9/11.

At best, all the data in our possession suggested a plausible scenario where the 'enemy of my enemy might be my friend,' that is, two enemies trying to determine how best to take advantage of each other." [*The fifteenth of the month used for date sorting purposes only.*]

—George Tenet with Bill Harlow, *At the Center of the Storm*, Pages 341–342

[**Note:** Days before we invaded Iraq, Tenet told Bush and Cheney that the CIA found no linkage between Hussein and 9/11.]

3/19/2003: Rep. Murtha: No Iraqi connection with Al-Qaeda

In an appearance on NBC's *Meet the Press* with Tim Russert on March 19, 2003, Representative Jack Murtha (D-PA) said: "There was no connection with al-Qaida, there was no connection with, with terrorism in Iraq itself."

—"Transcript for March 19: Gen. George Casey and Rep. John Murtha," *Meet the Press*, NBCNews.com, March 22, 2006

[Note: Without Bush and his administration's falsely claiming Hussein had WMD and was connected to 9/11 and Al-Qaeda, would Americans or our Congress have supported attacking Iraq?]

3/20/2003: UK's Cook: Blair's cleverly worded call to action on Iraq suggested, not alleged, Hussein ties with Al-Qaeda

Former House of Commons leader Robin Cook quoted Prime Minister Tony Blair's address to the UK on March 20, 2003, when Blair said: "'Dictators like Saddam, terrorist groups like al-Qa'ida, threaten the very existence of such a world. That is why I have asked our troops to go into action tonight.'"

Cook commented: "Tony [Blair] was far too clever to allege there was any affection between Saddam and al-Qa'ida. But he deliberately crafted a suggestive phrasing which in the minds of many viewers must have created an impression, and was designed to create *the* impression, that British troops were going to Iraq to fight a threat from al-Qa'ida."

—Robin Cook, *The Point of Departure*, Page 288

[Note: Tony Blair's comments called out not as facts but an attempt to create confusion.]

5/1/2003: George W. Bush suggesting a tie between Hussein and 9/11

"On May 1, 2003, aboard the USS *Abraham Lincoln*, President Bush announced that 'major combat operations' in Iraq had ended. The defeat of Saddam Hussein, he told the American people, was 'a crucial advance in the campaign against terror.' For the umpteenth time Bush once again bracketed Saddam and 9/11: 'The battle of Iraq is one victory in a war on terror that began on September 11th, 2001 and still goes on.' The president went on to describe the 9/11 attacks, 'the last phone calls, the cold murder of children, the searches in the rubble,' as if this had any bearing on the Iraq War. The president also made the definitive statement that Saddam was 'an ally of al-Qaeda,' something that his own intelligence agencies had determined was not the case before the war."

—Peter Bergen, *The Longest War*, Page 172

[Note: President Bush again suggesting a connection with Iraq and 9/11 without explicitly saying so.]

6/9/2003: Bin Laden didn't want to be "beholden" to Hussein

According to a *New York Times* article on June 9, 2003: "In separate debrief-ings, both [9/11 mastermind] Khalid Shaikh Mohammed and Abu Zubayd-ah, a high-level aide to Osama bin Laden, said that the Saudi billionaire had vetoed the idea of linking with Iraq because he didn't want to be beholden to Saddam Hussein."

—Peter Lance, *1000 Years For Revenge*, Pages 442–443

7/9/2003: Hussein saw Al-Qaeda as a threat and uncontrollable

In testimony before the 9/11 Commission on July 9, 2003, "A commission member, former Secretary of the Navy John Lehman, raised the Iraq-al Qaeda issue with Judith Yaphe, a veteran CIA Iraq expert.

Yaphe spoke of the 'unwillingness of Saddam and Osama to consider cooperation' and testified that while the Iraqi regime used Islamic extremists, it used only those groups it could control. So she did not think Saddam would work with al Qaeda. 'I think he saw him as a threat, Osama as a threat, rather than a potential partner.'"

—Stephen F. Hayes, *The Connection*, Pages 183–184

9/16/2003: Cheney failed to dismiss widely discredited claim that Hussein might have played role in 9/11

A *Boston Globe* article on September 16, 2003, discussed Cheney's appear-ance on NBC's *Meet the Press* two days earlier.

"'Vice President Dick Cheney, anxious to defend the [Bush] White House foreign policy amid ongoing violence in Iraq, stunned intelligence analysts and even members of his own administration this week by failing to dismiss a widely discredited claim: that Saddam Hussein might have played a role in the Sept. 11 attacks.'... 'Details that Cheney cited to make the case that the Iraqi dictator had ties to Al Qaeda have been dismissed by the CIA as having no basis, according to analysts and officials'"

—Stephen F. Hayes, *The Connection*, Page 19

[Note: Cheney's continued attempt to mislead our country by selling a widely discredited claim about Hussein and 9/11.]

9/17/2003: George W. Bush clarifies Cheney statement: Hussein "has been involved with al Qaeda"

Following a meeting with members of the Congressional Conference Com-mittee on Energy Legislation on September 17, 2003, President George W. Bush stated: "We've had no evidence that Saddam Hussein was involved with the September 11th [attack]. What the Vice President said was, is that he has been involved with al Qaeda. And al Zarqawi, al Qaeda operative, was in Baghdad."

—"Remarks by the President After Meeting with Members of the Congressional Conference Committee on Energy Legislation," George W. Bush—White House Archives, September 17, 2003

[Note: Bush trying to *clarify* a prior *misleading* statement while suggesting a link between Iraq, Al-Qaeda, and 9/11—a link that was never found.]

9/25/2003: White House concocted faked letter showing Iraq/Al-Qaeda link to 9/11 attacks

"In late September [2003], Tenet returned from a meeting at the White House with instructions for CIA....The White House had concocted a fake letter from [Iraqi intelligence head Tahir Jalil] Habbush to Saddam, backdated to July 1, 2001. It said that 9/11 ringleader Mohammed Atta had actually trained for his mission in Iraq—thus showing, finally, that there was an operational link between Saddam and al Qaeda, something the Vice President's Office had been pressing CIA to prove since 9/11 as a justification to invade Iraq.

There is no link. The letter also mentioned suspicious shipments to Iraq from Niger set up with al Qaeda's assistance.

The idea was to take the letter to Habbush and have him transcribe it in his own neat handwriting on a piece of Iraq government stationery, to make it look legitimate. CIA would then take the finished product to Baghdad and have someone release it to the media." [*The twenty-fifth of the month used for date sorting purposes only.*]

—Ron Suskind, *The Way of the World*, Page 371

[Note: A Bush White House forgery intended to deceive and defraud the American people into an unnecessary war with Iraq. If your loved one died in such a phony war, do you think Bush should have paid a price for such deception?]

1/9/2004: *NY Times*: Powell says he had "not seen smoking gun, concrete evidence" of Hussein ties to Al-Qaeda

According to a January 9, 2004, article in *The New York Times*: "Only in January 2004 did Secretary of State Colin L. Powell, long the only member of the Bush cabinet to enjoy the trust of foreign governments, finally acknowledge that he had 'not seen smoking gun, concrete evidence' backing up administration assertions and insinuations that Saddam had ties to Al-Qaeda."

—Jonathan Randal, *Osama*, Page 268

[**Note:** Powell being precise after his prior *misleading* and false words helped sell the Iraq War.]

2/2/2004: Senator Levin: Intel didn't show Iraq/Al-Qaeda link, George W. Bush administration exaggerated connection

Senator Carl Levin (D-MI) was interviewed by John Gibson on Fox News' *The Big Story* on February 2, 2004. Regarding a possible Al-Qaeda/Iraq link, "'The intel didn't say that there is a direct connection between al Qaeda and Iraq...That was not the intel. That's what this [Bush] administration exaggerated to produce. And so there are many instances where the administration went beyond the intelligence....I'm saying that the administration's statements were exaggerations of what was given to them by the analysts and the intelligence community.'"

—Stephen F. Hayes, *The Connection*, Page 182

3/15/2004: Prof. Pfiffner: George W. Bush "misled" US in implying there was a Hussein/9/11 connection

In the March 2004, *Presidential Studies Quarterly*, Professor James P. Pfiffner of George Mason University wrote: "'From the publicly available evidence, the president [Bush] misled the country in implying that there was a connection between Saddam and 9/11. The administration's claims about Iraq's nuclear capacity were based on dubious evidence that was presented in a misleading manner....Claims of Saddam's ability to deliver these weapons, however, were exaggerated. Finally, there was circumstantial and inconclusive evidence that in 2002 the intelligence community may have been under unusual pressure to support the administration's goals.'" [*The fifteenth of the month used for date sorting purposes only.*]

—Jeffrey Record, *Wanting War*, Pages 61–62

[**Note:** Another person saw Bush's deceptions that took America into war with Iraq.]

3/21/2004: Clarke: No evidence "ever" of Al-Qaeda, Iraq link

In an interview on *60 Minutes* on March 21, 2004, Clarke told journalist Lesley Stahl: "No. There's absolutely no evidence that Iraq was supporting al-Qaeda ever."

—"60 Minutes, 9/11: Before And After, Part 1," Search.alexanderstreet.com, 2004

4/22/2004: Congressman Ron Paul: No connection between Hussein and 9/11; real reasons for Iraq War include

"oil, neoconservative empire building, and our support for Israel"

In a speech on the House floor on April 22, 2004, Representative Ron Paul (R-TX) said: "Evidence has shown that there was no connection between Saddam Hussein and the guerilla attacks on New York and Washington, and since no weapons of mass destruction were found, other reasons are given for invading Iraq. The real reasons are either denied or ignored: oil, neoconservative empire building, and our support for Israel over the Palestinians."

—Ron Paul, *Foreign Policy of Freedom*, Pages 291–292

6/16/2004: 9/11 Commission report: No "collaborative relationship" between Iraq and Al-Qaeda

"The Sept. 11 commission reported yesterday [June 16, 2004] that it has found no 'collaborative relationship' between Iraq and al Qaeda, challenging one of the Bush administration's main justifications for the war in Iraq. Along with the contention that Saddam Hussein was stockpiling weapons of mass destruction, President Bush, Vice President Cheney and other top administration officials have often asserted that there were extensive ties between Hussein's government and Osama bin Laden's terrorist network; earlier this year, Cheney said evidence of a link was 'overwhelming.'"

—Walter Pincus and Dana Milbank, "Al Qaeda-Hussein Link Is Dismissed," *The Washington Post*, June 17, 2004

6/17/2004: George W. Bush: There "was a relationship between Iraq and al Qaeda"

In President Bush's June 17, 2004, remarks after meeting with his cabinet, when asked why the administration continued to insist that Hussein had a relationship with Al-Qaeda, when the same administration denies any connection between Saddam and 9/11, Bush answered:

"The reason I keep insisting that there was a relationship between Iraq and Saddam and al Qaeda, because there was a relationship between Iraq and al Qaeda. This administration never said that the 9/11 attacks were orchestrated between Saddam and al Qaeda.

We did say there were numerous contacts between Saddam Hussein and al Qaeda. For example, Iraqi intelligence officers met with bin Laden, the head of al Qaeda, in the Sudan. There's numerous contacts between the two.

I always said that Saddam Hussein was a threat. He was a threat because he had used weapons of mass destruction against his own people. He was a threat because he was a sworn enemy to the United States of America, just like al Qaeda. He was a threat because he had terrorist connections—not only al Qaeda connections, but other connections to terrorist organizations; Abu Nidal was one. He was a threat because he provided safe-haven for a terrorist like Zarqawi, who is still killing innocent inside of Iraq."

—Office of the Press Secretary, "President Discusses Economy, Iraq in Cabinet Meeting: Remarks by the President After Meeting with His Cabinet," George W. Bush—White House Archives, June 17, 2004

[Note: Bush continued to mislead our country about a relationship between 9/11, Al-Qaeda, and Iraq. No credible evidence of such a relationship was ever found.]

10/6/2004: Cheney doubles down on lie: "I have not suggested... connection between Iraq and 9/11."

"[A] number of mainstream articles and books have been published accusing Cheney of dishonesty and misleading statements about Iraq and weapons of mass destruction, about Iraq and the terrorist Mohamed Atta, about Iraq and aluminum tubes, about Iraq and uranium yellowcake. This was brought to a head by Cheney's shameless lie to Senator John Edwards [D-NC] in the 2004 vice presidential debate [as reported in *The Washington Post* on October 6, 2004]: 'The senator has got his facts wrong. I have not suggested there's a connection between Iraq and 9/11.'"

—Peter Dale Scott, *The Road to 9/11*, Page 232

[Note: See prior quotes of Dick Cheney suggesting there was a connection between Iraq and 9/11 dated 6/15/2002, 9/8/2002, and 3/16/2003.]

11/6/2005: George W. Bush administration chose to ignore that the Iraq, 9/11 claim was false

According to a *Washington Post* article on November 6, 2005: "The myth that Iraq and al-Qaeda were working together was not the result of an innocent and ignorant mistake by the White House. The president [Bush] and vice president [Cheney] ignored clear warnings, well before the war began—from the Pentagon's Defense Intelligence Agency and from the CIA, in classified reports given directly to the White House—that the claim was false."

—Al Gore, *The Assault on Reason*, Page 109

3/15/2006: CIA: "Greatest discrepancy" between administration statements and intel was in respect to relationship between Hussein, Al-Qaeda

"Paul R. Pillar was the CIA's national intelligence officer for the Near East and South Asia...According to him [in the March/April 2006 issue of *Foreign Affairs*], the 'greatest discrepancy between the [Bush] administration's public statements and the intelligence community's judgments' was with respect to 'the relationship between Saddam and al-Qaeda....The reason the connection got so much attention was that the administration wanted to hitch the Iraq expectation to the *war on terror* and the threat the American public feared most, thereby capitalizing on the country's militant post-9/11 mood.'"
[*The fifteenth of the month used for date sorting purposes only.*]

—Ian S. Lustick, *Trapped in the War on Terror*, Page 64

3/20/2006: George W. Bush: I didn't say there was a direct connection between Hussein and 9/11, only that he was a sponsor of terror

In a discussion about the war on terror on March 20, 2006, in Cleveland, Ohio, President Bush said: "'I don't think we ever said—at least I know I didn't say—that there was a direct connection between September the 11th and Saddam Hussein. We did say he was a state sponsor of terror.'"

—Transcript, "Bush Discusses War on Terror," CNN.com, March 20, 2006

[**Note:** Although Bush never said there was a *direct* connection between Hussein and 9/11, he implied so on 10/7/2002, 1/28/2003, 3/6/2003, 5/1/2003, 9/17/2003, and 6/17/2004.]

8/21/2006: George W. Bush both implies and does not imply connection between Hussein and 9/11

When questioned by a member of the press on August 21, 2006, about the connection between Hussein and 9/11, President Bush replied:

"Nothing, except for it's part of—and nobody has ever suggested in this administration that Saddam Hussein ordered the attack. Iraq was a—the lesson of September the 11th is, take threats before they fully materialize, Ken. Nobody has ever suggested that the attacks of September the 11th were ordered by Iraq. I have suggested, however, that resentment and the lack of hope create the breeding grounds for terrorists who are willing to use suiciders to kill to achieve an objective. I have made that case."

—"The President's News Conference: August 21, 2006," Weekly Compilation of Presidential Documents, August 28, 2006, Vol. 42, No. 34, Page 1492

[**Note:** Bush never said that Hussein ordered the attacks of 9/11, but he implied a relationship between Hussein and Al-Qaeda on 10/7/2002, 1/28/2003, 3/6/2003, 5/1/2003, 9/17/2003, and 6/17/2004.]

11/15/2007: Pentagon study: No "smoking gun" direct connection between Hussein, Al-Qaeda

A November 2007 "Pentagon-sponsored study based on 600,000 documents seized in Iraq 'found no *smoking gun* (i.e., direct connection) between Saddam's Iraq and al Qaeda.' The study also concluded that while Saddam's regime did provide some support to other terrorist groups in the Middle East, the 'predominant targets of Iraqi state terror operations were Iraqi citizens, both inside and outside Iraq.'" [*The fifteenth of the month used for date sorting purposes only.*]

—Jeffrey Record, *Wanting War*, Page 72

6/5/2008: Senate Select Committee concludes that Hussein turned down Al-Qaeda request years before the invasion of Iraq

"In June [5] 2008, the Senate Select Committee on Intelligence concluded... that there was no 'cooperative relationship' between Saddam and al-Qaeda. The committee also found that 'most of the contacts cited between Iraq and al-Qa'ida before the war by the intelligence community and policy makers have been determined not to have occurred.' The only meeting that had actually taken place was eight years before the invasion of Iraq, between Farouq Hijazi, a senior Iraqi intelligence official, and bin Laden in Sudan in early 1995. Once he was in U.S. custody, Hijazi told his American interrogators that he had been admonished by Saddam before the meeting not to negotiate or promise anything to the al-Qaeda leader but 'only to listen.' Bin Laden asked to open an office in Baghdad and for military training for his men. Those requests were turned down flat by Saddam."

—Peter Bergen, *The Longest War*, Page 151

[Note: More debunking of the Bush administration myth that there was some cooperative relationship between Hussein and Al-Qaeda.]

4. Bush: Saddam Hussein tried to buy uranium from Niger

BUSH AND A FEW senior staff told the American public that Hussein was trying to buy uranium in Niger (Africa) for Iraq's nuclear programs. Bush's own State Department and others concluded that story was unfounded in December 2001, while Bush and his minions continued marketing that fraud up through March 2003.

Some of the following quotes debunk the Niger/Hussein story, while the gray box quotes show Bush and his staff continuing to mislead and lie about an Iraq/Niger/uranium purchase.

10/10/2000: Documents claiming Iraq sought to purchase yellowcake uranium were forged and phony

"Documents in the Niger dossier [claiming Iraq sought to purchase yellow-cake uranium from Niger] were not just forged, they were full of errors. A letter dated October 10, 2000, was signed by [Niger's] Minister of Foreign Affairs Allele Elhadj Habibou—even though he had been out of office for more than a decade. Its September 28 postmark indicated that somehow the letter had been received nearly two weeks before it was sent. In another letter, President Tandja Mamadou's signature appeared to be phony. The accord signed by him referred to the Niger constitution of May 12, 1965, when a new constitution had been enacted in 1999. One of the letters was dated July 30, 1999, but referred to agreements that were not made until a year later. Finally, the agreement called for the five hundred tons of uranium to be transferred from one ship to another in international waters—a spectacularly difficult feat."

—Craig Unger, *The Fall of the House of Bush*, Pages 236–237

12/15/2001: State Dept.: "Niger [Iraq] deal was a fraud"

Following the November 2001 investigation by the US embassy in Niger into sales of uranium from Niger to Iraq, "State Department analysts... concluded that the Niger deal was a fraud.

In December 2001, Greg Thielmann, director for strategic proliferation and military affairs at the State Department's Bureau of Intelligence and Research (INR), reviewed Iraq's WMD program for Secretary of State Colin Powell. 'A whole lot of things told us that the report was bogus,' said Thielmann. 'This wasn't highly contested. There weren't strong advocates on the other side. It was done, shot down.'" [*The fifteenth of the month used for date sorting purposes only.*]

—Craig Unger, *The Fall of the House of Bush*, Page 229

2/5/2002: CIA issues suspicious Iraq/Niger report anyway

"On February 5, 2002...for reasons that remain unclear, the CIA issued a new report on the alleged Niger deal [to sell uranium to Iraq], one that provided significantly more detail, including what was said to be 'verbatim text' of the accord between Niger and Iraq. In the State Department, analysts were still suspicious of the reports."

—Craig Unger, *The Fall of the House of Bush*, Page 239

[**Note:** It is difficult to believe that the CIA overlooked the preceding 12/15/2001 quote from the State Department stating that the Niger/Iraq deal was found to be a fraud.]

2/15/2002: Envoy reported that Niger docs had been forged

On May 6, 2003, journalist Nicholas Kristof wrote in *The New York Times*, regarding the Niger-Iraq yellowcake situation: "'I'm told by a person involved in the Niger caper that more than a year ago the vice president's [Cheney's] office asked for an investigation of the uranium deal, so a former U.S. ambassador to Africa [Joe Wilson] was dispatched to Niger.

In February 2002, according to someone present at the meetings, that envoy reported to the C.I.A. and State Department that the information was unequivocally wrong and that the documents had been forged.'" [*The fifteenth of the month used for date sorting purposes only.*]

—Michael Isikoff and David Corn, *Hubris*, Pages 222–223

3/1/2002: State Department cable: Niger president would not want to "risk good relations" with US by trading with Iraq

"On March 1 [2002], the State Department weighed in with another cable, this one headed 'Sale of Niger Uranium to Iraq Unlikely.' Citing 'unequivocal' control of the mines, the cable asserted that President [Mamadou] Tandja of Niger would not want to risk good relations with the United States by trading with Iraq, and cited the prohibitive logistical problems in a transaction requiring '25 hard to conceal 10-ton-tractor trailers' that would have to travel a thousand miles and cross one international border before reaching the sea."

—Craig Unger, *The Fall of the House of Bush*, Page 241

3/4/2002: A high-level administration intel assessment: Niger/Iraq deal "unlikely," too many obstacles

"A high-level intelligence assessment by the Bush administration concluded in early 2002 that the sale of uranium from Niger to Iraq was 'unlikely' because of a host of economic, diplomatic, and logistical obstacles, according to a secret State Department memo [on March 4, 2002]."

—Frank Rich, *The Greatest Story Ever Sold*, Page 235

Wilson's NOT Ack page Code —
No deal

3/5/2002: Joe Wilson also invalidates Niger/Iraq claim; the sale is discredited more than half a dozen times

"A few days later [early March, 2002], [former ambassador Joe] Wilson returned from Niger and told CIA officials that he had found no evidence to support the story about the alleged uranium deal [with Iraq].

By now the Niger reports had been discredited more than half a dozen times—by the French in 2001, by the CIA in Rome and in Langley [Virginia], by the State Department's INR, by some analysts in the Pentagon, by the ambassador to Niger, by Wilson, and yet again by the State Department." [*The fifth of the month used for date sorting purposes only.*]

—Craig Unger, *The Fall of the House of Bush*, Page 241

10/1/2002: CIA NIE assessment includes "highly dubious" Niger/Iraq uranium claim as a footnote

On October 1, 2002, "CIA officials had referred to the [Niger/Iraq] uranium claim in the classified ninety-page National Intelligence Estimate on Iraqi weapons programs." However, "the CIA had included as a footnote to the assessment that the uranium allegations were 'highly dubious.'"

—Stefan Halper and Jonathan Clarke, *America Alone*, Pages 216–217

10/7/2002: Iraq/Niger claim dropped from George W. Bush speech

According to a *New York Times* article on July 13, 2003: "[A] claim that Saddam Hussein had tried to buy 550 tons of uranium ore from Niger had been dropped from a speech given by President Bush in Cincinnati [Ohio] back on October 7, 2002. CIA director George Tenet, the story said, had personally warned deputy national security adviser Steve Hadley that the claim couldn't be supported by solid intelligence."

—Scott McClellan, *What Happened*, Page 177

1/20/2003: George W. Bush submits report to Congress on Iraq's attempt to acquire uranium days before SOTU

"[O]n January 20 [2003], just eight days before the State of the Union address, President Bush submitted a report to Congress citing Iraq's attempts 'to acquire uranium and the means to enrich it.'"

—Craig Unger, *The Fall of the House of Bush*, Page 269

[Note: Bush's report to Congress flies directly in the face of the previous quotes that prove the charge that Iraq bought or tried to buy uranium from Africa were dubious or false.]

1/28/2003: George W. Bush attributed claim of Niger/Iraq uranium sale to UK government

"In January [28] 2003, President Bush said in his State of the Union speech that the British government had learned that Iraq 'had recently sought significant quantities of uranium from Africa.' Two months later, U.S. and allied troops invaded Iraq. Paul Pillar, who retired last year after 30 years at the CIA, said that the White House attributed the charge to the British because the CIA wouldn't vouch for it. 'U.S. analysts said it was just too squishy to use publicly,' said Pillar, who was national intelligence officer for the Near East and South Asia."

—Bob Drogin and Tom Hamburger, "Niger Uranium Rumors Wouldn't Die,"
Los Angeles Times, February 17, 2006

[**Note:** Bush claiming a fact even his own CIA did not believe.]

2/15/2003: George W. Bush attaches memo to IAEA Niger docs: White House can't confirm reports, have questions about some specific claims

In February 2003, "Jacques Baute, head of the International Atomic Energy Agency's Iraq nuclear verification office, examined electronic copies of the Niger [yellowcake uranium] documents that had finally been forwarded to the IAEA by the United States. Astonishingly, the Bush administration had attached a note to the documents. 'We cannot confirm these reports and have questions regarding some specific claims,' it said." [*The fifteenth of the month used for date sorting purposes only.*]

—Craig Unger, *The Fall of the House of Bush*, Page 289

2/17/2003: Chief of Iraqi nuclear matters: Niger docs "completely bogus"

On February 17, 2003, Jacques Baute, chief of Iraqi nuclear matters at the International Atomic Energy Agency, "concluded that the papers [alleging the sale of uranium from Niger to Iraq] were completely bogus."

—Michael Isikoff and David Corn, *Hubris*, Page 203

3/2/2003: IAEA says Iraq/Niger docs were forgeries

"On March 2 [2003], the International Atomic Energy Association (IAEA) reported that documents it had been given by the U.S. government purporting to show a uranium deal between Iraq and Niger were forgeries."

—Stephen F. Hayes, *Cheney*, Page 390

3/14/2003: Senator wants investigation: Niger yellowcake "fabrication" may be part of a "larger deception"

"On March 14 [2003], Senator Jay Rockefeller IV [D-WV], the ranking Democrat on the Senate Intelligence Committee, wrote a letter to FBI chief Robert Mueller asking for an investigation because 'the fabrication of these [Niger yellowcake] documents may be part of a larger deception campaign aimed at manipulating public opinion and foreign policy regarding Iraq.'"

—Craig Unger, *The Fall of the House of Bush*, Page 292

6/8/2003: Rice: Iraqi uranium claim based on UK intel

"On June 8 [2003], National Security Adviser Condoleezza Rice appeared on *Meet the Press* and was asked by Tim Russert if [President George W.] Bush should retract his [January 28, 2003] State of the Union sentence about Iraqi uranium shopping in Africa. She replied, 'The president quoted a British paper. We did not know at the time—no one knew at the time, in our circles—maybe someone knew down in the bowels of the agency, but no one in our circles knew that there were doubts and suspicions that this might be a forgery.'"

—Michael Isikoff and David Corn, *Hubris*, Pages 240–241

[**Note:** Rice was either ignorant or not telling the truth that many in the Bush administration thought or knew the uranium stories were probably untrue or a fraud as early as 12/15/2001, 2/15/2002, or 10/1/2002.]

7/7/2003: UK panel report questions Niger/Iraq sale

"That day [July 7, 2003], in London, the House of Commons foreign affairs committee released a tough report questioning the Blair government's prewar intelligence on Iraq.

The panel...questioned the September [24] 2002 British white paper's 'bald claim' that Iraq had tried to buy 'significant quantities of uranium from Africa.' The panel noted that government ministers had insisted there was 'other evidence' beyond the forged Niger documents to support the assertion, but the ministers had not disclosed what that evidence was—or whether they stood behind it....Bush's definitive [January 28, 2003] State of the Union remark—which attributed the yellowcake charge to British intelligence—had lost its foundation."

—Michael Isikoff and David Corn, *Hubris*, Pages 257–258

[**Note:** More debunking the false United States/British Iraq/Niger yellowcake claims.]

7/7/2003: Fleischer: "Now, we've long acknowledged" that the yellowcake story turned "out to be incorrect"

On July 7, 2003, White House Press Secretary Ari "Fleischer inadvertent-ly dropped a small bombshell: 'Now, we've long acknowledged—and this is old news, we've said this repeatedly—that the information on yellow-cake [uranium, being sold by Niger to Iraq] did, indeed, turn out to be incorrect.'"

—Scott McClellan, *What Happened*, Page 168

[**Note:** Bush's press secretary making up history given President Bush had discussed the attempted Iraq/Niger deal less than six months before, on 1/28/2003.]

7/11/2003: Tenet: Sixteen words in SOTU on uranium/Niger/Iraq "should never have been included"

On July 11, 2003, "the White House and the CIA accepted joint responsi-bility for the [misinformation in the January 28, 2003] State of the Union address, with Tenet's statement saying, 'These 16 words [suggesting Iraq attempted to obtain uranium from Africa] should never have been included in the text written for the President [Bush].'"

—Karl Rove, *Courage and Consequence*, Pages 325–326

[**Note:** The White House and CIA accepted *responsibility* for the *misinformation* they spread (that Iraq was trying to buy uranium from Africa) that helped garner public and congressional support for our attacking Iraq.]

Although the White House and the intelligence community knew or should have known as early as October 10, 2000, that the rumor about Iraq trying to buy Niger uranium was false, Bush in his statement of January 28, 2003 (less than two months before the invasion of Iraq), continued to say otherwise.

5. Bush: Saddam Hussein has nuclear programs

FROM THE TIME GEORGE W. Bush became president, and even after 9/11, he and others in his administration told the American people that Hussein *had* a nuclear program, and said, suggested, and implied that program could or would produce WMD. If so, that nuclear program was never found. Furthermore, when Bush and his administration were touting Hussein's nuclear program, Bush had intel that Iraq's nuclear program had ended years before.

The quotes in this section show Iraq did not have a nuclear program (at least none was ever found), while the gray box quotes illustrate how Bush and some of his staff pushed the rumor that Iraq had a nuclear program.

6/15/1991: An engineer on an Iraqi uranium enrichment program was told in 1991 that the nuclear program was over

According to Saad Tawfiq, an engineer who worked on a uranium-enrichment program under scientist Ja'afar Dia Jafar in Iraq, in June 1991, "Saad and other members of Jafar's team were called in to the presidential palace and told by Jafar that the [nuclear] program was over and that they must now get rid of all of the evidence of its existence. 'My orders were to destroy or hide all incriminating evidence, and leave only the equipment that could be shown to be dual-use technology.' In the space of seventy-two frantic hours, Saad and other scientists loaded equipment onto 150 tractor-trailers and escorted them out into the western desert....the truckloads were turned over to Saddam's Special Security force to conceal and bury." [*The fifteenth of the month used for date sorting purposes only.*]

—James Risen, *State of War*, Page 101

10/8/1997: IAEA to UN: No "discrepancies" in Iraq nuclear declarations of its past program

"In the report submitted to the [United Nations] Security Council on October 8, 1997...the [International Atomic Energy] agency declared that a 'technically coherent picture' of Iraq's past nuclear program had evolved, and that it saw no significant discrepancies between that picture and Iraq's latest declaration."

—Hans Blix, *Disarming Iraq*, Pages 28–29

1/30/2002: CIA: Iraq nuclear report *embellished* at Bush administration level

"On January 30, 2002, the agency [CIA] issued an unclassified report to Congress containing the phrase 'Baghdad may be attempting to acquire materials that could aid in reconstituting its nuclear-weapons program.' Still, it was not highlighted and it was couched in very ambiguous-sounding language.

Yet only a week or so later...as the item moved from intelligence professionals to the Bush inner circle, it made a Herculean leap in credibility....Secretary of State Colin Powell declared, 'With respect to the

249

nuclear program, there is no doubt that the Iraqis are pursuing it.' In fact, there was every doubt. It was a reckless charge."

—James Bamford, *A Pretext for War*, Pages 304–305

[**Note:** Powel misleading our country by turning doubt into no doubt.]

9/8/2002: Thielmann: Senior George W. Bush administration officials made statements about Hussein and nuclear weapons that were "dishonest"

"With no reason to think they were being lied to, the public was left to believe that Saddam Hussein had restarted his nuclear weapons program and was just six months away from having a working atomic bomb. 'Senior [Bush administration] officials made statements which I can only describe as dishonest,' said senior State Department intelligence official Gregory Thielmann, who saw much of the intelligence.

'They were distorting some of the information that we provided to make it seem more alarmist and more dangerous....I thought there were limits on how much one was willing to do in order to twist things.' The only thing left was for the national media to give the bogus information its imprimatur. Like clockwork, that happened the next morning, Sunday, September 8 [2002], when *The New York Times* published a major story under the stark headline 'U.S. Says Hussein Intensifies Quest for A-Bomb Parts.'"

—James Bamford, *A Pretext for War*, Page 323

[**Note:** Bush administration dishonest scare tactics.]

9/8/2002: Cheney asserts Hussein has reconstituted his nuclear program

Appearing on *Meet the Press* on September 8, 2002, Vice President "Cheney asserted that Saddam 'has indeed stepped up his capacity to produce and deliver biological weapons, that he has reconstituted his nuclear program to develop a nuclear weapon, that there are efforts under way inside Iraq to significantly expand his capability.'"

—Michael Isikoff and David Corn, *Hubris*, Page 34

[**Note:** No credible facts confirmed Cheney's assertion at the time or afterward.]

9/14/2002: George W. Bush implies to Congress and our country that Hussein has nuclear program; he didn't mention that the information came from 1996

"[O]n September 14 [2002], [President] Bush repeated his nuclear charge during his weekly radio address. 'Saddam Hussein has the scientists and infrastructure for a nuclear-weapons program, and has illicitly sought to purchase the equipment needed to enrich uranium for a nuclear weapon.' But, again, there was no new report.

The IAEA document he was referring to was from 1996, and it described a weapons program the inspectors had long ago destroyed. Off on the sidelines, George Tenet was one of the few who knew the truth. But instead of speaking out, he was quietly attempting to stick his finger in the dike by trying to persuade first the British and then the White House to stay away from the Italian Niger report [that fraudulently claimed Hussein was purchasing yellowcake for weapons of mass destruction development]."

—James Bamford, *A Pretext for War*, Page 322

[**Note:** Bush misleading our country by selling old news as current news.]

1/27/2003: IAEA: No known Iraqi nuclear program since 1990s

"The International Atomic Energy Agency (IAEA) had just issued a report taking issue with [Bush] administration claims that Iraq had an active nuclear program. 'We have to date found no evidence that Iraq has revived its nuclear weapon program since the elimination of the program in the 1990's,' Mohamed ElBaradei, the head of the agency, told the United Nations Security Council [on January 27, 2003]."

—Craig Unger, *The Fall of the House of Bush*, Pages 281–282

3/7/2003: IAEA: No evidence Iraq had revived its nuclear program; Niger/Iraq contract was not authentic

In a report to the United Nations Security Council on March 7, 2003, Director of the International Atomic Energy Agency Mohamed ElBaradei said: "[T]he IAEA had found no evidence or plausible indication of the revival of a nuclear weapons program in Iraq. He presented two stark pieces of information on matters that had recently emerged: First, the IAEA had concluded after extensive investigations that the much-publicized aluminum tubes Iraq had attempted to import were not likely to have been related to the manufacture of centrifuges for the enrichment of uranium. Second, the contract alleged to have been made between Iraq and Niger for the import of raw uranium—yellowcake—was not authentic."

—Hans Blix, *Disarming Iraq*, Pages 210–211

3/16/2003: Cheney: We believe Iraq *has* reconstituted nuclear weapons

In an appearance on NBC's *Meet the Press* on March 16, 2003, Vice President Cheney said the International Atomic Energy Agency, who had recently exposed the Niger documents as forgeries, had "'consistently underestimated or missed what it was Saddam Hussein was doing...We know [Saddam] has been absolutely devoted to trying to acquire nuclear weapons. And we believe he has, in fact, reconstituted nuclear weapons.'"

—Craig Unger, *The Fall of the House of Bush*, Page 292

[**Note:** Cheney's claim three days before we attacked Iraq was never confirmed.]

7/6/2003: Wilson: "some of the intelligence related to Iraq's nuclear weapons program was twisted to exaggerate the Iraqi threat"

"A column written by Joseph Wilson, the former ambassador to Gabon, was...published on Sunday, July 6 [2003], in *The New York Times*. Wilson had been sent by the CIA, at the behest of Cheney, in February 2002, to investigate claims that Hussein was attempting to buy 'yellowcake' uranium from the African nation of Niger in order to support a nuclear weapons building program. He unleashed a storm with his 1,452 words, which started, 'Did the Bush administration manipulate intelligence about Saddam Hussein's weapons programs to justify an invasion of Iraq? Based on my experience with the administration in the months leading up to the war, I have little choice but to conclude that some of the intelligence related to Iraq's nuclear weapons program was twisted to exaggerate the Iraqi threat.'"

—Ron Suskind, *The One Percent Doctrine*, Page 243

[**Note:** More twisted facts to exaggerate the Iraq threat.]

6. Bush: Saddam Hussein has biological and chemical weapons

GEORGE W. BUSH FANNED American fears by telling them that Hussein had biological and chemical weapons.

While instilling that fear, Bush neglected to mention that Presidents Reagan and H. W. Bush allowed America to sell biological and chemical weapons to Iraq in the past and exhibited little concern over Hussein using some of those chemical weapons against his own people and Iranians.

ATCC

Beginning in the mid-1980s, and under Presidents Reagan and H. W. Bush, Hussein bought potentially deadly chemical and biological agents from America. Many of those purchases went through our Department of Commerce. American company sales to Iraq included biological agents such as anthrax, bubonic plague, West Nile virus, plague-infected mouse tissue smears, and botulism.

The following quotes detail a few sales of those potentially deadly weapons to Iraq.

2/8/1985: Anthrax, bubonic plague among the biological agents Reagan, George H. W. Bush admins sold to Iraq

"The Reagan and Bush I administrations...authorized sales of deadly chemical and biological agents to Iraq [starting on February 8, 1985], including anthrax and bubonic plague."

> —Amy Goodman with David Goodman, *The Exception to the Rulers*, Page 34

9/29/1988: Riegle: ATCC shipped Class III pathogens to Iraq, including anthrax and a source of botulism to the Iraqi Ministry of Trade

"According to the Riegle Report, [on September 29, 1988] the American Type Culture Collection (ATCC) sent a shipment of Anthrax and a source of Botulism to the Iraqi Ministry of Trade (a pathogen produces disease):
'Materials Shipped: Bacillus anthracis (ATCC 240)
Batch# 05-14-63 (3 each)
Class III pathogen
Materials shipped: Clostridium botulinum Type A
Batch# 07-86 (3 each)
Class III pathogen.'"

> —Philip Taylor, *The War in Iraq—A Failure of Honesty*, Page 14

[**Note:** Class III pathogens are described as "readily transmitted and virulent agents."[73]]

3/15/1989: State Department: Terrorists still operating out of Iraq, a country working on chemical and biological weapons

"In March 1989, State Department officials told Secretary of State James Baker that Iraq was working on chemical and biological weapons and that terrorists were still operating out of Iraq."

> —Craig Unger, *House of Bush, House of Saud*, Page 81

---

73   "Exam Three—Mechanisms of Disease," Quizlet.com, accessed December 18, 2017

10/2/1989: George H. W. Bush directive normalizing relations with Iraq warns about sanctions if Iraq caught *using* illegal chemical or biological weapons

"President [H. W.] Bush had signed a Persian Gulf policy directive, NSD-26, on October 2, 1989. It declared that normal relations between the countries [US and Iraq] would serve long-term U.S. interests. The United States would propose economic and political incentives for Iraq to moderate its behavior.

The directive also mentioned that illegal *use* (not possession) of chemical or biological weapons would lead to economic and political sanctions. Sanctions would also result if Iraq breached International Atomic Energy Agency (IAEA) safeguards. NSD-26 went on to say the United States should look for opportunities to participate in Iraqi reconstruction, especially in the energy sector. Finally, the U.S. government should consider sales of nonlethal military assistance."

—Charles Duelfer, *Hide and Seek*, Page 60

10/15/1989: Private research foundation catalogues Iraq's chemical and biological weapons

"[I]n October 1989 the Washington Institute for Near East Policy, a private research foundation, issued a report entitled 'The Genie Unleashed,' which cataloged Iraq's chemical and biological weapons production and suggested that the West might already have lost the battle to halt the proliferation of such weapons.

The report stated: 'Significantly, Iraq has continued and even expanded its efforts since the cessation of fighting with Iran in July 1988,' and went on to say that international efforts to undermine the chemical weapons program by starving it of raw materials were increasingly irrelevant as Iraq was on the verge of becoming self-sufficient. 'Baghdad's willingness to invest substantial resources in its chemical and biological weapons programs suggests that its leaders believe that these programs will continue to be of tremendous strategic importance.'" [*The fifteenth of the month used for date sorting purposes only.*]

—Con Coughlin, *Saddam*, Page 243

1/17/1990: Congress-imposed US Export-Import Bank ban voided by George H. W. Bush; trade was the "central factor" in the US-Iraq relationship

"[T]he U.S. Congress had imposed U.S. Export-Import Bank financing restrictions on Iraq because of the Halabja massacre [in which chemical weapons were used on Kurds in March 1988].

On January 17, 1990, [President H. W.] Bush voided the prohibition with a stroke of a pen, stating that it was 'not in the national interest of the U.S.' [Secretary of State James] Baker then described trade as the 'central factor in the U.S.-Iraq relationship.'

During the Bush-Baker tenure, the United States became Iraq's largest supplier of nonmilitary goods, and Iraq became the United States['] second biggest trading partner in the Middle East."

—Antonia Juhasz, *The Bush Agenda*, Page 171

4/15/1990: Reagan administration provided Iraq with deadly bacteria, such as anthrax and botulism, and technology to extend range of SCUDs

"By April 1990, the Reagan Administration had:

*Approved exports that 'allowed Iraq to extend SCUD range far enough to hit allied soldiers in Saudi Arabia and Israeli civilians in Tel Aviv and Haifa.'

*Provided Iraq with deadly bacteria such as anthrax and a source of botulism." [*The fifteenth of the month used for date sorting purposes only.*]

—Philip Taylor, *The War in Iraq—A Failure of Honesty*, Page 15

[**Note:** The Reagan administration armed Iraq with biological weapons ten years before George W. Bush became president and gave the reason that because Hussein had biological weapons, he was a threat to America.]

10/15/1992: Riegle report: Disease producing, poisonous biological materials exported to Iraq, licensed by the US Department of Commerce

In their May 25, 1994, report titled "U.S. Chemical and Biological Warfare-Related Dual Use Exports to Iraq and their Possible Impact on the Health Consequences of the Gulf War," also known as "The Riegle Report": "In October 1992, the Committee on Banking, Housing, and Urban Affairs, which has Senate oversight responsibility for the Export Administration Act (EAA), held an Inquiry into the U.S. export policy to Iraq prior to the [1991] Persian Gulf War. During that hearing it was learned that U.N. Inspectors identified many U.S.-manufactured items exported pursuant to licenses issued by the U.S. Department of Commerce that were used to further Iraq's chemical and nuclear weapons development and missile delivery system development programs....we contacted a principal supplier [of biological materials] to determine what, if any, materials were exported to Iraq which might have contributed to an offensive or defensive biological warfare program. Records available from the supplier for the period from [March] 1985 until the present show that during this time, pathogenic (meaning 'disease producing'), toxigenic (meaning 'poisonous'), and other biological research materials were exported to Iraq pursuant to application and licensing by the U.S. Department of Commerce." [*The fifteenth of the month used for date sorting purposes only.*]

—Donald Wayne Riegle, Jr. and Alfonse M. D'Amato, "The Riegle Report," May 25, 1994, Pages 4, 22, 23

[**Note:** In the 1980s and early 1990s, the governments of Reagan and H. W. Bush provided Iraq with United States exports that furthered Iraq's chemical and nuclear weapons development and missile delivery system development programs.]

4/15/1993: UN confirms Iraq manufactured a form of mustard gas, and nerve agents Sarin and Tabun

According to "The Riegle Report," which was delivered to the Senate on February 9, 1994, regarding the health of Gulf War veterans, "In April 1993, weapons inspectors from the United Nations charged with locating all of Iraq's nuclear, chemical and biological weapons by U.N. Resolution 687, confirmed that in Muthanna, 65 miles northwest of Baghdad, Iraq manufactured a form of mustard gas as well as Sarin and Tabun, both nerve agents. This vast desert complex was the nucleus of Iraq's chemical weapons program." [*The fifteenth of the month used for date sorting purposes only.*]

—Donald Wayne Riegle, Jr. and Alfonse M. D'Amato, "The Riegle Report," May 25, 1994, Page 12

6/21/1995: Senator Riegle receives list from CDC director of the biological materials such as West Nile virus, botulinum, and plague-infected mouse tissue smears they had given to Iraq from 1984 through 1993

"In 1995, the Center for Disease Control & Prevention [CDC] provided to then-Senator Donald [Riegle] (D-Mich.) a complete list of all biological materials—including viruses, retroviruses, bacteria, and fungi—that the CDC provided to Iraq from Oct. 1, 1984 through Oct. 13, 1993."

—Dean Foust and John Carey, "A U.S. Gift to Iraq: Deadly Viruses," Bloomberg. com, September 20, 2002

[**Note:** Not only did our government convey to the Iraqi government dangerous biological materials that George W. Bush later blamed Hussein for having, but we also trained an Iraqi doctor at our CDC facilities to work with some of those materials.]

Here is a copy of that letter and its attachments.

 DEPARTMENT OF HEALTH & HUMAN SERVICES

Public Health Service

Centers for Disease Control
and Prevention (CDC)
Atlanta GA 30333

JUN 21 1995

The Honorable Donald W. Riegle, Jr.
United States Senate
Washington, D.C. 20510-2201

Dear Senator Riegle:

In 1993, at your request, the Centers for Disease Control and Prevention (CDC) forwarded to your office a listing of all biological materials, including viruses, retroviruses, bacteria, and fungi, which CDC provided to the government of Iraq from October 1, 1984, through October 13, 1993. Recently, in the course of reviewing our shipping records for a Freedom of Information Act (FOIA) request from a private citizen, we identified an additional shipment, on May 21, 1985, that was not included on the list that was provided to your office. Following this discovery, we conducted a thorough review of all of our shipping records and are confident that we have now included a listing of all shipments. A corrected list is enclosed (Note: the new information is italicized).

These additional materials were hand-carried by Dr. Mohammad Mahmud to Iraq after he had spent three months training in a CDC laboratory. Most of the materials were non-infectious diagnostic reagents for detecting evidence of infections to mosquito-borne viruses. Only two of the materials are on the Commodity Control List, i.e., *Yersinia pestis* (the agent of plague) and dengue virus. (The strain of plague bacillus was non-virulent, and CDC is currently petitioning the Department of Commerce to remove this particular variant from the list of controlled materials).

We regret that our earlier list was incomplete and appreciate your understanding.

Sincerely,

David Satcher, M.D., Ph.D.
Director

CDC SHIPMENTS TO IRAQ OCTOBER 1, 1984 THROUGH PRESENT

4/26/85	8 vials antigen and antisera (R. rickettsii and R. typhi)	Minister of Health Ministry of Health
	to diagnose rickettsial infections (non-infectious)	Baghdad, Iraq

5/21/85 Etiologic Agents
lyophilised arbovirus seed   Dr.   Mohammad   Imad

Al-Deen M. Mahmud
West Nile Fever Virus   Dept. of Microbiology
Lyophilised cultures of avirulent   College of Medicine
Yersinia pestis and   University of Basrah
Y. pseudotuberculosis (strain J)   Basrah, Iraq
0.5 ml Bhanja Virus (Ig 690)
0.5 ml Dengue Virus Type 2 (New Guinea C)
0.5 ml Dengue Virus Type 3 (H-87)
0.5 ml Hazara Virus (Pak IC 280)
0.5 ml Kemerovo Virus (Rio)
0.5 ml Langat Virus (TP 21)
0.5 ml Sandfly Fever/Naples Virus (original)
0.5 ml Sandfly Fever/Sicilian Virus (original)
0.5 ml Sindbis Virus (EgAr 339)
0.5 ml Tahyna Virus (Bardos 92)
0.5 ml Thogoto Virus (IT A)

Diagnostic Reagents and Associated Materials
2 vials each Y. pestis FA (+ & -)
  conjugates
2 vials Y. pestis Fraction 1 antigen
10 vials Y. pestis bacteriophage impregnated paper strips
5 plague-infected mouse tissue smears (fixed)
Various protocols for diagnostic bacteriology tests
23 X 0.5 ml Bhanja (Ig 690) antigen
22 X 0.5 ml Dengue Type 2 (New Guinea C) antigen
22 X 0.5 ml Dengue Type 3 (H-87) antigen
22 X 0.5 ml Hazara (Pak IC 280) antigen
23 X 0.5 ml Kemerovo (Rio) antigen
21 X 0.5 ml Langat (TP 21) antigen
24 X 0.5 ml Sandfly Fever/Naples (original) antigen
24 X 0.5 ml Sandfly Fever/Sicilian (original) antigen
23 X 0.5 ml Sindbis (EgAr 339) antigen
23 X 0.5 ml Tahyna (Bardos 92) antigen
20 X 0.5 ml Thogoto (IT A) antigen
23 X 0.5 ml Bhanja (Ig 690) antigen
23 X 0.5 ml West Nile (Eg 101) antigen
20 X 1.0 ml Normal SMB antigen
10 X 0.5 ml Normal SML antigen
5 X 1.0 ml Bhanja (Ig 690) antibody
5 X 1.0 ml Dengue Type 2 (New Guinea C) antibody
5 X 1.0 ml Dengue Type 3 (H-87) antibody
5 X 1.0 ml Hazara (Pak IC 280) antibody
5 X 1.0 ml Kemerovo (Rio) antibody
5 X 2.0 ml Langat (TP 21) antibody
5 X 1.0 ml Sandfly Fever/Naples (original) antibody
5 X 2.0 ml Sandfly Fever/Sicilian (original) antibody
5 X 1.0 ml Sindbis (EgAr 339) antibody
5 X 1.0 ml Tahyna (Bardos 92) antibody

5 X 1.0 ml Thogoto (IT A) antibody
5 X 1.0 ml West Nile (Eg 101) antibody
3 X 1.0 ml Normal NHIAF (SMB) antibody
3 X 1.0 ml Normal NHIAF (SML) antibody
1.0 ml A polyvalent grouping fluid
1.0 ml AFFA, etc. polyvalent grouping fluid
1.0 ml B polyvalent grouping fluid
1.0 ml BUN polyvalent grouping fluid
1.0 ml BWA polyvalent grouping fluid
1.0 ml C-1 polyvalent grouping fluid
1.0 ml C-2 polyvalent grouping fluid
1.0 ml CAL polyvalent grouping fluid
1.0 ml CAP polyvalent grouping fluid
1.0 ml CON polyvalent grouping fluid
1.0 ml GMA polyvalent grouping fluid
1.0 ml KEN polyvalent grouping fluid
1.0 ml PAL polyvalent grouping fluid
1.0 ml PAT polyvalent grouping fluid
1.0 ml PHL polyvalent grouping fluid
1.0 ml QRF polyvalent grouping fluid
1.0 ml Bnbios, etc. polyvalent grouping fluid
1.0 ml SIM polyvalent grouping fluid
2.0 ml TCR polyvalent grouping fluid
1.0 ml VSV polyvalent grouping fluid
1.0 ml polyvalent 1
1.0 ml polyvalent 2
1.0 ml polyvalent 3
1.0 ml polyvalent 4
1.0 ml polyvalent 5
1.0 ml polyvalent 6
1.0 ml polyvalent 7
1.0 ml polyvalent 8
1.0 ml polyvalent 9
1.0 ml polyvalent 10
1.0 ml polyvalent 11
1.0 ml Group B1 reagent
1.0 ml Bluetongue reagent
4 x 0.5 ml Dengue 1-4 set monoclonal antibodies
1.0 ml St. Louis Enc. (HSI-7) monoclonal antibody
1.0 ml Western Eq. Enc. (McMillan) monoclonal antibody

6/26/85	3 yeast cultures _Candida_ sp. (etiologic)	Dr. Mohammed S. Khider University of Baghdad
	College of Medicine	Department of Microbiology Baghdad, Iraq
3/10/86	1 vial Botulinum Toxoid # A-2 (non-infectious)	Dr. Rowil Shawil Georgis K.B.CH.B.D.F.H. Officers City Al-Muthanna Quartret 710 Street 13, Close 69, House 28/I Baghdad, Iraq
4/21/86	1 vial Botulinum Toxoid (non-infectious)	K.B.CH.B.D.F.H. Officers City Al-Muthanna Quartret 710 Street 13, Close 69, House 28/I Baghdad, Iraq
7/21/86	teaching supplies (non-infectious) CDC procedure manuals Zikak 54, House 97	Dr. Fagid Alfarhood Mahela 887 Hay Aljihad Kerk, Baghdad, Iraq
7/27/86	teaching supplies (non-infectious) CDC procedure manuals Zikak 54, House 97	Dr. Fagid Alfarhood Mahela 887 Hay Aljihad Kerk, Baghdad, Iraq
11/28/89	5.0 mls Enterococcus faecalis 5.0 mls Enterococcus faecium 5.0 mls Enterococcus avium 5.0 mls Enterococcus raffinosus 5.0 mls Enterococcus gallinarum 5.0 mls Enterococcus durans 5.0 mls Enterococcus hirae 5.0 mls Streptococcus bovis (etiologic)	Dr. Nadeel T. Al Hadithi University of Basrah College of Science Department of Biology Basrah, Iraq

7/1/1995: Iraqi Deputy Prime Minister: Biological weapons such as botulinum toxin, anthrax destroyed in October 1990, before war against Kuwait

On July 1, 1995, Iraqi Deputy Prime Minister Tariq "Aziz presented ten points describing that Iraq did, after all, have an offensive biological-weapons program.

Aziz suggested that Iraq had chosen not to reveal its existence before because it had all been eliminated and Baghdad was concerned that Washington would find this an excuse to attack Iraq again. Aziz stated that Iraq had produced botulinum toxin and anthrax at a facility called al Hakam. Large quantities of concentrated agent had been produced, but had never been put in weapons. Aziz also declared that all the agents had been destroyed in October 1990, before the war against Kuwait."

—Charles Duelfer, *Hide and Seek*, Page 106

1/20/2001: Republican George W. Bush inaugurated as president with Richard [Dick] Bruce Cheney as vice president

---

1/27/2003: Blix: Iraq declared it had destroyed leftover VX nerve gas in the summer of 1991

Regarding Iraq's use of chemical weapons, the Blix Report, issued on January 27, 2003, by Hans Blix, chief United Nations weapons inspector, read: "'Iraq has declared that it only produced VX [nerve gas] on a pilot scale, just a few tonnes and that the quality was poor and the product unstable. Consequently, it was said that the agent was never weaponised. Iraq said that the small quantity of agent remaining after the Gulf War was unilaterally destroyed in the summer of 1991.'"

—Tony Blair, *A Journey*, Page 414

2/5/2003: British Intelligence to Tenet: Hussein ended nuclear program in 1991, same year chemical weapons destroyed

"By early February [2003], the British were ready to deliver a report to the Americans. [MI6 Chief] Richard Dearlove flew to Washington to present the report to Tenet....The report stated that according to Habbush, Saddam had ended his nuclear program in 1991, the same year he destroyed his chemical weapons stockpile. Iraq had no intention, Habbush said, of restarting either program. As for biological weapons, Habbush had significant credibility—that program had been run by the Iraqi intelligence service. He said that since the destruction of the Al Hakam biological weapons facility in 1996, there was no biological weapons program. All of this turned out to be true." [*The fifth of the month used for date sorting purposes only.*]

—Ron Suskind, *The Way of the World*, Page 366

[Note: Bush got his war six weeks later, regardless.]

2/5/2003: Powell used an unreliable confession that Iraq had chemical, biological weapons in his 2003 UN speech obtained from *tortured* alleged Al-Qaeda leader

After being held in a floating prison in the Indian Ocean, alleged Al-Qaeda leader Ibn al-Sheikh al-Libi "was sent to Egypt for additional interrogation to extract a confession. Under torture, he gave a statement that Iraq had chemical and biological weapons and provided training to al Qaeda....In his address to the UN Security Council in February [5] 2003, Secretary of State Powell quoted at length from the 'confession' anonymously to make his case for the invasion of Iraq, even though, in a secret report, the CIA had concluded that the information was unreliable."

—Deepak Tripathi, *Overcoming the Bush Legacy in Iraq and Afghanistan*, Page 80

[Note: Powell selling the UN Security council on facts that were anything but.]

2/14/2003: Blix: Iraqi CB sample consistent with declaration

"On February 14, 2003, Blix told the [United Nations] Security Council that, of the chemical and biological samples the team had collected so far, three-fourths had been analyzed. All of the results had been consistent with Iraqi declarations."

—Deepak Tripathi, *Overcoming the Bush Legacy in Iraq and Afghanistan*, Page 63

[Note: The news that all the testing results had been consistent with Iraqi declarations was received by the United Nations Security Council five weeks before Bush attacked Iraq.]

3/6/2003: George W. Bush during press conference: Iraq continuing to hide biological, chemical agents

President George W. Bush, when elaborating on the threat of Iraq, during a press conference in the East Room on March 6, 2003: "Iraqi operatives continue to hide biological and chemical agents to avoid detection by inspectors. In some cases, these materials have been moved to different locations every 12 to 24 hours or placed in vehicles that are in residential neighborhoods....Saddam Hussein has a long history of reckless aggression and terrible crimes. He possesses weapons of terror. He provides funding and training and safe haven to terrorists—terrorists who would willingly use weapons of mass destruction against America and other peace-loving countries."

—"The President's News Conference, March 6, 2003," Weekly Compilation of Presidential Documents, March 10, 2003, Vol. 39, No. 10, Pages 295–296

[Note: Bush's assertions regarding Iraq having biological and chemical weapons were never confirmed, nor did he mention that if any existed, they may have come from the United States.]

5/28/2003: CIA paper: Iraqi mobile labs were biological labs; later acknowledged labs were to pump hydrogen into weather balloons

On May 28, 2003, the CIA issued "a paper stating that two trailers discovered in Iraq cinched the case that Iraq had mobile biological laboratories.... analysts later acknowledged that the trailers they had discovered were used to pump hydrogen into weather balloons; the weather balloons were to be used by the Iraqis to help gauge wind conditions for its conventional artillery."

—James Risen, *State of War*, Page 119

9/30/2004: Duelfer Report: No Iraqi plans for biological weapons program after 1996

The Iraq Survey Group, released its final report, the Duelfer Report, on September 30, 2004. "'ISG [Iraq Survey Group] found no direct evidence that Iraq, after 1996, had plans for a new BW [biological weapons] program or was conducting BW-specific work for military purposes.'"

—Philip Taylor, *The War in Iraq—A Failure of Honesty*, Page 1

7. Bush: Congress[74] knew what I knew when they voted to give me the power to attack Iraq

GEORGE W. BUSH SUPPORTED his decision to attack Iraq in part by saying that when Congress voted to give him the power to attack Iraq in the fall of 2002, they knew what he knew. That claim was false, as confirmed by the following quotes.

10/4/2002: CIA report released as Congress began debate on Iraq war resolution falsely stated that all intelligence experts agree Iraq seeking nukes

"The CIA's new white paper, 'Iraq's Weapons of Mass Destruction Programs,' was publicly released on October 4 [2002], just as senators and representatives were beginning the floor debate on the resolution that would authorize [President] Bush to launch a war against Iraq whenever he saw fit.... The white paper falsely stated that 'All intelligence experts agree that Iraq is seeking nuclear weapons,' ignoring the State Department's pointed dissent."

—Michael Isikoff and David Corn, *Hubris*, Pages 138–139

10/7/2002: Senator's response to George W. Bush's Ohio speech about justification for invading Iraq: "the administration's arguments do not add up"

From the Senate floor, Senator Russ Feingold in response to President Bush's Cincinnati speech: "Both in terms of justifications for an invasion and in terms of the mission and the plan for the invasion, the administration's arguments do not add up.

---

74   From the November 15, 2005, *New York Times* article titled "Decoding Mr. Bush's Denials, speaking about the misleading statements that led to war in Iraq, President Bush said, on November 14, 2005, that "everyone had the same intelligence he had—[former President] Mr. Clinton and his advisers, foreign governments, and members of Congress—and that all of them reached the same conclusions. The only part that is true is that Mr. Bush was working off the same intelligence Mr. Clinton had. But that is scary, not reassuring. The reports about Saddam Hussein's weapons were old, some more than 10 years old. Nothing was fresher than about five years, except reports that later proved to be fanciful. Foreign intelligence services did not have full access to American intelligence. But some had dissenting opinions that were ignored or not shown to top American officials. Congress had nothing close to the president's access to intelligence. The National Intelligence Estimate presented to Congress a few days before the vote on war [October 2002] was sanitized to remove dissent and make conjecture seem like fact."

They do not add up to a coherent basis for a new major war in the middle of our current challenging fight against the terrorism of Al Qaeda and related organizations. Therefore, I cannot support the resolution for the use of force before the Senate."

—Russ Feingold, *While America Sleeps*, Page 83

[**Note:** Feingold voted against the 2003 Iraq War resolution on October 11, 2002.[75]]

10/15/2003: CIA's Tenet: We allowed flawed information about Iraq to be presented to Congress; that never should have happened

Discussing Powell's February 5, 2003, speech to the United Nations, which supported going to war with Iraq, then-CIA Director Tenet wrote: "Our [CIA] goal…was to come up with rhetoric [for Powell's February 5, 2003, speech] that was both supported by underlying intelligence and worthy of what we all hoped would be a defining moment. Despite our efforts, a lot of flawed information still made its way into the speech. No one involved regrets that more than I do.…We allowed flawed information to be presented to Congress, the president [Bush], the United Nations, and the world. That never should have happened."

—George Tenet with Bill Harlow, *At the Center of the Storm*, Pages 373–383

[**Note:** Tenet apologizing for the *flawed information* in Powell's 2/5/2003 UN speech that helped stir our country to war six weeks later.]

1/28/2004: Senator Nelson: "The degree of specificity I was given a year and a half ago, prior to my vote [in favor of war in Iraq], was not only inaccurate; it was patently false."

"'We now know,' said Senator [Bill] Nelson [D-FL] in January [28] 2004, 'after the fact and on the basis of…[former Iraq Survey Group leader] Dr. [David] Kay's testimony today in the Senate Armed Services Committee, that the information [regarding WMDs in Iraq] was false; and not only that there were not weapons of mass destruction—chemical and biological—but there was no fleet of UAVs, unmanned aerial vehicles, nor was there any capability of putting UAVs on ships and transporting them to the Atlantic coast and launching them at U.S. cities on the eastern seaboard.… The degree of specificity I was given a year and a half ago, prior to my vote [in favor of war in Iraq], was not only inaccurate; it was patently false.'"

—James Bamford, *A Pretext for War*, Page 331

---

75   See Appendix B: Congressional Votes for the 2003 Iraq War.

[**Note:** A powerful accusation from a senator—that he voted for the Iraq War based on false information.]

2/19/2004: AF Lt. Col.: Congress was misled and lied to

According to a February 19, 2004, interview with retired Air Force Lt. Col. Karen Kwiatkowski: "'The OSP [Office of Special Plans] and the Vice President's office were critical in this propaganda effort—to convince Americans that there was some just requirement for preemptive war [in Iraq]....The Congress was misled, it was lied to. At a very minimum, that is a subversion of the Constitution. A preemptive war based on what we knew was not a pressing need is not what this country stands for.'"

—James Bamford, *A Pretext for War*, Pages 316–317

[**Note:** Congress was misled; it was lied to. Pretty clear and as damming as words could be.]

11/14/2005: George W. Bush: Everyone had the same intelligence we had including members of Congress

Speaking about the misleading statements that led to war in Iraq, President Bush said, on November 14, 2005, that "everyone had the same intelligence he had—[former President] Mr. Clinton and his advisers, foreign governments, and members of Congress—and that all of them reached the same conclusions.

The only part that is true is that Mr. Bush was working off the same intelligence Mr. Clinton had. But that is scary, not reassuring. The reports about Saddam Hussein's weapons were old, some more than 10 years old. Nothing was fresher than about five years, except reports that later proved to be fanciful. Foreign intelligence services did not have full access to American intelligence. But some had dissenting opinions that were ignored or not shown to top American officials. Congress had nothing close to the president's access to intelligence. The National Intelligence Estimate presented to Congress a few days before the vote on war [October 2002] was sanitized to remove dissent and make conjecture seem like fact."

—Editorial Staff, "Decoding Mr. Bush's Denials," *The New York Times*, November 15, 2005

[**Note:** More debunking the George W. Bush myth that Congress knew what he knew when it voted to give him the power to declare war in the fall of 2002.]

8/4/2006: Conyers: Substantial evidence George W. Bush and others in his administration misled Congress regarding justification for going to war with Iraq

The final draft of an investigation into the case for the Iraq invasion was led by Congressman John Conyers, Jr. (D-MI), and released on August 4, 2006. It stated: "'In brief, we have found that there is substantial evidence the President [Bush], the Vice President and other high ranking members of the Bush Administration misled Congress and the American people regarding the decision to go to war with Iraq; [and that they] misstated and manipulated intelligence information regarding the justification for such war'"

—Philip Taylor, *The War in Iraq—A Failure of Honesty*, Page 4

6/10/2008: George W. Bush, administration "executed a calculated and wide-ranging strategy to deceive the [US] citizens and Congress" into believing that the nation of Iraq posed an imminent threat and to justify the use of the Armed Forces against the nation of Iraq "in a manner damaging to our national security interests"

"In his conduct while President of the United States, George W. Bush...has both personally and acting through his agents and subordinates, together with the Vice President, executed a calculated and wide-ranging strategy to deceive the citizens and Congress of the United States into believing that the nation of Iraq posed an imminent threat to the United States in order to justify the use of the United States Armed Forces against the nation of Iraq in a manner damaging to our national security interests, thereby interfering with and obstructing Congress's lawful functions of overseeing foreign affairs and declaring war.

The means used to implement this deception were and continue to be, first, allowing, authorizing and sanctioning the manipulation of intelligence analysis by those under his direction and control, including the Vice President and the Vice President's agents, and second, personally making, or causing, authorizing and allowing to be made through highly-placed subordinates, including the President's Chief of Staff, the White House Press Secretary and other White House spokespersons, the Secretaries of State and Defense, the National Security Advisor, and their deputies and spokespersons, false and fraudulent representations to the citizens of the United States and Congress regarding an alleged urgent threat posed by Iraq, statements that were half-true, literally true but misleading, and/or made without a reasonable basis and with reckless indifference to their truth, as well as omitting to state facts necessary to present an accurate picture of the truth as follows:

(1) Notwithstanding the complete absence of intelligence analysis to support a claim that Iraq posed an imminent or urgent threat to the United States and the intelligence community's assessment that Iraq was in fact not likely to attack the United States unless it was itself attacked, President Bush, both personally and through his agents and subordinates, made, allowed and caused to be made repeated false representations to the citizens and Congress of the United States implying and explicitly stating that such a dire threat existed...

(2) In furtherance of his fraudulent effort to deceive Congress and the citizens of the United States into believing that Iraq and Saddam Hussein posed an imminent threat to the United States, the President allowed and authorized those acting under his direction and control, including Vice President Richard B. Cheney, former Secretary of Defense Donald Rumsfeld, and Lewis Libby, who reported directly to both the President and the Vice President, among others, to pressure intelligence analysts to tailor their assessments and to create special units outside of, and unknown to, the intelligence community in order to secretly obtain unreliable information, to manufacture intelligence, or to reinterpret raw data in ways that would support the Bush administration's plan to invade Iraq based on a false claim of urgency despite the lack of justification for such a preemptive action.

(3) The Senate Select Committee on Intelligence Report on Whether Public Statements Regarding Iraq by U.S. Government Officials Were Substantiated by Intelligence Information, which was released on June 5, 2008, concluded that: 'Statements by the President and the Vice President indicating that Saddam Hussein was prepared to give weapons of mass destruction to terrorist groups for attacks against the United States were contradicted by available intelligence information.'

Thus the President willfully and falsely misrepresented Iraq as an urgent threat requiring immediate action thereby subverting the national security interests of the United States by setting the stage for the loss of more than 4,000 United States servicemembers; the injuries to tens of thousands of U.S. soldiers; the deaths of more than 1,000,000 Iraqi citizens since the United States invasion; the loss of approximately $527 billion in war costs which has increased our Federal debt and the ultimate costs of the war between three trillion and five trillion dollars; the loss of military readiness within the United States Armed Services due to overextension, the lack of training and lack of equipment; the loss of United States credibility in world affairs; and the decades of likely blowback created by the invasion of Iraq."

—Article IV "Misleading the American People and Members of Congress To Believe Iraq Posed an Imminent Threat to the United States," of H.Res.1258 "RESOLUTION Impeaching George W. Bush, President of the United States, of high crimes and misdemeanors," introduced by Rep. Dennis J. Kucinich (D-OH-10), Congress.gov, June 10, 2008

6/26/2009: CIA Director Panetta: Top CIA officials "concealed significant actions" from Congress, and misled Congress

In a June 26, 2009, letter to CIA Director Leon E. Panetta, seven Democrats on the House Intelligence Committee said Panetta recently testified that "'top CIA officials have concealed significant actions from all Members of Congress, and misled Members for a number of years from 2001 to this week'" Democrats called on Panetta to publicly "correct" his May 15, 2009 statement that: "'Let me be clear: It is not our policy or practice to mislead Congress. That is against our laws and values'"

—Deirdre Walsh, Bob Kovach and Pam Benson, "House Dems: Panetta testified CIA has misled Congress repeatedly," CNN.com, July 9, 2009

When Congress voted in October 2002 to give George W. Bush the authority to attack Iraq, his administration had covered up and hidden important intel from Congress. The Bush administration hid the fact that it had no credible intel that Hussein was an immediate threat or danger to our country. His administration also hid the fact that it had no credible intel that Hussein had any connection with Al-Qaeda or 9/11, and hid the fact that it was pretty clear that what his administration had been saying, that Hussein had tried to buy a significant amount of uranium in Africa, was not true.

Even after all the falsehoods about the danger to our country from Hussein, some members of Congress looked closely at the "facts" the Bush administration was spewing and didn't believe them.

On October 10, 2002, 126 Democratic House party members (out of 208) voted "no" to giving Bush the power to attack Iraq, as did six Republicans (out of 223) and one Independent. There were three open House seats at the time.

The next day,[76] twenty-one Democratic senators (out of fifty) voted "no" to giving Bush the power to attack Iraq, as did one Republican (Lincoln Chafee) (out of forty-nine), and one independent (Jim Jeffords) (out of one).

---

76   See Appendix B: Congressional Votes for the 2003 Iraq War.

8. BUSH: SADDAM HUSSEIN GASSED HIS OWN AND OTHER PEOPLE

TRUE BUT MISLEADING. GEORGE W. Bush told Americans that Hussein was a threat to our country because he had gassed his own people as well as the Iranians. What George W. Bush didn't say was that his father, H. W. Bush, and President Reagan (and Rumsfeld) knew about those gassings even as their administrations continued to support Hussein.

Here are some sample quotes covering Iraq and United States history with chemical and biological weapons before George W. Bush became president.

12/20/1983: Rumsfeld meets Hussein, doesn't ask about Hussein's reported use of chemical weapons almost daily

"On December 20 [1983], Donald Rumsfeld travels to Baghdad as a [Reagan] presidential special envoy to meet Saddam Hussein. Although Iraq is using chemical weapons almost daily, Rumsfeld does not raise the issue with Saddam."

—Craig Unger, *House of Bush, House of Saud*, Page 302

3/5/1984: Despite Hussein's air force dropping thousands of chemical bombs on Iran and Halabja, Iraq, Reagan administration still supportive of Iraq

"From 1983 to 1988, the Iraqi air force dropped between 13,000 and 19,500 chemical bombs on Iran and on the Iraqi Kurdish city of Halabja.

On March 5, 1984, the U.S. State Department issued a public statement condemning Iraq's use of chemical weapons in the war against Iran. In private, however, the Reagan administration was eager to ensure that Hussein knew the U.S. government still supported his regime. Just four days after the public condemnation, the State Department told the Export-Import Bank that it should start granting short-term loans to Iraq 'for foreign relations purposes.'"

—Antonia Juhasz, *The Bush Agenda*, Pages 166–167

3/15/1984: US delegate to UN instructed to lobby for "no decision" on resolution condemning Iraq's proven use of chemical weapons

In March 1984, "European-based doctors examined Iranian troops and confirmed that they had been exposed to mustard gas [during combat in the Iran-Iraq War].

Iran followed up on these gas attacks with a draft resolution, calling on the United Nations Security Council to condemn Iraq's use of chemical weapons.

According to Joyce Battle from the National Security Archive, 'The U.S. delegate to the U.N. was instructed to lobby friendly delegations in order to obtain a general motion of *no decision* on the resolution.'" [*The fifteenth of the month used for date sorting purposes only.*]

—Philip Taylor, *The War in Iraq—A Failure of Honesty*, Page 7

3/24/1984: Rumsfeld reassures Iraq that US protests over Iraq's chemical weapons use shouldn't interfere with "warm relationship" between US and Iraq

"He [Middle East envoy Rumsfeld] returns [to Iraq] in March [24] 1984 to assure Iraq that U.S. protests against the use of chemical weapons should not interfere with a warm relationship between the two countries."

—Craig Unger, *House of Bush, House of Saud*, Page 302

[**Note:** Let me repeat: "He [Rumsfeld] returns [to Iraq] in March 1984 to assure Iraq that U.S. protests against [Iraq's] the use of chemical weapons should not interfere with a warm relationship between the two countries."]

11/15/1984: Despite the US openly condemning Iraq's use of chemical weapons against Iran, US restores diplomatic relations with Iraq

"Despite the fact that the United States had openly condemned Iraq's use of lethal chemical weapons against Iran, diplomatic relations between the two countries [US and Iraq] were fully restored in November 1984. (They had not existed since the 1967 Arab-Israeli War.)" [*The fifteenth of the month used for date sorting purposes only.*]

—Ricardo S. Sanchez with Donald T. Phillips, *Wiser in Battle*, Page 52

[**Note:** This is consistent with the fact that the United States supplied Iraq with biological materials.]

8/29/1988: Iraqi gassing affected nearly all of Kurdistan; nearly 3,000 Kurds gassed to death

The Anfal operations were a genocidal movement by the Iraqi regime against Kurds, which began in February 1988. "The entire civilian population of Kurdistan was in one way or another affected. Nearly one-and-a-half million people were displaced, and half the landmass of Kurdistan was depopulated. The savagery of the assaults on innocent civilians was unprecedented. Gas was the weapon of choice. In Bazi Gorge on 29 August, 1988, nearly 3,000 Kurds were gassed to death. All in all, the *Anfal* led to the death of nearly 200,000 civilians in a planned, methodically executed, genocide."

—Ali A. Allawi, *The Occupation of Iraq*, Pages 37–38

[Note: Three-thousand Kurds gassed to death by Iraq while President H. W. Bush looked the other way.]

9/29/1992: President George H. W. Bush looking the other way at Hussein's gassing Iraq and Iranians, and other dangerous behavior

"Republican administrations [of Reagan and H. W. Bush] over the past decade had propped up Saddam Hussein in his war against Iran, ignoring bountiful evidence of Hussein's horrors, [vice presidential candidate Al] Gore argued [in a speech on September 29, 1992]. Saddam Hussein, he exclaimed, 'had already launched poison gas attacks repeatedly, and [President H. W.] Bush looked the other way. He had already conducted extensive terrorism activities, and Bush had looked the other way. He was already deeply involved in the effort to acquire nuclear weapons and other weapons of mass destruction, and Bush knew it, but he looked the other way. Well, in my view, the Bush administration was acting in a manner directly opposite to what you would expect with all of the evidence that it had available to it at the time. Saddam Hussein's nature and intentions were perfectly visible.'"

—Stephen F. Hayes, *The Connection*, Pages 41–42

10/11/2001: George W. Bush saying the leader of Iraq was evil, in part because he gassed his own people

When questioned during a news conference on October 11, 2001, if there was any intention of widening the war to include Iraq, Syria, etc., President George W. Bush's reply was: "You mentioned Iraq. There's no question that the leader of Iraq is an evil man. After all, he gassed his own people. We know he's been developing weapons of mass destruction. And I think it's in his advantage to allow inspectors back in his country to make sure that he's conforming to the agreement he made, after he was soundly trounced in the Gulf War. And so we're watching him very carefully. We're watching him carefully."

—"The President's News Conference, October 11, 2001," Weekly Compilation of
Presidential Documents October 15, 2001, Vol. 37, No. 41, Page 1457

[Note: Left out of the statement was the inconvenient fact that President H. W. Bush and President Reagan knew about Hussein's gassing people in the 1980s while they continued to send Hussein biological pathogens and other support.]

3/13/2002: George W. Bush pointed out that Iraq gassed its own people

When asked during a news conference on March 13, 2002, if he would "take action against Iraq unilaterally," President George W. Bush stated: "One of the things I've said to our friends is that we will consult, that we will share our views of how to make the world more safe. In regards to Iraq, we're doing just that. Every world leader that comes to see me, I explain our concerns about a nation which is not conforming to agreements that it made in the past, a nation which has gassed her people in the past, a nation which has weapons of mass destruction and apparently is not afraid to use them. And so one of the—what the Vice President is doing is he's reminding people about this danger and that we need to work in concert to confront this danger. Again, all options are on the table, and—but one thing I will not allow is a nation such as Iraq to threaten our very future by developing weapons of mass destruction. They've agreed not to have those weapons; they ought to conform to their agreement, comply with their agreement."

—"President's News Conference, March 13, 2002," Weekly Compilation of Presidential Documents, March 18, 2002, Vol. 38, No. 11, Pages 407–410

9/26/2002: George W. Bush saying in part that Hussein gassed the Kurds

On the afternoon of September 26, 2002, President Bush said: "There would be 'no discussion, no debate, no negotiation' with the Iraqi dictator....Saddam had tortured his own citizens, gassed the Kurds, invaded his neighbors: 'There's no doubt his hatred is mainly directed at us. There's no doubt he can't stand us.' But one line in this speech grabbed worldwide attention: 'After all, this is a guy that tried to kill my dad [H. W. Bush] at one time.'"

—Michael Isikoff and David Corn, Hubris, Page 115

[Note: There has been speculation that George W. Bush attacked Iraq in part because Hussein tried to kill his father.]

9. BUSH: SADDAM HUSSEIN ATTACKED KUWAIT

TRUE BUT MISLEADING. GEORGE W. Bush told our country that Hussein was dangerous, in part because he attacked Kuwait in 1991. Bush, however, left out the fact that H. W. Bush's diplomat to Iraq, April Glaspie, might have accidentally or purposefully allowed or encouraged Hussein to attack Kuwait.

7/25/1990: Baker had official US spokesmen emphasize instruction "no opinion" on Arab-Arab conflicts

Ambassador Glaspie to President Hussein during a documented exchange on July 25, 1990: "I admire your extraordinary efforts to rebuild your country. I know you need funds. We understand that and our opinion is that you should have the opportunity to rebuild your country. But we have no opinion on the Arab-Arab conflicts, like your border disagreement with Kuwait.

I was in the American Embassy in Kuwait during the late 60's. The instruction we had during this period was that we should express no opinion on this issue and that the issue is not associated with America. James Baker has directed our official spokesmen to emphasize this instruction. We hope you can solve this problem using any suitable methods via [Arab League Secretary General Chedli] Klibi or via President Mubarak. All that we hope is that these issues are solved quickly."

—Special to The New York Times, "CONFRONTATION IN THE GULF; Excerpts From Iraqi Document on Meeting With U.S. Envoy," The New York Times, September 23, 1990

[Note: It seems reasonable that Hussein, upon hearing the United States Ambassador to Iraq say that the United States considers the Iraq/Kuwait border dispute an "Arab-Arab" problem, would think that the United States would not become involved if he invaded Kuwait.]

5/1/2001: Showing Hussein was dangerous because he, in part, attacked Kuwait in 1990

When speaking to the students and faculty of National Defense University on May 1, 2001, President George W. Bush brought up previous issues with Iraq: "When Saddam Hussein invaded Kuwait in 1990, the world joined forces to turn him back. But the international community would have faced a very different situation had Hussein been able to blackmail with nuclear weapons."

—Office of the Press Secretary, "Remarks by the President to Students and Faculty at National Defense University," George W. Bush—White House Archives, May 1, 2001

[Note: True, but Bush's comment sidesteps the fact that his dad's ambassador to Iraq might have accidentally given Hussein the green light to attack Kuwait.]

10. SUMMARY: BUSH USED CHERRY-PICKED AND MISLEADING INFORMATION TO TAKE OUR COUNTRY TO WAR WITH IRAQ

AS YOU HAVE READ, and as the following quotes will further confirm, George W. Bush and some in his administration took bits and pieces of information that were old, discredited, taken out of context, or false and turned that information into misleading and false information to make Hussein seem a greater danger to our country then he was reasonably thought to be.

10/11/2002: Senator Feingold prior to Iraq invasion vote: "a deliberate attempt to manufacture the notion of a Hussein-bin Laden connection and a reckless distortion of the likelihood of a direct WMD attack by Iraq"

Senator Russ Feingold on his reasoning for voting against the invasion of Iraq: "Given what we knew about Saddam Hussein (and we knew quite a lot), the important question was whether it made any sense for him to coordinate with the likes of Osama bin Laden or to guarantee his own destruction by launching an independent WMD attack on the United States. These were sincere questions to which I wanted sincere answers from the administration. Instead what we got from August [2002] until the vote in October [2002] and then right up until the invasion of Iraq in March 2003 was a deliberate attempt to manufacture the notion of a Hussein-bin Laden connection and a reckless distortion of the likelihood of a direct WMD attack by Iraq....

As false as the claims about WMD proved to be, it was the scam of the connection between Saddam and Al Qaeda that outraged me the most. Without that ploy, played out in an environment of fear, both literal and political, the invasion of Iraq would never have been authorized by the Senate."

—Russ Feingold, *While America Sleeps*, Page 78

1/30/2003: Powell's chief of staff on George W. Bush administration's WMD case: It was put together by "cherry-picking" everything from the NYT to the DIA

Larry Wilkerson, chief of staff to Secretary of State Powell, after reviewing the draft for Powell's upcoming February 5, 2003, United Nations speech on the Bush Administration's weapons of mass destruction case thought little of the case. According to Wilkerson: "'It was clear the thing was put together by cherry-picking everything from *The New York Times* to the DIA [Defense Intelligence Agency],' he said.

When Wilkerson and the team began to examine the underlying sources, they found that a Defense Intelligence Agency report was not being used properly, a CIA report was not being cited in a fair way, a referenced *New York Times* article was quoting a DIA report out of context....Much of the information in Libby's draft, Wilkerson concluded, had come from the Iraqi National Congress—laundered through [Undersecretary of Defense Douglas] Feith's operation at the Pentagon [the Office of Special Plans]."

—Michael Isikoff and David Corn, *Hubris*, Page 177

1/31/2003: State Dept.'s INR: Thirty-eight allegations against Hussein in Powell's upcoming speech were "weak" or "unsubstantiated"

"On January 31 [2003], the State Department's INR, which had been vetting the work-in-progress draft [for Powell's upcoming UN speech given on February 5, 2003], sent Powell a memo noting that thirty-eight allegations in the speech were 'weak' or 'unsubstantiated.'...Since not all of INR's objections were heeded, Powell would be presenting evidence at the UN that even his own specialists did not believe."

—Michael Isikoff and David Corn, *Hubris*, Page 179

[**Note:** Powell gave his UN speech knowing parts of it *might not* have been accurate.]

2/6/2003: Cambridge University analyst says UK dossier mentioned in Powell's speech about Iraq's deception "lifted" from ten-year-old article

On February 6, 2003, "The day after Powell's presentation [to the UN Security Council], a Cambridge University analyst revealed that the British government's dossier on Iraq, referred to in Powell's speech as 'the fine paper that the United Kingdom distributed yesterday, which describes in exquisite detail Iraqi deception activities,' was lifted from a ten-year-old article in *Middle East Review of International Affairs* and two articles in *Jane's Intelligence Review*, including spelling mistakes."

—Stefan Halper and Jonathan Clarke, *America Alone*, Page 215

5/6/2003: Kristoff: George W. Bush administration used intel in run up to Iraq War it knew was false

"On May 6 [2003], *New York Times* columnist Nicholas Kristof published a column suggesting that in the lead-up to the war [in Iraq] the [Bush] administration had used intelligence that it had known to be false. Citing anonymous sources, Kristof wrote that the Vice President's [Cheney's] office had asked for an investigation into a claim that Iraq had tried to buy uranium from Niger. As early as February 2002 the envoy had told the CIA and State Department that the information was 'unequivocally wrong' and that the documents associated with the claim had been forged."

—Condoleezza Rice, *No Higher Honor*, Pages 221–222

7/9/2003: Rumsfeld acknowledges George W. Bush administration acted against Iraq on the basis of an "imagined threat"

In testimony before the Senate Armed Services Committee on July 9, 2003, Rumsfeld "acknowledged that the [Bush] administration 'did not act in Iraq because we had discovered dramatic new evidence of Iraq's pursuit of weapons of mass murder. We acted because we saw the existing evidence in a new light, through the prism of our experience on September 11th.'

In other words, the administration acted on the basis of an *imagined* threat. It *supposed* the *possibility* of a future similar attack, armed this time with Iraqi-supplied weapons of mass destruction, and acted to foreclose that theoretical possibility."

—Jeffrey Record, *Wanting War*, Page 60

8/12/2003: Thielmann: George W. Bush administration "cherry-picking" State Dept. Information to use "whatever pieces of it that fit their overall interpretation"

According to an August 12, 2003, interview with Greg Thielmann, the State Department proliferation expert, the Bush Administration was "'convinced that Saddam was developing nuclear weapons, that he was reconstituting his program, and I'm afraid that's where they started,' he said. 'They were cherry-picking the information that we provided to use whatever pieces of it that fit their overall interpretation. Worse than that, they were dropping qualifiers and distorting some of the information that we provided to make it seem even more alarmist and dangerous than the information that we were giving them.' The impulse to push the conclusions was especially worrisome, he added, because the intelligence community, not wanting to be caught napping, already tends 'to overwarn, rather than underwarn.'"

—Thomas E. Ricks, *Fiasco*, Page 55

[**Note:** Another Bush administration official saying that Bush used incomplete and misleading information to sell the need to attack Iraq.]

10/8/2003: Gardiner: George W. Bush administration's case for war against Iraq was not bad intel, but a "$200 million PR campaign to deceive the American public"

"'It [the Bush Administration's case for the Iraq invasion] was not bad intelligence. It was much more. It was an orchestrated effort. It began before the war, was a major effort during the war, and continues as post-conflict distortions,' wrote [retired Air Force Colonel and military analyst Sam] Gardiner in a fifty-six-page self-published report [that was posted to the Internet on October 8, 2003]....It was a $200 million PR campaign to deceive the American public."

—Amy Goodman with David Goodman, *The Exception to the Rulers*, Pages 252–254

1/15/2004: Thielmann: George W. Bush administration grossly distorted intel on Iraq/Al-Qaeda connection, and Iraqi nuclear weapons issue

In the January-February 2004 issue of *Mother Jones*, State Department intelligence analyst Greg Thielmann said: "'The Al Qaeda connection and nuclear weapons issue were the only two ways that you could link Iraq to an imminent security threat to the U.S. And the [Bush] administration was grossly distorting the intelligence on both.'" [*The fifteenth of the month used for date sorting purposes only.*]

—Jeffrey Record, *Wanting War*, Page 53

[**Note:** Another Bush administration official saying Bush intentionally distributed distorted intel to take our country to war against Iraq.]

1/26/2004: Col. Kwiatkowski: Iraqi intel was cherry-picked

In a *Mother Jones* article on January 26, 2004, retired Air Force Lt. Col. Karen Kwiatkowski said, of David Wurmser's Policy Counterterrorism Evalua tion Group: "'They'd take a little bit of intelligence, cherry-pick it, make it sound much more exciting, usually by taking it out of context, often by juxtaposition of two pieces of information that don't belong together.'"

—James Bamford, *A Pretext for War*, Page 290

[**Note:** More deception.]

5/16/2004: Powell discussing his February 2003 speech to UN: The "sourcing was inaccurate and wrong and, in some cases, deliberately misleading"

In an appearance on NBC's *Meet the Press* on May 16, 2004, Powell discussed his February 5, 2003, speech to the UN in which he called for regime change in Iraq. Powell said: "'[T]he sourcing was inaccurate and wrong and, in some cases, deliberately misleading, and for that I am disappointed and I regret it.'"

—Karen DeYoung, *Soldier*, Page 508

[**Note:** Should Powell pay for *deliberately misleading* the UN in his speech that helped garner support for Bush's war against Iraq, or was that just a part of his job?]

7/7/2004: Senate report: CIA intel to justify Iraq invasion was "both unfounded and unreasonable"

The Senate Select Committee on Intelligence released the Report on the US Intelligence Community's Prewar Intelligence Assessments on Iraq on July 7, 2004.

"The unanimous 511-page report...concluded that the intelligence put forth by the agency [CIA] to justify going to war was both unfounded and unreasonable.

It painted a picture of a dysfunctional organization that continually rejected evidence that did not fit into its preconceived biases and that sometimes passed on flawed analysis based on dubious or discredited sources.

It even found instances in which analysts may have misrepresented information by submitting reports that distorted the facts in order to strengthen their case that Iraq possessed weapons of mass destruction, including nuclear programs."

—James Bamford, *A Pretext for War*, Page 381

[**Note:** More Bush administration fraud to sell America on the need to attack Iraq.]

3/31/2005: Robb-Silberman Commission: US asserted Hussein had reconstituted his nuclear weapons program, and biological and other weapons programs; "not one bit of it could be confirmed when the [Iraq] war was over"

"'In front of the whole world, the United States government asserted that Saddam Hussein had reconstituted his nuclear weapons program, had biological weapons and mobile biological weapon production facilities and was producing chemical weapons,' the Robb-Silberman commission noted six months later [on March 31, 2005]. 'And not one bit of it could be confirmed when the war was over.'"

—Thomas E. Ricks, *Fiasco*, Page 377

11/20/2005: *LA Times*: George W. Bush, Powell mischaracterized and exaggerated Iraqi informant Curveball's intel

Los Angeles Times Staff Writers Bob Drogin and John Goetz on November 20, 2005, penned an article "How U.S. Fell Under the Spell of 'Curveball,'" which states in part: "The German intelligence officials responsible for one of the most important informants on Saddam Hussein's suspected weapons of mass destruction say that the Bush administration and the CIA repeatedly exaggerated his claims during the run-up to the war in Iraq....

According to the Germans, President Bush mischaracterized Curveball's information when he warned before the war that Iraq had at least seven mobile factories brewing biological poisons. Then-Secretary of State Colin L. Powell also misstated Curveball's accounts in his prewar presentation to the United Nations on Feb. 5, 2003, the Germans said."

—Bob Drogin and John Goetz, "How U.S. Fell Under the Spell of 'Curveball'," *Los Angeles Times*, November 20, 2005

4/9/2006: Marine Lt. Gen. Newbold says he retired before Iraq invasion in part because George W. Bush administration used 9/11 to invent the Iraq War

In an article in *Time* magazine on April 9, 2006, "Marine Lieutenant General Gregory Newbold, the Pentagon's top operations officer from 2000 to October 2002...revealed that he retired four months before the invasion [of Iraq] in part because the [Bush] administration had used '9/11's tragedy to hijack our security' and fight 'an invented war' instead of 'the real enemy, Al Qaeda.'"

—Frank Rich, *The Greatest Story Ever Sold*, Page 218

[**Note:** Should Bush be held accountable for his invented need-to-attack-Iraq war?]

5/28/2008: McClellan: Iraq war sold to American people with sophisticated "political propaganda campaign"

"Former White House press secretary Scott McClellan writes in a new memoir [*What Happened: Inside the Bush White House and Washington's Culture of Deception*] that the Iraq war was sold to the American people with a sophisticated 'political propaganda campaign' led by President Bush and aimed at 'manipulating sources of public opinion' and 'downplaying the major reason for going to war.'"

—Michael D. Shear, "Ex-Press Aide Writes that Bush Misled U.S. on Iraq," *The Washington Post*, May 28, 2008

C. THE RISKS AND DAMAGES TO OUR COUNTRY FROM THE 2003 IRAQ WAR

MANY, INCLUDING RUMSFELD, THE European Parliament, and the UK intel committee, wrote about the potential risks to the US if we attacked Iraq. After we attacked, many of those warnings proved prescient.

10/15/2002: Rumsfeld handwrites "Parade of Horribles" list of twenty-nine possible bad outcomes if Iraq attacked; number thirteen, "US could fail to find WMD"

"[W]ith lawmakers persuaded about what would go wrong if America did not attack Iraq, [President] Bush and Cheney were confronted with a roster of what could go wrong if it did. Rumsfeld had scrawled out by hand a list of all the possible setbacks…Marked 'SECRET' and dated October 15 [2002], the three-page document became known as the 'Parade of Horribles' and cited twenty-nine possible bad outcomes.

Number one was that Bush would fail to win UN approval, meaning that 'potential coalition partners may be unwilling to participate.' Others included the entry of Israel into the war, a Turkish incursion into Kurdistan, eruption of the Arab street, disruption of oil markets, higher than expected collateral damage, and Iraqi use of weapons of mass destruction against American forces.

Number thirteen was 'US could fail to find WMD on the ground in Iraq and be unpersuasive to the world.'

Number nineteen was 'Rather than having the post-Saddam effort require 2 to 4 years, it could take 8 to 10 years, thereby absorbing US leadership, military and financial resources.'

And number twenty-seven was 'Iraq could experience ethnic strife among Sunni, Shia and Kurds.' Still, Rumsfeld was not opposing war. He concluded his list by noting that 'it is possible of course to prepare a similar illustrative list of all the potential problems that need to be considered if there is no regime change in Iraq.'"

—Peter Baker, *Days of Fire*, Pages 226–227

1/20/2003: German foreign minister: "military strike against… Baghdad" would have "disastrous consequences"; Germany rejects strike idea

In a UN Security Council meeting on January 20, 2003, German Foreign Minister Joschka Fischer said: "'We are greatly concerned that a military strike against the regime in Baghdad [Iraq] would involve considerable and unpredictable risks for the global fight against terrorism.' It would have 'disastrous consequences,' and Germany rejected the very idea."

—Karen DeYoung, *Soldier*, Pages 432–433

1/29/2003: European Parliament: Unilateral military action in Iraq could lead to deeper crisis in region

"On the 29th of January, 2003, the European Parliament passed a nonbinding resolution, which: 'Expresses its opposition to any unilateral military action and believes that a preemptive strike [in Iraq] would not be in accordance with international law and the UN Charter and would lead to a deeper crisis involving other countries in the region.'"

—Philip Taylor, *The War in Iraq—A Failure of Honesty*, Page 127

2/10/2003: UK intel committee warns Blair that an Iraq regime collapse risks transfer of chemical and biological material to Al-Qaeda

Former House of Commons leader Robin Cook said: "only a month before [leading the UK into war in Iraq, on February 10, 2003] the Prime Minister [Blair] had received an assessment that 'there was no intelligence that Iraq had provided CB materials to al-Qa'ida'. Even more startlingly, the Joint Intelligence Committee warned that 'in the event of imminent regime collapse there would be a risk of transfer of such material'.

We had to wait until the report of the Intelligence and Security Committee six months later before we learnt of these warnings. Tony Blair was entirely within his rights to set aside this advice, but it is extraordinary that he should make the risk of the transfer of the CB material to terrorists a centrepiece of his case for war, when he had just received an intelligence assessment that war might make such transfer more, not less, likely."

—Robin Cook, *The Point of Departure*, Page 289

3/15/2003: CIA: US occupation in Iraq cultivating terrorists

According to a declassified report prepared by the CIA in April 2006, titled "Trends in Global Terrorism: Implications for the United States:" "[T]he [March 2003] American occupation of Iraq became 'the cause celebre for jihadists, breeding a deep resentment of U.S. involvement in the Muslim world and cultivating supporters for the global jihadist movement.'" [*The fifteenth of the month used for date sorting purposes only.*]

—Tim Weiner, *Legacy of Ashes*, Pages 569–570

[**Note:** Given the CIA's concerns about the consequence of the US attacking Iraq, and given that Bush had no credible intel that Hussein had WMD, helped bin Laden or Al-Qaeda, or was involved in 9/11, what pushed Bush to attack Iraq?]

4/5/2003: George W. Bush said war was fought to prevent spread of world's most dangerous weapons, but chose not to protect Iraqi nuclear facilities looted in first days of war

"Seven nuclear facilities in Iraq have been damaged or effectively destroyed by the looting that began in the first days of April [2003], when U.S. ground forces thrust into Baghdad, according to U.S. investigators and others with detailed knowledge of their work. The Bush administration fears that technical documents, sensitive equipment and possibly radiation sources have been scattered. If so, there are potentially significant consequences for public health and the spread of materials to build a nuclear or radiological bomb. President Bush had said the war was fought to prevent the spread of 'the world's most dangerous weapons.'" [*The fifth of the month used for date sorting purposes only.*]

—Barton Gellman, "Seven Nuclear Sites Looted," *The Washington Post*, May 10, 2003

9/11/2003: Joint Intel Committee: Al-Qaeda threat "would be heightened by military action against Iraq"

"The [UK] Intelligence and Security Committee...revealed that the Joint Intelligence Committee had assessed [in a September 11, 2003, report] that the al-Qa'ida threat 'would be heightened by military action against Iraq.'"

—Robin Cook, *The Point of Departure*, Page 290

2/5/2004: *NY Times*: George W. Bush administration acknowledged that its "muscular post-9/11 foreign policy and military interventionism...damaged American prestige"

According to a *New York Times* article from February 5, 2004: "[T]he Bush administration was obliged to acknowledge that its muscular post-9/11 foreign policy and military interventionism had damaged American prestige abroad so thoroughly that 'it will take us many years of hard, focused work' to restore America's international standing. Particularly hurtful were disclosures in 2004 of torture and humiliation meted by Americans to prisoners in Iraq, Guantánamo, and Afghanistan."

—Jonathan Randal, *Osama*, Page 290

5/6/2004: Congressman Murtha: Abu Ghraib "destroyed our credibility in Iraq...Arab world"

Regarding the abuse of Iraqi prisoners at Abu Ghraib: "'We're not going to recover from this damage,' Congressman John Murtha [D-PA] announced [on May 6, 2004]. 'This one incident destroyed our credibility in Iraq and in all the Arab world.'"

—Donald Rumsfeld, *Known and Unknown*, Page 546

6/10/2004: Congressman Waxman sought review of State Dept. report that terrorist incidents lowest in thirty years; then Powell admitted terrorism at twenty year high

The State Department's Patterns of Global Terrorism 2003 report, released in April 2004, claimed that terrorist incidents had dropped to 190, the lowest in over thirty years. "But after Democratic congressman Henry Waxman (D-CA) sought a review of the report by the Congressional Research Service, Secretary [of State] Colin Powell was forced to admit that terrorism activity was actually at a twenty-year high. 'We are still trying to determine what went wrong with the data and why we didn't catch it,' said an embarrassed Powell [in a *Washington Post* article on June 10, 2004]. The corrected report finally admitted that the total number of terrorist incidents actually *rose* in 2003. There were 390 deaths, versus 307 in the first report."

—Peter Lance, *Cover Up*, Page 250

[**Note:** Was Bush again using Powell as part of his marketing deceit or were Powell's numbers another one of his accidental errors?]

1/13/2005: NIC report suggests that a war in Iraq would create terrorist haven

Regarding the National Intelligence Council's (NIC's) January 13, 2005, report on terrorism in Iraq: "President Bush has frequently described the Iraq war as an integral part of U.S. efforts to combat terrorism. But the council's report suggests the conflict has also helped terrorists by creating a haven for them in the chaos of war. 'At the moment,' NIC Chairman Robert L. Hutchings said, Iraq 'is a magnet for international terrorist activity.'"

—Dana Priest, "Iraq New Terror Breeding Ground," *The Washington Post*, January 14, 2005

7/18/2005: UK's Chatham House: Iraq situation provided "a boost to the al Qaeda network's propaganda, recruitment and fundraising"

"Perhaps the biggest and most serious aspect of the American failure in Iraq was highlighted in an 18 July 2005 paper published by Chatham House (formerly the Royal Institute of International Affairs).

International security experts noted that the situation in Iraq had provided 'a boost to the al Qaeda network's propaganda, recruitment and fundraising, caused a major split in the coalition, and provided an ideal targeting and training area for al Qaedalinked [sic] terrorists.'"

—Abdel Bari Atwan, *The Secret History of al Qaeda*, Page 215

4/15/2006: NIE: Iraq war a "cause celebre" for jihadists, and "is shaping a new generation of terrorist leaders and operatives"

"The [Bush] administration's own National Intelligence Estimate on 'Trends in Global Terrorism: implications for the United States,' circulated within the government in April 2006 and partially declassified in October, states that 'the Iraq War has become the *cause celebre* for jihadists… and is shaping a new generation of terrorist leaders and operatives.'" [*The fifteenth of the month used for date sorting purposes only.*]

—Peter Bergen and Paul Cruickshank, "The Iraq Effect: War has Increased Terrorism Sevenfold Worldwide," *Mother Jones*, March 1, 2007

3/1/2007: *Mother Jones*: Iraq War "has motivated jihadists"… making Al-Qaeda's "message of global struggle… more persuasive to militants"

On March 1, 2007, journalist Peter Bergen and terrorism analyst Paul Cruickshank published a study on the War in Iraq in *Mother Jones*.

They "concluded that the Iraq War 'has motivated jihadists around the world to see their particular struggle as part of a wider global jihad fought on behalf of the Islamic *umma*.'

They believed that it served as a catalyst, helping to globalize jihadism by making al Qaeda's 'message of global struggle even more persuasive to militants.'"

—Daveed Gartenstein-Ross, *Bin Laden's Legacy*, Page 112

5/31/2007: Senate committee pre-war assessment: American invasion of Iraq would bring instability to region that Al-Qaeda and Iran would exploit

In Appendix D of the Senate Select Committee on Intelligence's May 31, 2007, report under the "Additional Views of Chairman John D. Rockefeller IV, Senator Ron Wyden, Senator Bayh, And Senator Whitehouse":

"The Committee's report on the Intelligence Community's pre-war assessments on post-war Iraq reveals that there was a steady flow of cautionary judgments sent to senior policy officials in the Bush Administration warning that securing the peace in Iraq would be difficult and success uncertain.

The most chilling and prescient warning from the Intelligence Community prior to the war was that the American invasion would bring about instability in Iraq that would be exploited by Iran and al-Qa'ida terrorists....

What the Administration also kept from the American people were the sobering intelligence assessments it received at the time warning that the post-war transition could allow al-Qa'ida to establish the presence in Iraq and opportunity to strike at Americans it did not have prior to the invasion."

—"Report on prewar intelligence assessments about postwar Iraq, together with additional minority views," Senate Select Committee on Intelligence, May 31, 2007, Page 188

[**Note:** The Bush administration was told more than once that attacking Iraq would create more terrorism.]

7/17/2007: Sixteen different US spy services concluded bin Laden's terror network had been revitalized and the threat of attacks on U.S. itself had increased since 9/11

"[T]he National Intelligence Estimate (compiled by sixteen different agencies) found that bin Laden's terror network had been revitalized in the previous two years, and that the threat of attacks on the U.S. homeland had actually *increased* since 9/11."

—Peter Lance, *Triple Cross*, Page 510

9/12/2007: One of the world's think-tanks concludes Al-Qaeda "adaptable," threat from Islamist terrorism to "get worse"

"In September [12] 2007 one of the world's leading security think-tanks, the International Institute for Strategic Studies (IISS) warned that '*core* al Qaeda is proving adaptable and resilient,' concluding that 'the threat from Islamist terrorism...looks set to get worse.'"

—Abdel Bari Atwan, *The Secret History of al Qaeda*, Page 281

3/8/2008: Senator Rockefeller: George W. Bush administration approach to counterterrorism "undermining the security" by weakening US legal, moral authority

In March 8, 2008, Senator Jay Rockefeller (D-WV) said: "the Bush Administration's approach [to counterterrorism] was not only unnecessary, it was also undermining the security that it claimed to safeguard.

'The CIA's program damages our national security by weakening our legal and moral authority, and by providing al Qaeda and other terrorist groups a recruiting and motivational tool,' he said."

—Jane Mayer, *The Dark Side*, Page 330

4/17/2008: National Defense University study: Iraq War costing US allies; US standing as a moral leader damaged; negative impact on War on Terror

"An April [17] 2008 National Defense University study summarized the damage [caused by the war in Iraq]:

'Globally, U.S. standing among friends and allies has fallen.

Our status as a moral leader has been damaged by the war, the subsequent occupation of a Muslim nation, and various issues concerning the treatment of detainees.

At the same time, operations in Iraq have had a negative impact on all other efforts in the war on terror, which must bow to the priority of Iraq when it comes to manpower, materiel, and the attention of decisionmakers.

Our Armed Forces—especially the Army and Marine Corps—have been severely strained by the war in Iraq. Compounding all of these problems, our efforts there were designed to enhance national security, but they have become, at least temporarily, an incubator for terrorism and have emboldened Iran to expand its influence throughout the Middle East.'"

—Jeffrey Record, *Wanting War*, Page 4

10/29/2008: War expert says Al-Qaeda was not in Iraq before the war; "Islamic extremism and violence will be stronger as a result of the war"

In a *Washington Times* article on October 29, 2008, Iraq War expert Anthony H. Cordesman wrote:

"'Al Qeada may be largely defeated [in Iraq], but it did not exist [there] before the U.S. invasion, and Islamic extremism and violence will be stronger as a result of the war.'"

—Jeffrey Record, *Wanting War*, Page 169

This section's quotes have shown that attacking Iraq would increase terrorism, not lessen it.

D. INJURIES AND DEATHS FROM OUR ATTACKING IRAQ

HERE ARE SOME REPORTED estimates of the injuries and deaths that occurred because of our attacking Iraq in 2003.

10/29/2004: *Lancet* study: Nearly eighty percent of those killed by coalition air strikes were women and children

According to an October 29, 2004, study by the British medical journal *The Lancet*: "Most individuals reportedly killed by coalition forces were women and children....Violence accounted for most of the excess deaths and air strikes from coalition forces accounted for most violent deaths."

—Les Roberts, Riyadh Lafta, Richard Garfield, Jamal Khudhairi, and Gilbert Burnham, "Mortality before and after the 2003 invasion of Iraq: cluster sample survey," *The Lancet*, October 29, 2004

[**Note:** Did Bush consider the deaths of women and children unfortunate collateral damage of war or perhaps the acquisition cost of Iraqi oil?]

7/15/2005: Dossier of Civilian Casualties in Iraq from 2003–2005 shows 24,865 civilians killed, almost twenty percent of those are women and children

"The *Dossier of Civilian Casualties in Iraq, [2003–2005]*, published by Iraq Body Count in July 2005, shows 24,865 civilians killed, with women and children accounting for almost 20 per cent of civilian deaths.

Thirty per cent of civilian deaths occurred in the invasion phase; post-invasion, the number of civilians killed was almost twice as high in year two (11,351) as in year one (6,215).

US forces killed 37 per cent of civilian victims, post-invasion criminal violence accounted for 36 per cent of deaths and anti-occupation forces 9 per cent." [*The fifteenth of the month used for date sorting purposes only.*] [*Editor's note: the author incorrectly identified the starting date of the Dossier as 2002.*]

—Clare Short, *An Honourable Deception?*, Page 293

10/15/2006: *Lancet:* Estimated deaths in Iraq between March 2003 and July 2006 exceeded 650,000 people

In October 2006, the noted British medical journal *Lancet* "estimated that the total deaths in Iraq in the period between March 2003 and July 2006 *may have exceeded 650,000 people.*

The figure was astounding, as it easily surpassed all the previously published figures of casualties, which ranged from 50,000 (from the unofficial Iraq Body Count) to 100,000. The *Lancet* used statistically acceptable methods, which had been employed with good effect in other conflict zones. The report was immediately condemned by officials in Washington and London as being grossly exaggerated." [*The fifteenth of the month used for date sorting purposes only.*]

—Ali A. Allawi, *The Occupation of Iraq*, Page 450

[**Note:** The unnecessary deaths may have exceeded 650,000.]

8/31/2010: CNN: 4,400 US military personnel dead, 30,000 wounded by end of Iraq War

According to a CNN.com article on August 31, 2010: "At 5 p.m. ET [on August 31, 2010]—at a cost of more than 4,400 U.S. military personnel killed and 30,000 wounded—America's combat mission in Iraq officially drew to a close."

—Alan Silverleib, "U.S. Combat Mission in Iraq Ends," CNN.com, September 1, 2010

[**Note:** Over 4,000 American deaths because of Bush's war.]

10/22/2010: *The Guardian:* Leaked Pentagon docs show more than 100,000 killed in Iraq including 15,000 more previously unrecorded Iraq war deaths

"Leaked Pentagon files obtained by *the Guardian* contain details of more than 100,000 people killed in Iraq following the US-led invasion, including more than 15,000 deaths that were previously unrecorded. British ministers have repeatedly refused to concede the existence of any official statistics on Iraqi deaths....The mass of leaked documents provides the first detailed tally by the US military of Iraqi fatalities. Troops on the ground filed secret field reports over six years of the occupation, purporting to tot up every casualty, military and civilian....The logs record a total of 109,032 violent deaths between 2004 and 2009. It is claimed that 66,081 of these were civilians. A further 23,984 deaths are classed as 'enemy' and 15,196 as members of the Iraqi security forces. The logs also include the deaths of 3,771 US and allied soldiers."

—David Leigh, "Iraq War Logs Reveal 15,000 Previously Unlisted Civilian Deaths," *The Guardian*, October 22, 2010

10/22/2010: More than 109,000 violent deaths in Iraq war from 2004 to 2009

"Although US generals have claimed their army does not carry out body counts and British ministers still say no official statistics exist, the war logs [exposed by WikiLeaks on October 22, 2010] show these claims are untrue.

The field reports purport to identify all civilian and insurgent casualties, as well as numbers of coalition forces wounded and killed in action.

They give a total of more than 109,000 violent deaths from all causes between 2004 and the end of 2009. This includes 66,081 civilians, 23,984 people classed as 'enemy' and 15,196 members of the Iraqi security forces.

Another 3,771 dead US and allied soldiers complete the body count."

—Nick Davies, Jonathan Steele, and David Leigh, "Iraq War Logs: Secret Files Show How US Ignored Torture," *The Guardian*, October 22, 2010

6/7/2013: Estimates of the Iraq death toll range from 174,000 to over a million

"The results from a new poll commissioned by the British media watchdog group MediaLens exposed a startling disconnect between the realities of the Iraq War and public perceptions of it: Namely, what the Iraqi death toll was....These answers are, of course, way off the mark. Estimates of the death toll range from about 174,000 (Iraq Body Count, 3/19/13) to over a million (Opinion Business Research, cited in Congressional Research Service, 10/7/10). Even at the times of those U.S. polls, death estimates were far beyond the public's estimates."

—Rebecca Hellmich, "How Many Iraqis Died in the Iraq War?," Fair.org, June 7, 2013

[**Note:** One estimate was that over a million people died because of Bush's Iraq war.]

10/16/2013: A study reported in BBC.com "concludes that more than 60% of the estimated 461,000 excess deaths were directly attributable to violence, with the rest associated with the collapse of infrastructure and other indirect causes"

"About half a million people died in Iraq as a result of war-related causes between the US-led invasion in 2003 and mid-2011, an academic study suggests....The study—by researchers from the University of Washington, Johns Hopkins University, Simon Fraser University and Mustansiriya University—covers March 2003 until June 2011, six months before the US withdrawal....The study concludes that more than 60% of the estimated 461,000 excess deaths were directly attributable to violence, with the rest associated with the collapse of infrastructure and other indirect causes.

These include the failures of health, sanitation, transportation, communication and other systems."

—"Iraq study estimates war-related deaths at 461,000," BBC.com, October 16, 2013

10/16/2013: 405,000 deaths attributable to Iraq War include heart attacks and ruined sanitation, hospitals

"The survey responses point to around 405,000 deaths attributable to the war and occupation in Iraq from 2003 to 2011. At least another 56,000 deaths should be added to that total from households forced to flee Iraq, the study authors estimate. More than 60 percent of the excess deaths of men, women, and children reported from 2003 to 2011 were the direct result of shootings, bombings, airstrikes, or other violence, according to the study. The rest came indirectly, from stress-related heart attacks or ruined sanitation and hospitals."

—Dan Vergano, "Half-Million Iraqis Died in the War, New Study Says," National-Geographic.com, October 16, 2013

E. COSTS RELATED TO OUR ATTACKING IRAQ

THE ESTIMATED COSTS RELATED to the 2003 Iraq War vary greatly.

1/9/2006: *Christian Science Monitor* article states the cost of the Iraq War to "probably be more than $2 trillion"

According to an article in the *Christian Science Monitor* on January 9, 2006: "In an independent analysis of the current, long-term, direct, and indirect costs of the Iraq War, Nobel Prize-winning economist Joseph E. Stiglitz and Harvard scholar Linda Bilmes concluded that the total costs of the war, compared with costs incurred by the U.S. government had the war not been launched, would probably be more than $2 trillion.

This conclusion was based on assumptions that U.S. troops will remain in Iraq for four more years, but at decreasing levels, and that the federal government will have to bear interest costs on loans made to finance the war, sharply higher recruitment costs for the armed forces, the cost of equipment replacement, the costs of health care for injured veterans, and tax revenues lost as a result of reduced years of productive labor by servicemen and -women killed and wounded in the war."

—Ian S. Lustick, *Trapped in the War on Terror*, Page 23

10/24/2007: CBO estimates Iraq War monetary cost at $2.4 trillion through 2017

"In October [24] 2007, the Congressional Budget Office [CBO] estimated that the monetary costs of the Iraq War could reach $2.4 trillion through 2017."

—Ricardo S. Sanchez with Donald T. Phillips, *Wiser in Battle*, Page 455

3/13/2008: *The Guardian:* Iraq War costs US $3 trillion in its first five years; Another $3 trillion to others

According to a March 13, 2008, article in *The Guardian*: "The total cost of the Iraq War in its first five years was estimated to be $3 trillion to the United States and a similarly colossal amount to the rest of the world."

—Deepak Tripathi, *Overcoming the Bush Legacy in Iraq and Afghanistan*, Pages 16–17

9/5/2010: Professors' follow-up calculation of Iraq War cost to US comes in at more than $3 trillion

Professors Joseph Stiglitz and Linda Bilmes "followed up their 2008 book [*The Three Trillion Dollar War: the True Cost of the Iraq Conflict*] with a September [5] 2010 *Washington Post* column, published as the United States ended what it dubbed its 'combat operations' in Iraq, arguing that their $3 trillion calculation was in fact too low—a notable claim, since the $3 trillion estimate had been markedly higher than previous projections."

—Daveed Gartenstein-Ross, *Bin Laden's Legacy*, Page 113

12/25/2011: Costs of Iraq War: $1.7 trillion through Fiscal Year 2013; $7 trillion by 2053

"We drew from sources including various news reports, The Brookings Institute's Iraq Index, and the Costs of War Project to document money and blood spent on the Iraq war between 2003 and 2011.

[1] 189,000: Direct war deaths, which doesn't include the hundreds of thousands more that died due to war-related hardships.

[2] 4,488: U.S. service personnel killed directly.

[3] 32,223: Troops injured (not including PTSD [Post-traumatic stress disorder]).

[4] 134,000: Civilians killed directly.

[5] 655,000: Persons who have died in Iraq since the invasion that would not have died if the invasion had not occurred.

[6] 150: Reporters killed.

[7] 2.8 million: Persons who remain either internally displaced or have fled the country.

[8] $1.7 trillion: Amount in war expenses spent by the U.S. Treasury Department as through Fiscal Year 2013.

[9] $5,000: Amount spent per second.

[10] $350,000: Cost to deploy one American military member.

[11] $490 billion: Amount in war benefits owed to war veterans.

[12] $7 trillion: Projected interest payments due by 2053 (because the war was paid for with borrowed money).

[13] $20 billion: Amount paid to KBR [Kellogg Brown and Root], contractor responsible for equipment and services.

[14] $3 billion: Amount of KBR payments Pentagon auditors considered 'questionable.'

[15] $60 billion: Amount paid for reconstruction, (which was ruled largely a waste due to corruption and shoddy work.)

[16] $4 billion: Amount owed to the U.S. by Iraq before the invasion.

[17] 1.6 million: Gallons of oil used by U.S. forces each day in Iraq (at $127.68 a barrel).

[18] $12 billion: Cost per month of the war by 2008.

[19] $7 billion: Amount owed to Iraq by the U.S. after the war (mostly due to fraud).

[20] $20 billion: Annual air conditioning cost.

[21] Missing: $546 million in spare parts; 190,000 guns, including 110,000 AK-47s.

[22] 40 percent: Increase in Iraqi oil production.

[23] $5 billion: Revenue from Iraqi oil in 2003.

[24] $85 billion: Revenue from Iraqi oil in 2011.

[25] $150 billion: Amount oil companies are expected to invest in oil development over the next decade.

[26] $75 billion: Approximate amount expected to go to American subcontracting companies, largest of all Halliburton.

[27] 0: Nuclear Weapons of Mass Destruction found (though a bunch of chems were discovered).

Perhaps most importantly, **this list doesn't account for the emotional damage** caused to service members and their families as well as the destruction to the homes, social fabric, and psyche of the Iraqi people."
[*The twenty-fifth of the month used for date sorting purposes only.*]

—Michael B Kelley and Geoffrey Ingersoll, "The Staggering Cost of the Last Decade's US War in Iraq—In Numbers," BusinessInsider.com, June 20, 2014

[Note: The costs of a war stemming from presidential deceit.]

F. RECAP

AFTER GEORGE W. BUSH was sworn in as president, he and his administration began telling Congress, the American people, and others specific reasons why Hussein was a unique and immediate threat to our country. The reasons given were effective, many in Congress believed the scare tactics, and Bush got his war. However, as you have read, most of those reasons were not true.

Here are a few of the quotes you have read, including gray box quotes, quotes that are misleading, without credible basis, or false.

— 9/19/2002: "On September 19 [2002], the president [Bush] met with 11 House members in the Cabinet Room. 'The war on terrorism is going okay; we are hunting down al Qaeda one-by-one,' Bush began. 'The biggest threat, however, is Saddam Hussein and his weapons of mass destruction. He can blow up Israel and that would trigger an international conflict....We will take over the oil fields early—and mitigate the oil shock'"
[Note: Six months before Bush invaded Iraq, he is talking about taking over the Iraq oil fields.]

— 10/7/2002: Referring to a speech made by President Bush on October 7, 2002, Senator Bob Graham (D-FL) said that President Bush's rhetoric was misleading: "These claims [of an Iraq/Al-Qaeda connection] were effective. At the time, a poll showed that 70 percent of Americans believed that Saddam Hussein was involved in or directly responsible for the attacks of September 11; rather than disabusing people of the notion, the President tried to solidify it. Instead of using his presidency to teach America about the real terrorist threats we faced, Bush was using it to mislead the country in order to build support for a war against an unrelated threat."

— 2/14/2003: "Saddam [Hussein] had presented a massive document to the UN [in December 2002], claiming that he had no WMD. Hans Blix had corroborated this, by stating to the Security Council on 14 February, 2003, that the UN team had found no WMD in Iraq."

— 3/16/2003: On March 16, 2003, Vice President Cheney appeared on NBC's *Meet the Press* and "told Tim Russert that Saddam was hoarding unconventional weapons and had 'a long-standing relationship' with al-Qaeda. Cheney dismissed the IAEA's finding that Saddam had not revived its nuclear weapons program. 'We believe,' Cheney said, 'he has, in fact, reconstituted nuclear weapons.'"
[**Note:** Cheney misleading America three days before we invaded Iraq.]

— 1/28/2004: "'We now know,' said Senator [Bill] Nelson [D-FL] in January [28] 2004, 'after the fact and on the basis of...[former Iraq Survey Group leader] Dr. Kay's testimony today in the Senate Armed Services Committee, that the information [regarding weapons of mass destruction in Iraq] was false; and not only that there were not weapons of mass destruction—chemical and biological—but there was no fleet of UAVs, unmanned aerial vehicles, nor was there any capability of putting UAVs on ships and transporting them to the Atlantic coast and launching them at U.S. cities on the eastern seaboard....The degree of specificity I was given a year and a half ago, prior to my vote [in favor of war in Iraq], was not only inaccurate; it was patently false.'"

— 2/19/2004: According to a February 19, 2004, interview with retired Air Force Lt. Col. Karen Kwiatkowski: "'The OSP and the Vice President's office were critical in this propaganda effort—to convince Americans that there was some just requirement for preemptive war [in Iraq]....The Congress was misled, it was lied to. At a very minimum, that is a subversion of the Constitution. A preemptive war based on what we knew was not a pressing need is not what this country stands for.'"

As this chapter has shown, Bush and top people in his administration relentlessly misled and lied to the American people, inflating and fabricating the danger to our country from Hussein and his said-to-have weapons of mass destruction.

Bush knew or must have known his march to war was based on lies and purposeful misinformation.

Regardless of his reason for taking our country into the Iraq War, be it for oil, to protect our country (with no credible intel supporting that fear), to become a war president, to gain his father's favor, or to spread some fanciful notion of democracy in Iraq or the Middle East, Bush knew there was no credible intelligence or justification for his Iraq War.

SUMMARY

AFTER COMPILING THIS BOOK, I asked myself how could one person, President George W. Bush, given the supposed checks and balances of the three branches of our federal government, have caused so much unnecessary pain, death, and destruction to our people, our country, and to others around the world.

Answers to the following questions might help us understand Bush's actions in the crimes I assert he committed.

What was going on in George W. Bush's mind when he all but ignored the flood of well-documented threats posed by Osama bin Laden and Al-Qaeda and instead focused on Hussein, Hussein's never-found weapons of mass destruction, and Iraq's oil?

Given all the threats George W. Bush was told about Osama bin Laden and Al-Qaeda coming to attack our country, some of which Bush was told about even before he became president, how could he have not made protecting us from those threats his number one job from the day he took office?

What was going through Bush's mind when he had people tortured? Did he think he was above the law or did he care?

Why did Bush sell the American people and Congress on an unnecessary war with Iraq based on old, inflated, and fabricated information that Hussein's supposed weapons of mass destruction were a danger to our country?

Did George W. Bush take our country to war against Iraq mainly or solely for oil by intentionally making up the dangers about Hussein as a road to that oil?

If Bush did take our country to war for oil, did he do so for our national oil security, or for his personal or friends' profit?

If Bush attacked Iraq to protect our access to oil for our national security, did he feel his deception in taking us to war for oil justified the deaths of so many?

Unfortunately, I don't believe that answers to such questions will ever be known.

CRIME 1: CRIMINAL NEGLIGENCE 9/11

As focused as President Bush was on removing Hussein from office, on Hussein's supposed weapons of mass destruction, and on Iraqi oil, what did he think about the many warnings he received regarding bin Laden and Al-Qaeda coming to attack our country prior to 9/11?

As Bush was well aware of those threats, how could he not have treated them with great concern when, for example, President Clinton told Bush on December 16, 2000, that Al-Qaeda was one of "the biggest security problems" he would face as president; or when, on December 20, 2000, counterterrorism czar Clarke and his team briefed incoming Secretary of State Powell on intel that Al-Qaeda was planning direct attacks against the United States; or on January 25, 2001, five days into his presidency, when Clarke sent Rice a memo and an attachment mentioning bin Laden and Al-Qaeda 117 times;[77] or when he received the June 28, 2001, CIA Alert Memorandum stating in part that the latest intelligence indicated the probability, not possibility, of imminent Al-Qaeda attacks, that they would "have dramatic consequences on [our] governments or cause major casualties"; or when, on August 6, 2001, Bush's PDB was titled "Bin Laden Determined to Strike in the US"?

The intel about the dangers from bin Laden and Al-Qaeda was accurate, and we were indeed struck by Al-Qaeda on September 11, 2001.

In a look back at 9/11, one might ask if the director of the CIA, or of the Phoenix office of the FBI, or the two members of the 9/11 Commission knew what they were talking about when they suggested that 9/11 could have or should have been prevented; or Tenet saying that his July 10, 2001, meeting with Rice was a tremendous lost opportunity to prevent or disrupt the 9/11 attacks; or Thomas Kean, Republican and Chair of the 9/11 Commission, and Lee Hamilton, Democrat and Vice Chair of the 9/11 Commission, telling *Meet The Press* on April 4, 2004, "the 9/11 attacks could have been prevented."

---

77   See Richard Clarke's January 25, 2001, memo and attachment.

Perhaps George W. Bush gave us the answer as to why he didn't act on the threats of bin Laden or Al-Qaeda until it was too late. As reported in Peter Baker's book *Days of Fire*, Bush admitted, when looking back on his President's Daily Brief of August 6, 2001 ("Bin Laden Determined to Strike in the U.S."), that he did not react with alarm to the bin Laden and Al-Qaeda warnings as he should have. He did not summon the directors of the FBI and the CIA. He did not order heightened alerts. "I didn't feel that sense of urgency," Bush said.

Was Bush's focus so directed at Iraqi oil and Hussein that he didn't even listen to the real terrorist dangers?

Regardless, Bush's lack of urgency in the face of so many dire warnings about bin Laden and Al-Qaeda only increased the odds that we would be attacked, which we were on 9/11.

CRIME 2: TORTURING PRISONERS AND SENDING THEM TO BE TORTURED BY OTHERS

IT SEEMS ODD TO put together a chapter on the president of the United States approving, if not promoting, torturing prisoners under his control, especially when he was stating on different occasions that neither he nor his administration tortured people.

When Bush said on March 1, 2003, "Damn right," when Tenet asked if he had permission to use enhanced interrogation techniques, including waterboarding a prisoner, did Bush care about the law or was torturing people an exciting way for him to exercise his presidential power? If Bush had known that torturing was a crime but he did it anyway to protect our country, would he accept the consequences of his actions?

Did Bush know or care when former CIA Agent Baer told the *New Statesman* on May 17, 2004, "If you want a serious interrogation, you send a prisoner to Jordan. If you want them to be tortured, you send them to Syria. If you want someone to disappear, never to see them again, you send them to Egypt"? What about when George W. Bush stated on June 26, 2003, that "Torture anywhere is an affront to human dignity everywhere," and, on June 26, 2004, when Bush said: "Freedom from torture is an inalienable human right"?

CRIME 3: INTENTIONAL DECEIT/DECEIVING OUR COUNTRY INTO UNNECESSARILY ATTACKING IRAQ

DID THE UGLINESS, DEATH, and destruction of war occur to President George W. Bush when he sent the world's most powerful army—powered mainly by young Americans thinking they were protecting our country from weapons of mass destruction—to fight a country that some knowledgeable people in his government and the intelligence community said was not an immediate threat to the US?

Why did Bush and his administration mislead the American public, our Congress, and many others around the world about the immediate danger of Hussein when he had no credible intel that Iraq was an immediate threat to America?

What was in Bush's mind, for example, when Cheney said in a speech on August 26, 2002, that "there is no doubt that Saddam Hussein now *has* weapons of mass destruction"; or when Cheney told the American people, on March 16, 2003, that Hussein "*has*, in fact, reconstituted nuclear weapons"; or when, on March 17, 2003, Bush told our nation that "the Iraq regime *continues to possess* and conceal some of the most lethal weapons ever devised"; or when, on March 26, 2003, George W. Bush responded to a question at MacDill Air Force Base with, "We are also taking every action we can to prevent the Iraqi regime from using *its hidden* weapons of mass destruction?"

There was an inkling of that deceit, albeit after Bush's war began, when Powell said on December 13, 2004, "If I had known there were no stockpiles [of WMD in Iraq], I never would have said there were stockpiles."

Few would have thought that prior to March 19, 2003, the fear of Hussein that Bush and his administration were creating and selling was not based on credible intel or facts.

Did Bush care about the horrors of war when he attacked Iraq, or did he blindly go to war against Iraq to get their oil? If so, does it matter why?

Could the following quote from *Payback*,[78] a book by David P. Barash and Judith Eve Lipton, in part on the strategy of *redirected aggression*, explain Bush's taking our country to war on his misleading and false premises?

> **"George W. Bush and his Administration were not stooges at all, but quite brilliant. They read the need of most Americans at the time: to hit someone, hard, so as to redirect their suffering and anger [from 9/11]. The evidence is overwhelming that for the Bush Administration's 'neocons,' the September 11 attacks were not the reason for the Iraq War; rather, it was a convenient excuse for doing something upon which they had already decided. Their accomplishment—if such is the correct word—was identifying the post-9/11 mood of the American people, and manipulating this mood, brilliantly, toward war."**

It's difficult to fathom the extent of the death and destruction caused by George W. Bush's three crimes, but his legacy of death and destruction are of Olympic proportions.

— An estimated 2,977 people killed by the attacks on 9/11, and thousands more injured or incapacitated that day. In addition, hundreds if not thousands have died and will die early from the toxic air from the collapse of the Twin Towers and its aftermath.

— By one count, there were 4,400 United States personnel killed and 30,000 wounded in the Iraq War as of August 31, 2010; tens of thousands more wounded physically and emotionally crippled by participating in that war; millions of Americans and their families destroyed, devastated, and/or traumatized by 9/11 and Bush's 2003 Iraq War.

— As many as 650,000 deaths or more from Bush's Iraq War, deaths that wouldn't have occurred but for that war.

— Many of our civil rights, and the civil rights of others around the world, were curtailed due to the fear created by 9/11, a fear used by some as an opportunity to weaken our liberties.

_____

78   Barash and Lipton, Payback: *Why We Retaliate, Redirect Aggression, and Take Revenge*, Page 11

— Three to seven trillion dollars in costs to our country from 9/11 and the 2003 invasion of Iraq. Those unnecessary trillions were and will be added to our national debt, a sum burdening our future, the future of our children, and perhaps of generations to come.

— Bush's torture of prisoners puts American soldiers captured in future wars at greater risk of being tortured.

— The loss of America's prestige and moral authority from Bush's unnecessary Iraq War and torturing prisoners will hurt our country in the years ahead.

— Sixteen different US spy agencies on September 24, 2006, concluded that the American invasion and occupation of Iraq since March 2003 has helped spawn a new generation of Islamic radicals— effectively increasing the terror threat in the years after 9/11—and that the Bush administration tortured detainees and that torture wasn't effective in securing intel otherwise unavailable.

Because America invaded a sovereign country without credible reason and tortured prisoners, how can we say without hypocrisy that other countries shouldn't do the same to other nations or to us? What moral authority do we have to tell others it is wrong to torture?

IN CONCLUSION

BASED ON MY RESEARCH and supported by the preceding quotes and information, I submit that President George W. Bush is guilty of three crimes— criminal negligence (or the equivalent), torture, and murder/crimes against humanity. Hopefully the quotes in these pages have provided you with enough information to decide for yourself the degree, if any, of Bush's culpability for his actions.

Regardless of how I or others see what I submit are Bush's criminal acts, some will continue to argue that while he wasn't a perfect president, at least he rid the world of the tyrant, Hussein. Yes, he did, but for what reason, by what method, and at what cost?

In addition to the unnecessary deaths and wounding of thousands of brave Americans, hundreds of thousands of others died and were injured from Bush's unnecessary Iraq invasion. The trillions of dollars Bush's war has cost has and will continue to be added to our national debt. A debt saddling our future.

In conclusion, I believe the *evidence* in this book shows Bush's three crimes were reckless, dishonest, and tragically unnecessary.

I rest my case.

METHODOLOGY

1. www.911Plus.org

Many of the quotes in this book were taken from the online searchable database www.911Plus.org, which I created.

The 911Plus.org database contains over 7,800 quotes from 130 published books and other sources. That database was put together over a period of three and a half years and was built to be nonpartisan, using quotes from authors on all sides of the political spectrum.

For the methodology behind that database, go to www.911Plus.org/Methodology.

2. Dates of quotes

If a quote on one day alludes to or mentions events that took place on a specific earlier day or days, depending on the context, the quote is recorded on either the earlier date(s), the later date, or both.

3. Some shortened quotes

A handful of quotes in this book are slightly shorter than the corresponding quotes in the 911Plus.org database. The shortening of those few quotes occurred because of brevity considerations. The words taken out of the quotes should not have changed the intent or the meaning of those quotes.

4. Accuracy of quotes

The quotes in this book have been checked for accuracy. In addition, I have tried to pick quotes from authors and sources that seem mainstream and/or reliable, although some authors do paraphrase the words of others, sometimes altering meanings.

5. Speeches

George W. Bush's presidential speeches, compiled from George W. Bush—White House Archives online, are considered any remarks he made when he spoke in front of an undefined number of people, either alone or with other individuals, and include, but are not limited to, State of the Union speeches, radio addresses, press conferences, commencement ceremonies, meetings, remarks, tours, toasts, photo opportunities, visits, and events.

6. **Context of quotes**

    None of the quotes should have been taken out of context.

7. **Editing style notes for this book**

    Newspaper and broadcast names, book titles, and all source information are italicized in this book. Quote marks are used for report and article titles. Months in dates [January 1, 2010, for example] are not abbreviated unless they are shown that way in quoted material.

8. **Notes**

    My author notes will be offset from the quotes under the source.

    [**Note:** Quick brown dog jumped the fence.]

    Headlines

    The names, titles, and other pieces of information in the quote headlines are shortened for brevity.

9. **Quotes counted for the Bibliography**

    Quotes are counted in the Bibliography unless they are summarized as partial quotes for recapping or are a duplicate.

10. **Inconsistencies in spellings**

    Different sources spell words and acronyms like US/U.S., advisor/adviser, and Osama/Usama in a variety of ways. Outside of quotes, these words will be spelled consistently, even if they vary from the spelling within the quote. The names of the terrorist organization Al-Qaeda and its then-leader Osama bin Laden (when not in quoted text) are "Al-Qaeda" and "Osama bin Laden" or "bin Laden." The names of other individuals, such as El Sayyid Nosair, may also have different spellings within quotes.

11. **Ellipses**

    Ellipses are used for quotes that have been shortened. Ellipses are used with no spaces at either end[t...t] to show that parts of the original quote have been removed, but there will be no ellipsis at the beginning of a quote that starts in the middle of the original text. Instead, a bracket [] will be used to capitalize the first letter if text is started from the middle of a quote.

12. Brackets

Brackets are used for a variety of reasons. Some information in brackets [] has been included to clarify information within a quote, like the year of a date mentioned, full names and job titles, to correct spelling errors, and spell out acronyms.

13. Use of defined words and acronyms

When an obscure word or acronym appears, it will normally be defined in a footnote or within the quote the first time it is used.

14. Terminology for Combatants

The terms "unlawful enemy combatants" and "enemy combatants" are used interchangeably.

15. Bibliography

The Bibliography for published books is in alphabetical order by author's name; the other sources are alphabetical by source title or organization.

16. The quotes in this book

There are assuredly millions of quotes that could have been found and picked for this book, but the quotes herein should represent a fair, albeit small, selection that reasonably reflect the context of the times, places, and events mentioned.

APPENDIX A

GEORGE W. BUSH'S PRESIDENTIAL CABINET[79]

THE CABINET MEMBERS FROM President George W. Bush's first administration are noted in bold

1.	Secretary of State	**A. Gen. Colin L. Powell, 2001–2005** B. Condoleezza Rice, 2005–2009
2.	Secretary of the Treasury	**A. Paul H. O'Neill, 2001–2002** **B. John W. Snow, 2003–2006** C. Henry M. Paulson, 2006–2009
3.	Secretary of Defense	**A. Donald H. Rumsfeld, 2001–2006** B. Robert M. Gates, 2006–2009
4.	Attorney General	**A. John Ashcroft, 2001–2005** B. Alberto Gonzales, 2005–2007 C. Michael B. Mukasey, 2007–2009
5.	Secretary of the Interior	**A. Gale Norton, 2001–2006** B. Dirk Kempthorne, 2006–2009
6.	Secretary of Agriculture	**A. Ann M. Veneman, 2001–2005** B. Mike Johanns, 2005–2007 C. Ed Schafer, 2008–2009
7.	Secretary of Commerce	**A. Don Evans, 2001–2005** B. Carlos M. Gutierrez, 2005–2009
8.	Secretary of Labor	**A. Elaine Chao, 2001–2009**
9.	Secretary of Health and Human Services	**A. Tommy G. Thompson, 2001–2005** B. Michael O. Leavitt, 2005–2009
10.	Secretary of Homeland Security	**A. Tom Ridge, 2003–2005** B. Michael Chertoff, 2005–2009

---

79 "GEORGE W. BUSH—ADMINISTRATION," MillerCenter.org, accessed June 7, 2020. Names as shown on the website.

11.	Secretary of Housing and Urban Development	**A. Melquiades Martinez, 2001–2003** B. Alphonso Jackson, 2004–2008 C. Steve Preston, 2008–2009
12.	Secretary of Transportation	**A. Norman Y. Mineta, 2001–2006** B. Mary E. Peters, 2006–2009
13.	Secretary of Energy	**A. Spencer Abraham, 2001–2005** B. Samuel W. Bodman, 2005–2009
14.	Secretary of Education	**A. Rod Paige, 2001–2005** B. Margaret Spellings, 2005–2009
15.	Secretary of Veterans Affairs	**A. Anthony Principi, 2001–2005** B. R. James Nicholson, 2005–2007 C. James B. Peake, 2007–2009

APPENDIX B

CONGRESSIONAL VOTES FOR THE 2003 IRAQ WAR

"AUTHORIZATION FOR USE OF Military Force Against Iraq Resolution of 2002" (HJRes 114) was voted on by the US House of Representatives[80] on October 10, 2002, and by the US Senate[81] on October 11, 2002. The following is how each Senator and each Congress member voted on that resolution.

I. US Senate	AYEs	NAYs	No Vote	Vacant Seat	Total
Democratic	29	21	0	0	50
Republican	48	1	0	0	49
Independent	0	1	0	0	1
Senate Totals (% of totals)	77 (77%)	23 (23%)	0	0	100
II. US House of Representatives	AYEs	NAYs	No Vote	Vacant Seat	Total
Democratic	81	126	1[82]	3[83]	211
Republican	215	6	2[84]	0	223
Independent	0	1	0	0	1
House Totals (% of totals)	296 (68.05%)	133 (30.57%)	3 (.69%)	3 (.69%)	435

---

80   "Final Vote Results For Roll Call 455," Clerk.House.gov, accessed December 24, 2015

81   "Roll Call Vote 107th Congress—2nd Session...Question: On the Joint Resolution (H.J.Res. 114)," Senate.gov, accessed December 24, 2015

82   Ortiz (D-TX)

83   Ohio—3rd and 17th Districts; Hawaii—2nd District

84   Roukema (R-NJ), and Stump (R-AZ)

U.S. Senate Vote Count

	A. AYEs	B. NAYs	C. No Vote	D. Totals (minus vacant)
Democratic	29	21	0	50
Republican	48	1	0	49
Independent	0	1	0	1
Vacant Seats	0	0	0	0
Totals	**77**	**23**	**0**	**100**

A. Senate—AYEs—77

1. Wayne Allard
   (R-CO)

2. George Allen
   (R-VA)

3. Max Baucus
   (D-MT)

4. Evan Bayh
   (D-IN)

5. Robert Bennett
   (R-UT)

6. Joseph Biden
   (D-DE)

7. Kit Bond
   (R-MO)

8. John Breaux
   (D-LA)

9. Sam Brownback
   (R-KS)

10. Jim Bunning
    (R-KY)

11. Conrad Burns
    (R-MT)

12. Ben Campbell
    (R-CO)

13. Maria Cantwell
    (D-WA)

14. Jean Carnahan
    (D-MO)

15. Thomas Carper
    (D-DE)

16. Maxwell Cleland
    (D-GA)

17. Hillary Clinton
    (D-NY)

18. Thad Cochran
    (R-MS)

19. Susan Collins
    (R-ME)

20. Larry Craig
    (R-ID)

21. Michael Crapo
(R-ID)

22. Tom Daschle
(D-SD)

23. Mike DeWine
(R-OH)

24. ChristopherDodd
(D-CT)

25. Pete Domenici
(R-NM)

26. Byron Dorgan
(D-ND)

27. John Edwards
(D-NC)

28. John Ensign
(R-NV)

29. Michael Enzi
(R-WY)

30. Dianne Feinstein
(D-CA)

31. Peter Fitzgerald
(R-IL)

32. Bill Frist
(R-TN)

33. Phil Gramm
(R-TX)

34. Chuck Grassley
(R-IA)

35. Judd Gregg
(R-NH)

36. Chuck Hagel
(R-NE)

37. Tom Harkin
(D-IA)

38. Orrin Hatch
(R-UT)

39. Jesse Helms
(R-NC)

40. Fritz Hollings
(D-SC)

41. Tim Hutchinson
(R-AR)

42. Kay Hutchison
(R-TX)

43. Jim Inhofe
(R-OK)

44. Tim Johnson
(D-SD)

45. John Kerry
(D-MA)

46. Herb Kohl
(D-WI)

47. Jon Kyl
(R-AZ)

48. Mary Landrieu
(D-LA)

49. Joseph Lieberman (D-CT)

50. Blanche Lincoln
(D-AR)

51. Trent Lott
(R-MS)

52. Richard Lugar
(R-IN)

53. John McCain
(R-AZ)

54. Mitch McConnell
(R-KY)

55. Zell Miller
(D-GA)

56. Frank Murkowski (R-AK)

57. Bill Nelson
    (D-FL)

58. Ben Nelson
    (D-NE)

59. Don Nickles
    (R-OK)

60. Harry Reid
    (D-NV)

61. Pat Roberts
    (R-KS)

62. Jay Rockefeller
    (D-WV)

63. Rick Santorum
    (R-PA)

64. Chuck Schumer
    (D-NY)

65. Jeff Sessions
    (R-AL)

66. Richard Shelby
    (R-AL)

67. Bob Smith
    (R-NH)

68. Gordon Smith
    (R-OR)

69. Olympia Snowe
    (R-ME)

70. Arlen Specter
    (R-PA)

71. Ted Stevens
    (R-AK)

72. Craig Thomas
    (R-WY)

73. Fred Thompson
    (R-TN)

74. Strom Thurmond
    (R-SC)

75. Robert Torricelli
    (D-NJ)

76. George Voinovich
    (R-OH)

77. John Warner
    (R-VA)

B. Senate—NAYs—23

1. Daniel Akaka
   (D-HI)

2. Jeff Bingaman (D-NM)

3. Barbara Boxer
   (D-CA)

4. Robert Byrd
   (D-WV)

5. Lincoln Chafee
   (R-RI)

6. Kent Conrad
   (D-ND)

7. Jon Corzine
   (D-NJ)

8. Mark Dayton
   (D-MN)

9. Richard Durbin
   (D-IL)

10. Russell Feingold
    (D-WI)

11. Bob Graham
    (D-FL)

12. Daniel Inouye
    (D-HI)

13. Jim Jeffords
    (I-VT)

14. Ted Kennedy
    (D-MA)

15. Patrick Leahy
    (D-VT)

16. Carl Levin
    (D-MI)

17. Barbara Mikulski
    (D-MD)

18. Patty Murray
    (D-WA)

19. John Reed
    (D-RI)

20. Paul Sarbanes
    (D-MD)

21. Debbie Stabenow (D-MI)

22. Paul Wellstone (D-MN)

23. Ron Wyden
    (D-OR)

U.S. HOUSE OF REPRESENTATIVES VOTE

	A. AYEs	B. NAYs	C. No Vote	D. Totals (minus vacant)
Democratic	81	126	1	208
Republican	215	6	2	223
Independent	0	1	0	1
Vacant Seats	0	0	0	3
Totals	296	133	3	435

A. House—AYEs—296

1. Gary Ackerman
   (D-NY)

2. Robert Aderholt
   (R-AL)

3. Todd Akin
   (R-MO)

4. Rob Andrews
   (D-NJ)

5. Richard Armey
   (R-TX)

6. Spencer Bachus
   (R-AL)

7. Richard Baker
   (R-LA)

8. Cass Ballenger
   (R-NC)

9. James Barcia
   (D-MI)

10. Bob Barr
    (R-GA)

11. Roscoe Bartlett
    (R-MD)

12. Joe Barton
    (R-TX)

13. Charles Bass
    (R-NH)

14. Ken Bentsen
    (D-TX)

15. Doug Bereuter
    (R-NE)

16. Shelley Berkley
    (D-NV)

17. Howard Berman
    (D-CA)

18. Robert Berry
    (D-AR)

19. Judy Biggert
    (R-IL)

20. Michael Bilirakis
    (R-FL)

21. Sanford Bishop
    (D-GA)

22. Rod Blagojevich
    (D-IL)

23. Roy Blunt
    (R-MO)

24. Sherry Boehlert
    (R-NY)

25. John Boehner
    (R-OH)

26. Henry Bonilla
    (R-TX)

27. Mary Bono Mack
    (R-CA)

28. John Boozman
    (R-AR)

29. Robert Borski
    (D-PA)

30. Leonard Boswell
    (D-IA)

31. Rick Boucher
    (D-VA)

32. Allen Boyd
    (D-FL)

33. Kevin Brady
    (R-TX)

34. Henry Brown
    (R-SC)

35. Ed Bryant
    (R-TN)

36. Richard Burr
    (R-NC)

37. Dan Burton
    (R-IN)

38. Steve Buyer
    (R-IN)

39. Herbert (Sonny) Leon Callahan
    (R-AL)

40. Ken Calvert
    (R-CA)

41. Dave Camp
    (R-MI)

42. Chris Cannon
    (R-UT)

43. Eric Cantor
    (R-VA)

44. Shelley Capito
    (R-WV)

45. Brad Carson
    (D-OK)

46. Michael Castle
    (R-DE)

47. Steve Chabot
    (R-OH)

48. Saxby Chambliss
    (R-GA)

49. Robert Clement
    (D-TN)

50. Howard Coble
    (R-NC)

51. Mac Collins
    (R-GA)

52. Larry Combest
    (R-TX)

53. John Cooksey
    (R-LA)

54. Christopher Cox
    (R-CA)

55. Bud Cramer
    (D-AL)

56. Phil Crane
    (R-IL)

57. Ander Crenshaw
(R-FL)

58. Joe Crowley
(D-NY)

59. Barbara Cubin
(R-WY)

60. John Culberson
(R-TX)

61. Duke Cunningham
(R-CA)

62. Jim Davis
(D-FL)

63. Jo Ann Davis (R-VA)

64. Tom Davis
(R-VA)

65. Nathan Deal
(R-GA)

66. Tom DeLay
(R-TX)

67. Jim DeMint
(R-SC)

68. Peter Deutsch
(D-FL)

69. Lincoln Diaz-Balart
(R-FL)

70. Norm Dicks
(D-WA)

71. Cal Dooley
(D-CA)

72. John Doolittle
(R-CA)

73. David Dreier
(R-CA)

74. Jennifer Dunn
(R-WA)

75. Chet Edwards
(D-TX)

76. Vernon Ehlers
(R-MI)

77. Robert Ehrlich
(R-MD)

78. Jo Ann Emerson
(R-MO)

79. Eliot Engel
(D-NY)

80. Phil English
(R-PA)

81. Bob Etheridge
(D-NC)

82. Terry Everett
(R-AL)

83. Mike Ferguson
(R-NJ)

84. Jeff Flake
(R-AZ)

85. Ernie Fletcher
(R-KY)

86. Mark Foley
(R-FL)

87. Randy Forbes
(R-VA)

88. Harold Ford
(D-TN)

89. Vito Fossella
(R-NY)

90. Rodney Frelinghuysen
(R-NJ)

91. Jonas Frost
(D-TX)

92. Elton Gallegly
(R-CA)

93. Greg Ganske
(R-IA)

94. George Gekas
(R-PA)

95. Dick Gephardt
(D-MO)

96. Jim Gibbons
(R-NV)

97. Wayne Gilchrest
(R-MD)

98. Paul Gillmor
(R-OH)

99. Benjamin Gilman
(R-NY)

100. Virgil Goode
(R-VA)

101. Bob Goodlatte
(R-VA)

102. Bart Gordon
(D-TN)

103. Porter Goss
(R-FL)

104. Lindsey Graham
(R-SC)

105. Kay Granger
(R-TX)

106. Sam Graves
(R-MO)

107. Gene Green
(D-TX)

108. Mark Green
(R-WI)

109. Jim Greenwood
(R-PA)

110. Felix Grucci
(R-NY)

111. Gil Gutknecht
(R-MN)

112. Ralph Hall
(D-TX)[85]

113. James Hansen
(R-UT)

114. Jane Harman
(D-CA)

115. Melissa Hart
(R-PA)

116. Danny Hastert
(R-IL)

117. Doc Hastings
(R-WA)

118. Robin Hayes
(R-NC)

119. John Hayworth
(R-AZ)

120. Joel Hefley
(R-CO)

121. Wally Herger
(R-CA)

122. Baron Hill
(D-IN)

123. Van Hilleary
(R-TN)

124. Dave Hobson
(R-OH)

125. Joseph Hoeffel
(D-PA)

126. Pete Hoekstra
(R-MI)

---

85   Switched to Republican on January 5, 2004, History.House.gov, accessed January 24, 2019

127. Tim Holden
(D-PA)

128. Stephen Horn
(R-CA)

129. Steny Hoyer
(D-MD)

130. Kenny Hulshof
(R-MO)

131. Duncan Hunter
(R-CA)

132. Henry Hyde
(R-IL)

133. John Isakson
(R-GA)

134. Steve Israel
(D-NY)

135. Darrell Issa
(R-CA)

136. Ernest Istook
(R-OK)

137. William Jefferson
(D-LA)

138. Bill Jenkins
(R-TN)

139. Chris John
(D-LA)

140. Nancy Johnson
(R-CT)

141. Sam Johnson
(R-TX)

142. Timothy Johnson
(R-IL)

143. Walter Jones
(R-NC)

144. Paul Kanjorski
(D-PA)

145. Ric Keller
(R-FL)

146. Sue Kelly
(R-NY)

147. Mark Kennedy
(R-MN)

148. Patrick Kennedy
(D-RI)

149. Brian Kerns
(R-IN)

150. Ron Kind
(D-WI)

151. Pete King
(R-NY)

152. Jack Kingston
(R-GA)

153. Mark Kirk
(R-IL)

154. Joe Knollenberg (R-MI)

155. Jim Kolbe
(R-AZ)

156. Ray LaHood
(R-IL)

157. Nick Lampson
(D-TX)

158. Tom Lantos
(D-CA)

159. Tom Latham
(R-IA)

160. Steven LaTourette
(R-OH)

161. Jerry Lewis
(R-CA)

162. Ron Lewis
(R-KY)

163. John Linder
(R-GA)

164. Frank LoBiondo
(R-NJ)

165. Nita Lowey
(D-NY)

166. Ken Lucas
(D-KY)

167. Frank Lucas
(R-OK)

168. William Luther
(D-MN)

169. Stephen Lynch
(D-MA)

170. Carolyn Maloney
(D-NY)

171. Donald Manzullo
(R-IL)

172. Ed Markey
(D-MA)

173. Frank Mascara
(D-PA)

174. Jim Matheson
(D-UT)

175. Carolyn McCarthy
(D-NY)

176. Jim McCrery
(R-LA)

177. John McHugh
(R-NY)

178. Scott McInnis
(R-CO)

179. Mike McIntyre
(D-NC)

180. Buck McKeon
(R-CA)

181. Michael McNulty
(D-NY)

182. Marty Meehan
(D-MA)

183. John Mica
(R-FL)

184. Jeff Miller
(R-FL)

185. Gary Miller
(R-CA)

186. Dan Miller
(R-FL)

187. Dennis Moore
(D-KS)

188. Jerry Moran
(R-KS)

189. John Murtha
(D-PA)

190. Sue Myrick
(R-NC)

191. George Nethercutt
(R-WA)

192. Bob Ney
(R-OH)

193. Anne Northup
(R-KY)

194. Charles Norwood
(R-GA)

195. Jim Nussle
(R-IA)

196. Tom Osborne
(R-NE)

197. Doug Ose
(R-CA)

198. C.L. "Butch" Otter
(R-ID)

199. Michael Oxley
(R-OH)

200. Bill Pascrell
(D-NJ)

201. Mike Pence
(R-IN)

202. Collin Peterson
(D-MN)

203. John Peterson
(R-PA)

204. Tom Petri
(R-WI)

205. David Phelps
(D-IL)

206. Chip Pickering
(R-MS)

207. Joseph Pitts
(R-PA)

208. Todd Platts
(R-PA)

209. Richard Pombo
(R-CA)

210. Earl Pomeroy
(D-ND)

211. Rob Portman
(R-OH)

212. Deborah Pryce
(R-OH)

213. Adam Putnam
(R-FL)

214. Jack Quinn
(R-NY)

215. George Radanovich
(R-CA)

216. Jim Ramstad
(R-MN)

217. Ralph Regula
(R-OH)

218. Denny Rehberg
(R-MT)

219. Thomas Reynolds
(R-NY)

220. Bob Riley
(R-AL)

221. Timothy Roemer
(D-IN)

222. Hal Rogers
(R-KY)

223. Mike Rogers
(R-MI)

224. Dana Rohrabacher (R-CA)

225. Ileana Ros-Lehtinen
(R-FL)

226. Mike Ross
(D-AR)

227. Steven Rothman
(D-NJ)

228. Ed Royce
(R-CA)

229. Paul Ryan
(R-WI)

230. Jim Ryun
(R-KS)

231. Max Sandlin
(D-TX)

232. Jim Saxton
(R-NJ)

233. Bob Schaffer
(R-CO)

234. Adam Schiff
(D-CA)

235. Ed Schrock
(R-VA)

236. James Sensenbrenner
(R-WI)

237. Pete Sessions
(R-TX)

238. John Shadegg
(R-AZ)

239. Clay Shaw
(R-FL)

240. Christopher Shays
(R-CT)

241. Brad Sherman
(D-CA)

242. Don Sherwood
(R-PA)

243. John Shimkus
(R-IL)

244. Ronnie Shows
(D-MS)

245. Bill Shuster
(R-PA)

246. Rob Simmons
(R-CT)

247. Mike Simpson
(R-ID)

248. Joseph Skeen
(R-NM)

249. Ike Skelton
(D-MO)

250. Chris Smith
(R-NJ)

251. Lamar Smith
(R-TX)

252. Nick Smith
(R-MI)

253. Adam Smith
(D-WA)

254. Mark Souder
(R-IN)

255. John Spratt
(D-SC)

256. Karen Stearns
(R-FL)

257. Charles Stenholm
(D-TX)

258. John Sullivan
(R-OK)

259. John Sununu
(R-NH)

260. John Sweeney
(R-NY)

261. Tom Tancredo
(R-CO)

262. John Tanner
(D-TN)

263. Ellen Tauscher
(D-CA)

264. Billy Tauzin
(R-LA)

265. Gene Taylor
(D-MS)

266. Charles Taylor
(R-NC)

267. Lee Terry
(R-NE)

268. Bill Thomas
(R-CA)

269. Mac Thornberry
(R-TX)

270. John Thune
(R-SD)

271. Karen Thurman
(D-FL)

272. Todd Tiahrt
(R-KS)

273. Pat Tiberi
(R-OH)

274. Pat Toomey
(R-PA)

275. Jim Turner
(D-TX)

276. Fred Upton
(R-MI)

277. David Vitter
(R-LA)

278. Greg Walden
(R-OR)

279. Jim Walsh
(R-NY)

280. Zach Wamp
(R-TN)

281. Wes Watkins
(R-OK)

282. J.C. Watts, Jr.
(R-OK)

283. Henry Waxman
(D-CA)

284. Anthony Weiner
(D-NY)

285. Dave Weldon
(R-FL)

286. Curt Weldon
(R-PA)

287. Jerry Weller
(R-IL)

288. Robert Wexler
(D-FL)

289. Ed Whitfield
(R-KY)

290. Roger Wicker
(R-MS)

291. Joe Wilson
(R-SC)

292. Heather Wilson
(R-NM)

293. Frank Wolf
(R-VA)

294. Albert Wynn
(D-MD)

295. W. Bill Young
(R-FL)

296. Don Young
(R-AK)

B. House—NAYs—133

1. Neil Abercrombie (D-HI)

2. Tom Allen
(D-ME)

3. Joe Baca
(D-CA)

4. Brian Baird
(D-WA)

5. John Baldacci
(D-ME)

6. Tammy Baldwin
(D-WI)

7. Thomas Barrett
(D-WI)

8. Xavier Becerra
(D-CA)

9. Earl Blumenauer
(D-OR)

10. David Bonior
(D-MI)

11. Robert Brady
(D-PA)

12. Corrine Brown
(D-FL)

13. Sherrod Brown
(D-OH)

14. Lois Capps
(D-CA)

15. Michael Capuano
(D-MA)

16. Benjamin Cardin
(D-MD)

17. Julia Carson
(D-IN)

18. Lacy Clay
(D-MO)

19. Eva Clayton
(D-NC)

20. Jim Clyburn
(D-SC)

21. Gary Condit
(D-CA)

22. John Conyers
(D-MI)

23. Jerry Costello
(D-IL)

24. William Coyne
(D-PA)

25. Elijah Cummings
(D-MD)

26. Danny Davis
(D-IL)

27. Susan Davis
(D-CA)

28. Peter DeFazio
(D-OR)

29. Diana DeGette
(D-CO)

30. Bill Delahunt
(D-MA)

31. Rosa DeLauro
(D-CT)

32. John Dingell
(D-MI)

33. Lloyd Doggett
(D-TX)

34. Mike Doyle
(D-PA)

35. John Duncan
(R-TN)

36. Anna Eshoo
(D-CA)

37. Lane Evans
(D-IL)

38. Sam Farr
(D-CA)

39. Chaka Fattah
(D-PA)

40. Bob Filner
(D-CA)

41. Barney Frank
(D-MA)

42. Charles Gonzalez
(D-TX)

43. Luis Gutierrez
(D-IL)

44. Alice Hastings
    (D-FL)

45. Earl Hilliard
    (D-AL)

46. Maurice Hinchey
    (D-NY)

47. Rubén Hinojosa
    (D-TX)

48. Rush Holt
    (D-NJ)

49. Mike Honda
    (D-CA)

50. Darlene Hooley
    (D-OR)

51. John Hostettler
    (R-IN)

52. Amo Houghton
    (R-NY)

53. Jay Inslee
    (D-WA)

54. Jesse Jackson
    (D-IL)

55. Sheila Jackson-Lee (D-TX)

56. Eddie Johnson
    (D-TX)

57. Stephanie Jones
    (D-OH)

58. Marcy Kaptur
    (D-OH)

59. Dale Kildee
    (D-MI)

60. Carolyn Kilpatrick
    (D-MI)

61. Jerry Kleczka
    (D-WI)

62. Dennis Kucinich
    (D-OH)

63. John LaFalce
    (D-NY)

64. Jim Langevin
    (D-RI)

65. Rick Larsen (D-WA)

66. John Larson
    (D-CT)

67. Jim Leach
    (R-IA)

68. Barbara Lee
    (D-CA)

69. Sander Levin
    (D-MI)

70. John Lewis
    (D-GA)

71. William Lipinski
    (D-IL)

72. Zoe Lofgren
    (D-CA)

73. James Maloney
    (D-CT)

74. Robert Matsui
    (D-CA)

75. Karen McCarthy
    (D-MO)

76. Betty McCollum
    (D-MN)

77. Jim McDermott
    (D-WA)

78. Jim McGovern
    (D-MA)

79. Cynthia McKinney
    (D-GA)

80. Mark Meek
(D-FL)

81. Gregory Meeks
(D-NY)

82. Bob Menendez
(D-NJ)

83. Juanita Millender-McDonald
(D-CA)

84. George Miller (D-CA)

85. Alan Mollohan
(D-WV)

86. Jim Moran
(D-VA)

87. Constance Morella
(R-MD)

88. Jerrold Nadler
(D-NY)

89. Grace Napolitano
(D-CA)

90. Richard Neal
(D-MA)

91. James Oberstar
(D-MN)

92. Dave Obey
(D-WI)

93. John Olver
(D-MA)

94. Major Owens
(D-NY)

95. Frank Pallone
(D-NJ)

96. Ed Pastor
(D-AZ)

97. Ron Paul
(R-TX)

98. Donald Payne
(D-NJ)

99. Nancy Pelosi
(D-CA)

100. David Price
(D-NC)

101. Nick Rahall
(D-WV)

102. Charles Rangel
(D-NY)

103. Silvestre Reyes
(D-TX)

104. Lynn Rivers
(D-MI)

105. Ciro Rodriguez
(D-TX)

106. Lucille Roybal-Allard
(D-CA)

107. Bobby Rush
(D-IL)

108. Martin Sabo
(D-MN)

109. Loretta Sanchez
(D-CA)

110. Bernie Sanders
(I-VT)

111. Thomas Sawyer
(D-OH)

112. Jan Schakowsky (D-IL)

113. Bobby Scott
(D-VA)

114. Jose Serrano
(D-NY)

115. Louise Slaughter
(D-NY)

116. Vic Snyder
(D-AR)

117. Hilda Solis
(D-CA)

118. Pete Stark
(D-CA)

119. Ted Strickland
(D-OH)

120. Bart Stupak
(D-MI)

121. Bennie Thompson
(D-MS)

122. Mike Thompson
(D-CA)

123. John Tierney
(D-MA)

124. Ed Towns
(D-NY)

125. Mark Udall
(D-CO)

126. Tom Udall
(D-NM)

127. Nydia Velazquez (D-NY)

128. Peter Visclosky (D-IN)

129. Maxine Waters
(D-CA)

130. Diane Watson
(D-CA)

131. Mel Watt
(D-NC)

132. Lynn Woolsey
(D-CA)

133. David Wu
(D-OR)

APPENDIX C

SUMMARY OF "THE NATIONAL COMMISSION ON TERRORIST ATTACKS UPON THE UNITED STATES" (ALSO KNOWN AS THE 9-11 COMMISSION)

9/11 Commission

"The National Commission on Terrorist Attacks Upon the United States (also known as the 9-11 Commission), an independent, bipartisan commission created by congressional legislation and the signature of President George W. Bush [on November 27,] 2002, is chartered to prepare a full and complete account of the circumstances surrounding the September 11, 2001 terrorist attacks, including preparedness for and the immediate response to the attacks.

The Commission is also mandated to provide recommendations designed to guard against future attacks."[86]

— The Commission released its final report, [567 pages] titled "THE 9/11 COMMISSION REPORT: FINAL REPORT OF THE NATIONAL COMMISSION ON TERRORIST ATTACKS UPON THE UNITED STATES," July 22, 2004;

— The Commission closed August 21, 2004;

— As of September 6, 2017, a link to the full 9/11 Commission report could be found at http://govinfo.library.unt.edu/911/report/index.htm

---

86   National Commission on Terrorist Attacks Upon the United States, "Complete 9/11 Commission Report," GovInfo.org, http://govinfo.library.unt.edu/911/about/bio_thompson.htm, accessed June 5, 2017

Makeup of the 9/11 Commission

Dr. Philip Zelikow was named the Executive Director on January 27, 2003, the day the commission convened.[87]

9/11 Comission

Republican Party	Democratic Party
Thomas H. Kean, Chair—R (Former Governor of New Jersey)	Lee H. Hamilton, Vice Chair—D (Former Congressman representing Indiana's 9th District)
Fred F. Fielding—R (Lawyer and former U.S. presidential Counsel)	Richard Ben-Veniste—D (Lawyer and Chief of the Watergate Task Force of the Watergate Special Prosecutor's Office)
Slade Gorton—R (Former Senator from Washington State)	Jamie S. Gorelick—D (Lawyer and former U.S. Deputy Attorney General)
John F. Lehman—R (Secretary of the Navy under President Reagan)	Bob Kerrey—D (Former Senator from Nebraska)
James R. Thompson—R (Lawyer and former Governor of Illinois)	Timothy J. Roemer—D (Former Indiana Congressman representing the 3rd District)

---

87   "9/11 Commission Convenes, Names Executive Director," WilsonCenter.org, January 27, 2003

April 3, 2014, Vote to Declassify Senate Intelligence Committee Report on Torture–Eleven to Three in Favor, One Present vote

	For[88]	Opposed[89]
	A.	**B.**
1.	**Dianne Feinstein** California—D *Chairman*	**Marco Rubio** [90] Florida—R
2.	**John D. Rockefeller IV** West Virginia—D	**James E. Risch**[91] Idaho—R
3.	**Saxby Chambliss**[92] Georgia—R *Vice Chairman*	**Daniel Coats**[93] Indiana—R
4.	**Martin Heinrich** New Mexico—D	
5.	**Angus King, Jr.** Maine—I	
6.	**Susan Collins**[94] Maine—R	
7.	**Mark Udall** Colorado—D[95]	

88   Liz Halloran, "Who's Who In Senate-CIA Report Showdown," NPR.org, April 3, 2014

89   Bradley Klapper, "Senate committee OKs release of CIA torture report," APnews.com, April 4, 2014, accessed January 6, 2016

90   Jeremy Herb, "Senate Intel panel approves CIA report," TheHill.com, April 3, 2014, accessed January 6, 2016

91   Ibid.

92   Ibid.

93   Ibid.

94   Ibid.

95   "Intelligence Committee Votes to Declassify CIA Report (Updated)," Blogs.Rollcall.com, April 3, 2014

8.	**Ron Wyden** Oregon—D	**Tom Coburn—Voted Present**[96] Oklahoma—R[97][98]
9.	**Barbara A. Mikulski** Maryland—D	
10.	**Mark Warner** Virginia—D	
11.	**Richard Burr** North Carolina—R[99]	

96   According to the article "Voting Present as a Legislative Tactic," on The Congressional Institute website, "When a bill or amendment is up for a vote, a Representative may vote 'aye', 'no', or 'present', which is a refusal to take sides. A 'present' vote does not count toward or against the passage of a bill, but it contributes toward the quorum, which is the minimum number of Members required in attendance for the body to conduct business legally."

97   Liz Halloran, "Who's Who In Senate-CIA Report Showdown," KPBS.org, April 3, 2014

98   Steven T. Dennis and Niels Lesniewski, "Intelligence Committee Votes to Declassify CIA Report (Updated)," Blogs.Rollcall.com, April 3, 2014

99   Renee Schoof and David Lightman—Mcclatchy Washington Bureau, "Sen. Richard Burr: Torture report is attempt to 'smear' Bush administration," CharlotteObserver.com, December 9, 2014

APPENDIX D

SUMMARY OF THE TWENTY FINDINGS OF THE SENATE INTELLIGENCE COMMITTEE REPORT ON TORTURE; APRIL 3, 2014

THE FOLLOWING EXCERPTS ARE from the "Findings and Conclusions" of the Senate Intelligence Committee report on torture, "Report of the Senate Select Committee on Intelligence Committee Study of the Central Intelligence Agency's Detention and Interrogation Program together with Foreword by Chairman Feinstein and Additional and Minority Views" pages x-xxvi, followed by the Congressional vote on April 3, 2014, to declassify the report.

"#1: The CIA's use of its enhanced interrogation techniques was not an effective means of acquiring intelligence or gaining cooperation from detainees....

For example, according to CIA records, seven of the 39 CIA detainees known to have been subjected to the CIA's enhanced interrogation techniques produced no intelligence while in CIA custody....CIA officers regularly called into question whether the CIA's enhanced interrogation techniques were effective, assessing that the use of the techniques failed to elicit detainee cooperation or produce accurate intelligence."

"#2: The CIA's justification for the use of its enhanced interrogation techniques rested on inaccurate claims of their effectiveness....

The Committee reviewed 20 of the most frequent and prominent examples of purported counterterrorism successes that the CIA has attributed to the use of its enhanced interrogation techniques, and found them to be wrong in fundamental respects....The examples provided by the CIA included numerous factual inaccuracies....Some of the plots that the CIA claimed to have 'disrupted' as a result of the CIA's enhanced interrogation techniques were assessed by intelligence and law enforcement officials as being infeasible or ideas that were never operationalized."

"#3: The interrogations of CIA detainees were brutal and far worse than the CIA represented to policymakers and others.

Beginning with the CIA's first detainee, Abu Zubaydah, and continuing with numerous others, the CIA applied its enhanced interrogation techniques with significant repetition for days or weeks at a time. Interrogation techniques such as slaps and 'wallings' (slamming detainees against a wall) were used in combination, frequently concurrent with sleep deprivation and nudity....At least five CIA detainees were subjected to 'rectal rehydration' or rectal feeding without documented medical necessity....One interrogator told another detainee that he would never go to court, because 'we can never let the world know what I have done to you.'"

"#4: The conditions of confinement for CIA detainees were harsher than the CIA had represented to policymakers and others....

CIA detainees at the COBALT detention facility were kept in complete darkness and constantly shackled in isolated cells with loud noise or music and only a bucket to use for human waste. Lack of heat at the facility likely contributed to the death of a detainee. The chief of interrogations described COBALT as a 'dungeon.'...Multiple psychologists identified the lack of human contact experienced by detainees as a cause of psychiatric problems."

"#5: The CIA repeatedly provided inaccurate information to the Department of Justice, impeding a proper legal analysis of the CIA's Detention and Interrogation Program....

The Department of Justice did not conduct independent analysis or verification of the information it received from the CIA. The department warned, however, that if the facts provided by the CIA were to change, its legal conclusions might not apply. When the CIA determined that information it had provided to the Department of Justice was incorrect, the CIA rarely informed the department."

"#6: The CIA has actively avoided or impeded congressional oversight of the program.

The CIA did not brief the leadership of the Senate Select Committee on Intelligence on the CIA's enhanced interrogation techniques until September 2002, after the techniques had been approved and used....Briefings to the full Committee beginning on September 6, 2006, also contained numerous inaccuracies, including inaccurate descriptions of how interrogation techniques were applied and what information was obtained from CIA detainees....A year after being briefed on the program, the House and Senate Conference Committee considering the Fiscal Year 2008 Intelligence Authorization bill voted to limit the CIA to using only interrogation techniques authorized by the Army Field Manual. That legislation was approved by the Senate and the House of Representatives in February 2008, and was vetoed by President Bush on March 8, 2008."

"#7: The CIA impeded effective White House oversight and decision-making.

The CIA provided extensive amounts of inaccurate and incomplete information related to the operation and effectiveness of the CIA's Detention and Interrogation Program to the White House, the National Security Council principals, and their staffs. This prevented an accurate and complete understanding of the program by Executive Branch officials, thereby impeding oversight and decision-making....In briefings for the National Security Council principals and White House officials, the CIA advocated for the continued use of the CIA's enhanced interrogation techniques, warning that '[t]ermination of this program will result in loss of life, possibly extensive.'"

"#8: The CIA's operation and management of the program complicated, and in some cases impeded, the national security missions of other Executive Branch agencies....

The CIA withheld or restricted information relevant to these agencies' missions and responsibilities, denied access to detainees, and provided inaccurate information on the CIA's Detention and Interrogation Program to these agencies....The CIA denied specific requests from FBI Director Robert Mueller III for FBI access to CIA detainees that the FBI believed was necessary to understand CIA detainee reporting on threats to the U.S. Homeland.... The ODNI was provided with inaccurate and incomplete information about the program, preventing the director of national intelligence from effectively carrying out the director's statutory responsibility to serve as the principal advisor to the president on intelligence matters. The inaccurate information provided to the ODNI by the CIA resulted in the ODNI releasing inaccurate information to the public in September 2006."

"#9: The CIA impeded oversight by the CIA's Office of Inspector General....

The CIA did not brief the OIG [Office of Inspector General] on the program until after the death of a detainee, by which time the CIA had held at least 22 detainees at two different CIA detention sites. Once notified, the OIG reviewed the CIA's Detention and Interrogation Program and issued several reports, including an important May 2004 'Special Review' of the program that identified significant concerns and deficiencies. During the OIG reviews, CIA personnel provided OIG with inaccurate information on the operation and management of the CIA's Detention and Interrogation Program, as well as on the effectiveness of the CIA's enhanced interrogation techniques. The inaccurate information was included in the final May 2004 Special Review, which was later declassified and released publicly, and remains uncorrected."

"#10: The CIA coordinated the release of classified information to the media, including inaccurate information concerning the effectiveness of the CIA's enhanced interrogation techniques....

The deputy director of the CIA's Counterterrorism Center wrote to a colleague in 2005, shortly before being interviewed by a media outlet, that 'we either get out and sell, or we get hammered, which has implications beyond the media. [C]ongress reads it, cuts our authorities, messes up our budget...we either put out our story or we get eaten. [T]here is no middle ground.' The same CIA officer explained to a colleague that 'when the [Washington Post]/[New York T]imes quotes *senior intelligence official,* it's us...authorized and directed by opa [CIA's Office of Public Affairs].'"

"#11: The CIA was unprepared as it began operating its Detention and Interrogation Program more than six months after being granted detention authorities....

The CIA was not prepared to take custody of its first detainee. In the fall of 2001, the CIA explored the possibility of establishing clandestine detention facilities in several countries....As it began detention and interrogation operations, the CIA deployed personnel who lacked relevant training and experience. The CIA began interrogation training more than seven months after taking custody of Abu Zubaydah, and more than three months after the CIA began using its 'enhanced interrogation techniques.' CIA Director George Tenet issued formal guidelines for interrogations and conditions of confinement at detention sites in January 2003, by which time 40 of the 119 known detainees had been detained by the CIA."

"#12: The CIA's management and operation of its Detention and Interrogation Program was deeply flawed throughout the program's duration, particularly so in 2002 and early 2003....

In 2005, the chief of the CIA's BLACK detention site, where many of the detainees the CIA assessed as 'high-value' were held, complained that CIA Headquarters 'managers seem to be selecting either problem, underperforming officers, new, totally inexperienced officers or whomever seems to be willing and able to deploy at any given time,' resulting in 'the production of mediocre or, I dare say, useless intelligence....' Numerous CIA officers had serious documented personal and professional problems—including histories of violence and records of abusive treatment of others—that should have called into question their suitability to participate in the CIA's Detention and Interrogation Program, their employment with the CIA, and their continued access to classified information. In nearly all cases, these problems were known to the CIA prior to the assignment of these officers to detention and interrogation positions."

"#13: Two contract psychologists devised the CIA's enhanced interrogation techniques and played a central role in the operation, assessments, and management of the CIA's Detention and Interrogation Program. By 2005, the CIA had overwhelmingly outsourced operations related to the program....

Neither psychologist had any experience as an interrogator, nor did either have specialized knowledge of al-Qa'ida, a background in counterterrorism, or any relevant cultural or linguistic expertise....In 2005, the psychologists formed a company specifically for the purpose of conducting their work with the CIA. Shortly thereafter, the CIA outsourced virtually all aspects of the program.... In 2007, the CIA provided a multi-year indemnification agreement to protect the company and its employees from legal liability arising out of the program. The CIA has since paid out more than $1 million pursuant to the agreement."

"#14: CIA detainees were subjected to coercive interrogation techniques that had not been approved by the Department of Justice or had not been authorized by CIA Headquarters.

Prior to mid-2004, the CIA routinely subjected detainees to nudity and dietary manipulation. The CIA also used abdominal slaps and cold water dousing on several detainees during that period. None of these techniques had been approved by the Department of Justice. At least 17 detainees were subjected to CIA enhanced interrogation techniques without authorization from CIA Headquarters....Although these incidents were recorded in CIA cables and, in at least some cases were identified at the time by supervisors at CIA Headquarters as being inappropriate, corrective action was rarely taken against the interrogators involved."

"#15: The CIA did not conduct a comprehensive or accurate accounting of the number of individuals it detained, and held individuals who did not meet the legal standard for detention. The CIA's claims about the number of detainees held and subjected to its enhanced interrogation techniques were inaccurate....

CIA statements to the Committee and later to the public that the CIA detained fewer than 100 individuals, and that less than a third of those 100 detainees were subjected to the CIA's enhanced interrogation techniques, were inaccurate. The Committee's review of CIA records determined that the CIA detained at least 119 individuals, of whom at least 39 were subjected to the CIA's enhanced interrogation techniques....A full accounting of CIA detentions and interrogations may be impossible, as records in some cases are non-existent, and, in many other cases, are sparse and insufficient."

"#16: The CIA failed to adequately evaluate the effectiveness of its enhanced interrogation techniques....

There are no CIA records to indicate that any of the reviews independently validated the 'effectiveness' claims presented by the CIA, to include basic confirmation that the intelligence cited by the CIA was acquired from CIA detainees during or after the use of the CIA's enhanced interrogation techniques. Nor did the reviews seek to confirm whether the intelligence cited by the CIA as being obtained 'as a result' of the CIA's enhanced interrogation techniques was unique and 'otherwise unavailable,' as claimed by the CIA, and not previously obtained from other sources."

"#17: The CIA rarely reprimanded or held personnel accountable for serious and significant violations, inappropriate activities, and systemic and individual management failures....

CIA managers who were aware of failings and shortcomings in the program but did not intervene, or who failed to provide proper leadership and management, were also not held to account....On two occasions in which the CIA inspector general identified wrongdoing, accountability recommendations were overruled by senior CIA leadership. In one instance, involving the death of a CIA detainee at COBALT, CIA Headquarters decided not to take disciplinary action against an officer involved because, at the time, CIA Headquarters had been 'motivated to extract any and all operational information' from the detainee."

"#18: The CIA marginalized and ignored numerous internal critiques, criticisms, and objections concerning the operation and management of the CIA's Detention and Interrogation Program....

These concerns were regularly overridden by CIA management, and the CIA made few corrective changes to its policies governing the program. At times, CIA officers were instructed by supervisors not to put their concerns or observations in written communications. In several instances, CIA officers identified inaccuracies in CIA representations about the program and its effectiveness to the Office of Inspector General, the White House, the Department of Justice, the Congress, and the American public. The CIA nonetheless failed to take action to correct these representations, and allowed inaccurate information to remain as the CIA's official position."

"#19: The CIA's Detention and Interrogation Program was inherently unsustainable and had effectively ended by 2006 due to unauthorized press disclosures, reduced cooperation from other nations, and legal and oversight concerns....

From the beginning of the program, the CIA faced significant challenges in finding nations willing to host CIA clandestine detention sites. These challenges became increasingly difficult over time....By 2006, press disclosures, the unwillingness of other countries to host existing or new detention sites, and legal and oversight concerns had largely ended the CIA's ability to operate clandestine detention facilities....By March 2006, the program was operating in only one country. The CIA last used its enhanced interrogation techniques on November 8, 2007. The CIA did not hold any detainees after April 2008."

"#20: The CIA's Detention and Interrogation Program damaged the United States' standing in the world, and resulted in other significant monetary and non-monetary costs.

The CIA's Detention and Interrogation Program created tensions with U.S. partners and allies, leading to formal *demarches* to the United States, and damaging and complicating bilateral intelligence relationships....More broadly, the program caused immeasurable damage to the United States' public standing, as well as to the United States' longstanding global leadership on human rights in general and the prevention of torture in particular. CIA records indicate that the CIA's Detention and Interrogation Program cost well over $300 million in non-personnel costs....To encourage governments to clandestinely host CIA detention sites, or to increase support for existing sites, the CIA provided millions of dollars in cash payments to foreign government officials."

APPENDIX E

BIBLIOGRAPHY AND REFERENCES PER SOURCE: PUBLISHED BOOKS, ONLINE MEDIA, GOVERNMENT RESOURCES, AND OTHER SOURCES

THE FOLLOWING BIBLIOGRAPHY CONTAINS the number of different sources used[100] and the number of times a quote was pulled from each referenced published work.

In total, the 586 quotes in this book came from 151 different sources.

	Number of Sources	Number of Quotes Used
I. Published Books	90	396
II. Media	38	103
III. Government Resources	13	76
IV. Other Sources	10	11
Totals	**151**	**586**

---

100   Only quotes with dates and headlines are included in this count, and excludes quotes in chapter Recaps, footnotes, and other areas of the book.

I. Published Books

	Quote Source	Number of times referenced
1.	**Aid, Matthew M.** *The Secret Sentry: The Untold History of the National Security Agency.* Bloomberg Press, 2009.	4
2.	**Allawi, Ali A.** *The Occupation of Iraq: Winning the War, Losing the Peace.* Yale University Press, 2008.	7
3.	**Atwan, Abdel Bari** *The Secret History of al Qaeda.* University of California Press, 2006.	3
4.	**Baker, Peter** *Days of Fire: Bush and Cheney in the White House.* Doubleday, 2013.	6
5.	**Bamford, James** *A Pretext for War; 9/11, Iraq, and the Abuse of America's Intelligence Agencies.* Anchor Books, 2008.	16
6.	**Bamford, James** *The Shadow Factory: The NSA from 9/11 to Eavesdropping on America.* Anchor Books, 2009.	2
7.	**Bassiouni, M. Cherif** *The Institutionalization of Torture by the Bush Administration: Is Anyone Responsible?.* Intersentia, 2010.	15
8.	**Benjamin, Daniel and Simon, Rep. Steve** *The Age of Sacred Terror: Radical Islam's War Against America.* Random House, 2003.	2
9.	**Bergen, Peter** *Holy War, Inc.: Inside the Secret World of Osama Bin Laden.* Free Press, 2008.	2
10.	**Bergen, Peter** *The Longest War: The Enduring Conflict between America and Al-Qaeda.* Free Press, 2011.	8
11.	**Bergen, Peter** *The Osama bin Laden I Know: An Oral History of al Qaeda's Leader.* Simon & Schuster, 2006.	2

	Quote Source	Number of times referenced
12.	**Blair, Tony** *A Journey: My Political Life.* Knopf Doubleday Publishing Group, 2010.	1
13.	**Blix, Hans** *Disarming Iraq: The Search for Weapons of Mass Destruction.* Pantheon, 2004.	4
14.	**Bumiller, Elisabeth** *Condoleezza Rice: An American Life: A Biography.* Random House, 2007.	7
15.	**Bush, George W.** *Decision Points.* Crown Publishing, 2004.	2
16.	**Cheney, Dick** *In My Time: A Personal and Political Memoir.* Threshold Editions, 2011.	2
17.	**Clarke, Richard A.** *Against All Enemies: Inside America's War on Terror.* Free Press, 2004.	2
18.	**Cockburn, Andrew** *Rumsfeld: His Rise, Fall, and Catastrophic Legacy.* Scribner, 2007.	3
19.	**Coll, Steve** *Ghost Wars: The Secret History of the CIA, Afghanistan and bin Laden, from the Soviet Invasion to September 11, 2001.* Penguin Books, 2004.	9
20.	**Cook, Robin F.** *The Point of Departure: Why One of Britain's Leading Politicians Resigned over Tony Blair's Decision to Go to War in Iraq.* Simon & Schuster, 2007.	3
21.	**Corn, David and Isikoff, Michael** *Hubris: The Inside Story of Spin, Scandal, and the Selling of the Iraq War.* Crown Publishers, 2007.	14
22.	**Coughlin, Con** *Saddam: His Rise and Fall.* Harper Perennial, 2001.	2
23.	**DeYoung, Karen** *Soldier: The Life of Colin Powell.* Alfred A. Knopf Publishing, 2006.	9

	Quote Source	Number of times referenced
24.	**Duelfer, Charles A.** *Hide and Seek: The Search for Truth in Iraq.* PublicAffairs Books, 2009.	3
25.	**Farmer, John** *The Ground Truth.* Riverhead Hardcover, 2009.	2
26.	**Feingold, Russ** *While America Sleeps: A Wake-up Call for the Post-9/11 Era.* Broadway Books, 2013.	2
27.	**Foreign Affairs,** *The U.S. vs. al Qaeda: A History of the War on Terror.* Council on Foreign Relations, 2011.	1
28.	**Gartenstein-Ross, Daveed** *Bin Laden's Legacy: Why We're Still Losing the War on Terror.* Wiley, John & Sons, Inc., 2011.	2
29.	**Gellman, Barton** *Angler: The Cheney Vice Presidency.* Penguin Press, 2008.	2
30.	**Gertz, Bill** *Breakdown: How America's Intelligence Failures Led to September 11.* The Regnery Publishing, Inc., 2002.	2
31.	**Goldsmith, Jack** *The Terror Presidency: Law and Judgment Inside the Bush Administration.* W. W. Norton & Company, 2009.	1
32.	**Goodman, Amy and Goodman, David** *The Exception to the Rulers: Exposing Oily Politicians, War Profiteers, and the Media That Love Them.* Hyperion, 2004.	4
33.	**Gordon, Michael R. and Trainor, Bernard E.** *Cobra II: The Inside Story of the Invasion and Occupation of Iraq.* Vintage Books, 2007.	2
34.	**Gore, Al** *The Assault on Reason.* Penguin Group Publishing, 2007.	4

	Quote Source	Number of times referenced
35.	**Graham, Bob and Nussbaum, Jeff** *Intelligence Matters: The CIA, the FBI, Saudi Arabia, and the Failure of America's War on Terror.* University Press of Kansas, 2004.	2
36.	**Gutman, Roy** *How We Missed the Story: Osama Bin Laden, the Taliban, and the Hijacking of Afghanistan.* USIP Press Books, 2008.	3
37.	**Haass, Richard** *War of Necessity, War of Choice: A Memoir of Two Iraq Wars.* Simon & Schuster, 2010.	2
38.	**Halper, Stefan and Clarke, Jonathan** *America Alone: The Neo-Conservative and the Global Order.* Cambridge University Press, 2005.	6
39.	**Harlow, Bill and Tenet, George** *At the Center of the Storm: My Years at the CIA.* Harper Perennial, 2008.	7
40.	**Hayes, Stephen F.** *Cheney: The Untold Story of America's Most Powerful and Controversial Vice President.* HarperCollins Publishers, 2009.	4
41.	**Hayes, Stephen F.** *The Connection: How al Qaeda's Collaboration with Saddam Hussein Has Endangered America.* HarperCollins, 2003.	5
42.	**Jarecki, Eugene** *The American Way of War: Guided Missiles, Misguided Men, and a Republic in Peril.* Free Press, 2008.	2
43.	**Juhasz, Antonia** *The Bush Agenda: Invading the World, One Economy at a Time.* Regan Books, 2006.	6
44.	**Juhasz, Antonia** *The Tyranny of Oil: The World's Most Powerful Industry— and What We Must Do to Stop It.* HarperCollins Publishers, 2008.	8

	Quote Source	Number of times referenced
45.	**Kaplan, Lawrence F. and Kristol, William** *The War Over Iraq: Saddam's Tyranny and America's Mission.* Encounter Books, 2003.	2
46.	**Kiriakou, John and Ruby, Michael** *The Reluctant Spy: My Secret Life in the CIA's War on Terror.* Bantam Books, 2010.	1
47.	**Lance, Peter** *1000 Years for Revenge: International Terrorism and the FBI–the Untold Story.* Harper Paperbacks, 2004.	8
48.	**Lance, Peter** *Cover Up: What the Government Is Still Hiding About the War on Terror.* HarperCollins Publishers, 2005.	3
49.	**Lance, Peter** *Triple Cross: How Bin Laden's Master Spy Penetrated the CIA, the Green Berets, and the FBI.* Regan Books, 2006.	12
50.	**Lustick, Ian S.** *Trapped in the War on Terror.* University of Pennsylvania Press, 2006.	2
51.	**Margulies, Peter** *Law's Detour: Justice Displaced in the Bush Administration.* NYU Press, 2010.	1
52.	**Mayer, Jane** *The Dark Side: The Inside Story of How the War on Terror Turned into a War on American Ideals.* Doubleday, 2008.	20
53.	**McClellan, Scott** *What Happened: Inside the Bush White House and Washington's Culture of Deception.* Public Affairs Press, 2008.	4
54.	**McDermott, Terry** *Perfect Soldiers: The 9/11 Hijackers: Who They Were, Why They Did It.* Vanguard Press, 2006.	1

	Quote Source	Number of times referenced
55.	**Miniter, Richard** *Losing Bin Laden: How Bill Clinton's Failures Unleashed Global Terror.* The Regnery Publishing Inc., 2004.	5
56.	**Paul, Ron** *A Foreign Policy Of Freedom: Peace, Commerce, And Honest Friendship.* Foundation for Rational Economics and Education, 2007.	1
57.	**Paust, Jordan** *Beyond the Law: The Bush Administration's Unlawful Responses in the "War" on Terror.* Cambridge University Press, 2007.	8
58.	**Phillips, Donald T. and Sanchez, Ricardo S.** *Wiser in Battle: A Soldier's Story.* HarperCollins Publishers, 2008.	7
59.	**Posner, Gerald** *Why America Slept: The Failure to Prevent 9/11.* Ballantine Books, 2004.	3
60.	**Powers, Thomas** *The Military Error: Baghdad and Beyond in America's War of Choice.* New York Review Books, 2008.	5
61.	**Purdum, Todd S.** *A Time of Our Choosing: America's War in Iraq.* Times Books, 2003.	1
62.	**Randal, Jonathan C.** *Osama: The Making of a Terrorist.* Anchor Books, 2005.	3
63.	**Rashid, Ahmed** *Descent Into Chaos: The U.S. and the Disaster in Pakistan, Afghanistan, and Central Asia.* Penguin, 2009.	1
64.	**Record, Jeffrey** *Wanting War: Why the Bush Administration Invaded Iraq.* Potomac Books, Inc., 2010.	7
65.	**Reeve, Simon** *The New Jackals: Ramzi Yousef, Osama bin Laden, and the Future of Terrorism.* Vintage Books, 2002.	4

	Quote Source	Number of times referenced
66.	**Rice, Condoleezza** *No Higher Honor: A Memoir of My Years in Washington.* Crown Publishers, 2010.	4
67.	**Rich, Frank** *The Greatest Story Ever Sold: The Decline and Fall of Truth in Bush's America.* Penguin Group, Inc., 2006.	5
68.	**Ricks, Thomas** *Fiasco: The American Military Adventure in Iraq.* Penguin Press, 2006.	2
69.	**Riedel, Bruce** *The Search for al Qaeda: Its Leadership, Ideology, and Future.* Brookings Institution Press, 2008.	1
70.	**Risen, James** *State of War: The Secret History of the CIA and the Bush Administration.* Free Press, 2006.	2
71.	**Rove, Karl** *Courage and Consequence: My Life as a Conservative in the Fight.* Simon & Schuster, 2010.	1
72.	**Rumsfeld, Donald** *Known and Unknown: A Memoir.* Sentinel/Penguin Group, 2011.	4
73.	**Scheuer, Michael, Ph.D.** *Through Our Enemies' Eyes: Osama bin Laden, Radical Islam, and the Future of America.* Potomac Books, 2007.	1
74.	**Scott, Peter Dale** *The Road to 9/11: Wealth, Empire, and the Future of America.* University of California, 2008.	2
75.	**Shenon, Philip** *The Commission: The Uncensored History of the 9/11 Investigation.* Twelve Books, 2008.	11
76.	**Short, Clare** *An Honourable Deception?: New Labor, Iraq, and the Misuse of Power.* Free Press, 2005.	2

	Quote Source	Number of times referenced
77.	**Suskind, Ron** *The One Percent Doctrine: Deep Inside America's Pursuit of Its Enemies Since 9/11*. Simon & Schuster, 2007.	1
78.	**Suskind, Ron** *The Way of the World: A Story of Truth and Hope in an Age of Extremism*. HarperCollins Publishers, 2008.	2
79.	**Taylor, Philip** *The War in Iraq–A Failure of Honesty: Top secret documents prove that many of the justifications for the invasion of Iraq, were presented deceptively*. BookSurge Publishing, 2008.	10
80.	**Tripathi, Deepak** *Overcoming the Bush Legacy in Iraq and Afghanistan*. Potomac Books, Inc., 2010.	5
81.	**Unger, Craig** *House of Bush, House of Saud: The Secret Relationship Between the World's Two Most Powerful Dynasties*. Scribner, 2004.	16
82.	**Unger, Craig** *The Fall of the House of Bush: The Untold Story of How a Band of True Believers Seized the Executive Branch, Started the Iraq War, and Still Imperils America's Future*. Simon & Schuster, 2007.	14
83.	**Weiner, Tim** *Legacy of Ashes: The History of the CIA*. Random House, 2008.	1
84.	**Woodward, Bob** *Bush at War*. Simon & Schuster, 2003.	1
85.	**Woodward, Bob** *Obama's Wars*. Simon & Schuster, 2010.	1
86.	**Woodward, Bob** *Plan of Attack: The Definitive Account of the Decision to Invade Iraq*. Simon & Schuster, 2004.	8

	Quote Source	Number of times referenced
87.	**Woodward, Bob** *State of Denial: Bush at War, Part III.* Simon & Schuster, 2007.	2
88.	**Wright, Lawrence** *The Looming Tower: Al Qaeda and the Road to 9/11.* Vintage Books, 2007.	3
89.	**Yoo, John** *War By Other Means: An Insider's Account of the War on Terror.* Atlantic Monthly Press, 2006.	2
90.	**Zelizer, Julian E.** *The Presidency of George W. Bush: A First Historical Assessment.* Princeton University Press, 2010.	1

Subtotal	# of Sources	# of Quotes Used
I. Published Books	90	396

II. Media—Online Publications

	Quote Sources	Number of times referenced
1.	ABCNews.go.com	4
2.	Aljazeera.com	1
3.	BBC.com	2
4.	*Berkeley Daily Planet, The*	1
5.	Bloomberg.com	1
6.	*Boston Globe, The*	1
7.	Brown.edu	2
8.	BusinessInsider.com	1
9.	CBSNews.com	2
10.	CNN.com (Cable News Network)	8
11.	C-SPAN.org	1
12.	*Daily Mail (UK)*	1
13.	Fair.org	1
14.	*Guardian, The*	6
15.	*Huffington Post, The*	1
16.	*Independent, The*	2
17.	*Lancet, The*	1
18.	*Los Angeles Times*	5
19.	*McClatchy Newspapers, The*	1
20.	*Mother Jones*	1
21.	*Nation, The*	3
22.	NationalGeographic.com	1
23.	*National Journal*	1
24.	NBCNews.com	3
25.	*New York Times, The*	24
26.	*New Yorker, The*	2
27.	Newsmax.com	1
28.	*PBS Frontline*	4
29.	PubRecord.org	1
30.	Salon.com	1

	Quote Sources	Number of times referenced
31.	*San Diego Union-Tribune, The*	1
32.	Slate.com	1
33.	*Telegraph, The*	1
34.	*Time* magazine	1
35.	*Times of London, The* (thetimes.co.uk)	2
36.	*USA Today*	1
37.	*Wall Street Journal, The*	1
38.	*Washington Post, The*	11

Subtotal	# of Sources	# of Quotes Used
II. Online Media	38	103

III. Government Resources Online

	Quote Sources	Number of times referenced
1.	9/11 Commission	12
2.	Congress.gov	5
3.	Federation of American Scientists	2
4.	George W. Bush—White House Archives	32
5.	Intelligence.Senate.gov	2
6.	Jimmy Carter Library	1
7.	National Security Archive, The	8
8.	Office of the Inspector General in the US Department of Justice (OIG.Justice.gov)	1
9.	Riegle Report, The	2
10.	Senate Select Committee on Intelligence	1
11.	United States Senate Armed Services Committee	1
12.	US Government Printing Office	3
13.	Weekly Compilation of Presidential Documents	6

Subtotal	# of Sources	# of Quotes Used
III. Governement Resources	13	76

IV. Other Sources

	Quote Sources	Number of times referenced
1.	American Presidency Project, The (Presidency. UCSB.edu)	2
2.	Archive.org	1
3.	Archive.commondreams. org	1
4.	Institute for the Analysis of Global Security, The (IAGS.org)	1
5.	International Committee of the Red Cross (ICRC)	1
6.	IraqInquiry.org.uk	1
7.	James A. Baker III Institute for Public Policy at Rice University	1
8.	NSarchive.gwu.edu	1
9.	ScholarlyCommons.law. Northwestern.edu	1
10.	Search.alexanderstreet. com	1

Subtotal	# of Sources	# of Quotes Used
IV. Other Sources	10	11

ACKNOWLEDGMENTS

I wish to thank the following people who offered assistance, information, suggestions, criticisms, and helped mold my thinking about putting this book together, and together, and together…

My thanks to:

— Steven Gaskin, who with our team spent three-plus years combing through over 130 books and many other sources about 9/11 and related issues, and for putting up with me and our arm wrestling over what should be included or not in the 911plus.org database, the foundation of this work.

— David Adhicary, Kamy Akhavan, Patrick Andes, Rocky Butler, Robert Frcek, Jeannie Gorman, Jeff Gould, Erick Hansen, Greg Hansen, Peter Hoffman, Bob Howard, Deyonne Jones, Mike Marvin, Peter Thatcher, John Willheim, and Bill Zimmerman, and for those I forgot to mention, I apologize.

— David Barash, who, on seeing the many quotes I had assembled, counseled me astutely that my early drafts needed more definition.

— All the authors of the works I used as sourced quotes. Given they number over ninety, I won't repeat their names, but you have seen their pointed quotes throughout this book.

— Jeff Berg, who believed enough in this work that he set up a meeting with me and Tyson Cornell, CEO of Rare Bird.

— Richard A. Clarke for penning his insightful foreword to this work.

— A. R. Hawarden, of A&M Consulting and Services LLC, who for some years typed, challenged, and retyped the words and format in this work over and over. Without her steadfast help, this book probably wouldn't have been finished in my lifetime. In sum, she made putting this book together possible.

And lastly:

— I would like to thank Tyson Cornell, Hailie Johnson, and the staff at Rare Bird Books in downtown Los Angeles. They stepped in to publish this book when other publishers thought the book *interesting* but not for them.

ABOUT THE AUTHOR

STEVEN C. MARKOFF WAS born in Los Angeles in 1943. He graduated from Los Angeles City College in 1964 with an Associate in Arts degree. Mr. Markoff is a successful entrepreneur. He has had an interest in business since he was six and in business law since his teens.

His business interests include the TCL Chinese Theatre in Hollywood (famous for both its celebrity handprints in the concrete sidewalk and its film premieres).

Mr. Markoff joined the board of the ACLU Foundation of Southern California in 1979. The factual and political views he learned about the ACLU led to the founding of the A-Mark Foundation in 1997—the not-for-profit parent of free searchable databases and nonpartisan information sites. In 2004, Mr. Markoff founded ProCon.org, another not-for-profit website that researches and posts the pros and cons of controversial issues.

1. The A-Mark Foundation [www.amarkfoundation.org], a 501(c)(3) operating foundation, was founded in 1997 by the author, and chaired by him: The Foundation has produced and lists on its website reports and other websites covering such diverse topics such as:

    — AboutTrump.org: A free searchable database containing thousands of sourced quotes from and related to Donald Trump before and after he became president.

    — SecondAmendment.org [secondamendment.org]: Many pieces of the puzzle that make up our individual rights to arms.

    — Was the ACA (Obamacare) Negotiated by the Democrats in Secret?: Some facts about the 427-day process of turning the ACA (Obamacare) into law, including final vote tallies, the "if you like your doctor" statements, the compromises, and its nineteen taxes, penalties, fees, revenue enhancements, and deduction eliminations.

2. ProCon.org [www.procon.org], a 501(c)(3) public charity founded by the author and his wife in 2004: The charity provides free and unbiased, professionally researched pro, con, and related information on more than fifty controversial issues. Such topics include:

— Alternative Energy: Can Alternative Energy Effectively Replace Fossil Fuels?

— Is a College Education Worth It?: Information about the pros and cons of a college education, including its costs and benefits.

— Illegal Immigration: "Should the Government Allow Immigrants Who Are Here Illegally to Become US Citizens?"

ProCon.org was acquired by Encyclopaedia Britannica in May 2020.

3. The author's other books in progress:

— The ACLU and the US Supreme Court: The Union's Wins and Losses at the Court During its First 100 years: Much has been written about the ACLU, but few know what it does or how it does what it does. The work will come in two different stand-alone formats: a three-volume, 2,400-page work, which covers 1,100-plus cases decided by the US Supreme Court where the ACLU was involved during the first ninety-five years of the Union's centennial. Additionally, the work includes how each of the forty-five Supreme Court Justices voted on each of the 1,100-plus cases, and the wins and losses of the ACLU by vote tally (i.e., nine to zero, eight to one, six to three) and by decade. The work offers no opinions about the ACLU, but provides the information for others to analyze and debate. Erwin Chemerinsky, Dean of the Boalt Hall School of Law at Berkeley, wrote the foreword for the work. The second format is a handbook of about 200 pages containing all the data and charts from the three-volume work except it only has the analyses of three of the 1,100-plus cases (as examples).

— Official Anti-Jewish Acts Throughout History (410 B.C.E. to Dec. 31, 2000): For several thousand years, Jews have been discriminated against in many parts of the world. What isn't well known or well documented is the depth and breadth of that discrimination. This reference book set's goal is to find and list, with brief summaries in English, all the Official Anti-Jewish Acts in the world through the year 2000. The author and his researchers continue poring through books on the topic and contacting international libraries, Jewish organizations, and expert resources to compile, so far, almost 3,000 Official Anti-Jewish Acts from over forty different countries and geographic areas.

Mr. Markoff lives in the Los Angeles area with his wife Jadwiga Zabawska, a retired physician.

He can be reached via email at scmarkoff@aol.com

INDEX

Scott Ritter
Iraq Confidential

1) NO WMD "& blew
Three UN"

2) Bush beaked out
inspectors
SH - infilt. by CIA -
Butler
3) met c SH —— wanted
to cooperate — hire
info on terrorist
financing "

Saddam Hussein —
An side with Trump wanted
to overthrow, Bush
turned down —
Syria — drag into

Andrea Card —
warned GW
above for cooperation
and fear of overreach
Pulled Russia
more to get her
in virtual hospital
Smell overheard Bush
narrative